Advanced Multimedia Programming

Steve Rimmer

Windcrest®/ McGraw-Hill

New York   San Francisco   Washington, D.C.   Auckland   Bogotá
Caracas   Lisbon   London   Madrid   Mexico City   Milan
Montreal   New Delhi   San Juan   Singapore
Sydney   Tokyo   Toronto

This book is dedicated to the newest members of our family. . .
. . . before building a house, always count the groundhogs.

© 1995 by **Windcrest**.
Published by Windcrest, an imprint of McGraw-Hill, Inc.
The name "Windcrest" is a registered trademark of McGraw-Hill, Inc.

pbk   1 2 3 4 5 6 7 8 9 0 DOC/DOC 9 9 8 7 6 5
hc   1 2 3 4 5 6 7 8 9 0 DOC/DOC 9 9 8 7 6 5

Library of Congress Cataloging-in-Publication Data
Rimmer, Steve.
        Advanced multimedia programming / by Steve Rimmer.
            p.   cm.
        Includes index.
        ISBN 0-07-911897-6   ISBN 0-07-911898-4 (pbk.)
        1. Multimedia systems.   I. Title.
    QA76.575.R55   1994
    006.6—dc20   94-13523
                                                    CIP

Acquisitions editor: Brad Shepp
Editorial team: Joanne Slike, Executive Editor
                David M. McCandless, Supervising Editor
                Emily Glossbrenner, Book Editor
Production team: Katherine G. Brown, Director
                Susan E. Hansford, Coding
                Jan Fisher, Desktop Operator
                Nancy K. Mickley, Proofreading
                Joanne Woy, Indexer
Design team: Jaclyn J. Boone, Designer   9118984
                Brian Allison, Associate Designer   WK2

Contents

sources and are believed to be in the public domain. They are provided here at no cost for your interest, and as sample files for use with applications in this book.

➤ The author accepts no responsibility for any loss, damage, or expense caused by your application of the information in this book, however it's caused.

Purchaser's rights

If you have bought this book, you have bought the following rights to use the code herein for your applications:

➤ You're free to extract code fragments from this book as you require and incorporate them into programs that you write. You may distribute these programs freely in their executable form, so that they can be run by other users but not readily decompiled, disassembled, or linked into other applications.

➤ You may not distribute any of the source code from this book as source code, in either human- or machine-readable form.

➤ In distributing executable application files that contain functions or variations on function from this book, you are not required to pay any additional royalties, or get explicit written permission. No credit need be given to this book.

➤ You may not distribute any of the applications, utilities, documentation, or complete packages on the companion CD-ROM for this book without explicit written permission from Alchemy Mindworks Inc.

➤ The music, sounds, graphics, and movies on the companion CD-ROM for this book were obtained from public domain

Getting help

One of the drawbacks to writing microcomputer software on your own is that if you get really stuck, there's typically no one you can ask for help. If you get really stuck with something in a computer book, you should be able to contact its author. Sadly, this frequently involves an extensive wait for things to make it through the post. Technology waits for no one.

If you get into a bind with something in this book, you can reach me at the following e-mail addresses:

CompuServe   70451,2734

Internet   alchemy@accesspt.north.net

BBS   1-905-729-4609

All of these numbers are subject to change—the BBS number will almost certainly change shortly after this book is released. If you're unable to connect to the bulletin board, dial the number given above with a voice telephone and listen for the phone company's recording for the new number.

The bulletin board is an open system. It runs at up to 9600 baud v.32, eight data bits, no parity, and one stop bit.

You'll find Alchemy Mindworks' toll-free ordering and technical support numbers in the Graphic Workshop for Windows package on the companion CD-ROM for this book. Please don't call these numbers for help with this book. I'm not usually there.

Depending on my general level of work, deadlines, and groundhogs, I can usually reply to questions about the programs in books like this one within 48 hours. As a rule, I'm not usually able to help with modifications to the code or with questions only tangentially related to it.

1

Getting started

CHAPTER 1

"You can always spot the pioneers—they're the ones with the arrows in their backs."
—Graffiti

THIS book is to some extent a sequel. It's a companion volume to my earlier book *Multimedia Programming for Windows*, also published by Windcrest/McGraw Hill. Whereas *Multimedia Programming for Windows* deals largely with the Windows multimedia facilities, this book expands on them somewhat and fills in some of the elements that Windows doesn't include. It offers you tools to deal with animation, screen savers, and the newer resources for Video for Windows, among other things.

While everything in this book is wholly self-standing, you'll probably find aspects of it a lot easier to understand if you've previously read *Multimedia Programming for Windows*. Many of the underlying concepts of the Windows implementation of multimedia facilities— elements like RIFF (resource interchange file format) files, sampled sound, and so on—are discussed in detail in that book.

The expression "computer science" may be pretty close to a contradiction in terms. Writing software is far more an art form than a science. It's creative—in much the same way that painting or writing music is creative—and the people who turn out to be particularly good at it usually have a much more artistic nature than a scientific one. Much as painting involves looking at a blank canvas and seeing on it the image in one's imagination, so too does writing software require that one begin with a blank screen or window and imagine the application that will eventually occupy it.

Most areas of application development presuppose some structural limitations on the sort of software you can write. The perhaps unreasonable requirement that applications actually do something, and more frequently that they do something specific and productive, is by its nature a bit restrictive. For example, if you write a database application, it will forever have a nagging tendency to want to work with data of some sort.

One of the really great things about multimedia as an area of application design—assuming that you want to consider it as such—is

that it's singularly ill-defined and very open-ended. Multimedia can encompass anything you can imagine, as long as it's reasonably amusing and can't be exported to a spreadsheet. Multimedia elements include sound, graphics, animation, music, and anything else you can think of to use as a medium.

If you're able to get a job in which the description of your position includes the word *multimedia*, you should be able to do absolutely anything you like and be paid very well for it.

Multimedia under Windows is perhaps a bit more restrictive—or perhaps just somewhat more clearly defined. As it stands, Windows has no true multimedia capabilities. It does, however, have all sorts of strategically placed internal hooks to allow multimedia extensions to be bolted onto it. When they're in place, the Windows multimedia extensions are singularly flexible. They integrate well into conventional Windows software and offer a library of system calls to handle things like playing sounds and music, displaying video sequences, selecting compact disc audio tracks, and so on.

It would be unrealistic to imagine that the Windows multimedia extensions are everything there is to multimedia. They are, however, a particularly comfortable place to start.

⇨ Noise & where it comes from

Multimedia as it exists under Windows is really a collection of discrete resources. Among these resources are system calls to do the following:

> ➤ Record and play back sampled sound as WAV (wave) files.

> ➤ Record and play back sequenced music as MIDI (musical instrument digital interface) files.

> ➤ Record and play back digital video as AVI (audio video interleave) files.

> ➤ Manage unusual input devices, such as joysticks.

> ➤ Select and play compact disc audio tracks.

The latter function won't turn up in this book—it is discussed exhaustively in *Multimedia Programming for Windows*.

Each of the complex file types that can be handled by the Windows multimedia extensions—WAV files for sampled sound, MIDI files for sequenced music, and AVI files for Video for Windows movies—is supported by various levels of system calls under the Windows multimedia extensions. In each case, the Windows media control interface (MCI) can treat these files as black boxes—you can hand the path to a multimedia file to MCI, tell MCI to play it, and understand almost nothing about what's really going on in the process.

Windows will also allow you to work with these multimedia elements at a much lower level. You can play back multimedia files in an environment that requires you to understand almost everything that's going on in excruciatingly fine detail. This would be a considerable inconvenience if, for example, you merely want to have your computer make some noise when an application opens. It's almost essential if you want to do something more than the canned interfaces that the Windows multimedia extensions provide for.

Here's a real-world example of how understanding what really happens in the Windows multimedia extensions can be essential in getting around the facilities not included in Windows' higher-level multimedia calls. The easiest way to play instrumental sequenced music from a MIDI file is to hand the file to the Windows MCI interface, discussed in detail in Chapter 6. The code to play a MIDI file under MCI typically runs to fewer than two dozen lines, and contains no surprises.

There's a much more complex way of playing MIDI files—that is, by splitting each file into its discrete elements (its MIDI *messages*) and sending each message to the MIDI interface of your computer directly. Software to do this will run to many hundreds of lines of code, and for applications that simply play MIDI music, will do nothing more than the two dozen lines of code required to play MIDI files through the MCI interface.

If you want to have some MIDI music hardwired into an application, however, the MCI interface will prove all but useless. The MCI

interface wants to play music stored as MIDI files on disk. A MIDI file stored as a resource object or a list of instructions in data will not be of interest to it. You'll need to know how to work at the lower level of the Windows MIDI interface in order to transcend these sorts of limitations.

Figure 1-1 illustrates the main window of PLAYSONG, one of the applications discussed in detail in this book. The PLAYSONG application illustrates how to work at the lowest level of MIDI under Windows by playing a selection of three traditional Celtic fiddle tunes without recourse to a MIDI file. However, even PLAYSONG's main window illustrates a facility which is not available through the MCI interface. The three combo boxes shown in Fig. 1-1 allow you to select the voices the music will be played in. This requires some understanding of how MIDI works and the actual structure of MIDI note information.

Figure 1-1

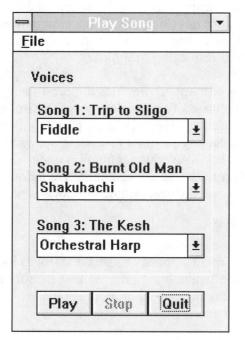

The PLAYSONG application.

Whereas *Multimedia Programming for Windows* deals largely with the higher-level interfaces to multimedia elements provided by Windows, this book gets into the really poorly documented bits of multimedia—the low-level calls and other pseudosecrets of sound and light under Windows.

One of the curious aspects of developing software under Windows is that almost everything that's interesting to do requires at least some recourse to facilities Windows does not provide, or does not provide in an easily usable manner. While it seems a bit too cynical to suggest that the only good software is that which is difficult to write, it's easy to imagine the authors of the Windows multimedia extensions believing that.

Some of the aspects of multimedia touched on in this book don't have anything at all to do with the Windows multimedia extensions. Specifically, Windows' multimedia facilities don't add anything to Windows' resources for dealing with still graphics. Displaying pictures under Windows has always been monumentally confusing, with numerous apparently conflicting approaches available and almost no guidance in the Windows software development kit documentation on how to weed through them. One of the elements discussed in this book is a workable approach to displaying graphics.

Actually, Chapters 4 and 5 on bitmapped graphics do more than merely talk about looking at pictures. They explore ways to display pictures so that they can't be missed. Beyond simply painting pictures on your screen, they deal with having pictures tile, wipe, split-screen, and plummet into a window. They also cover animation under Windows—with an introduction to the all-but-unheard-of Windows joystick interface on the side—and the creation of Windows screen savers.

Windows screen savers are one of the real growth industries in commercial software at the moment. One spreadsheet starts to look pretty much like another after a while, but being the first person in your office to have flying toasters or tribbles on your screen is something genuinely worth pursuing.

Finally, the last chapter of this book deals with new resources of the Microsoft Video for Windows Software Development Kit (SDK) Version 1.1. Whereas the initial introduction of Video for Windows was a programmer's nightmare just this side of a John Carpenter movie, the new software development kit offers relatively effortless access to just about everything imaginable under Video for Windows.

It might well be argued that none of the sample applications discussed in this book is likely to be of much use as it stands. One of the challenges of multimedia is that it's a canvas so large and so blank as to make the blankness of lesser canvases seem almost overcrowded by comparison. While you're unlikely to find any of these sample applications useful, you can extract functions from them for your own multimedia software. Think of them more as paint than as pictures.

Hardware & software

The programs in this book were written using Borland C++ for Windows. In most cases, you'll be able to compile them more or less as they are under other Windows C compilers. There are minor things you will want to modify—we'll discuss them in detail.

All of the source code, resource elements, DEF files, and PRJ files for the sample programs in this book are included on the companion CD-ROM. If you install the source code on your hard drive as discussed in the README.TXT file for the CD-ROM, you should be able to compile the programs without any difficulty. This is a good place to start when you begin writing your own multimedia applications.

Should you decide to start from scratch, creating your own project files, keep in mind how these applications expect your compiler to be set up:

➤ The *memory model* should be small or medium.

➤ The *default char type* should be unsigned.

➤ The *register variables* should be off.

➤ The *jump optimization* should be off.

The project files for the sample applications in this book are set up with a particular directory structure in mind. If you have a different directory structure on your hard drive, be sure to change the directories for the libraries and include files in each of the projects. Otherwise your compiler will inundate you with warnings and errors.

Here's a list of the directory paths that apply to these applications:

> Borland C++ for Windows should be installed in C:\BC.

> The source code for this book should be installed in C:\BC\SMPW.

> The include file path should include C:\BC\INCLUDE for all the applications in this book.

> The include file path should also include C:\VFWDK\INC for the Video for Windows applications in the last chapter of this book.

> The library path should include C:\BC\LIB.

All of the sample applications in this book make calls to the Windows multimedia extensions, as provided by the Microsoft Multimedia Development Kit illustrated in Fig. 1-2.

You must install the Multimedia Development Kit on your hard drive before compiling any of the applications in this book. You might also need to install a few drivers through the Control Panel Drivers applet before some of them will work correctly. Driver issues are discussed in appropriate sections throughout this book.

The Video for Windows software discussed in Chapter 7 requires the Video for Windows Software Development Kit Version 1.1. It also requires that you have Version 1.1 of Video for Windows installed on your hard drive.

If you attempt to compile the applications in this book and encounter warnings or errors, there may be something wrong with your compiler setup. One exception to this are the warnings generated by the Video for Windows Software Development Kit dealt with in the last chapter of the book. These messages are spurious and can be ignored.

Figure 1-2

The Microsoft Multimedia Development Kit.

There are a few things about the applications discussed in this book that are peculiar to Borland's C++ implementation. They're all cosmetic, and if you'll be working with a different implementation of C, such as one of Microsoft's languages, you can simply delete the Borland-related elements. Specifically, Borland's BWCC.DLL custom control library is used to create drop shadows in most of the application windows and dialogs that appear in this book. It generates message dialogs and manages a bitmap in the About dialog of most of the applications.

Here's what you will need to change in the source code in this book in order to use it with a non-Borland language:

> Each of the application source code files in this book includes the BWCC.H header file. This #include directive must be deleted for non-Borland languages.

> Each application calls BWCCGetVersion in its WinMain function. Remove this call.

> Most of the applications have RC files that include Borland custom button controls with the type BorBtn. Replace these with conventional Windows buttons.

> A few of the applications use other Borland custom controls, such as BorCheck check boxes. Replace these with conventional Windows controls of the same types.

> All of the applications' RC files include BorShade custom controls. These are drop shadows, and have no function other than making the application look attractive and state-of-the-art. Replace them with conventional Windows rectangles, or just delete them.

> With the exception of the BMP-FX application in Chapter 4, each of the RC files in this book has an About dialog with a Borland button having the resource ID 801. This is a particularly exotic use of the Borland button facility—it displays a bitmap. You can delete these buttons for non-Borland languages. Chapter 4 discusses alternate ways to display a bitmap in a dialog.

Finally, each of the source code listings in this book includes the following macro definition:

```
#define DoMessage(hwnd,string) BWCCMessageBox(hwnd,string,"Message",\
                       MB_OK ¦ MB_ICONINFORMATION)
```

To compile one of the applications in this book with a non-Borland language, you would change this a bit:

```
#define DoMessage(hwnd,string) MessageBox(hwnd,string,"Message",\
                       MB_OK ¦ MB_ICONINFORMATION)
```

The DoMessage macro is used to display simple dialogs. As it stands, it uses the BWCCMessageBox call provided by BWCC.DLL to create a message dialog that's more or less consistent in appearance with the other dialogs of the applications presented in this book. You can change this to use the conventional Windows MessageBox API call for situations in which BWCC.DLL isn't available.

Working with the applications in this book also involves some hardware considerations. To begin with, you'll need a fairly high-end computer to make much of the software in this book work. An 80386 system is arguably the bottom of the list—a 486 system will be an improvement, and a Pentium machine wouldn't be wholly wasted. A fast accelerated video card is essential for Video for Windows. A minimum of 8 megabytes of memory will allow you to avoid all sorts of nasty limitations of Windows' multimedia extensions, with 16 megabytes being highly desirable. Plan on having lots of free hard drive space.

You'll need a CD-ROM reader to access the source code for this book, much of the Microsoft Windows Multimedia Development Kit's components, and all of the Video for Windows Software Development Kit.

Many of the applications in this book require a Windows-compatible sound card. As discussed in Chapter 2, most of the sample source code in this book was developed on one of the cheapest and grottiest sound cards in the known universe—it was subsequently tested on more substantial hardware to make sure it didn't have any hidden predilection toward the extreme low end. While I don't necessarily recommend that you buy a low-end $75 sound card—unless you find yourself confronted with a situation like the one described in Chapter 2—keep in mind that Windows-compatible sound hardware is available for just about any Visa balance.

The magazine reviews dealing with sound cards periodically have a lot to say about the very high-end systems, such as the Turtle Beach cards. Some of these are breathtaking. If you have a lot of money you would like to part with, you should buy one. Be aware that you don't have to do so, however.

If you want to play with the beach ball in cheap sunglasses discussed in Chapter 5, you'll need a joystick. The beach ball is illustrated in Fig. 1-3.

Figure 1-3

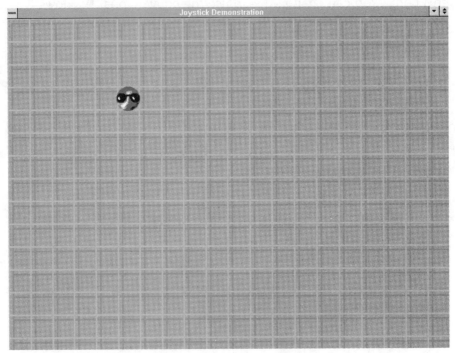

A beach ball in cheap sunglasses.

Joysticks, like sound cards, come in flavors ranging from Diet Pepsi to Dom Perignon. Unlike sound cards, even really high-end joysticks aren't all that expensive. I used a Gravis joystick for the beach ball application—it cost ten dollars more than the cheap ones, but it didn't make the beach ball seasick—a laudable achievement.

⇨ Making it work

The sample programs in this book are written in ANSI C, as opposed to the much more trendy C++. As its name implies, C++ is a superset of conventional C. A C++ compiler has a C compiler hiding

inside it. You can use a C++ compiler to compile C source code by simply pretending the C++ extensions don't exist.

If you prefer to write in C++ rather than C, you can add the additional bits to the source code in this book to make it into C++ fairly simply. Alternately, languages like Borland C++ allow you to freely mix C and C++ functions—you can use the functions presented in this book as they stand and add your own code in C++.

There's nothing about C++ that creates inherently better code. What C++ offers is inherently better structures for the organization of large projects being worked on by multiple programmers. The modest applications in this book wouldn't benefit from the facilities of C++.

This book will help you access the facilities of Windows multimedia extensions, the Multimedia Development Kit and the Video for Windows Software Development Kit. It won't teach you to program in C. If you're new to C-language programming, attempting to learn it by reading this book would be analogous to learning how to swim by jumping into the deep end of the pool—while carrying an anchor. Should all this be new to you, you'll find the process of learning to program in C a great deal easier if you put this book aside for a week or two and begin with one of the many excellent texts available for introductory C programming.

The same is true of learning to write Windows applications in C, should you hitherto have written C-language programs exclusively under DOS, or another non-Windows environment. Plunging into multimedia probably wouldn't be the most effortless introduction to the craft.

It's a great deal easier to learn to write software by tinkering with existing source code than it is to write your own from scratch. You can attain a grasp of multimedia under Windows—and perhaps even a satisfactory hammerlock on it—by modifying and adding to the sample applications in this book until they become the applications you have in mind.

Multimedia is one of the best unexplored jungles left in Windows application design. Unlike some of the lesser jungles, it has no plastic

trees, mechanical snakes, or digitally enhanced charging elephants. All the creatures are real. All the fangs and claws and poisonous crawling beasties are real too, of course—that's the way of jungles. There'd be no glory in exploring them if they were really just back entrances to Disneyland.

This book will give you the provisions for an extended safari into multimedia under Windows.

2

Wave files

CHAPTER 2

"Dogs come when you call. Cats have answering machines."
—Graffiti

ONE of the most interesting and frequently used aspects of multimedia under Windows is the facility to play wave files. The wave file format allows sound bites to be reproduced through a suitable sound card with anything up to CD-quality audio. You can use wave files to make your computer speak, to generate attention-getting special effects, to add sounds to system events under Windows, and to have selected applications plead piteously for their lives when you select Exit from the File menu.

This latter invocation of the Windows multimedia extensions is far from dignified, but it makes ostensibly serious packages, like Excel or Word, a lot more agreeable. I find that Windows seems to better express itself if quotations from old Warner Brothers' cartoons pop up occasionally. For example, one of the systems here has Elmer Fudd say "Be vewy, vewy quiet. I'm hunting wabbits" when anything from the Windows Accessories group is launched. Perhaps it should say "Be vewy, vewy quiet. I'm hunting pwotected mode faults."

As discussed in detail in *Multimedia Programming for Windows*, the structure and variations on both wave files themselves and the system calls used to manipulate wave file playback under Windows are somewhat awe-inspiring. While it all eventually makes a perverse sort of sense, the facilities for working with canned sounds under Windows are by no means transparent.

This chapter covers several of the less than obvious applications of wave files and wave file sound under Windows. Perhaps more so than for any other chapter in this book, you'll probably find the corresponding section of *Multimedia Programming for Windows* to be all but essential if you aren't otherwise intimately familiar with Windows' multimedia extensions. Digitized sound isn't particularly intuitive to work with at the best of times, and wave files in particular seem intended to confuse the unwary.

You absolutely must have a sound card installed in your system to use the sample applications discussed in this chapter. While some limited access to wave sounds is possible through the Windows speaker driver—a somewhat lamentable bit of code that will attempt to reproduce digital audio through the squeaker-speaker of a PC—the speaker driver does not function with the higher-end MCI sound interface used here. It's unclear whether this is because of a technological limitation or out of a sense of decorum.

As an aside, I should note that while high-end sound cards are still reasonably expensive, lesser hardware with names you've never heard of is available to suit any budget. It's also available to suit any system. One of the reasons that most of my computers have sound cards is that I've bought quite a number of them in hopes of finding one that would work correctly with the machine I usually use to develop applications on. Possibly because that machine is rather thick with peripherals, all the really good sound cards I tried encountered hardware conflicts when they were plugged into it.

The situation looked hopeless, until one day Greg up at the computer shop in the next village mentioned that he had the ultimate in sound cards, a bit of fiberglass suitable for even the most uncooperative system. Called Zoltrix, as I recall, it was a clone of a clone of a SoundBlaster. It did not have the most stunning sound quality, but the whole works, including two speakers and some funky software, cost less than a hundred dollars. Perhaps predictably, it sang while all its far more expensive predecessors only coughed and complained.

There are times when only the cheapest sound card will do.

Wave file resources

The most familiar use of wave audio for most Windows users will be as WAV files, sounds that can be loaded and played from disk. This is a handy form to store them in if you'll be adding new dimensions in message beeps to your dialog boxes, but it's perhaps less than ideal should you want to build canned sounds into your software. Having a plethora of WAV files accompanying your application is both less

than professional and not the optimum use of your system resources. Opening and loading a discrete wave file from disk is relatively time-consuming.

Handling canned sounds as discrete files also offers the opportunity for them to be accidentally deleted or modified.

In addition to living in WAV files, canned sounds can be stored as resource list items in an application's EXE file. This means that a stored sound can be fetched with a call to LoadResource, used, and then discarded. The time required to fetch a resource item is significantly shorter than would be required to load a discrete WAV file from disk. While it's certainly possible to delete or modify resource objects—the Resource Workshop application that accompanies Borland C++ for Windows will manage it for you—allowing that it might done accidentally is stretching a point.

Unfortunately, the Windows multimedia extensions don't offer the same degree of flexibility in playing wave file sounds stored as resources as they do for sounds stored in discrete disk files. The MCI interface, for example, insists on dealing with disk files. You can play a wave file sound stored in memory through the low-level waveOut calls discussed at length in *Multimedia Programming for Windows*— and touched on later in this chapter—but you'd have to undertake some data swapping to arrange it. The waveOut calls want to deal with raw sound samples, while a wave file sound stored as a resource is really a complete WAV file, couched in RIFF chunks.

The sndPlaySound function is actually designed to accept wave file data stored in a buffer, as well as WAV files on disk. It does embody some limitations, as we'll discuss in a moment, and some of them can actually be somewhat daunting for complex applications involving playing canned sounds. However, there's no simpler way to play sounds loaded from the resource list of your application if all you really want to do is make some noise.

The sndPlaySound function accepts two arguments, as shown here:

```
sndPlaySound(LPSTR pointer,WORD flags)
```

Depending on how it's to be used, the pointer argument to sndPlaySound can point to either the file name of a WAV file to be played from disk or to a buffer that contains the contents of a WAV file loaded into memory. This latter case also applies to wave file sounds fetched by LoadResource.

The flags argument of sndPlaySound allows you to define how the function will treat its first argument, and how it will play the sound so specified. The following are the flags that sndPlaySound recognizes. Note that you can OR together multiple flags.

SND_SYNC   Tells sndPlaySound to play the specified sound and return when the sound is complete.

SND_ASYNC   Tells sndPlaySound to play the specified sound and return immediately. If the pointer argument passed to sndPlaySound is not a path to a disk file, the sound must remain locked in memory until it terminates.

SND_NODEFAULT   Tells sndPlaySound to play nothing if the specified sound can't be loaded or played. Without this flag in place, sndPlaySound will play a default sound specified in your WIN.INI file if it can't play the sound you've asked for.

SND_MEMORY   Tells sndPlaySound that its pointer argument points to a sound stored in memory, rather than to a file name.

SND_LOOP   Tells sndPlaySound to play the specified sound repeatedly until it's explicitly stopped or until you yank the plug for your computer from the wall in desperation.

SND_NOSTOP   Tells sndPlaySound to return immediately if a sound is currently playing.

The sndPlaySound call will return a true value if it has successfully initiated the playing of a sound; otherwise it will return a false. If its

pointer argument is NULL, it will immediately stop playing the current sound. You can use the SND_NOSTOP flag to test whether a sound is currently playing.

The primary limitation to sndPlaySound is that it embodies no mechanism to notify your application when a sound terminates. As such, short of waiting in a loop until sndPlaySound with the SND_NOSTOP flag installed says that all is silent, it's impossible to use sndPlaySound to string multiple sounds together. This approach, of polling the sound system, is exceedingly wasteful of resources under Windows. If you undertake it, Windows will put a hex on your cat and make it live forever—no foolin'.

The sndPlaySound function would typically be used to play a single sound for situations in which it really does matter when the sound ends. With the exception of the sound information itself, should you be playing a sound in memory, sndPlaySound will clean up after itself, freeing any internal storage and closing the Windows sound drivers automatically as soon as the sound has been played.

Figure 2-1 illustrates an About dialog from one of the applications discussed in this book. They all look pretty much like this. What Fig. 2-1 doesn't illustrate is that when this dialog opens, a wave file sound will play.

As with most clever dialogs, most of the work involved in the About dialog in Fig. 2-1 is performed by its message handler. In this case, there's also a bit of conspiracy involved in the resource script for the application in question.

To begin with, here's how you would include a wave file in a resource script:

```
AboutWave RCDATA ABOUT.WAV
```

This will create a resource list object called AboutWave with the contents of the ABOUT.WAV file stored in it. This resource list object can subsequently be called by the LoadResource function.

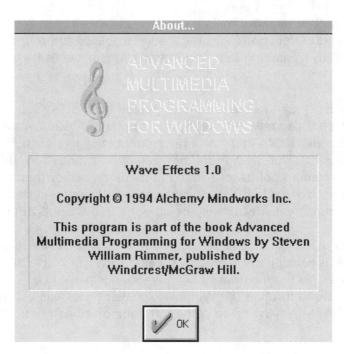

Figure 2-1

An About dialog.

With a suitable wave file ensconced in its resource list, an application can load it into memory and play it like this:

```
HANDLE sound;
LPSTR psound;
HANDLE handle;
if((handle=FindResource(hInst,"AboutWave",RT_RCDATA)) != NULL) {
        if((sound=LoadResource(hInst,handle)) != NULL) {
                if((psound=LockResource(sound)) != NULL}
                        sndPlaySound(psound,SND_ASYNC |
                        SND_MEMORY | SND_NOSTOP);
                }
        }
}
```

This bit of code begins by locating a handle to the resource in question with FindResource. The LoadResource call loads the wave file in question into memory—or just returns a handle to the wave file

if it's already in memory from a previous instance. The LockResource function locks the loaded resource and returns a far pointer to it, something that sndPlaySound can use as its pointer argument.

Note the flags used as the second argument to sndPlaySound. The SND_ASYNC flag tells sndPlaySound to play the AboutWave sound asynchronously, such that it will return immediately after the sound begins playing. The SND_MEMORY flag tells sndPlaySound that its pointer argument points to a sound in memory, rather than to a file name. The SND_NOSTOP flag says not to interrupt a currently playing sound, which will rarely be an issue in this application.

The SND_ASYNC flag will be ignored if the sound device in your computer is actually the Windows speaker driver, because the speaker driver can't play asynchronous sounds. Sounds played by sndPlaySound through the Windows speaker driver will cause the system they're playing on to come to a temporary halt until silence returns.

This does not apply to systems with real sound cards, of course.

On a system that can play sounds asynchronously, it's also very important to keep in mind that when the foregoing bit of code is complete, there will probably still be a sound in the midst of being played. Windows typically runs in protected mode, which means that attempts by an application to access memory it does not own—even if the application in question just wants to read from it—will cause a protected mode fault. This will occur, for example, if sndPlaySound is playing a sound in memory and the buffer the sound lives in is unlocked or freed before the sound terminates.

You should always make sure that a sound in memory initiated by sndPlaySound is finished before you call UnlockResource to unlock its buffer. The most reliable way to do this is to call sndPlaySound with its pointer argument set to NULL prior to calling UnlockResource.

Here's how you'd deal with the objects created by the foregoing bit of code:

```
sndPlaySound(NULL,SND_SYNC);
UnlockResource(sound);
FreeResource(sound);
```

Now, this might present you with some logistical difficulties, depending on how you'll actually be using sndPlaySound. If the second code fragment discussed here immediately follows the first, the sound being played will be terminated instantly, and all will be silent. Ideally there should be some mechanism for waiting at least until the sound in question is complete, but as discussed earlier, sndPlaySound doesn't allow for this.

In using sndPlaySound as a noisemaker in a dialog box, the delay between starting the sound and closing the dialog will be however long it takes for someone to click on the OK button. This serves admirably as a delay to let the sound play. In most cases the sound will terminate naturally, but it's still a good idea to call sndPlaySound a second time, just in case someone is exceedingly quick belting the OK button.

Note that in a complete message handler for a dialog, the code to load and play a sound would naturally occur in the WM_INITDIALOG case, and the code to terminate it would occur in the WM_COMMAND case. Because local variables in a message handler only survive for the life of one message—being objects on the stack—it's important that the sound and psound be declared static, lest Windows find that it's being asked to unlock and free dead air.

The following is a somewhat abbreviated message handler for the About dialog of any of the applications in this book.

```
DWORD FAR PASCAL AboutDlgProc(HWND hwnd,WORD message,
    WORD wParam,LONG lParam)
{
    static HANDLE sound;
    static LPSTR psound;
    HANDLE handle;
    POINT point;

    switch(message) {
```

```
        case WM_INITDIALOG:
            if((handle=FindResource(hInst,"AboutWave",
            RT_RCDATA)) != NULL) {
                if((sound=LoadResource(hInst,handle)) != NULL) {
                    if((psound=LockResource(sound)) != NULL)
                        sndPlaySound(psound,SND_ASYNC |
                        SND_MEMORY | SND_NOSTOP);
                }
            }
            return(FALSE);
        case WM_COMMAND:
            switch(wParam) {
                case IDOK:

                    sndPlaySound(NULL,SND_SYNC);
                    if(psound != NULL) UnlockResource(sound);
                    if(sound != NULL) FreeResource(sound);
                    EndDialog(hwnd,wParam);
                    return(FALSE);

            }
            break;

    }

    return(FALSE);
}
```

Another limitation of sndPlaySound is that it can typically only be counted upon to reliably play sounds occupying about 100 kilobytes. It's also not a good idea to use it to play stereo sounds, as not all sound cards handle these correctly.

⇨ An evening with the MCI interface

Most sound cards have audio input jacks as well as places to connect your stereo or speakers. In most cases you can plug a microphone or high-level audio jack into your sound card and make wave files of

your own. The ability to record wave files is fundamental to most applications that use canned sounds under Windows.

If you need a few wave files to add specific sounds or words to an application, you can record them using any of a number of available tools—the Microsoft WaveEdit application makes a workable wave file recorder. It offers facilities to fine-tune recorded wave files as well.

There are certainly reasons for building the facility to record sound into your own applications. If you'd like your software to be able to listen as well as speak, you'll have to teach it how to get friendly with the input jack of your sound card.

In theory, recording wave files should be no more difficult than playing them. The MCI interface, discussed at length in conjunction with playing wave files in *Multimedia Programming for Windows*, also offers facilities to input audio. The implementation looks relatively effortless. It's not, of course—nothing ever works this easily in practice.

The MCI interface is the most flexible and easiest to deal with of Windows' various levels of multimedia facilities. It offers to work with a variety of media types, does most of the file handling and such for you, and will even notify a particular window of its activities. It's capable of some fairly impressive functions, as we'll get to in greater detail when we look at Video for Windows in Chapter 7.

Playing a wave file with the MCI interface is exceedingly easy:

```
MCI_OPEN_PARMS mciopen;
MCI_PLAY_PARMS mciplay;
DWORD rtrn;
char b[STRINGSIZE+1];
int id=-1;

mciopen.lpstrDeviceType="waveaudio";
mciopen.lpstrElementName=path;
if(mciSendCommand(0,MCI_OPEN,MCI_OPEN_TYPE ¦
                MCI_OPEN_ELEMENT,
        (DWORD)(LPVOID)&mciopen) != 0L)
```

```
                return(-1);

        id=mciopen.wDeviceID;

        mciplay.dwCallback=(DWORD)hwnd;
        if((rtrn=mciSendCommand(id,MCI_PLAY,MCI_NOTIFY,
            (DWORD)(LPVOID)&mciplay)) != 0L) {
                mciSendCommand(id,MCI_CLOSE,0,NULL);
                        return(-1);
        }

        return(id);
```

All communication from an application to the MCI interface is
handled through the mciSendCommand function. Its arguments are
as follows:

```
    mciSendCommand(id,message,param1,param2)
```

The id argument to mciSendCommand is an ID value representing
an opened MCI device. This will be zero if the device has not yet
been opened, as in the first instance of mciSendCommand in the
foregoing code fragment. An ID value will be returned in the
wDeviceID element of the MCI_OPEN_PARMS object passed to
mciSendCommand when it's used to open a device.

The message argument to mciSendCommand will be the MCI
message to be sent to the MCI interface. There are quite a few of
these—the ones that appeared in the preceding code fragment are
MCI_OPEN to open a device and associate a file with it, MCI_PLAY
to set the file playing, and MCI_CLOSE to close the device.

The param1 argument to mciSendCommand consists of a set of
flags telling the MCI interface what the other arguments to the
function mean. Usually there will be flags to indicate which elements
in the structure passed to mciSendCommand are to be considered
valid. Additional flags instruct the MCI interface on the finer points of
playing the file in question. For example, the MCI_NOTIFY flag used
in the second instance of mciSendCommand in the foregoing code

fragment tells MCI to notify the specified window when the wave file in question finishes playing.

The param2 argument to mciSendCommand is typically a far pointer to a data structure. The structure to be used varies with the function mciSendCommand is being asked to perform. It's exceedingly important to use the structure that matches the MCI message you pass in the message argument of mciSendCommand, lest MCI start overwriting bits of your stack and other useful elements of Windows.

Note also that more recently developed applications of MCI, such as Video for Windows, typically use variations on the common MCI data structures discussed in the Microsoft Multimedia Development Kit documentation. In these instances too, it's important that you use the data structures that MCI is expecting.

As an aside, while sndPlaySound is hardwired into the Windows multimedia extensions, the MCI facilities are handled by drivers loaded through the Drivers applet of the Control Panel. Figure 2-2 illustrates the Windows Control Panel with the MCI drivers installed.

You must install these drivers before you can use the MCI functions discussed in this chapter. This is also true for other MCI applications,

Figure 2-2

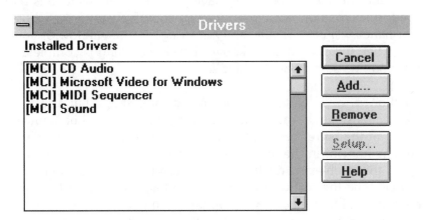

The MCI drivers in the Windows Control Panel Drivers applet.

such as the Video for Windows applications covered in Chapter 7. The drivers are included with Windows—just click on Add to access the standard Windows driver list.

If you dig through the MCI message lists in the Windows Multimedia Development Kit documentation, you'll encounter one called MCI_RECORD. This purports to tell the MCI interface to input audio—or whatever is appropriate to the device you've opened—store it in a buffer, and ultimately write it out to a suitable file. This would seem to be a fairly painless interface to handle recording. It is, in fact, although you'll have to clamp a fair bit of extra software onto it to make it into a complete wave recorder.

The MCI interface is by default asynchronous. The code fragment to play wave file sounds discussed earlier will return as soon as the sound begins playing. It will play the sound in the background and send a message informing the window of your choice that the jig's up when the sound stops. This allows an application using MCI to play sounds to go about its business doing other things while sounds are playing.

The same is true for other media accessible through MCI, such as MIDI files and AVI movies.

One obvious distinction between playing and recording sound is that in the former case the MCI interface can know how long the whole performance will be and can send a message to the window of your choice when it's over. It can't know when a recording is complete unless you find some way to tell it so.

In addition, a wave file to be played can be stored in a buffer of known dimensions, because the size of the wave file will be known. The size of the buffer required to store sound data as it's recorded cannot be known. In the wave file recorder discussed later in this chapter, this problem is dealt with by determining the maximum recording time the software will permit and allocating a buffer large enough to hold that much sound. In fact, you needn't actually do so explicitly—the MCI interface will handle all its internal buffering for you.

If you skip ahead to the MIDI recorder application discussed in
Chapter 6, you'll encounter an alternate approach to this situation.
The MIDI recorder will record virtually any amount of MIDI music by
constantly expanding its buffer as it records. This is practical for MIDI
messages, which don't represent a continuous stream of data. It's
trickier to handle in recording waveform audio—it's well beyond the
scope of the MCI interface as well.

To begin with, this is how you'd set up the MCI interface to start
recording sound:

```
MCI_OPEN_PARMS mciopen;
MCI_RECORD_PARMS mcirecord;
int id;

mciopen.lpstrDeviceType="waveaudio";
mciopen.lpstrElementName="";
if(mciSendCommand(0,MCI_OPEN,MCI_OPEN_TYPE |
    MCI_OPEN_ELEMENT,(DWORD)(LPVOID)&mciopen) != 0L)
        return(-1);

id=mciopen.wDeviceID;

mcirecord.dwTo=MAXRECORDTIME;
mcirecord.dwCallback=(DWORD)hwnd;
if(mciSendCommand(id,MCI_RECORD,MCI_TO | MCI_NOTIFY,
    (DWORD)(LPVOID)&mcirecord) != 0L) {
        mciSendCommand(soundID,MCI_CLOSE,0,NULL);
}

return(id);
```

The first call to mciSendCommand handles opening the MCI
waveaudio device, just as it did in the sample code fragment for
playing sound. In this case no wave file will be associated with the
device.

The second call to mciSendCommand starts the MCI interface
recording audio. The dwTo element of the MCI_RECORD_PARMS
object passed to it must contain the maximum recording time in

milliseconds. In this case, the MCI interface will notify the window referenced by the dwCallback element of the MCI_RECORD_PARMS object at such time as the maximum recording time has been reached, if recording isn't terminated manually first.

Because mciSendCommand is asynchronous, the function that this code fragment is part of will return as soon as recording is initiated. Control will return to the calling window, which can wait for a button click or other conventional bit of Windows user input to signal that the recording should be stopped. To stop a waveaudio recording, you would send the MCI_STOP message using mciSendCommand.

Here's the correct syntax to stop a wave that is being recorded:

```
MCI_GENERIC_PARMS mcigen;


mcigen.dwCallback=hwnd;
mciSendCommand(id,MCI_STOP,MCI_NOTIFY ¦ MCI_WAIT,
        (DWORD)(LPVOID)&mcigen);
```

The id argument to mciSendCommand would be the value returned by the code fragment that initiated recording, as discussed earlier.

Thus far I've mentioned that MCI is prepared to notify the message handler of the window of your choice when a wave file stops playing or recording, but I haven't explained the mechanism by which this happens. The notification occurs in the MCI_STOP call as well. When MCI wants to indicate that its song has lapsed into silence, it sends an MM_MCINOTIFY message to the window in question. This assumes that the MCI_NOTIFY flag was used when the sound was initially played or began recording, and that the dwCallback element of the data structure involved contained a valid HWND window handle for the window to receive the message.

An MM_MCINOTIFY message has the device ID value for the MCI device in question in the low-order word of its lParam argument, and it has a constant in its wParam argument. The constant will be one of the following:

MCI_NOTIFY_ABORTED   The function was aborted.

MCI_NOTIFY_SUCCESSFUL   The function was successful.

MCI_NOTIFY_SUPERSEDED   A new command took over the device
                         before the current one could be
                         completed.

MCI_NOTIFY_FAILURE   A device error occurred.

When an MM_MCINOTIFY message appears, the message handler
for the window that receives it should typically shut down the MCI
device in question. Here's a typical MM_MCINOTIFY message
handler:

```
case MM_MCINOTIFY:
    mciSendCommand(LOWORD(lParam),MCI_STOP,MCI_WAIT ,NULL);
    break;
```

The MCI_WAIT flag tells mciSendCommand not to return until the
MCI_STOP function has been completed. As an aside, if you apply this
flag to an MCI_PLAY or MCI_RECORD function, the MCI interface will
behave synchronously—it will not return control of the computer to
your application until the operation has been performed; that is, until
playing or recording terminates. You'll rarely want to do this.

Once a sound has been successfully recorded, you'll probably want to
write it to a WAV file. The MCI interface will be pleased to handle
this, as well:

```
MCI_SAVE_PARMS mcisave;

mcisave.lpfilename=FILENAME;
if(mciSendCommand(id,MCI_SAVE,MCI_SAVE_FILE,
    (DWORD)(LPVOID)&mcisave) != 0L)
        return(FALSE);

return(TRUE);
```

The id argument to mciSendCommand is the device ID returned by
the code fragment that initiated the recording. The FILENAME
constant is the name to write the file to—typically a name returned
from a dialog to prompt you for a file name. The result of all this will

be a Windows WAV file, suitable for use with any of the wave-playing
functions offered by the Windows multimedia extensions, or for
attachment to one of the system events that Windows supports
making noise for.

⇨ The wave file recorder

Figure 2-3 illustrates the main window of the WAVEREC application.
It's not the most complex of Windows applications. The upper left
area indicates the current wave file name—it defaults to
UNTITLED.WAV. The upper right area displays a running time
counter when a recording is in progress.

Figure 2-3

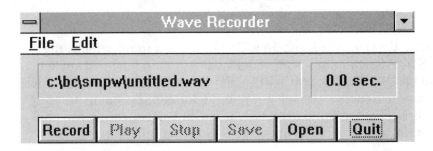

The WAVEREC application.

Figure 2-4 illustrates the WAVEREC.CPP source code file. Figure 2-5
illustrates WAVEREC.RC, its resource script. In addition to these files,
you'll need PRJ and DEF files for WAVEREC, and the WAV and BMP
files included in WAVEREC.RC. You will find all these files on the
companion CD-ROM for this book.

Figure 2-4   *The WAVEREC.CPP source code.*

```
/*
            Wave Recorder
            Copyright (c) 1993 Alchemy Mindworks Inc.
*/
#include <windows.h>
#include <stdio.h>
#include <stdlib.h>
#include <dir.h>
```

```
#include <ctype.h>
#include <alloc.h>
#include <string.h>
#include <io.h>
#include <bwcc.h>
#include <dos.h>
#include <errno.h>
#include <math.h>
#include <commdlg.h>
#include <mmsystem.h>


#define say(s)    MessageBox(NULL,s,"Yo...",MB_OK ¦ MB_ICONSTOP);
#define saynumber(f,s)    {char b[128]; sprintf((LPSTR)b,(LPSTR)f,s); \
                    MessageBox(NULL,b,"Debug Message",MB_OK ¦ MB_ICONSTOP); \
                    }


#define ItemName(item,string)    { dlgH=GetDlgItem(hwnd,item); \
                            SetWindowText(dlgH,(LPSTR)string); \
                            }


#define ItemOn(item)     { dlgH=GetDlgItem(hwnd,item); \
                    EnableWindow(dlgH,TRUE); \
                    EnableMenuItem(hmenu,item,MF_ENABLED);\
                    }


#define ItemOff(item)     { dlgH=GetDlgItem(hwnd,item); \
                    EnableWindow(dlgH,FALSE); \
                    EnableMenuItem(hmenu,item,MF_GRAYED);\
                    }


#define STRINGSIZE      128               /* how big is a string? */

#define THETIMER        1

#define MAIN_OPEN       101
#define MAIN_ABOUT      102

#define MAIN_RECORD     202
#define MAIN_PLAY       203
#define MAIN_STOP       204
#define MAIN_SAVE       205
#define MAIN_EXIT       206

#define MAIN_MESSAGE    401
#define MAIN_TIME       402

#define MAXRECORDTIME   30000      /* 30 seconds */

#define UpdateRecordTime(hwnd,n)   { char bxx[STRINGSIZE+1];\
                                wsprintf(bxx,"%u.%u sec.",n/10,n%10);\
                                ItemName(MAIN_TIME,bxx);\
                                }
```

Figure 2-4   *Continued.*

```
#define SetUntitledFile(hwnd)   { getcwd(soundpath,STRINGSIZE-16);\
                                 lstrcat(soundpath,"\\UNTITLED.WAV");\
                                 strlwr(soundpath);\
                                 ItemName(MAIN_MESSAGE,soundpath);\
                                 }

#define DoMessage(hwnd,string)       BWCCMessageBox(hwnd,string,"Message",\
                                       MB_OK | MB_ICONINFORMATION)

#define SetSoundPath(hwnd,bxx)       { lstrcpy(soundpath,bxx);\
                                 strlwr(soundpath);\
                                 ItemName(MAIN_MESSAGE,soundpath);\
                                 }

#ifndef max
#define max(a,b)           (((a)>(b))?(a):(b))
#endif
#ifndef min
#define min(a,b)           (((a)<(b))?(a):(b))
#endif

/* prototypes */
DWORD FAR PASCAL SelectProc(HWND hwnd,WORD message,WORD wParam,LONG lParam);
DWORD FAR PASCAL AboutDlgProc(HWND hwnd,WORD message,WORD wParam,LONG lParam);
DWORD FAR PASCAL MessageDlgProc(HWND hwnd,WORD message,WORD wParam,LONG lParam);

int RecordWave(HWND hwnd);
int PlayWave(HWND hwnd,int id);
int GetOpenFileName(HWND hwnd,LPSTR path);
int GetSaveFileName(HWND hwnd,LPSTR path);
int SaveWave(HWND hwnd,LPSTR path,int id);
int OpenWave(HWND hwnd,LPSTR path);
int CloseWave(HWND wnd,int id);

void SayLoadedSound(HWND hwnd,int flag);
void lmemset(LPSTR s,int n,unsigned int size);
void CentreWindow(HWND hwnd);

/* globals */
char szAppName[] = "WaveRecorder";
HANDLE hInst;

int soundID=-1;

char soundpath[256];

#pragma warn -par
int PASCAL WinMain(HANDLE hInstance,HANDLE hPrevInstance,
                LPSTR lpszCmdParam,int nCmdShow)
{
        FARPROC dlgProc;
```

```
        int r=0;

        BWCCGetVersion();

        hInst=hInstance;

        dlgProc=MakeProcInstance((FARPROC)SelectProc,hInst);
        r=DialogBox(hInst,"MainScreen",NULL,dlgProc);

        FreeProcInstance(dlgProc);

        return(r);
}

DWORD FAR PASCAL SelectProc(HWND hwnd,WORD message,WORD wParam,LONG lParam)
{
        static unsigned int recordtime,playtime;
        PAINTSTRUCT ps;
        HICON hIcon;
        FARPROC lpfnDlgProc;
        POINT point;
        MCI_GENERIC_PARMS mcigen;
        HMENU hmenu;
        HWND dlgH;
        char b[STRINGSIZE+1];

        switch(message) {
                case MM_MCINOTIFY:
                        KillTimer(hwnd,THETIMER);
                        mciSendCommand(LOWORD(lParam),MCI_STOP,MCI_WAIT,NULL);
                        ItemName(MAIN_MESSAGE,soundpath);
                        UpdateRecordTime(hwnd,recordtime);

                        hmenu=GetMenu(hwnd);
                        ItemOn(MAIN_RECORD);
                        ItemOn(MAIN_PLAY);
                        ItemOff(MAIN_STOP);
                        ItemOn(MAIN_SAVE);
                        ItemOn(MAIN_OPEN);

                        SayLoadedSound(hwnd,TRUE);
                        break;
                case WM_CTLCOLOR:
                        if(HIWORD(lParam)==CTLCOLOR_STATIC ||
                           HIWORD(lParam)==CTLCOLOR_DLG) {
                                SetBkColor(wParam,RGB(192,192,192));
                                SetTextColor(wParam,RGB(0,0,0));

                                ClientToScreen(hwnd,&point);
                                UnrealizeObject(GetStockObject(LTGRAY_BRUSH));
                                SetBrushOrg(wParam,point.x,point.y);

                                return((DWORD)GetStockObject(LTGRAY_BRUSH));
```

Figure 2-4   *Continued.*

```
                        }
                        if(HIWORD(lParam)==CTLCOLOR_BTN) {
                                SetBkColor(wParam,RGB(192,192,192));
                                SetTextColor(wParam,RGB(0,0,0));

                                ClientToScreen(hwnd,&point);
                                UnrealizeObject(GetStockObject(BLACK_BRUSH));
                                SetBrushOrg(wParam,point.x,point.y);

                                return((DWORD)GetStockObject(BLACK_BRUSH));
                        }
                        break;
                case WM_SYSCOMMAND:
                        switch(wParam & 0xfff0) {
                                case SC_CLOSE:
                                        SendMessage(hwnd,WM_COMMAND,MAIN_EXIT,0L);
                                        break;
                        }
                        break;
                case WM_TIMER:
                        if(playtime==0xffffU) {
                                ++recordtime;
                                UpdateRecordTime(hwnd,recordtime);
                        }
                        else {
                                ++playtime;
                                UpdateRecordTime(hwnd,playtime);
                        }
                        break;
                case WM_INITDIALOG:
                        hIcon=LoadIcon(hInst,szAppName);
                        SetClassWord(hwnd,GCW_HICON,(WORD)hIcon);
                        waveOutSetVolume(0,0xffffffffL);

                        recordtime=0;

                        hmenu=GetMenu(hwnd);

                        ItemOn(MAIN_OPEN);
                        ItemOn(MAIN_RECORD);
                        ItemOff(MAIN_PLAY);
                        ItemOff(MAIN_STOP);
                        ItemOff(MAIN_SAVE);

                        SetUntitledFile(hwnd);
                        UpdateRecordTime(hwnd,recordtime);
                        CentreWindow(hwnd);
                        break;
                case WM_PAINT:
                        BeginPaint(hwnd,&ps);
```

```
                    EndPaint(hwnd,&ps);
                    break;
            case WM_COMMAND:
                    switch(wParam) {
                            case MAIN_SAVE:
                                    if(GetSaveFileName(hwnd,b)) {
                                            SaveWave(hwnd,b,soundID);
                                            SetSoundPath(hwnd,b);
                                    }
                                    break;
                            case MAIN_RECORD:
                                    soundID=CloseWave(hwnd,soundID);
                                    ItemOff(MAIN_RECORD);
                                    if((soundID=RecordWave(hwnd)) != -1) {
                                            recordtime=0;
                                            playtime=0xffffU;
                                            SetTimer(hwnd,THETIMER,100,NULL);

                                            hmenu=GetMenu(hwnd);
                                            ItemOn(MAIN_STOP);
                                            ItemOff(MAIN_RECORD);
                                            ItemOff(MAIN_PLAY);
                                            ItemOff(MAIN_SAVE);
                                            ItemOff(MAIN_OPEN);

                                            SetUntitledFile(hwnd);
                                            UpdateRecordTime(hwnd,recordtime);
                                    }
                                    else {
                                            SayLoadedSound(hwnd,FALSE);
                                            soundpath[0]=0;
                                            DoMessage(hwnd,
                                                "Can't initiate recording")
                                    }
                                    ItemName(MAIN_MESSAGE,soundpath);
                                    break;
                            case MAIN_OPEN:
                                    soundID=CloseWave(hwnd,soundID);
                                    SayLoadedSound(hwnd,FALSE);
                                    SetUntitledFile(hwnd);
                                    recordtime=0;
                                    if(GetOpenFileName(hwnd,b)) {
                                            if((soundID=OpenWave(hwnd,b)) != -1) {
                                                    SayLoadedSound(hwnd,TRUE);
                                                    SetSoundPath(hwnd,b);
                                            } else
                                                    DoMessage(hwnd,
                                                        "Can't open that file");
                                    }

                                    break
                            case MAIN_STOP:
                                    if(soundID != -1) {
```

Figure 2-4   *Continued.*

```
                                              mcigen.dwCallback=hwnd;
                                              mciSendCommand(soundID,MCI_STOP,
                                                  MCI_NOTIFY | MCI_WAIT,
                                                  (DWORD)(LPVOID)&mcigen);
                                          }
                                          break;
                                  case MAIN_PLAY:
                                          if(soundID != -1) {
                                                  if(PlayWave(hwnd,soundID)) {
                                                          playtime=0;
                                                          UpdateRecordTime(hwnd,
                                                              playtime);
                                                          SetTimer(hwnd,THETIMER,
                                                              100,NULL);

                                                          hmenu=GetMenu(hwnd);

                                                          ItemOff(MAIN_RECORD);
                                                          ItemOff(MAIN_PLAY);
                                                          ItemOn(MAIN_STOP);
                                                          ItemOff(MAIN_SAVE);
                                                          ItemOff(MAIN_OPEN);
                                                  } else DoMessage(hwnd,"Can't play");
                                          }
                                          break
                                  case MAIN_ABOUT:
                                          if((lpfnDlgProc=MakeProcInstance((FARPROC)
                                              AboutDlgProc,hInst)) != NULL) {
                                                  DialogBox(hInst,"AboutBox",
                                                      hwnd,lpfnDlgProc);
                                                  FreeProcInstance(lpfnDlgProc);
                                          }
                                          break;
                                  case MAIN_EXIT:
                                          SendMessage(hwnd,WM_COMMAND,MAIN_STOP,0L);
                                          soundID=CloseWave(hwnd,soundID);
                                          PostQuitMessage(0);
                                          break;
                          }
                          break;
                  }

          return(FALSE);
  }

  DWORD FAR PASCAL AboutDlgProc(HWND hwnd,WORD message,WORD wParam,LONG lParam)
  {
          static HANDLE sound;
          static LPSTR psound;
          HANDLE handle;
          POINT point;
```

```
        switch(message) {
                case WM_INITDIALOG:
                        if((handle=FindResource(hInst,
                            "AboutWave",RT_RCDATA)) != NULL) {
                                if((sound=LoadResource(hInst,handle)) != NULL) {
                                        if((psound=LockResource(sound)) != NULL)
                                                sndPlaySound(psound,SND_ASYNC |
                                                    SND_MEMORY | SND_NOSTOP);
                                }
                        }
                        CentreWindow(hwnd);
                        return(FALSE);
                case WM_CTLCOLOR:
                        if(HIWORD(lParam)==CTLCOLOR_STATIC ||
                            HIWORD(lParam)==CTLCOLOR_DLG) {
                                SetBkColor(wParam,RGB(192,192,192));
                                SetTextColor(wParam,RGB(0,0,0));

                                ClientToScreen(hwnd,&point);
                                UnrealizeObject(GetStockObject(LTGRAY_BRUSH));
                                SetBrushOrg(wParam,point.x,point.y);

                                return((DWORD)GetStockObject(LTGRAY_BRUSH));

                        }
                        if(HIWORD(lParam)==CTLCOLOR_BTN) {
                                SetBkColor(wParam,RGB(192,192,192));
                                SetTextColor(wParam,RGB(0,0,0));

                                ClientToScreen(hwnd,&point);
                                UnrealizeObject(GetStockObject(BLACK_BRUSH));
                                SetBrushOrg(wParam,point.x,point.y);

                                return((DWORD)GetStockObject(BLACK_BRUSH));
                        }
                        break;
                case WM_COMMAND:
                        switch(wParam) {
                                case IDOK:
                                        sndPlaySound(NULL,SND_SYNC);
                                        if(psound != NULL) UnlockResource(sound);
                                        if(sound != NULL) FreeResource(sound);
                                        EndDialog(hwnd,wParam);
                                        return(FALSE);
                        }
                        break;
        }

        return(FALSE);
}

void lmemset(LPSTR s,int n,unsigned int size)
```

39

Figure 2-4 *Continued.*

```
{
        unsigned int i;

        for(i=0;i<size;++i) *s++=n;
}

void SayLoadedSound(HWND hwnd,int flag)
{
        HMENU hmenu;
        HWND dlgH;

        hmenu=GetMenu(hwnd);

        if(flag) {
                ItemOn(MAIN_PLAY);
                ItemOn(MAIN_SAVE);
        }
        else {
                ItemOff(MAIN_PLAY);
                ItemOff(MAIN_SAVE);
        }
}

int GetOpenFileName(HWND hwnd,LPSTR path)
{
        OPENFILENAME ofn;
        char szDirName[256],szFileTitle[256],szFilter[256];

        getcwd(szDirName,sizeof(szDirName)-1);

        lstrcpy(szFilter,"*.WAV");

        lmemset((LPSTR)&ofn,0,sizeof(OPENFILENAME));

        lstrcpy(path,"*.WAV");
        szFileTitle[0]=0;

        ofn.lStructSize=sizeof(OPENFILENAME);
        ofn.hwndOwner=hwnd;
        ofn.lpstrFilter="All files (*.*)\000*.*\000Wave files (*.WAV)\000*.WAV\000";
        ofn.lpstrFile=path;
        ofn.nFilterIndex=2;
        ofn.nMaxFile=STRINGSIZE;
        ofn.lpstrFileTitle=szFileTitle;
        ofn.nMaxFileTitle=sizeof(szFileTitle);
        ofn.lpstrInitialDir=szDirName;
        ofn.Flags=OFN_PATHMUSTEXIST | OFN_HIDEREADONLY;
        ofn.lpstrTitle="Open File";
        ofn.lpstrDefExt="WAV";

        if(!GetOpenFileName(&ofn)) {
```

```
                path[0]=0;
                return(0);
        } else return(1);
}
int GetSaveFileName(HWND hwnd,LPSTR path)
{
        OPENFILENAME ofn;
        char szDirName[256],szFileTitle[256],szFilter[256];

        getcwd(szDirName,sizeof(szDirName)-1);

        lstrcpy(szFilter,"*.WAV");

        lmemset((LPSTR)&ofn,0,sizeof(OPENFILENAME));

        lstrcpy(path,"*.WAV");
//      path[0]=0;
        szFileTitle[0]=0;

        ofn.lStructSize=sizeof(OPENFILENAME);
        ofn.hwndOwner=hwnd;
        ofn.lpstrFilter="Wave files (*.WAV)\000*.WAV\000";
        ofn.lpstrFile=path;
        ofn.nFilterIndex=2;
        ofn.nMaxFile=STRINGSIZE;
        ofn.lpstrFileTitle=szFileTitle;
        ofn.nMaxFileTitle=sizeof(szFileTitle);
        ofn.lpstrInitialDir=szDirName;
        ofn.Flags=OFN_OVERWRITEPROMPT | OFN_HIDEREADONLY;
        ofn.lpstrTitle="Save File";

        if(!GetSaveFileName(&ofn)) {
                path[0]=0;
                return(0);
        } else return(1);
}

int OpenWave(HWND hwnd,LPSTR path)
{
        MCI_OPEN_PARMS mciopen;
        DWORD rtrn;
        char b[STRINGSIZE+1];

        mciopen.lpstrDeviceType="waveaudio";
        mciopen.lpstrElementName=path;
        if((rtrn=mciSendCommand(0,MCI_OPEN,MCI_OPEN_TYPE |
        MCI_OPEN_ELEMENT,(DWORD)(LPVOID)&mciopen)) != 0L) {
            mciGetErrorString(rtrn,(LPSTR)b,STRINGSIZE);
            DoMessage(hwnd,b);
            return(-1);
        }

        return(mciopen.wDeviceID);
```

Figure 2-4   *Continued.*

```
        }

int SaveWave(HWND hwnd,LPSTR path,int id)
{
        MCI_SAVE_PARMS mcisave;
        DWORD rtrn;
        char b[STRINGSIZE+1];

        mcisave.lpfilename=path;
        if((rtrn=mciSendCommand(id,MCI_SAVE,MCI_SAVE_FILE,
            (DWORD)(LPVOID)&mcisave)) != 0L) {
                mciGetErrorString(rtrn,(LPSTR)b,STRINGSIZE);
                DoMessage(hwnd,b);
                return(0);
        }

        return(1);
}

int CloseWave(HWND wnd,int id)
{
        MCI_GENERIC_PARMS mcigen;

        if(soundID != -1) {
                mciSendCommand(id,MCI_CLOSE,MCI_WAIT,(DWORD)(LPVOID)&mcigen);
        }
        return(-1);
}

int RecordWave(HWND hwnd)
{
        MCI_OPEN_PARMS mciopen;
        MCI_RECORD_PARMS mcirecord;
        DWORD rtrn;
        char b[STRINGSIZE+1];
        int sndID;

        mciopen.lpstrDeviceType="waveaudio";
        mciopen.lpstrElementName="";
        if((rtrn=mciSendCommand(0,MCI_OPEN,MCI_OPEN_TYPE |
            MCI_OPEN_ELEMENT,(DWORD)(LPVOID)&mciopen)) != 0L) {
                mciGetErrorString(rtrn,(LPSTR)b,STRINGSIZE);
                DoMessage(hwnd,b);
                return(-1);
        }

        sndID=mciopen.wDeviceID;

        mcirecord.dwTo=MAXRECORDTIME;
        mcirecord.dwCallback=(DWORD)hwnd;
        if((rtrn=mciSendCommand(sndID,MCI_RECORD,MCI_TO |
```

```
                    MCI_NOTIFY,(DWORD)(LPVOID)&mcirecord)) != 0L) {
                        mciSendCommand(soundID,MCI_CLOSE,0,NULL);
                        mciGetErrorString(rtrn,(LPSTR)b,STRINGSIZE);
                        DoMessage(hwnd,b);
                        return(-1);
                }

                return(sndID);
        }

int PlayWave(HWND hwnd,int id)
{
        MCI_PLAY_PARMS mciplay;
        DWORD rtrn;
        char b[STRINGSIZE+1];

        mciplay.dwCallback=(DWORD)hwnd;
        mciplay.dwFrom=0L;
        if((rtrn=mciSendCommand(id,MCI_PLAY,MCI_FROM |
            MCI_NOTIFY,(DWORD)(LPVOID)&mciplay)) != 0L) {
                mciGetErrorString(rtrn,(LPSTR)b,STRINGSIZE);
                DoMessage(hwnd,b);
                return(FALSE);
        }

        return(TRUE);
}

void CentreWindow(HWND hwnd)
{
        RECT rect;
        unsigned int x,y;

        GetWindowRect(hwnd,&rect);
        x=(GetSystemMetrics(SM_CXSCREEN)-(rect.right-rect.left))/2;
        y=(GetSystemMetrics(SM_CYSCREEN)-(rect.bottom-rect.top))/2;
        SetWindowPos(hwnd,NULL,x,y,rect.right-rect.left,
            rect.bottom-rect.top,SWP_NOSIZE);
}
```

The WAVEREC.RC resource script.

Figure 2-5

```
MainScreen DIALOG 9, 24, 184, 48
STYLE WS_POPUP | WS_CAPTION | WS_SYSMENU | WS_MINIMIZEBOX
CAPTION "Wave Recorder"
MENU MainMenu
BEGIN
        CONTROL "", -1, "BorShade", BSS_GROUP | WS_CHILD | WS_VISIBLE, 8, 4, 124, 16
        LTEXT "", 401, 12, 8, 116, 8, WS_CHILD | WS_VISIBLE | WS_GROUP
        PUSHBUTTON "Quit", 206, 148, 28, 28, 12, WS_CHILD | WS_VISIBLE | WS_TABSTOP
        PUSHBUTTON "Open", 101, 120, 28, 28, 12, WS_CHILD | WS_VISIBLE | WS_TABSTOP
        PUSHBUTTON "Save", 205, 92, 28, 28, 12, WS_CHILD | WS_VISIBLE | WS_TABSTOP
```

43

Figure 2-5   *Continued.*

```
        PUSHBUTTON "Stop", 204, 64, 28, 28, 12, WS_CHILD ¦ WS_VISIBLE ¦ WS_TABSTOP
        PUSHBUTTON "Play", 203, 36, 28, 28, 12, WS_CHILD ¦ WS_VISIBLE ¦ WS_TABSTOP
        PUSHBUTTON "Record", 202, 8, 28, 28, 12, WS_CHILD ¦ WS_VISIBLE ¦ WS_TABSTOP
        CONTROL "", 102, "BorShade", 32769 ¦ WS_CHILD ¦ WS_VISIBLE, 136, 4, 40, 16
        CTEXT "", 402, 140, 8, 32, 8, WS_CHILD ¦ WS_VISIBLE ¦ WS_GROUP
END

MainMenu MENU
BEGIN
        POPUP "&File"
        BEGIN
                MENUITEM "&Open", 101
                MENUITEM "&Save", 205
                MENUITEM "&About", 102
                MENUITEM SEPARATOR
                MENUITEM "E&xit", 206
        END

        POPUP "&Edit"
        BEGIN
                MENUITEM "&Record", 202
                MENUITEM "&Play", 203
                MENUITEM "&Stop", 204
        END

END

AboutBox DIALOG 18, 18, 184, 180
STYLE WS_POPUP ¦ WS_CAPTION
CAPTION "About..."
BEGIN
        CONTROL "", 102, "BorShade", BSS_GROUP ¦ WS_CHILD ¦ WS_VISIBLE ¦ WS_TABSTOP,
            8, 68, 168, 76
        CTEXT "Wave Recorder 1.0\n\nCopyright (c) 1994 Alchemy Mindworks Inc.\n\n
            This program is part of the book Advanced Multimedia Programming for
            Windows by Steven William Rimmer, published by Windcrest/McGraw Hill.",
            -1, 12, 72, 160, 68, WS_CHILD ¦ WS_VISIBLE ¦ WS_GROUP
        CONTROL "Button", IDOK, "BorBtn", BS_DEFPUSHBUTTON ¦ WS_CHILD ¦ WS_VISIBLE ¦
            WS_TABSTOP, 74, 152, 32, 20
        CONTROL "Button", 801, "BorBtn", BS_PUSHBUTTON ¦ WS_CHILD ¦ WS_VISIBLE ¦
            WS_TABSTOP, 36, 8, 32, 20
END

1801 BITMAP "smpw.bmp"

AboutWave RCDATA "ABOUT.WAV"
WaveRecorder ICON
BEGIN
        '00 00 01 00 01 00 20 20 10 00 00 00 00 00 E8 02'
        '00 00 16 00 00 00 28 00 00 00 20 00 00 00 40 00'
```

```
'00 00 01 00 04 00 00 00 00 00 80 02 00 00 00 00'
'00 00 00 00 00 00 10 00 00 00 00 00 00 00 00 00'
'00 00 00 00 BF 00 00 BF 00 00 00 BF BF 00 BF 00'
'00 00 BF 00 BF 00 BF BF 00 00 C0 C0 C0 00 80 80'
'80 00 00 00 FF 00 00 FF 00 00 00 FF FF 00 FF 00'
'00 00 FF 00 FF 00 FF FF 00 00 FF FF FF 00 77 77'
'77 77 77 77 77 77 77 77 77 77 77 77 77 77 7F 88'
'88 88 88 88 88 88 88 88 88 88 88 88 88 87 7F F8'
'88 88 88 88 88 88 88 88 88 88 88 88 88 87 7F F7'
'77 77 77 77 77 77 77 77 77 77 77 77 78 87 7F F7'
'77 77 77 77 77 77 77 77 77 77 77 77 78 87 7F F7'
'77 77 77 77 77 77 77 77 77 77 77 77 78 87 7F F7'
'77 FF FF FF FF FF FF FF FF FF FF 77 78 87 7F F7'
'77 1F FF FF FF FF FF FF FF FF FF 77 78 87 7F F7'
'77 11 99 99 99 99 99 99 99 99 FF 77 78 87 7F F7'
'77 11 99 99 99 99 99 99 99 99 FF 77 78 87 7F F7'
'77 11 99 99 99 99 99 99 99 99 FF 77 78 87 7F F7'
'77 11 99 99 99 99 99 99 99 99 FF 77 78 87 7F F7'
'77 11 99 99 99 99 99 99 99 99 FF 77 78 87 7F F7'
'77 11 99 99 99 99 99 99 99 99 FF 77 78 87 7F F7'
'77 11 99 99 99 99 99 99 99 99 FF 77 78 87 7F F7'
'77 11 99 99 99 99 99 99 99 99 FF 77 78 87 7F F7'
'77 11 99 99 99 99 99 99 99 99 FF 77 78 87 7F F7'
'77 11 99 99 99 99 99 99 99 99 FF 77 78 87 7F F7'
'77 11 99 99 99 99 99 99 99 99 FF 77 78 87 7F F7'
'77 11 99 99 99 99 99 99 99 99 FF 77 78 87 7F F7'
'77 11 99 99 99 99 99 99 99 99 FF 77 78 87 7F F7'
'77 11 99 99 99 99 99 99 99 99 FF 77 78 87 7F F7'
'77 11 99 99 99 99 99 99 99 99 FF 77 78 87 7F F7'
'77 11 11 11 11 11 11 11 11 11 FF 77 78 87 7F F7'
'77 11 11 11 11 11 11 11 11 11 1F 77 78 87 7F F7'
'77 77 77 77 77 77 77 77 77 77 77 77 78 87 7F F7'
'77 77 77 77 77 77 77 77 77 77 77 77 78 87 7F F7'
'77 77 77 77 77 77 77 77 77 77 77 77 78 87 7F FF'
'FF FF FF FF FF FF FF FF FF FF FF FF F8 87 7F FF'
'FF FF FF FF FF FF FF FF FF FF FF FF FF 87 77 77'
'77 77 77 77 77 77 77 77 77 77 77 77 77 77 00 00'
'00 00 00 00 00 00 00 00 00 00 00 00 00 00 00 00'
'00 00 00 00 00 00 00 00 00 00 00 00 00 00 00 00'
'00 00 00 00 00 00 00 00 00 00 00 00 00 00 00 00'
'00 00 00 00 00 00 00 00 00 00 00 00 00 00 00 00'
'00 00 00 00 00 00 00 00 00 00 00 00 00 00 00 00'
'00 00 00 00 00 00 00 00 00 00 00 00 00 00 00 00'
'00 00 00 00 00 00 00 00 00 00 00 00 00 00 00 00'
'00 00 00 00 00 00 00 00 00 00 00 00 00 00 00 00'
'00 00 00 00 00 00 00 00 00 00 00 00 00 00 00'
END
```

The WAVEREC application is typical of the programs discussed in
this book, and if you're familiar with its basic structure you'll find
most of the later source code to be pretty easily understood. Its main

window is handled as a dialog, as called from the WinMain function of WAVEREC.CPP. Note the call to BWCCGetVersion preceding the one to DialogBox. As mentioned in Chapter 1, the applications in this book use the Borland BWCC.DLL library to beset themselves with fancy bitmapped buttons and drop shadows. Calling BWCCGetVersion ensures that the BWCC.DLL library is accessible as soon as the application boots up.

The SelectProc function serves as a message handler for the main window of WAVEREC. While some of the message types it deals with are specific to this application, most of them will turn up in all the programs in this book. The first of these in WAVEREC is WM_CTLCOLOR.

For reasons that might make light party chatter for archaeologists 3,000 years hence, Windows applications are no longer considered to be state-of-the-art unless their windows have grey backgrounds. There are actually a number of ways to arrive at this—the technology of greyness is discussed in detail in my book *Constructing Windows Dialogs*. Responding to WM_CTLCOLOR messages by returning a brush handle to the Windows stock light-grey brush works admirably.

The WM_INITDIALOG case of the SelectProc message handler takes care of whatever initialization is required for the dialog. It begins by loading the application icon and using SetClassWord to install it— one of the drawbacks to creating the main window of a Windows application as a dialog is that this won't be handled automatically for you. The ItemOn and ItemOff calls are actually macros, defined at the top of the WAVEREC.CPP listing. They take care of enabling or disabling menu items and buttons.

Note that in WAVEREC—as in most of the other applications in this book—the menu functions are duplicated by buttons. Most users will find the buttons quicker and easier to deal with, but experience suggests that omitting a menu bar from Windows software will typically call down the wrath of the Windows purists. The ItemOn and ItemOff macros deal with both menu items and buttons—it's important to call GetMenu before you use one.

The SetUntitledFile macro in the WM_INITDIALOG handler defines the initial file title. The UpdateRecordTime call sets the initial running time display. Finally, the CentreWindow function, defined later in WAVEREC.CPP, places the WAVEREC window in the center of your screen.

The WM_TIMER handler of SelectProc will be called once every tenth of a second when a wave file is playing or being recorded—we'll look at how this gets going in a moment. It actually has no effect on either recording or playing back, but merely serves to make the numbers change in the running time display. The MCI interface doesn't provide a way to have a function called periodically while an MCI function is proceeding. Using WM_TIMER messages—or one of the precision timer functions discussed in Chapter 3—is the only way to handle this task.

Note that even though the WM_TIMER messages handled by SelectProc are generated and processed asynchronously, they're still dealt with by the same processor that's running your computer as a whole. A beast of finite resources, the processor will encounter difficulties maintaining MCI recording if the code in your WM_TIMER handler requires a significant amount of time to execute.

The WM_COMMAND handler of SelectProc dispatches commands to the rest of the WAVEREC application, as generated by the buttons and menu items of its main window. Because the buttons and their corresponding menu items have the same resource ID numbers, only one set of handlers is needed. For example, an identical WM_COMMAND message with its wParam argument set to MAIN_SAVE will be generated if Save is selected from the WAVEREC File menu, or if you click on its Save button.

The MAIN_RECORD section of the WM_COMMAND message handler deals with starting a recording. It begins by calling CloseWave to deal with a previously recorded wave file, if one exists. The CloseWave function will do nothing if the device ID passed to it as its second argument is null, and it always returns a NULL value.

The RecordWave function does essentially what was discussed earlier in this chapter to start a recording through the MCI interface. If you look at its declaration later on in WAVEREC.CPP, you'll notice that it

does a bit more error handling than the earlier hypothetical code fragment, displaying a dialog with a description of what went wrong if the attempt to begin recording is unsuccessful.

Having said this, it's worth noting that while the canned error messages provided by the MCI interface are certainly better than cryptic error codes, they're not always wholly lucid. For example, the messages will recommend that users of the MCI interface contact the sound card manufacturer for things like driver problems. Sound card manufacturers no doubt appreciate this.

The RecordWave function will return an MCI device ID if it's successful, or a −1 if it's not. Assuming that all is well, the SetTimer API call is used to start a stream of WM_TIMER messages appearing at SelectProc at intervals of 100 milliseconds.

There are two fairly important things to keep in mind about WM_TIMER messages. The first is that Windows is able to provide only a finite number of timers. If other applications currently running under Windows are using timers for their own purposes, a further call to SetTimer could fail. Although the timer facility doesn't do anything particularly essential in this case, it's worth checking to be sure a call to SetTimer has succeeded if your software will misbehave without its WM_TIMER messages. The SetTimer function will return a false value if it was unable to start up the timer it was asked for.

A second important characteristic of Windows' timers is that they're only somewhat accurate. While a timer set to send WM_TIMER messages every hundred milliseconds will average 10 messages per second, it's unlikely that they will occur at precisely the same intervals. Perturbations in the Windows message queue will usually delay some messages longer than others. This problem will be addressed in greater detail in Chapter 3 when we deal with the precision timer facilities of the Windows multimedia extensions.

The MAIN_STOP section of the WM_COMMAND handler of SelectProc deals with stopping either wave recording or playing, depending on what's happening at the moment. The operation of this section is a bit more complex than it seems. As explained earlier in this chapter, mciSendCommand sends an MCI_STOP message to the MCI

interface. However, because this command includes the MCI_NOTIFY flag, an MM_MCINOTIFY message will be sent back to SelectProc. The MM_MCINOTIFY handler can be found at the top of SelectProc. It will stop the timer initiated by SetTimer and close the waveaudio device previously opened by RecordWave or PlayWave. It will also make some cosmetic adjustments to the main window of WAVEREC, enabling and disabling some menu items and buttons.

The MAIN_SAVE section of the WM_COMMAND handler takes care of saving a recorded wave file to disk. It makes a call to the GetSaveFileName function declared later on in WAVEREC.CPP to fetch a file name, and then uses SaveWave to write the current wave file to disk. The SaveWave function uses the MCI interface to handle the mechanics of storing recorded sound in a proper wave file, as illustrated earlier in this chapter.

The GetSaveFileName function makes a call to the Windows COMMDLG.DLL library to display a standard Save As dialog. For a more complete discussion of Windows' common dialogs, see my book *Constructing Windows Dialogs*.

The MAIN_PLAY section of the WM_COMMAND handler of SelectProc allows a previously recorded wave to be played, such that users of WAVEREC will be able to hear what they've wrought and decide whether it deserves to be preserved for posterity on disk. It calls PlayWave, which uses the basic MCI calls for wave playing discussed earlier in this chapter.

The About dialog of WAVEREC is called forth from the MAIN_ABOUT case of the SelectProc WM_COMMAND message handler. Messages for the About dialog are handled by AboutProc, immediately below SelectProc in WAVEREC.CPP. Note that the bitmap at the top of the dialog, illustrated in Fig. 2-1, is handled as a nonclickable Borland bitmap button, managed through BWCC.DLL. This is a somewhat unconventional use of the facility. If you're using the code in this book with a language other than Borland C++, you might want to take a look at Chapter 4 for a discussion of displaying bitmaps using more conventional techniques.

It's unlikely that you'll want to write a stand-alone wave recorder like WAVEREC as a serious application—countless similar programs exist.

However, you can extract the wave recording techniques discussed in this chapter for use in larger packages. The modular nature of the MCI interface makes it pretty effortless to pour the recording features of WAVEREC into your own software.

One of the limitations of the WAVEREC application as it stands—and, arguably, as a platform upon which to build a more elaborate wave file recorder and editor—is the somewhat "closed shop" of the MCI interface. It will record and play wave files, read them from disk, and write them back again, but it will not allow you ready access to the buffered sound samples it has in memory. This makes the prospect of modifying wave files handled by MCI somewhat impractical. Dealing with sampled sound at its elemental level requires a different set of functions from the multimedia extensions. You'll have to come to terms with RIFF files and with sound samples that give no quarter nor expect any.

We'll take a look at the violent, brutish world of wave files below the veneer of civilization in the next section of this chapter.

 # Wave file special effects

Sampled sound in its most basic sense consists of a list of values representing the instantaneous amplitude of complex waveforms. In a wave file, these can take one of four forms. A simple 8-bit wave file with monaural sound will consist of a string of single-byte values ranging from 0 through 255. A 16-bit wave file will consist of a string of signed word values ranging from −32,767 to 32,768. A stereo wave file will be structured like a monaural wave file, except that each sample will consist of two values, one for each channel. Quadraphonic wave files, mercifully, don't exist.

Digital sound processing allows you to modify the nature of a sampled sound by algorithmically processing its samples. This is a science which has grown to significant dimensions in the past few decades—the phone company, for example, is particularly interested in any technology that will allow it to squeeze more sound into a confined bandwidth. Other applications of complex algorithmic signal processing include noise reduction and digital echo machines.

In this section we will look at several fairly elementary special effects that can be wrought on the sampled sounds of wave files. We will also look at the functions you'll need to deal with wave files at their most basic level, such that their sound samples will become accessible. None of this will impress the phone company, by the way, which surpassed this rudimentary level of sound processing back when the only use of windows was as a place to chuck the family cat when it began to get underfoot.

Figure 2-6 illustrates the main window of WAVE-FX, a simple Windows application to experiment with sound processing. WAVE-FX will read and write wave files using the low-level RIFF file functions alluded to earlier, draw an *envelope graph* of a wave, and apply your choice of three sound-effects filters to the wave file in memory. Specifically, it will *reverse* a wave file, apply a *low-pass filter* to it, or add *echo* to it.

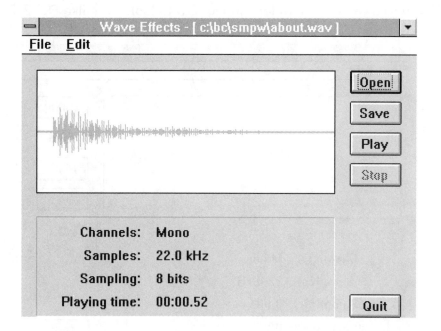

Figure 2-6

The WAVE-FX application.

The simplest of the wave file effects is reversing a sound—that is, manipulating its samples such that it plays backwards. Most natural acoustic sounds have a characteristic envelope that looks more or less like the one illustrated in Fig. 2-6. The event that initially causes the sound happens, and the sound is immediately at its loudest volume. The energy imparted by whatever created the sound subsequently decays, and the sound gets progressively softer. This envelope is common to things like guitar notes, drum beats, the sound of a horse's hoof on stone, a cough, or the noise the aforementioned cat might have made being chucked out a window.

One of the remarkable things about cats leaving through a window is that they always land on their feet—although sometimes not until after the third or fourth bounce. A cat bouncing will create a more complex sound envelope than the one in Fig. 2-6.

Reversing a wave file involves nothing more than copying its samples to a new buffer in the reverse order that they'd naturally appear in. This would cause the envelope in Fig. 2-6 to look more like Fig. 2-7.

Figure 2-7

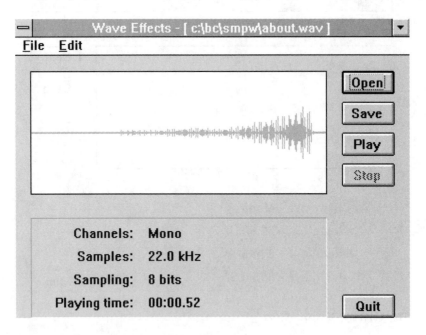

A reversed wave file in WAVE-FX.

There are virtually no natural acoustic phenomena that produce sounds with an envelope like the one in Fig. 2-7—that is, a sound that gets gradually louder and then suddenly becomes silent. Sound is created by imparting energy to something that can be made to vibrate. Vibrations may die out gradually, but it's difficult to imagine a situation in which energy could be added to a vibrating object gradually, and then suddenly removed all at once.

The unlikelihood of a sound like the one in Fig. 2-7 occurring naturally makes reversed sounds particularly unusual and interesting. Some while back it was all the rage to work them into music by recording normal sounds on a half-track reel-to-reel tape recorder and turning the tape over. You can't do this with a conventional tape recorder—a half-track stereo recorder has only two tracks on its tape, and the tape is only recorded in one direction.

One of the most interesting of these bits of tape manipulation is the percussive introduction to Queen of Dreams on the Strawbs' Grave New World album. For the faithful, it's available on compact disc, but only in Japan as far as I know.

Low-pass filtering a digital sound is considerably less involved than it might seem. In electronic terms, a low-pass filter is a circuit that allows low frequencies to pass unattenuated but obstructs higher frequencies. Higher frequencies in a sampled sound are represented by data that changes more rapidly as the samples are stepped through. In comparing two adjacent samples, a greater difference between their amplitudes indicates a higher frequency in the waveform they're part of.

To apply a digital low-pass filter to a sampled sound, then, you would integrate the adjoining samples by averaging them and applying a portion of the error between them to each. Increasing the amount of integration would, in effect, reduce the corner frequency of the filter.

A low-pass filter will make a sound seem less distinct—if you reduce the corner frequency sufficiently, the sound in question will seem to be at the far end of a bad phone line.

Effects involving echo are perhaps the most interesting of the things you can do to sound. Aside from simple reverberation, many of the guitar effects that appear in popular music use small amounts of delayed sound mixed with the original signal. While much of the theory of delay effects is well beyond the scope of this book, you might want to experiment with some variations on the reverberation filter discussed in this chapter, should you want to expand on the basic effects presented here.

In its simplest sense, you can add reverberation to a sound by duplicating each sample farther along in the string of samples, typically reduced in amplitude somewhat to simulate the original sound decaying. Radically different echo characteristics can be obtained by varying the rate of decay and the delay between each sample and its first echo.

The WAVE-FX application allows you to experiment interactively with the three effects filters it offers. Having loaded a sound into WAVE-FX, you can call up the dialogs illustrated in Fig. 2-8 to see what the effects filters make your wave file sound like, and how they affect its visual envelope diagram.

The flexibility of the Windows wave file format can be a bit of a nuisance for software that wants to work with wave files at the sample level. Samples can be either 8 or 16 bits wide, and in either mono or stereo, for a total of four possible permutations. The WAVE-FX source code is relatively long as it stands, and in order to keep it from getting any more so, the version of WAVE-FX discussed in this chapter is limited to working with 8-bit monaural wave files. This is possibly not the best format for experimenting with sound effects— any filter that actually modifies the amplitude of the sound samples in a wave file will tend to create somewhat crunchy sounds due to the rounding errors inherent in 8-bit numbers. If you find WAVE-FX interesting and want to expand its facilities into a real-world application, you'll probably want to give it the capability of working with the other three wave file formats.

For a more complete discussion of the variations on wave files see *Multimedia Programming for Windows*.

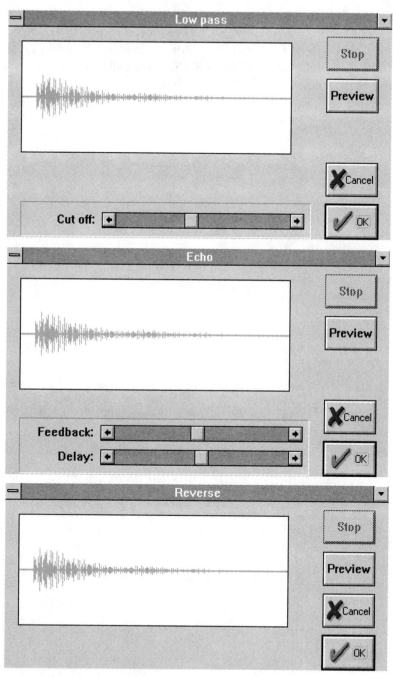

Figure 2-8

The WAVE-FX filter dialogs.

Figure 2-9 illustrates the WAVE-FX.CPP source code file. Figure
2-10 illustrates WAVE-FX.RC, its resource script. In addition to these
files, you'll need PRJ and DEF files for WAVE-FX, and the WAV and
BMP files included in WAVE-FX.RC. You will find all these files on
the companion CD-ROM for this book.

Figure 2-9   *The WAVE-FX.CPP source code.*

```
/*
     Wave Effects
     Copyright (c) 1993 Alchemy Mindworks Inc.
*/
#include <windows.h>
#include <stdio.h>
#include <stdlib.h>
#include <dir.h>0
#include <ctype.h>
#include <alloc.h>
#include <string.h>
#include <io.h>
#include <bwcc.h>
#include <dos.h>
#include <errno.h>
#include <math.h>
#include <commdlg.h>
#include <mmsystem.h>

#define    say(s)     MessageBox(NULL,s,"Yo...",MB_OK | MB_ICONSTOP);
#define    saynumber(f,s)     {char b[128]; sprintf((LPSTR)b,(LPSTR)f,s); \
            MessageBox(NULL,b,"Debug Message",MB_OK | MB_ICONSTOP); \
            }

#define    ItemName(item,string)     { dlgH=GetDlgItem(hwnd,item); \
            SetWindowText(dlgH,(LPSTR)string); \
            }

#define    ItemOn(item)     { dlgH=GetDlgItem(hwnd,item); \
            EnableWindow(dlgH,TRUE); \
            EnableMenuItem(hmenu,item,MF_ENABLED);\
            }

#define    ItemOff(item)     { dlgH=GetDlgItem(hwnd,item); \
            EnableWindow(dlgH,FALSE); \
            EnableMenuItem(hmenu,item,MF_GRAYED);\
            }

#define    STRINGSIZE    128          /* how big is a string? */

#define    THETIMER    1

#define    MAIN_OPEN    101
```

```
#define    MAIN_SAVE      102
#define    MAIN_SAVEAS    103
#define    MAIN_ABOUT     104
#define    MAIN_EXIT      199

#define    MAIN_PLAY      201
#define    MAIN_STOP      202

#define    MAIN_LOWPASS   203
#define    MAIN_ECHO      204
#define    MAIN_REVERSE   205

#define    INFO_CHANNELS 401
#define    INFO_SAMPLES  402
#define    INFO_SAMPLING 403
#define    INFO_PLAYTIME 404

#define    INFO_WAVELEFT 16          /* where the wave diagram goes */
#define    INFO_WAVETOP  16
#define    INFO_WAVEWIDE 320
#define    INFO_WAVEDEEP 128

#define    FX_PREVIEW     701
#define    FX_FEEDBACK    702
#define    FX_DELAY       703
#define    FX_CUTOFF      704
#define    FX_STOP        799

#define    MIN_FEEDBACK   1
#define    MAX_FEEDBACK   24
#define    MIN_DELAY      16
#define    MAX_DELAY      8192
#define    MIN_CUTOFF     1
#define    MAX_CUTOFF     8

#define    SetUntitledFile(hwnd) { char sxx[STRINGSIZE+1];\
               getcwd(soundpath,STRINGSIZE-16);\
               lstrcat(soundpath,"\\UNTITLED.WAV");\
               strlwr(soundpath);\
               wsprintf(sxx,"Wave Effects - [ %s ]",(LPSTR)soundpath);\
               SetWindowText(hwnd,sxx);\
               }

#define    DoMessage(hwnd,string) BWCCMessageBox(hwnd,string,"Message",\
               MB_OK | MB_ICONINFORMATION)

#define    SetSoundPath(hwnd,bxx) { char sxx[STRINGSIZE+1];\
               lstrcpy(soundpath,bxx);\
               strlwr(soundpath);\
               wsprintf(sxx,"Wave Effects - [ %s ]",(LPSTR)soundpath);\
               SetWindowText(hwnd,sxx);\
               }
```

Figure 2-9 *Continued.*

```
#define     UpdateGraph(hwnd) { RECT rectxx;\
                SetRect(&rectxx,INFO_WAVELEFT,INFO_WAVETOP,\
                 INFO_WAVELEFT+INFO_WAVEWIDE,\
                 INFO_WAVETOP+INFO_WAVEDEEP);\
                InvalidateRect(hwnd,&rectxx,TRUE);\
              }

#define     GetSample(lpsxx,nxx)         ((SAMPLE)lpsxx->wavepointer[nxx])
#define     PutSample(lpsxx,nxx,smpxx)  lpsxx->wavepointer[nxx]=\
                                        (char)max(min(smpxx,255),0)
#define     ClampSample(nxx)             max(min(nxx,255),0)

#ifndef max
#define max(a,b)            (((a)>(b))?(a):(b))
#endif
#ifndef min
#define min(a,b)            (((a)<(b))?(a):(b))
#endif

typedef struct {
    char name[STRINGSIZE+1];
    PCMWAVEFORMAT waveformat;
    HPSTR wavepointer;
    unsigned long datasize;
    GLOBALHANDLE wavehandle;
    GLOBALHANDLE waveheader;
    LPWAVEHDR pwaveheader;
    HWAVEOUT hwaveout;
    } SOUND;

typedef SOUND FAR *LPSOUND;

typedef int SAMPLE;

/* prototypes */
DWORD FAR PASCAL SelectProc(HWND hwnd,WORD message,WORD wParam,LONG lParam);
DWORD FAR PASCAL AboutDlgProc(HWND hwnd,WORD message,WORD wParam,LONG lParam);
DWORD FAR PASCAL ReverseDlgProc(HWND hwnd,WORD message,WORD wParam,LONG lParam);
DWORD FAR PASCAL EchoDlgProc(HWND hwnd,WORD message,WORD wParam,LONG lParam);
DWORD FAR PASCAL LowpassDlgProc(HWND hwnd,WORD message,WORD wParam,LONG lParam);

DWORD HandleCtlColour(HWND hwnd,WORD wParam,DWORD lParam);

LPSOUND OpenWave(HWND hwnd,LPSTR path);
LPSOUND DestroyWave(LPSOUND lpsound);
LPSOUND DuplicateWave(LPSOUND lpsource);
LPSOUND ReverseWave(LPSOUND lpsource);
LPSOUND EchoWave(LPSOUND lpsource,int delay,int feedback);
LPSOUND LowpassWave(LPSOUND lpsource,int cutoff);

LPSOUND DoReverse(HWND hwnd,LPSOUND lpsound);
```

```
LPSOUND DoEcho(HWND hwnd,LPSOUND lpsound);
LPSOUND DoLowpass(HWND hwnd,LPSOUND lpsound);

unsigned long GetWaveSampleCount(LPSOUND lpsound);

int PlayWave(HWND hwnd,LPSOUND lpsound);
int GetAmplitude(LPSOUND lpsound,unsigned long sample);
int HandleScroll(HWND hwnd,WORD wParam,DWORD lParam);
int GetOpenFileName(HWND hwnd,LPSTR path);
int GetSaveFileName(HWND hwnd,LPSTR path);
int WriteWave(HWND hwnd,LPSTR path,LPSOUND lpsound);
int LockWave(LPSOUND lpsound);
int IsSuitableWave(LPSOUND lpsound);

void UnlockWave(LPSOUND lpsound);
void AddInfo(HWND hwnd,LPSOUND lpsound);
void DrawWave(HDC hdc,unsigned int x,unsigned int y,LPSOUND lpsound);
void SayLoadedSound(HWND hwnd,int flag);
void SayPlayingSound(HWND hwnd,int flag);
void lmemset(LPSTR s,int n,unsigned int size);
void CentreWindow(HWND hwnd);

/* globals */
char szAppName[] = "WaveEffects";
HANDLE hInst;
LPSTR messagehook;
char soundpath[256];

#pragma warn -par
int PASCAL WinMain(HANDLE hInstance,HANDLE hPrevInstance,
        LPSTR lpszCmdParam,int nCmdShow)
{
    FARPROC dlgProc;
    int r=0;

    BWCCGetVersion();

    if(lstrlen(lpszCmdParam)) messagehook=lpszCmdParam;
    else messagehook=NULL;

    hInst=hInstance;

    dlgProc=MakeProcInstance((FARPROC)SelectProc,hInst);
    r=DialogBox(hInst,"MainScreen",NULL,dlgProc);

    FreeProcInstance(dlgProc);

    return(r);
}

DWORD FAR PASCAL SelectProc(HWND hwnd,WORD message,WORD wParam,LONG lParam)
{
    static LPSOUND lpsound;
```

Figure 2-9   *Continued.*

```
LPSOUND lptemp;
PAINTSTRUCT ps;
HICON hIcon;
FARPROC lpfnDlgProc;
HMENU hmenu;
HWND dlgH;
HDC hdc;
char b[STRINGSIZE+1];

switch(message) {
    case MM_WOM_DONE:
        waveOutUnprepareHeader((HWAVEOUT)wParam,
            (LPWAVEHDR)lParam,sizeof(WAVEHDR));
        waveOutClose((HWAVEOUT)wParam);
        if(lpsound->waveheader != NULL) {
            GlobalUnlock(lpsound->waveheader);
            GlobalFree(lpsound->waveheader);
            lpsound->waveheader=NULL;
        }

        SayPlayingSound(hwnd,FALSE);
        break;
    case WM_CTLCOLOR:
        return(HandleCtlColour(hwnd,wParam,lParam));
    case WM_SYSCOMMAND:
        switch(wParam & 0xfff0) {
            case SC_CLOSE:
                SendMessage(hwnd,WM_COMMAND,MAIN_EXIT,0L);
                break;
        }
        break;
    case WM_INITDIALOG:
        hIcon=LoadIcon(hInst,szAppName);
        SetClassWord(hwnd,GCW_HICON,(WORD)hIcon);
        waveOutSetVolume(0,0xffffffffL);

        lpsound=NULL;

        hmenu=GetMenu(hwnd);

        ItemOn(MAIN_OPEN);

        ItemOff(MAIN_PLAY);
        ItemOff(MAIN_STOP);
        ItemOff(MAIN_SAVE);
        ItemOff(MAIN_LOWPASS);
        ItemOff(MAIN_ECHO);
        ItemOff(MAIN_REVERSE);

        SetUntitledFile(hwnd);
```

```
        if(messagehook != NULL) {
            lstrcpy(b,messagehook);
            strlwr(b);
            if((lpsound=OpenWave(hwnd,b)) != NULL) {
                if(!IsSuitableWave(lpsound)) {
                    lpsound=DestroyWave(lpsound);
                    DoMessage(hwnd,
                        "Unsuitable wave format");
                }
                else {
                    AddInfo(hwnd,lpsound);
                    SayLoadedSound(hwnd,TRUE);
                    SetSoundPath(hwnd,b);
                }
            }
        }
        CentreWindow(hwnd);
        break;
    case WM_PAINT:
        hdc=BeginPaint(hwnd,&ps);
        DrawWave(hdc,INFO_WAVELEFT,INFO_WAVETOP,lpsound);
        EndPaint(hwnd,&ps);
        break;
    case WM_COMMAND:
        switch(wParam) {
            case MAIN_LOWPASS:
                if((lptemp=DoLowpass(hwnd,lpsound)) != NULL) {
                    lpsound=DestroyWave(lpsound);
                    lpsound=lptemp;
                    UpdateGraph(hwnd);
                }
                break;
            case MAIN_ECHO:
                if((lptemp=DoEcho(hwnd,lpsound)) != NULL) {
                    lpsound=DestroyWave(lpsound);
                    lpsound=lptemp;
                    UpdateGraph(hwnd);
                }
                break;
            case MAIN_REVERSE:
                if((lptemp=DoReverse(hwnd,lpsound)) != NULL) {
                    lpsound=DestroyWave(lpsound);
                    lpsound=lptemp;
                    UpdateGraph(hwnd);
                }
                break;
            case MAIN_SAVE:
                fnsplit(soundpath,NULL,NULL,b,NULL);
                if(stricmp(b,"untitled"))
                    WriteWave(hwnd,b,lpsound);
                else SendMessage(hwnd,WM_COMMAND,
                    MAIN_SAVEAS,0L);
                break;
```

61

Figure 2-9   *Continued.*

```
case MAIN_SAVEAS:
    if(GetSaveFileName(hwnd,b)) {
        if(WriteWave(hwnd,b,lpsound)) {
            SetSoundPath(hwnd,b
        }
        else
            DoMessage(hwnd,
                "Error writing file");
    }
    break;
case MAIN_OPEN:
    lpsound=DestroyWave(lpsound);
    SayLoadedSound(hwnd,FALSE);
    SetUntitledFile(hwnd);
    if(GetOpenFileName(hwnd,b)) {
        if((lpsound=OpenWave(hwnd,b)) != NULL) {
            if(!IsSuitableWave(lpsound)) {
                lpsound=
                    DestroyWave(lpsound);
                DoMessage(hwnd,
                    "Unsuitable wave format");
            }
            else {
                AddInfo(hwnd,lpsound);
                UpdateGraph(hwnd);
                SayLoadedSound(hwnd,TRUE);
                SetSoundPath(hwnd,b);
            }
        } else
            DoMessage(hwnd,"Can't open that file");
    }

    break;
case MAIN_STOP:
    if(lpsound != NULL &&
        lpsound->wavehandle != NULL)
            waveOutReset(lpsound->hwaveout);
    break;
case MAIN_PLAY:
    if(lpsound != NULL &&
        lpsound->wavehandle != NULL) {
        if(PlayWave(hwnd,lpsound)) {
            SayPlayingSound(hwnd,TRUE);
        } else DoMessage(hwnd,"Can't play");
    }
    break;
case MAIN_ABOUT:
    if((lpfnDlgProc=MakeProcInstance((FARPROC)
        AboutDlgProc,hInst)) != NULL) {
        DialogBox(hInst,"AboutBox",
            hwnd,lpfnDlgProc);
```

```
                          FreeProcInstance(lpfnDlgProc);
                    }
                    break;
                 case MAIN_EXIT:
                    SendMessage(hwnd,WM_COMMAND,MAIN_STOP,0L);
                    lpsound=DestroyWave(lpsound);
                    PostQuitMessage(0);
                    break;

            }
            break;

    }

    return(FALSE);
}

LPSOUND DoLowpass(HWND hwnd,LPSOUND lpsound)
{
    FARPROC lpfnDlgProc;
    LPSTR oldmessagehook;
    int r;

    oldmessagehook=messagehook;
    messagehook=(LPSTR)lpsound;
    if((lpfnDlgProc=MakeProcInstance((FARPROC)LowpassDlgProc,hInst)) != NULL) {
        r=DialogBox(hInst,"LowpassBox",hwnd,lpfnDlgProc);
        FreeProcInstance(lpfnDlgProc);
    }
    lpsound=(LPSOUND)messagehook;
    messagehook=oldmessagehook;

    if(r==IDOK) return(lpsound);
    else return(NULL);
}

DWORD FAR PASCAL LowpassDlgProc(HWND hwnd,WORD message,WORD wParam,LONG lParam)
{
    static LPSOUND lpsound;
    PAINTSTRUCT ps;
    HWND dlgH;
    HDC hdc;
    int cutoff;

    switch(message) {
        case MM_WOM_DONE:
            waveOutUnprepareHeader((HWAVEOUT)wParam,
                (LPWAVEHDR)lParam,sizeof(WAVEHDR));
            waveOutClose((HWAVEOUT)wParam);
            if(lpsound->waveheader != NULL) {
                GlobalUnlock(lpsound->waveheader);
                GlobalFree(lpsound->waveheader);
                lpsound->waveheader=NULL;
            }
```

Figure 2-9   *Continued.*

```
            SayPlayingSound(hwnd,FALSE);
            break;
    case WM_INITDIALOG:
        lpsound=NULL;
        SayPlayingSound(hwnd,FALSE);

        dlgH=GetDlgItem(hwnd,FX_CUTOFF);
        SetScrollRange(dlgH,SB_CTL,MIN_CUTOFF,MAX_CUTOFF,FALSE);
        SetScrollPos(dlgH,SB_CTL,(MIN_CUTOFF+MAX_CUTOFF)/2,TRUE);

        CentreWindow(hwnd);
        return(FALSE);
    case WM_HSCROLL:
        HandleScroll(hwnd,wParam,lParam);
                    break;
    case WM_CTLCOLOR:
        return(HandleCtlColour(hwnd,wParam,lParam));
    case WM_PAINT:
        hdc=BeginPaint(hwnd,&ps);
        if(lpsound==NULL)
            DrawWave(hdc,INFO_WAVELEFT,INFO_WAVETOP,
                (LPSOUND)messagehook);
        else
            DrawWave(hdc,INFO_WAVELEFT,INFO_WAVETOP,lpsound);
        EndPaint(hwnd,&ps);
        break;
    case WM_COMMAND:
        switch(wParam) {
            case FX_STOP:
                if(lpsound != NULL &&
                    lpsound->wavehandle != NULL)
                        waveOutReset(lpsound->hwaveout);
                break;
            case FX_PREVIEW:
                cutoff=GetScrollPos(GetDlgItem(hwnd,
                    FX_CUTOFF),SB_CTL);

                if((lpsound=LowpassWave((LPSOUND)messagehook,
                    cutoff)) != NULL) {
                    UpdateGraph(hwnd);

                    if(PlayWave(hwnd,lpsound)) {
                        SayPlayingSound(hwnd,TRUE);
                    } else DoMessage(hwnd,"Can't play");
                } else DoMessage(hwnd,"Can't process");
                break;
            case IDOK:
                SendMessage(hwnd,WM_COMMAND,FX_STOP,0L);
                cutoff=GetScrollPos(GetDlgItem(hwnd,
                    FX_CUTOFF),SB_CTL);
```

```
                    messagehook=(LPSTR)LowpassWave((LPSOUND)
                        messagehook,cutoff);
                    EndDialog(hwnd,wParam);
                    return(FALSE);
                case IDCANCEL:
                    SendMessage(hwnd,WM_COMMAND,FX_STOP,0L);
                    EndDialog(hwnd,wParam);
                    return(FALSE);
            }
            break;
    }

    return(FALSE);
}

LPSOUND DoEcho(HWND hwnd,LPSOUND lpsound)
{
    FARPROC lpfnDlgProc;
    LPSTR oldmessagehook;
    int r;

    oldmessagehook=messagehook;
    messagehook=(LPSTR)lpsound;
    if((lpfnDlgProc=MakeProcInstance((FARPROC)EchoDlgProc,hInst)) != NULL) {
        r=DialogBox(hInst,"EchoBox",hwnd,lpfnDlgProc);
        FreeProcInstance(lpfnDlgProc);
    }
    lpsound=(LPSOUND)messagehook;
    messagehook=oldmessagehook;

    if(r==IDOK) return(lpsound);
    else return(NULL);
}

DWORD FAR PASCAL EchoDlgProc(HWND hwnd,WORD message,WORD wParam,LONG lParam)
{
    static LPSOUND lpsound;
    PAINTSTRUCT ps;
    HDC hdc;
    HWND dlgH;
    int delay,feedback;

    switch(message) {
        case MM_WOM_DONE:
            waveOutUnprepareHeader((HWAVEOUT)wParam,
                (LPWAVEHDR)lParam,sizeof(WAVEHDR));
            waveOutClose((HWAVEOUT)wParam);
            if(lpsound->waveheader != NULL) {
                GlobalUnlock(lpsound->waveheader);
                GlobalFree(lpsound->waveheader);
                lpsound->waveheader=NULL;
            }
```

Figure 2-9 *Continued.*

```
            SayPlayingSound(hwnd,FALSE);
            break;
        case WM_INITDIALOG:
            lpsound=NULL;

            dlgH=GetDlgItem(hwnd,FX_FEEDBACK);
            SetScrollRange(dlgH,SB_CTL,MIN_FEEDBACK,MAX_FEEDBACK,FALSE);
            SetScrollPos(dlgH,SB_CTL,(MIN_FEEDBACK+MAX_FEEDBACK)/2,TRUE);

            dlgH=GetDlgItem(hwnd,FX_DELAY);
            SetScrollRange(dlgH,SB_CTL,MIN_DELAY,MAX_DELAY,FALSE);
            SetScrollPos(dlgH,SB_CTL,(MIN_DELAY+MAX_DELAY)/2,TRUE);

            SayPlayingSound(hwnd,FALSE);

            CentreWindow(hwnd);
            return(FALSE);
        case WM_HSCROLL:
            HandleScroll(hwnd,wParam,lParam);
            break;
        case WM_CTLCOLOR:
            return(HandleCtlColour(hwnd,wParam,lParam));
        case WM_PAINT:
            hdc=BeginPaint(hwnd,&ps);
            if(lpsound==NULL)
                DrawWave(hdc,INFO_WAVELEFT,INFO_WAVETOP,
                    (LPSOUND)messagehook);
            else
                DrawWave(hdc,INFO_WAVELEFT,INFO_WAVETOP,lpsound);
            EndPaint(hwnd,&ps);
            break;
        case WM_COMMAND:
            switch(wParam) {
                case FX_STOP:
                    if(lpsound != NULL && lpsound->wavehandle != NULL)
                        waveOutReset(lpsound->hwaveout);
                    break;
                case FX_PREVIEW:
                    delay=GetScrollPos(GetDlgItem(hwnd,FX_DELAY),SB_CTL);
                    feedback=GetScrollPos(GetDlgItem(hwnd,
                        FX_FEEDBACK),SB_CTL);

                    if((lpsound=EchoWave((LPSOUND)messagehook,
                        delay,feedback)) != NULL) {
                        UpdateGraph(hwnd);

                        if(PlayWave(hwnd,lpsound)) {
                                SayPlayingSound(hwnd,TRUE);
                        } else DoMessage(hwnd,"Can't play");
                    } else DoMessage(hwnd,"Can't echo");
```

```
                    break;
                case IDOK:
                    SendMessage(hwnd,WM_COMMAND,FX_STOP,0L);
                    delay=GetScrollPos(GetDlgItem(hwnd,
                        FX_DELAY),SB_CTL);
                    feedback=GetScrollPos(GetDlgItem(hwnd,
                        FX_FEEDBACK),SB_CTL);
                    messagehook=(LPSTR)EchoWave((LPSOUND)messagehook,
                        delay,feedback);
                    EndDialog(hwnd,wParam);
                    return(FALSE);
                case IDCANCEL:
                    SendMessage(hwnd,WM_COMMAND,FX_STOP,0L);
                    EndDialog(hwnd,wParam);
                    return(FALSE);
            }
            break;
    }

    return(FALSE);
}

LPSOUND DoReverse(HWND hwnd,LPSOUND lpsound)
{
    FARPROC lpfnDlgProc;
    LPSTR oldmessagehook;
    int r;

    oldmessagehook=messagehook;
    messagehook=(LPSTR)lpsound;
    if((lpfnDlgProc=MakeProcInstance((FARPROC)ReverseDlgProc,hInst)) != NULL) {
        r=DialogBox(hInst,"ReverseBox",hwnd,lpfnDlgProc);
        FreeProcInstance(lpfnDlgProc);
    }
    lpsound=(LPSOUND)messagehook;
    messagehook=oldmessagehook;

    if(r==IDOK) return(lpsound);
    else return(NULL);
}

DWORD FAR PASCAL ReverseDlgProc(HWND hwnd,WORD message,WORD wParam,LONG lParam)
{
    static LPSOUND lpsound;
    PAINTSTRUCT ps;
    HDC hdc;

    switch(message) {
        case MM_WOM_DONE:
            waveOutUnprepareHeader((HWAVEOUT)wParam,(LPWAVEHDR)lParam,
                sizeof(WAVEHDR));
            waveOutClose((HWAVEOUT)wParam);
            if(lpsound->waveheader != NULL) {
```

Figure 2-9   *Continued.*

```
                GlobalUnlock(lpsound->waveheader);
                GlobalFree(lpsound->waveheader);
                lpsound->waveheader=NULL;
            }

            SayPlayingSound(hwnd,FALSE);
            break;
        case WM_INITDIALOG:
            lpsound=NULL;
            SayPlayingSound(hwnd,FALSE);
            CentreWindow(hwnd);
            return(FALSE);
        case WM_CTLCOLOR:
            return(HandleCtlColour(hwnd,wParam,lParam));
        case WM_PAINT:
            hdc=BeginPaint(hwnd,&ps);
            if(lpsound==NULL)
                DrawWave(hdc,INFO_WAVELEFT,INFO_WAVETOP,
                    (LPSOUND)messagehook);
            else
                DrawWave(hdc,INFO_WAVELEFT,INFO_WAVETOP,lpsound);
            EndPaint(hwnd,&ps);
            break;
        case WM_COMMAND:
            switch(wParam) {
                case FX_STOP:
                    if(lpsound != NULL && lpsound->wavehandle != NULL)
                        waveOutReset(lpsound->hwaveout);
                    break;
                case FX_PREVIEW:
                    if((lpsound=ReverseWave((LPSOUND)messagehook))
                        != NULL) {
                        UpdateGraph(hwnd);

                        if(PlayWave(hwnd,lpsound)) {
                                SayPlayingSound(hwnd,TRUE);
                        } else DoMessage(hwnd,"Can't play");
                    } else DoMessage(hwnd,"Can't reverse");
                    break;
                case IDOK:
                    SendMessage(hwnd,WM_COMMAND,FX_STOP,0L);
                    messagehook=(LPSTR)ReverseWave((LPSOUND)messagehook);
                    EndDialog(hwnd,wParam);
                    return(FALSE);
                case IDCANCEL:
                    SendMessage(hwnd,WM_COMMAND,FX_STOP,0L);
                    EndDialog(hwnd,wParam);
                    return(FALSE);
            }
            break;
    }
```

```
        return(FALSE);
}

DWORD FAR PASCAL AboutDlgProc(HWND hwnd,WORD message,WORD wParam,LONG lParam)
{
    static HANDLE sound;
    static LPSTR psound;
    HANDLE handle;

    switch(message) {
        case WM_INITDIALOG:
            If((handle=FindResource(hInst,
                "AboutWave",RT_RCDATA)) != NULL) {
                if((sound=LoadResource(hInst,handle)) != NULL) {
                    if((psound=LockResource(sound)) != NULL)
                        sndPlaySound(psound,SND_ASYNC |
                        SND_MEMORY | SND_NOSTOP);
                }
            }
            CentreWindow(hwnd);
            return(FALSE);
        case WM_CTLCOLOR:
            return(HandleCtlColour(hwnd,wParam,lParam));
        case WM_COMMAND:
            switch(wParam) {
                case IDOK:
                    sndPlaySound(NULL,SND_SYNC);
                    if(psound != NULL) UnlockResource(sound);
                    if(sound != NULL) FreeResource(sound);
                    EndDialog(hwnd,wParam);
                    return(FALSE);
            }
            break;
    }

    return(FALSE);
}

void lmemset(LPSTR s,int n,unsigned int size)
{
    unsigned int i;

    for(i=0;i<size;++i) *s++=n;
}

void SayLoadedSound(HWND hwnd,int flag)
{
    HMENU hmenu;
    HWND dlgH;

    hmenu=GetMenu(hwnd);

    ItemOff(MAIN_STOP);
```

Figure 2-9   *Continued.*

```
        if(flag) {
            ItemOn(MAIN_PLAY);
            ItemOn(MAIN_SAVE);
            ItemOn(MAIN_LOWPASS);
            ItemOn(MAIN_ECHO);
            ItemOn(MAIN_REVERSE);
        }
        else {
            ItemOff(MAIN_PLAY);
            ItemOff(MAIN_SAVE);
            ItemOff(MAIN_LOWPASS);
            ItemOff(MAIN_ECHO);
            ItemOff(MAIN_REVERSE);
        }
    }

    void SayPlayingSound(HWND hwnd,int flag)
    {
        HMENU hmenu;
        HWND dlgH;

        hmenu=GetMenu(hwnd);

        if(flag) {
            ItemOn(MAIN_STOP);
            ItemOff(MAIN_PLAY);
            ItemOff(MAIN_SAVE);
            ItemOff(MAIN_LOWPASS);
            ItemOff(MAIN_ECHO);
            ItemOff(MAIN_REVERSE);

            ItemOn(FX_STOP);
            ItemOff(FX_PREVIEW);
            ItemOff(FX_FEEDBACK);
            ItemOff(FX_DELAY);
            ItemOff(FX_CUTOFF);
        }
        else {
            ItemOff(MAIN_STOP);
            ItemOn(MAIN_PLAY);
            ItemOn(MAIN_SAVE);
            ItemOn(MAIN_LOWPASS);
            ItemOn(MAIN_ECHO);
            ItemOn(MAIN_REVERSE);

            ItemOff(FX_STOP);
            ItemOn(FX_PREVIEW);
            ItemOn(FX_FEEDBACK);
            ItemOn(FX_DELAY);
            ItemOn(FX_CUTOFF);
        }
    }
```

```
int GetOpenFileName(HWND hwnd,LPSTR path)
{
    OPENFILENAME ofn;
    char szDirName[256],szFileTitle[256],szFilter[256];

    getcwd(szDirName,sizeof(szDirName)-1);

    lstrcpy(szFilter,"*.WAV");

    lmemset((LPSTR)&ofn,0,sizeof(OPENFILENAME));

    lstrcpy(path,"*.WAV");
    szFileTitle[0]=0;

    ofn.lStructSize=sizeof(OPENFILENAME);
    ofn.hwndOwner=hwnd;
    ofn.lpstrFilter="All files (*.*)\000*.*\000Wave files (*.WAV)\000*.WAV\000";
    ofn.lpstrFile=path;
    ofn.nFilterIndex=2;
    ofn.nMaxFile=STRINGSIZE;
    ofn.lpstrFileTitle=szFileTitle;
    ofn.nMaxFileTitle=sizeof(szFileTitle);
    ofn.lpstrInitialDir=szDirName;
    ofn.Flags=OFN_PATHMUSTEXIST | OFN_HIDEREADONLY;
    ofn.lpstrTitle="Open File";
    ofn.lpstrDefExt="WAV";

    if(!GetOpenFileName(&ofn)) {
        path[0]=0;
        return(0);
    } else return(1);
}

int GetSaveFileName(HWND hwnd,LPSTR path)
{
    OPENFILENAME ofn;
    char szDirName[256],szFileTitle[256],szFilter[256];

    getcwd(szDirName,sizeof(szDirName)-1);

    lstrcpy(szFilter,"*.WAV");

    lmemset((LPSTR)&ofn,0,sizeof(OPENFILENAME));

    lstrcpy(path,"*.WAV");
    szFileTitle[0]=0;

    ofn.lStructSize=sizeof(OPENFILENAME);
    ofn.hwndOwner=hwnd;
    ofn.lpstrFilter="Wave files (*.WAV)\000*.WAV\000";
    ofn.lpstrFile=path;
    ofn.nFilterIndex=2;
```

Figure 2-9   *Continued.*

```
        ofn.nMaxFile=STRINGSIZE;
        ofn.lpstrFileTitle=szFileTitle;
        ofn.nMaxFileTitle=sizeof(szFileTitle);
        ofn.lpstrInitialDir=szDirName;
        ofn.Flags=OFN_OVERWRITEPROMPT | OFN_HIDEREADONLY;
        ofn.lpstrTitle="Save File";

        if(!GetSaveFileName(&ofn)) {
            path[0]=0;
            return(0);
        } else return(1);
}

void CentreWindow(HWND hwnd)
{
        RECT rect;
        unsigned int x,y;

        GetWindowRect(hwnd,&rect);
        x=(GetSystemMetrics(SM_CXSCREEN)-(rect.right-rect.left))/2;
        y=(GetSystemMetrics(SM_CYSCREEN)-(rect.bottom-rect.top))/2;
        SetWindowPos(hwnd,NULL,x,y,rect.right-rect.left,
            rect.bottom-rect.top,SWP_NOSIZE);
}

unsigned long GetWaveSampleCount(LPSOUND lpsound)
{
        return(lpsound->datasize);
}

void DrawWave(HDC hdc,unsigned int x,unsigned int y,LPSOUND lpsound)
{
        HBRUSH oldbrush;
        HPEN hpen,oldpen;
        char huge *p;
        unsigned long nextsample;
        long afactor;
        unsigned int i,amp;

        if(lpsound==NULL) return;

        oldpen=SelectObject(hdc,GetStockObject(BLACK_PEN));
        oldbrush=SelectObject(hdc,GetStockObject(WHITE_BRUSH));
        Rectangle(hdc,x,y,x+INFO_WAVEWIDE,y+INFO_WAVEDEEP);
        SelectObject(hdc,oldpen);

        hpen=CreatePen(PS_SOLID,1,RGB(0,255,0));
        oldpen=SelectObject(hdc,hpen);

        nextsample=lpsound->datasize/(long)(INFO_WAVEWIDE-2);
        afactor=(255L/(long)(INFO_WAVEDEEP-2));
```

```
        if((p=(HPSTR)GlobalLock(lpsound->wavehandle)) != NULL) {
            for(i=0;i<(INFO_WAVEWIDE-2);++i) {
                amp=(unsigned int)max(labs(((long)p[0]-128L) / afactor),1L);

                MoveTo(hdc,x+i+1,max(y+((INFO_WAVEDEEP-2)/2)-amp+1,y+1));
                LineTo(hdc,x+i+1,min(y+((INFO_WAVEDEEP-2)/2)+
                    amp+1,y+INFO_WAVEDEEP-1));
                p+=nextsample;
            }
            GlobalUnlock(lpsound->wavehandle);
        }

    SelectObject(hdc,oldbrush);
    SelectObject(hdc,oldpen);

    DeleteObject(hpen);
}

void AddInfo(HWND hwnd,LPSOUND lpsound)
{
    HWND dlgH;
    char b[STRINGSIZE+1];
    double pt;
    int min,sec,hun;

    if(lpsound->waveformat.wf.nChannels==1) lstrcpy(b,"Mono");
    else lstrcpy(b,"Stereo");
    ItemName(INFO_CHANNELS,b);

    wsprintf(b,"%u.%1.1u kHz",
        (int)(lpsound->waveformat.wf.nSamplesPerSec / 1000L),
        (int)(lpsound->waveformat.wf.nSamplesPerSec % 1000L)/100);
    ItemName(INFO_SAMPLES,b);

    wsprintf(b,"%u bits",lpsound->waveformat.wBitsPerSample);
    ItemName(INFO_SAMPLING,b);

    pt=(double)lpsound->datasize/
    ((double)lpsound->waveformat.wf.nSamplesPerSec*
    (double)lpsound->waveformat.wf.nBlockAlign);

    min=(int)(pt/60);
    sec=(int)(pt-60*(double)min);
    hun=(int)((pt-floor(pt))*100);
    wsprintf(b,"%02.2u:%02.2u.%02.2u",min,sec,hun);
    ItemName(INFO_PLAYTIME,b);
}

LPSOUND DuplicateWave(LPSOUND lpsource)
{
    LPSOUND lpsound;

    if((lpsound=(LPSOUND)malloc(sizeof(SOUND)))==NULL)
        return(DestroyWave(lpsound));
```

Figure 2-9   *Continued.*

```c
    memcpy((char *)lpsound,(char *)lpsource,sizeof(SOUND));

    if((lpsound->wavehandle=GlobalAlloc(GMEM_MOVEABLE |
        GMEM_ZEROINIT,lpsource->datasize)) == NULL)
            return(DestroyWave(lpsound));

    return(lpsound);
}

#pragma warn -par
int WriteWave(HWND hwnd,LPSTR path,LPSOUND lpsound)
{
    HMMIO h;
    MMCKINFO mmParent;
    HPSTR p;
    char b[STRINGSIZE+1];

    lstrcpy(b,path);
    if((h=mmioOpen(path,NULL,MMIO_WRITE | MMIO_CREATE)) == NULL)
        return(FALSE);

    mmParent.fccType=mmioFOURCC('W','A','V','E');
    if(mmioCreateChunk(h,(LPMMCKINFO)&mmParent,MMIO_CREATERIFF)) {
        mmioClose(h,0);
        remove(b);
        return(FALSE);
    }

    mmParent.ckid=mmioFOURCC('f','m','t',' ');
        mmParent.cksize=sizeof(PCMWAVEFORMAT);
    if(mmioCreateChunk(h,(LPMMCKINFO)&mmParent,0)) {
        mmioClose(h,0);
        remove(b);
        return(FALSE);
    }

    if(mmioWrite(h,(HPSTR)&lpsound->waveformat,sizeof(PCMWAVEFORMAT))
        != sizeof(PCMWAVEFORMAT)) {
        mmioClose(h,0);
        remove(b);
        return(FALSE);
    }

    if(mmioAscend(h,&mmParent,0)) {
        mmioClose(h,0);
        remove(b);
        return(FALSE);
    }

    mmParent.ckid=mmioFOURCC('d','a','t','a');
    mmParent.cksize=lpsound->datasize;
```

```
        if(mmioCreateChunk(h,(LPMMCKINFO)&mmParent,0)) {
            mmioClose(h,0);
            remove(b);
            return(FALSE);
        }

        if((p=(HPSTR)GlobalLock(lpsound->wavehandle))==NULL) {
            mmioClose(h,0);
            remove(b);
            return(FALSE);
            }

        if(mmioWrite(h,p,lpsound->datasize) != lpsound->datasize) {
            mmioClose(h,0);
            remove(b);
            return(FALSE);
        }

        GlobalUnlock(lpsound->wavehandle);

        mmioClose(h,0);

        return(TRUE);
}
#pragma warn +par

LPSOUND OpenWave(HWND hwnd,LPSTR path)
{
        LPSOUND lpsound;
        HMMIO h;
        MMCKINFO mmParent,mmSub;
        int n;

        if((lpsound=(LPSOUND)malloc(sizeof(SOUND)))==NULL) {
            DoMessage(hwnd,"Can't allocate memory");
            return(DestroyWave(lpsound));
        }

        lmemset((LPSTR)lpsound,0,sizeof(SOUND));
        lstrcpy(lpsound->name,path);

        if((h=mmioOpen(path,NULL,MMIO_READ)) == NULL) {
            DoMessage(hwnd,"Error opening file");
            return(DestroyWave(lpsound));
        }

        mmParent.fccType=mmioFOURCC('W','A','V','E');
        if(mmioDescend(h,(LPMMCKINFO)&mmParent,NULL,MMIO_FINDRIFF)) {
            mmioClose(h,0);
            DoMessage(hwnd,"Error descending file");
            return(DestroyWave(lpsound));
        }
```

Figure 2-9   *Continued.*

```
mmSub.ckid=mmioFOURCC('f','m','t',' ');
if(mmioDescend(h,(LPMMCKINFO)&mmSub,(LPMMCKINFO)&mmParent,MMIO_FINDCHUNK)) {
    mmioClose(h,0);
    DoMessage(hwnd,"Error descending file");
    return(DestroyWave(lpsound));
}

n=min((unsigned int)mmSub.cksize,sizeof(PCMWAVEFORMAT));
if(mmioRead(h,(LPSTR)&lpsound->waveformat,n) != n) {
    mmioClose(h,0);
    DoMessage(hwnd,"Error reading file");
    return(DestroyWave(lpsound));
}

if(lpsound->waveformat.wf.wFormatTag != WAVE_FORMAT_PCM) {
    mmioClose(h,0);
    DoMessage(hwnd,"Error int file structure");
    return(DestroyWave(lpsound));
}

mmioAscend(h,&mmSub,0);

mmSub.ckid=mmioFOURCC('d','a','t','a');
if(mmioDescend(h,(LPMMCKINFO)&mmSub,(LPMMCKINFO)&mmParent,MMIO_FINDCHUNK)) {
    mmioClose(h,0);
    DoMessage(hwnd,"Error descending file");
    return(DestroyWave(lpsound));
}

lpsound->datasize=mmSub.cksize;
if((lpsound->wavehandle=GlobalAlloc(GMEM_MOVEABLE |
    GMEM_ZEROINIT,mmSub.cksize)) == NULL) {
    mmioClose(h,0);
    DoMessage(hwnd,"Memory allocation error");
    return(DestroyWave(lpsound));
}

if((lpsound->wavepointer=(HPSTR)GlobalLock(lpsound->wavehandle)) == NULL) {
    mmioClose(h,0);
    DoMessage(hwnd,"Memory locking error");
    return(DestroyWave(lpsound));
}

if(mmioRead(h,lpsound->wavepointer,mmSub.cksize) != mmSub.cksize) {
    GlobalUnlock(lpsound->wavehandle);
    mmioClose(h,0);
    DoMessage(hwnd,"Error reading file");
    return(DestroyWave(lpsound));
}

GlobalUnlock(lpsound->wavehandle);
```

```
    mmioClose(h,0);

    return(lpsound);
}

LPSOUND DestroyWave(LPSOUND lpsound)
{
    if(lpsound==NULL) return(NULL);

    if(lpsound->hwaveout != NULL) {
        waveOutUnprepareHeader(lpsound->hwaveout,lpsound->pwaveheader,
            sizeof(WAVEHDR));
        waveOutClose(lpsound->hwaveout);
    }

    if(lpsound->wavehandle != NULL) GlobalFree(lpsound->wavehandle);
    if(lpsound->waveheader != NULL) GlobalFree(lpsound->waveheader);

    free((char *)lpsound);
    return(NULL);
}

int PlayWave(HWND hwnd,LPSOUND lpsound)
{
    char b[STRINGSIZE+1];
    int rtrn;

    if((lpsound->wavepointer=(HPSTR)GlobalLock(lpsound->wavehandle)) == NULL) {
        DoMessage(hwnd,"Memory locking error");
        return(FALSE);
    }

    if((lpsound->waveheader=GlobalAlloc(GMEM_MOVEABLE | GMEM_SHARE,
        (long)sizeof(WAVEHDR))) == NULL) {
        GlobalUnlock(lpsound->wavehandle);
        DoMessage(hwnd,"Memory allocation error");
        return(FALSE);
    }

    if((lpsound->pwaveheader=(LPWAVEHDR)GlobalLock(lpsound->waveheader))==NULL) {
        GlobalUnlock(lpsound->wavehandle);
        DoMessage(hwnd,"Memory locking error");
        return(FALSE);
    }

    if((rtrn=waveOutOpen((LPHWAVEOUT)&lpsound->hwaveout,WAVE_MAPPER,
        (LPWAVEFORMAT)&lpsound->waveformat,(LONG)hwnd,0L,CALLBACK_WINDOW)) != 0) {
        GlobalUnlock(lpsound->waveheader);
        GlobalUnlock(lpsound->wavehandle);
        waveOutGetErrorText(rtrn,(LPSTR)b,STRINGSIZE);
        DoMessage(hwnd,b);
        return(FALSE);
    }
```

Figure 2-9   *Continued.*

```
lpsound->pwaveheader->lpData=(LPSTR)lpsound->wavepointer;
lpsound->pwaveheader->dwBufferLength=lpsound->datasize;
lpsound->pwaveheader->dwFlags=0L;
lpsound->pwaveheader->dwLoops=0L;
if((rtrn=waveOutPrepareHeader(lpsound->hwaveout,
    lpsound->pwaveheader,sizeof(WAVEHDR))) != 0) {
    GlobalUnlock(lpsound->waveheader);
    waveOutUnprepareHeader(lpsound->hwaveout,
        lpsound->pwaveheader,sizeof(WAVEHDR));
    waveOutClose(lpsound->hwaveout);
    lpsound->hwaveout=NULL;
    GlobalUnlock(lpsound->wavehandle);
    waveOutGetErrorText(rtrn,(LPSTR)b,STRINGSIZE);
    DoMessage(hwnd,b);
    return(FALSE);
}

if((rtrn=waveOutWrite(lpsound->hwaveout,lpsound->pwaveheader,
    sizeof(WAVEHDR))) != 0) {
    GlobalUnlock(lpsound->waveheader);
    waveOutUnprepareHeader(lpsound->hwaveout,
        lpsound->pwaveheader,sizeof(WAVEHDR));
    waveOutClose(lpsound->hwaveout);
    lpsound->hwaveout=NULL;
    GlobalUnlock(lpsound->wavehandle);
    waveOutGetErrorText(rtrn,(LPSTR)b,STRINGSIZE);
    DoMessage(hwnd,b);
    return(FALSE);
}

return(TRUE);
}

LPSOUND LowpassWave(LPSOUND lpsource,int cutoff)
{
    SAMPLE smp[2*MAX_CUTOFF+1],tsmp;
    LPSOUND lpsound;
    unsigned long samples,n;
    int i;

    cutoff=cutoff*2;

    if((lpsound=DuplicateWave(lpsource))==NULL)
        return(DestroyWave(lpsound));

    if(!LockWave(lpsource)) return(DestroyWave(lpsound));

    if(!LockWave(lpsound)) return(DestroyWave(lpsound));

    samples=GetWaveSampleCount(lpsource);
    cutoff=(MAX_CUTOFF*2+1)-cutoff;
```

```
    for(i=0;i<cutoff;++i) smp[i]=128;

    for(n=0L;n<samples;++n) {
        for(i=cutoff-1;i>0;--i) smp[i]=smp[i-1];
        smp[0]=GetSample(lpsource,n);

        for(tsmp=0,i=0;i<cutoff;++i) tsmp+=smp[i];
        tsmp=tsmp/cutoff;
        PutSample(lpsound,n,tsmp);
    }

    UnlockWave(lpsound);
    UnlockWave(lpsource);

    return(lpsound);
}

LPSOUND ReverseWave(LPSOUND lpsource)
{
    LPSOUND lpsound;
    unsigned long samples,n;

    if((lpsound=DuplicateWave(lpsource))==NULL)
        return(DestroyWave(lpsound));

    if(!LockWave(lpsource)) return(DestroyWave(lpsound));

    if(!LockWave(lpsound)) return(DestroyWave(lpsound));

    samples=GetWaveSampleCount(lpsource);
    for(n=0L;n<samples;++n)
        PutSample(lpsound,n,GetSample(lpsource,samples-n-1));

    UnlockWave(lpsound);
        UnlockWave(lpsource);

    return(lpsound);
}

LPSOUND EchoWave(LPSOUND lpsource,int delay,int feedback)
{
    LPSOUND lpsound;
    SAMPLE smp,tsmp;
    unsigned long samples,n,echo;

    if((lpsound=DuplicateWave(lpsource))==NULL)
        return(DestroyWave(lpsound));

    if(!LockWave(lpsource)) return(DestroyWave(lpsound));

    if(!LockWave(lpsound)) return(DestroyWave(lpsound));

    samples=GetWaveSampleCount(lpsource);
```

Figure 2-9 *Continued.*

```
        for(n=0L;n<samples;++n)
            PutSample(lpsound,n,0);

        for(n=0L;n<samples;++n) {
            smp=GetSample(lpsource,n);
            tsmp=GetSample(lpsound,n);
            PutSample(lpsound,n,ClampSample(smp+tsmp));

        for(echo=n+delay;n+echo < samples;echo+=delay) {
            smp=(smp*feedback)/(feedback+1);
            if(!smp) break;
            tsmp=GetSample(lpsound,echo)-128;
            PutSample(lpsound,echo,ClampSample(128+(tsmp+(smp-128)))/2);
        }
    }

    UnlockWave(lpsound);
    UnlockWave(lpsource);

    return(lpsound);
}

DWORD HandleCtlColour(HWND hwnd,WORD wParam,DWORD lParam)
{
    POINT point;
    HBRUSH hBrush;

    if(HIWORD(lParam)==CTLCOLOR_STATIC ||
       HIWORD(lParam)==CTLCOLOR_DLG) {
        hBrush=GetStockObject(LTGRAY_BRUSH);
            SetBkColor(wParam,RGB(192,192,192));
        SetTextColor(wParam,RGB(0,0,0));

        ClientToScreen(hwnd,&point);
        UnrealizeObject(hBrush);
        SetBrushOrg(wParam,point.x,point.y);

        return((DWORD)hBrush);

    }
    if(HIWORD(lParam)==CTLCOLOR_BTN) {
        hBrush=GetStockObject(LTGRAY_BRUSH);
        SetBkColor(wParam,RGB(192,192,192));
        SetTextColor(wParam,RGB(0,0,0));

        ClientToScreen(hwnd,&point);
        UnrealizeObject(hBrush);
        SetBrushOrg(wParam,point.x,point.y);

        return((DWORD)hBrush);
    }
```

```
        return(FALSE);
}

#pragma warn -par
int HandleScroll(HWND hwnd,WORD wParam,DWORD lParam)
{
        HWND dlgH;
        int pos,minpos,maxpos,jump;

        dlgH=(HWND)HIWORD(lParam);
        pos = GetScrollPos(dlgH,SB_CTL);
        GetScrollRange(dlgH,SB_CTL,&minpos,&maxpos);
        jump=(maxpos-minpos)/10;

        switch(wParam) {
            case SB_LINEUP:
                pos-=1;
                break;
            case SB_LINEDOWN:
                pos+=1;
                break;
            case SB_PAGEUP:
                pos-=jump;
                break;
            case SB_PAGEDOWN:
                pos+=jump;
                break;
            case SB_THUMBPOSITION:
                pos=LOWORD(lParam);
                break;
        }

        if(pos < minpos) pos=minpos;
        else if(pos > maxpos) pos=maxpos;

        if(pos != GetScrollPos(dlgH,SB_CTL)) {
            SetScrollPos(dlgH,SB_CTL,pos,TRUE);
        }

        return(pos);
}
#pragma warn +par

int LockWave(LPSOUND lpsound)
{
        if((lpsound->wavepointer=(HPSTR)GlobalLock(lpsound->wavehandle)) == NULL)
            return(FALSE);
        else
            return(TRUE);
}

void UnlockWave(LPSOUND lpsound)
{
```

Figure 2-9   *Continued.*

```
      GlobalUnlock(lpsound->wavehandle);
}

int IsSuitableWave(LPSOUND lpsound)
{
      if(lpsound->waveformat.wBitsPerSample==8 &&
         lpsound->waveformat.wf.nChannels==1) return(TRUE);
      else
         return(FALSE);
}
```

Figure 2-10   *The WAVE-FX.RC resource script.*

```
MainScreen DIALOG 9, 24, 212, 144
STYLE WS_POPUP ¦ WS_CAPTION ¦ WS_SYSMENU ¦ WS_MINIMIZEBOX
CAPTION "Wave Effects"
MENU MainMenu
BEGIN
        PUSHBUTTON "Open", 101, 176, 8, 28, 12, WS_CHILD ¦ WS_VISIBLE ¦ WS_TABSTOP
        PUSHBUTTON "Save", 102, 176, 24, 28, 12, WS_CHILD ¦ WS_VISIBLE ¦ WS_TABSTOP
        PUSHBUTTON "Stop", 202, 176, 56, 28, 12, WS_CHILD ¦ WS_VISIBLE ¦ WS_TABSTOP
        PUSHBUTTON "Play", 201, 176, 40, 28, 12, WS_CHILD ¦ WS_VISIBLE ¦ WS_TABSTOP
        PUSHBUTTON "Quit", 199, 176, 124, 28, 12, WS_CHILD ¦ WS_VISIBLE ¦ WS_TABSTOP
        CONTROL "", -1, "BorShade", 32769 ¦ WS_CHILD ¦ WS_VISIBLE, 8, 84, 160, 52
        RTEXT "Channels:", -1, 12, 88, 52, 8, SS_RIGHT ¦ WS_CHILD ¦
            WS_VISIBLE ¦ WS_GROUP
        LTEXT "", 401, 72, 88, 92, 8, WS_CHILD ¦ WS_VISIBLE ¦ WS_GROUP
        RTEXT "Samples:", -1, 12, 100, 52, 8, SS_RIGHT ¦ WS_CHILD ¦
            WS_VISIBLE ¦ WS_GROUP
        LTEXT "", 402, 72, 100, 92, 8, WS_CHILD ¦ WS_VISIBLE ¦ WS_GROUP
        RTEXT "Sampling:", -1, 12, 112, 52, 8, SS_RIGHT ¦ WS_CHILD ¦
            WS_VISIBLE ¦ WS_GROUP
        LTEXT "", 403, 72, 112, 92, 8, WS_CHILD ¦ WS_VISIBLE ¦ WS_GROUP
        RTEXT "Playing time:", -1, 12, 124, 52, 8, SS_RIGHT ¦ WS_CHILD ¦
            WS_VISIBLE ¦ WS_GROUP
        LTEXT "", 404, 72, 124, 92, 8, WS_CHILD ¦ WS_VISIBLE ¦ WS_GROUP
END


MainMenu MENU
BEGIN
        POPUP "&File"
        BEGIN
                MENUITEM "&Open", 101
                MENUITEM "&Save", 102
                MENUITEM "Save &as", 103
                MENUITEM "&About", 104
                MENUITEM SEPARATOR
                MENUITEM "E&xit", 199
        END
```

```
        POPUP "&Edit"
        BEGIN
                MENUITEM "&Play", 201
                MENUITEM "&Stop", 202
                MENUITEM SEPARATOR
                MENUITEM "&Low pass", 203
                MENUITEM "&Echo", 204
                MENUITEM "&Reverse", 205
        END

END


AboutBox DIALOG 18, 18, 184, 180
STYLE WS_POPUP | WS_CAPTION
CAPTION "About..."
BEGIN
        CONTROL "", 102, "BorShade", BSS_GROUP | WS_CHILD | WS_VISIBLE | WS_TABSTOP,
            8, 68, 168, 76
        CTEXT "Wave Effects 1.0\n\nCopyright © 1994 Alchemy Mindworks Inc.\n\n
            This program is part of the book Advanced Multimedia Programming for
            Windows by Steven William Rimmer, published by Windcrest/McGraw Hill.",
            -1, 12, 72, 160, 68, WS_CHILD | WS_VISIBLE | WS_GROUP
        CONTROL "Button", IDOK, "BorBtn", BS_DEFPUSHBUTTON | WS_CHILD | WS_VISIBLE |
            WS_TABSTOP, 74, 152, 32, 20
        CONTROL "Button", 801, "BorBtn", BS_PUSHBUTTON | WS_CHILD | WS_VISIBLE |
            WS_TABSTOP, 36, 8, 32, 20
END


WaveEffects ICON
BEGIN
        '00 00 01 00 01 00 20 20 10 00 00 00 00 00 E8 02'
        '00 00 16 00 00 00 28 00 00 00 20 00 00 00 40 00'
        '00 00 01 00 04 00 00 00 00 00 80 02 00 00 00 00'
        '00 00 00 00 00 00 10 00 00 00 00 00 00 00 00 00'
        '00 00 00 00 BF 00 00 BF 00 00 00 BF BF 00 BF 00'
        '00 00 BF 00 BF 00 BF BF 00 00 C0 C0 C0 00 80 80'
        '80 00 00 00 FF 00 00 FF 00 00 00 FF FF 00 FF 00'
        '00 00 FF 00 FF 00 FF FF 00 00 FF FF FF 00 77 77'
        '77 77 77 77 77 77 77 77 77 77 77 77 77 77 7F 88'
        '88 88 88 88 88 88 88 88 88 88 88 88 88 87 7F F8'
        '88 88 88 88 88 88 88 88 88 88 88 88 88 87 7F F7'
        '77 77 77 77 77 77 77 77 77 77 77 77 78 87 7F F7'
        '77 77 77 77 77 77 77 77 77 77 77 77 78 87 7F F7'
        '77 77 77 77 77 77 77 77 77 77 77 77 78 87 7F F7'
        '77 77 77 77 77 77 77 77 77 77 77 77 78 87 7F F7'
        '77 77 77 77 77 77 77 77 77 77 77 77 78 87 7F F7'
        '77 77 77 77 77 77 77 77 77 77 77 77 78 87 7F F7'
        '77 77 77 77 77 77 77 77 77 77 77 77 78 87 7F F7'
        '77 77 FF 77 77 77 77 FF 77 77 FF 77 78 87 7F F7'
        '77 78 8F 77 77 77 78 8F 77 78 8F 77 78 87 7F F7'
        '77 78 8F 77 77 77 78 8F F7 78 87 77 78 87 7F F7'
        '77 78 8F 77 77 77 77 88 F7 88 F7 77 78 87 7F F7'
        '77 78 8F 77 77 77 77 88 FF 88 77 77 78 87 7F F7'
```

Figure 2-10 *Continued.*

```
                '77 78 8F FF FF 77 77 78 88 87 77 77 78 87 7F F7'
                '77 78 88 88 8F 77 77 77 88 F7 77 77 78 87 7F F7'
                '77 78 88 88 87 77 77 77 88 FF 77 77 78 87 7F F7'
                '77 78 8F 77 77 77 77 78 88 8F F7 77 78 87 7F F7'
                '77 78 8F 77 77 77 77 88 F7 88 F7 77 78 87 7F F7'
                '77 78 8F FF FF FF 77 88 77 88 FF 77 78 87 7F F7'
                '77 78 88 88 88 8F 78 8F 77 78 8F 77 78 87 7F F7'
                '77 78 88 88 88 87 78 87 77 78 87 77 78 87 7F F7'
                '77 77 77 77 77 77 77 77 77 77 77 77 78 87 7F F7'
                '77 77 77 77 77 77 77 77 77 77 77 77 78 87 7F F7'
                '77 77 77 77 77 77 77 77 77 77 77 77 78 87 7F F7'
                '77 77 77 77 77 77 77 77 77 77 77 77 78 87 7F F7'
                '77 77 77 77 77 77 77 77 77 77 77 77 78 87 7F F7'
                '77 77 77 77 77 77 77 77 77 77 77 77 78 87 7F FF'
                'FF FF FF FF FF FF FF FF FF FF FF FF F8 87 7F FF'
                'FF FF FF FF FF FF FF FF FF FF FF FF FF 87 77 77'
                '77 77 77 77 77 77 77 77 77 77 77 77 77 77 00 00'
                '00 00 00 00 00 00 00 00 00 00 00 00 00 00 00 00'
                '00 00 00 00 00 00 00 00 00 00 00 00 00 00 00 00'
                '00 00 00 00 00 00 00 00 00 00 00 00 00 00 00 00'
                '00 00 00 00 00 00 00 00 00 00 00 00 00 00 00 00'
                '00 00 00 00 00 00 00 00 00 00 00 00 00 00 00 00'
                '00 00 00 00 00 00 00 00 00 00 00 00 00 00 00 00'
                '00 00 00 00 00 00 00 00 00 00 00 00 00 00 00 00'
                '00 00 00 00 00 00 00 00 00 00 00 00 00 00 00'
END


1801 BITMAP "smpw.bmp"

AboutWave RCDATA "ABOUT.WAV"

ReverseBox DIALOG 9, 24, 228, 100
STYLE WS_POPUP | WS_CAPTION | WS_SYSMENU | WS_MINIMIZEBOX
CAPTION "Reverse"
BEGIN
        CONTROL "OK", IDOK, "BorBtn", BS_DEFPUSHBUTTON | WS_CHILD |
            WS_VISIBLE | WS_TABSTOP, 188, 76, 32, 20
        CONTROL "Cancel", IDCANCEL, "BorBtn", BS_PUSHBUTTON |
            WS_CHILD | WS_VISIBLE | WS_TABSTOP, 188, 52, 32, 20
        CONTROL "Preview", 701, "BorBtn", BS_PUSHBUTTON | WS_CHILD |
            WS_VISIBLE | WS_TABSTOP, 188, 28, 32, 20
        CONTROL "Stop", 799, "BorBtn", BS_PUSHBUTTON | WS_CHILD |
            WS_VISIBLE | WS_TABSTOP, 188, 4, 32, 20
END


EchoBox DIALOG 9, 24, 228, 124
STYLE WS_POPUP | WS_CAPTION | WS_SYSMENU | WS_MINIMIZEBOX
CAPTION "Echo"
BEGIN
        CONTROL "OK", IDOK, "BorBtn", BS_DEFPUSHBUTTON | WS_CHILD |
```

```
            WS_VISIBLE | WS_TABSTOP, 188, 100, 32, 20
        CONTROL "Cancel", IDCANCEL, "BorBtn", BS_PUSHBUTTON | WS_CHILD |
            WS_VISIBLE | WS_TABSTOP, 188, 76, 32, 20
        CONTROL "Preview", 701, "BorBtn", BS_PUSHBUTTON | WS_CHILD |
            WS_VISIBLE | WS_TABSTOP, 188, 28, 32, 20
        SCROLLBAR 703, 56, 106, 120, 9
        CONTROL "", -1, "BorShade", 32769 | WS_CHILD | WS_VISIBLE,
            8, 88, 172, 32
        RTEXT "Delay:", -1, 12, 106, 40, 8, SS_RIGHT | WS_CHILD |
            WS_VISIBLE | WS_GROUP
        CONTROL "Stop", 799, "BorBtn", BS_PUSHBUTTON | WS_CHILD |
            WS_VISIBLE | WS_TABSTOP, 188, 4, 32, 20
        SCROLLBAR 702, 56, 92, 120, 9, SBS_HORZ | WS_CHILD | WS_VISIBLE
        RTEXT "Feedback:", -1, 12, 92, 40, 8, SS_RIGHT | WS_CHILD |
            WS_VISIBLE | WS_GROUP
END

LowpassBox DIALOG 9, 24, 228, 124
STYLE WS_POPUP | WS_CAPTION | WS_SYSMENU | WS_MINIMIZEBOX
CAPTION "Low pass"
BEGIN
        CONTROL "OK", IDOK, "BorBtn", BS_DEFPUSHBUTTON | WS_CHILD | WS_VISIBLE |
            WS_TABSTOP, 188, 100, 32, 20
        CONTROL "Cancel", IDCANCEL, "BorBtn", BS_PUSHBUTTON | WS_CHILD | WS_VISIBLE
            WS_TABSTOP, 188, 76, 32, 20
        CONTROL "Preview", 701, "BorBtn", BS_PUSHBUTTON | WS_CHILD | WS_VISIBLE |
            WS_TABSTOP, 188, 28, 32, 20
        SCROLLBAR 704, 56, 106, 120, 9, SBS_HORZ | WS_CHILD | WS_VISIBLE
        CONTROL "", -1, "BorShade", 32769 | WS_CHILD | WS_VISIBLE, 8, 100, 172, 20
        RTEXT "Cut off:", -1, 12, 106, 40, 8, SS_RIGHT | WS_CHILD |
            WS_VISIBLE | WS_GROUP
        CONTROL "Stop", 799, "BorBtn", BS_PUSHBUTTON | WS_CHILD | WS_VISIBLE |
            WS_TABSTOP, 188, 4, 32, 20
END
```

As with WAVEREC, the message handler for the main window of WAVE-FX is the SelectProc function. Most of what it does is similar to the tasks performed by the principal message handler in WAVEREC. Note that the MM_MCINOTIFY case has been replaced by a handler for MM_WOM_DONE. This is an analogous function— it's the message used by the low-level wave file output functions of the Windows multimedia extensions to indicate that a wave file has stopped playing.

The WAVE-FX application defines a data object called SOUND to keep track of the elements involved in maintaining a list of sound samples in memory, and it defines LPSOUND as a far pointer to a

SOUND object. The MAIN_OPEN case of the WM_COMMAND handler in SelectProc calls the OpenWave function to load into memory the samples and associated information from a wave file on disk, and to fill in a SOUND object pertaining to the wave file. The OpenWave function illustrates that most terrifying of all the monsters of Windows' multimedia extensions, a RIFF file handler.

The OpenWave function returns a pointer to a SOUND object. To keep the code in WAVE-FX as portable as possible, it allocates a buffer for the SOUND object to live in, rather than using a hardwired SOUND structure stored as a static variable somewhere. This will make it relatively easy to apply the functions in WAVE-FX to your own applications. A SOUND object returned by any of the functions in WAVE-FX that return LPSOUND pointers should be passed to DestroyWave when it's no longer required.

For a complete discussion of RIFF files and the mmio functions dealing with them, refer to my book *Multimedia Programming for Windows*. If you're really new to RIFF files—and insist on knowing exactly what OpenWave is up to—you might want to take a look at it. For most applications, you can simply let OpenWave summon forth its demons and then walk off with a loaded SOUND object when the spells are cooling. When it's all over with, the returned SOUND object will contain the following information:

```
typedef struct {
        char name[STRINGSIZE+1];
        PCMWAVEFORMAT waveformat;
        HPSTR wavepointer;
        unsigned long datasize;
        GLOBALHANDLE wavehandle;
        GLOBALHANDLE waveheader;
        LPWAVEHDR pwaveheader;
        HWAVEOUT hwaveout;
        } SOUND;
```

The name element of a SOUND object is the file name of the wave file that was loaded. The waveformat element is a PCMWAVEFORMAT structure, a header read from a wave file that defines its sample type, playing time, and other characteristics. This

is also covered in detail in *Multimedia Programming for Windows* and will thus be ignored here. The wavepointer element is a pointer to the wave file's samples when the wavehandle GLOBALHANDLE object of the SOUND in question has been locked—it's returned initially unlocked, and the wavepointer element is undefined.

The wavehandle GLOBALHANDLE object references an unlocked global memory buffer containing sound samples. The waveheader, pwaveheader, and hwaveout elements are used internally by the mmio functions that make OpenWave and WriteWave work—you can largely ignore them if you'll be using these functions as is for your own software. Once again, they're dealt with in detail in *Multimedia Programming for Windows*.

The MAIN_OPEN handler in SelectProc calls IsSuitableWave after it has successfully opened a wave file with OpenWave. The IsSuitableWave function, also defined in WAVE-FX.CPP, will return true for wave files having 8-bit monaural samples and false for any other sort of wave files, as WAVE-FX only knows how to deal with the former types of sounds. You can eliminate this function if you expand WAVE-FX to deal with all four wave file formats.

Once a wave file is in memory, it can be graphed with a call to DrawWave. This is something else lifted bodily from *Multimedia Programming for Windows* and probably deserving of no further elaboration here. The DrawWave function is called from the WM_PAINT handler of SelectProc. It will be called whenever the area of the main window of WAVE-FX containing the wave envelope graph is made invalid. A macro defined at the top of the WAVE-FX.CPP source file, UpdateGraph, does just that.

The PlayWave function is called from the MAIN_PLAY section of the WM_COMMAND handle of SelectProc. It's defined toward the end of WAVE-FX.CPP. PlayWave uses the multimedia extension waveOut functions to play a wave file in memory, rather than the MCI interface, which only wants to play wave files that reside on disk. It will start playing a wave file defined by a SOUND object, and send an MM_WOM_DONE message back to the window specified by the HWND object passed to it when it's done—in this case, the window's message handler will be SelectProc.

The remaining bits of interest in WAVE-FX are its filters. They all have roughly the same structure. Each one is a dialog to control the filter's qualities and graph the resulting sound. The filters work with copies of the original wave file loaded into memory, such that if you click on Cancel in one of the Filter dialogs, the original wave will remain unaltered. Each of the Filter dialogs has a Preview button to show what the effects of the filter and its attendant settings will be on the wave file in question. Clicking on Preview will modify the wave in question—or, more precisely, a copy of it—and then play and graph the resulting sound.

The EchoDlgProc function is typical of the message handler for one of the Filter dialogs. Because wave audio will be played from this dialog by its Preview button, a WM_WOM_DONE handler is required to deal with messages sent back when a wave played by PlayWave terminates. The WM_INITDIALOG handler sets up the controls in the dialog and positions the window.

If the Preview button in the Echo dialog is clicked, such that a WM_COMMAND message with its wParam argument set to FX_PREVIEW appears, the EchoDlgProc function will fetch the delay and feedback values that determine the echo characteristics by reading the dialog's scroll bar controls. It will then call EchoWave, which does the actual work. The EchoWave function returns an LPSOUND pointer to the sound it has modified. In fact, EchoWave will return a pointer to a new SOUND object that it creates.

You can find EchoWave down near the end of WAVE-FX.CPP. It's actually pretty simple in operation—it copies each sample from the original SOUND object to the new SOUND object, and then repeats it along the sample buffer at intervals specified by the delay argument, attenuated by a factor specified by the feedback argument.

The future of noise

As with WAVEREC earlier in this chapter, you probably won't want to create an application dedicated to making wave files sound stranger

than they do in real life—there are numerous such programs about. After a time they start to seem like a sonic onslaught, calculated to make your ears go on strike.

The modular nature of the sound handlers in WAVE-FX should make it a good place to lift functions for your own software, however. WAVE-FX will provide you with everything you need to handle wave file audio at the lowest level Windows provides. As low-level things are wont to be, dealing with wave files like this is brutish and inelegant. However, it will avail you of total control over every hiccup and phasor blast in your wave file sounds.

Coming up with wave files worth the effort, of course, is something that a book can't really help you with. Hearing is very much an art form—one that is perhaps even more demanding still than writing software.

Windows timers
A very short chapter

"Have you ever considered how much the AT&T logo looks like a Death Star?"
—Graffiti

ONE of the least inspiring features of the Windows multimedia extensions is their ability to bring precision timing of very short intervals to your software. Although the timer functions are crucial to several of the applications that appear later in this book, they are somehow difficult to get excited about. Everyone seems to get along well enough without them.

In fact, the absence of a way to handle short intervals of time in a useful fashion under Windows can be quite troubling. You probably won't appreciate just how bad Windows is at handling time without the multimedia timer calls until you start getting immersed in the problem.

The simplest way to pause for a while in software—and one dating back to the dark prehistory of microcomputer software development—is to use a timing loop. Here's an example of one:

```
int i;
for(i=0;i<10000;++i);
```

This little wonder doesn't do anything, but it takes a finite amount of time to do it. There are two significant drawbacks to this arrangement.

The first problem with simple timing loops is that they will wait for variable periods of time, depending on the speed of the processor in your computer. A system with a Pentium processor will run this loop in something like six percent of the time required to execute it on an old-style 8088-based system—assuming you can still find an old-style 8088-based system that hasn't been converted into a flower pot.

Under Windows, this loop will take varying amounts of time to execute over multiple iterations even on the same machine, as Windows' time slicing is somewhat erratic in an absolute sense.

The second drawback to timing loops is that it's difficult to make anything else happen while they're waiting. Although you could install some sort of repetitive function in the loop, the time required by the function would affect the time occupied by the timing loop.

Timing loops were popular back in the late seventies for systems like the Apple II. Although heavily cloned, all Apple IIs were based on the same processor, and thus could be counted on to run at the same speed. I suspect there's a special dynamic link library buried somewhere in Windows that detects timing loops in Windows applications and pops up a dialog with a really insulting message if it finds one.

The second approach to measuring time on a PC is to use the internal system interrupt clock. Although it's not documented in most Windows development packages, this approach is workable as far as it goes. Perhaps unbeknownst to most Windows users, a PC maintains a hardware interrupt that executes repeatedly every 18.2 milliseconds. This maintains the time-of-day clock in your computer as a long integer incremented with each "tick" of the clock. You can read this integer by executing a 1CH DOS interrupt call from within a Windows application.

In most cases, executing DOS interrupts from within a Windows application is a bit like toasting hotdogs over a nuclear power plant, but this particular instance is quite safe. All the hotdogs involved are completely cholesterol-free.

As you might imagine, this approach has its drawbacks as well. The principal one is that the shortest interval of time that can be measured this way is one clock tick, or 18.2 milliseconds. While this might seem to be a relatively short time for most humans, it's an eternity to a computer. It's by no means adequate for the sorts of timing required by the applications discussed in this book.

If you've read Chapter 1, you're probably thinking "Zounds! This is easy!" or words to that effect. The SetTimer function of Windows will send WM_TIMER messages to the window of your choice with a resolution of one millisecond. It takes very little imagination to

appreciate that these can be used to increment a counter and keep track of time.

In theory, this should be entirely true. It might well be that thinking it so, the authors of Windows decided that better timing functions weren't required. In fact, it doesn't work at all well because when SetTimer sends a WM_TIMER message to a window, it essentially calls SendMessage. While SendMessage jumps the Windows message queue, it must still interact with the message-handling kernel to some extent. Windows' internal time management functions don't operate at particularly regular intervals due to the vagaries of time slicing and task yielding in a nonpreemptive multitasking environment. As such, while the timer instigated by SetTimer might well send its messages at precise intervals, they won't reach the destination window with anything like the same degree of accuracy.

In fact, the accuracy of WM_TIMER messages is typically dreadful.

For playing music or timing fairly short periods for visual effects—two tasks covered in this book—the accuracy of WM_TIMER messages is wholly inadequate. The solution to this problem lies in one of the least well-documented areas of the Windows multimedia extension, its suite of timer functions.

⇨ The mother of all clocks

While a bit more elaborate in use than in theory, the multimedia timer functions have two basic applications. They can be used to read the system time, and hence the elapsed time between two events, with great accuracy. Second, they can be used to cause a function to be called at precise intervals. Because having an accurate timer running on a single-processor computer eats a measurable amount of processor overhead, you can set the accuracy of a multimedia timer to minimize its effect on the performance of your computer.

All the timer functions provided by the multimedia extensions begin with time.

Because the timer services of the multimedia extensions are somewhat draining on the resources of your computer, Windows would prefer that it not be asked to deal with its timers at all except when doing so is absolutely necessary. To this end, you should always call timeBeginPeriod just before using any of the time functions, and then timeEndPeriod as soon as they are no longer required.

Perhaps the simplest—and frequently the most useful—of the timer functions is timeGetTime. It returns a long integer containing the number of milliseconds that have elapsed since Windows was started. This value could in theory wrap past zero. For this to happen, however, Windows would have to run continuously for more than four billion milliseconds, or about a month and a half.

You can work out the duration of an event in milliseconds by calling timeGetTime just prior to the event, and then again after the event, and calculating the difference in the values returned by the two calls.

The timeGetTime function can be used to create accurate timing loops, as explained in Chapter 4. You'll often want something to take no less than a predetermined time, but also no longer than necessary if it requires more than the defined interval. To implement this with timeGetTime, you'd do the following:

```
DWORD timestart,timenow;
timestart=timeGetTime();
/* the code for your task goes here */
while((timenow=timeGetTime()) < timestart+INTERVAL);
```

The INTERVAL constant is the minimum time in milliseconds that the task to be performed should occupy.

The somewhat complicated-looking while loop in this example repeatedly calls timeGetTime and compares its return value with the initial time value before the task began, plus the number of milliseconds the whole affair should take. If the task turns out to have occupied more than INTERVAL milliseconds, the loop will terminate immediately. If it occupied less time, the loop will keep calling timeGetTime until its return value indicates that the interval has expired.

The really adventurous facility of the multimedia timer functions is their capacity for having a user-defined function called at periodic intervals. Complicated to implement, restrictive in what it can do, and somewhat difficult to find a use for, this is a resource which nonetheless can prove essential in some Windows applications. One such application is PLAYSONG, a MIDI music player that's covered in Chapter 6.

To set up a timer to call the function of your choice, use timeSetEvent. Here's how it's called:

```
timeSetEvent(delay,resolution,function,user,flags);
```

The delay argument to timeSetEvent is the number of milliseconds between calls to the function in question. This value must fall within the resolution of the particular timer. You can determine this range with a call to timeGetDevCaps, which is discussed at the end of this chapter.

The resolution argument to timeSetEvent is the resolution of the timer to be used to call your function. Smaller resolution values will increase the accuracy of the timer, but they'll also increase the amount of system overhead the whole circus requires.

The function argument to timeSetEvent is a callback to the function that the timer will call. This is, in fact, where things really get awkward, as we'll discuss in a moment.

The user argument to timeSetEvent is any 32-bit value you'd like passed to your function. You can leave it NULL if you don't need this facility.

Finally, the flags argument to timeSetEvent should be either TIME_ONESHOT to have your function called once, or TIME_PERIODIC to have it called repeatedly.

The timeSetEvent returns an ID value for the timer set up to call your function, or NULL if the timer couldn't be created. You should call timeKillEvent to clear a timer set by timeSetEvent as soon as it's no longer required. The argument to timeKillEvent should be the ID value returned by timeSetEvent.

The reason that timeSetEvent is such a python in your cornflakes to work with is this: it requires that the function it calls be in a dynamic link library having a fixed code segment, rather than in the code for your application itself. This allows your function to be called with a minimum of overhead, as Windows won't have to go searching for its code segment with each call.

The function called by a timer—and passed as the function argument to timeSetEvent—must be of the following form. Note that it need not be named TimeFunc—you can call it anything you like:

```
void FAR PASCAL TimeFunc(unsigned int id,unsigned int msg,
    DWORD dwUser,DWORD dw1,DWORD dw2)
```

The id argument to TimeFunc will be the same as the ID value returned by timeSetEvent when the timer in question was initiated. The msg argument is meaningless and should be ignored. The dwUser argument will contain whatever the user argument to timeSetEvent did. The dw1 and dw2 arguments are also meaningless, and should be ignored. You might want to place the following line before the declaration for your TimeFunc function to disable Borland C++'s warnings about unused arguments:

```
#pragma argsused
```

A somewhat restricted list of the Windows system calls can be included in the function called through timeSetEvent. Here's the whole works:

> PostMessage

> imeGetSystemTime

> timeGetTime

> timeSetEvent

> timeKillEvent

> midiOutShortMsg

> midiOutLongMsg

> OutputDebugStr

Attempting to make any other system calls from within a TimeFunc function will usually crash your application in one of a number of particularly fatal ways.

The TimeFunc function's limited range of capabilities might seem to severely limit what you can do with the timer event facility. So it does. You might find yourself hard pressed periodically to think of a function call that can confine itself to these slender resources. As mentioned earlier in this chapter, one such function can be found in the PLAYSONG application discussed in Chapter 6.

Finally, the timeGetDevCaps function will return information about the timer resources in your system. It should be called like this:

```
TIMECAPS tc;
timeGetDevCaps(&tc,sizeof(TIMECAPS));
```

The timeGetDevCaps will return zero if it was successful, or the constant TIMERR_NOCANDO if it's not. It's hard to imagine a condition under which it would be unable to complete its task.

A TIMECAPS object looks like this:

```
typedef struct {
        WORD wPeriodMin;
        WORD wPeriodMax;
        } TIMECAPS;
```

The two WORD values in a TIMECAPS structure define the minimum and maximum periods available for setting timers on your system. As of this writing, these values appear to be hardwired at 1 and 65,535 for all systems. Whether you call timeGetDevCaps and check them against any timers you plan to set might be considered optional.

Graphics

"Big game hunting is a form of natural selection . . .. The bulletproof tigers will survive to reproduce."
—Graffiti

THE nature of mainstream media has changed gradually with time. Graphics—the visual media—were everything you'd ever want in a form of expression for a long while. Stretching from the heyday of cave painting along to the Pre-Raphaelite painters, pictures once represented the only really permanent record of how things were. The other media of the day, such as sound, couldn't really be recorded, but only written down in a sort of coded pictographic form.

We're wont to forget that practical recorded sound is quite a bit younger than this century.

The Windows multimedia extensions seem to have embraced the newer media with a passion, perhaps to the exclusion of graphics. Pictures, after all, have been a part of personal computers for ages, while sound is a relatively new phenomenon. We'll allow that what has traditionally emerged from the tiny internal speaker of a PC shouldn't be classified as sound. With some imagination and more than a little goodwill, it might work its way up to being noise.

While bolting the multimedia extensions onto your applications will provide you with lots of functions to work with sound—as well as with a number of other facilities, such as the precision timers discussed in Chapter 3—pictures are largely your problem. If you wet your feet in the icy waters of Windows programming before opening this book, you probably have a sense of just how complicated pictures can be in Windows software.

Unfortunately, bitmapped graphic images under Windows are a perfect example of those areas in which Windows device independence begins to fall apart, and in which, as a consequence, the architecture of Windows has been patched and meddled with to get around a few of its internal limitations. The inherent problem in working with graphics is that they're large. The more interesting they get, the larger they become. Large objects require meaningful dollops

of processor resources and time to work with, things which Windows hands out reluctantly if it must hand them out at all.

Vastly complicating the issue of graphics is the great, yawning chasm of graphic display hardware under which Windows might find itself running. To as great a degree as possible, a Windows application must be able to display its graphics on anything from a standard VGA card plugged into an 80286 system from Sears right on up to a true-color, accelerated Super VGA card with more modes than most politicians have alibis. Of course, this is impossible, but Windows is constrained to try.

The result of this profusion of options and potential hardware bottlenecks is that Windows will not provide you with a particularly linear approach to displaying graphics. There is, for example, no visual equivalent to the sndPlaySound function that turned up in Chapter 2. Windows requires that you choose a strategy for displaying graphics based on your knowledge of the nature of your graphics, an appreciation of the sorts of hardware that your software might be run on, and the unwritten understanding that Windows probably won't be able to do everything the software development toolkit books say it can.

This chapter deals with some real-world graphics for Windows software. Chapter 5 looks at several more exotic graphic applications, including animation and screen savers. In both cases, however, everything that happens uses the low-level graphic functions of Windows. Typically less user-friendly than a 30-foot royal ball python with a surplus of venom, Windows' tools for working with bitmapped graphics in your applications will require some serious concentration.

Bitmaps & displays

A sheet of paper with something printed on it is a species of bitmap. While this page probably looks fairly solid, its type is really comprised of very tiny particles of ink. If you could look closely enough at its surface, you would find the page to be an irregular matrix of dots.

In computer terms, any image formed out of discrete elements is referred to as a *bitmap*. In fact, this name is somewhat incorrect—it harks back to the days when all graphics were black and white, and each dot in a matrix was either on or off. In this sort of graphic, each dot really is represented by one bit. Graphics with color require multiple bits to represent each dot—graphics with a lot of color can require multiple bytes.

Each dot in a matrix of a bitmap is called a *pixel*, unless you work for IBM, in which case it's called a *pel*. There's no obvious reason for this distinction, save perhaps that employees of IBM are predisposed to like three-letter acronyms.

Figure 4-1 illustrates a simple bitmapped graphic. The image of the parrot looks fairly solid. The fragment showing just the head reveals the image's true structure, that of a matrix of square pixels.

Your eye is a bitmapped device, as is the monitor of your computer. In fact, pretty well everything that's capable of displaying graphics can be regarded as a bitmap. While there are nonbitmapped graphics—we'll touch on them later in this chapter—they only exist in a theoretical sense, and must ultimately be rendered as bitmaps if you want to see them.

The simple bitmap in Fig. 4-1 is black and white—it only supports two colors. Note that black and white to a computer is significantly different from what we regard as black and white, the latter being in fact grey-scale images.

A black and white bitmap stores eight pixels in one byte. A black and white bitmapped graphic with the dimensions 640 by 480 pixels would require 38,400 bytes to store it.

If you set up Windows with a standard VGA screen driver—which is how it comes out of the box—it will display things using a 16-color graphic screen having the dimensions 640 by 480 pixels. Each pixel will require four bits, or half a byte. A four-bit number has 16 possible permutations. This means that the memory requirements for the bitmap that represents what's on such a screen is 153,600 bytes.

Figure 4-1

The structure of a bitmapped graphic.

The 256-color Super VGA graphic modes supported by most reasonable display cards offer the capability of displaying fairly convincing photo-realistic bitmaps. In fact, as we'll touch on in a moment, this is managed with a degree of cheating that can have some curious side effects. A 256-color bitmap stores each pixel in one byte—a 640 by 480 pixel, 256-color bitmap requires 307,200 pixels to store it.

Many of the latest generation of accelerated display cards offer high-color and true-color display modes in addition to their 256-color modes. High color allows for bitmaps with up to 32,768 or 65,536 potential colors, in which each pixel requires two bytes to store it. True color allows for 16,777,216 possible colors—each pixel in a true-color bitmap requires three bytes to store it. A high-color bitmap with the dimensions 640 by 480 pixels requires 614,400 bytes of storage. A true-color bitmap of the same dimensions requires 921,600 bytes, or the better part of a megabyte of memory, to store a single picture.

In fact, there are a few real-world considerations to keep in mind about these broad classes of bitmaps. First of all, whether they're stored on disk as BMP files or in memory as bitmaps, a bitmapped graphic must also carry around a header to define its dimensions, color palette, and several other useful criteria. This header will increase somewhat the storage requirements just outlined.

Second, while there are high-color screen modes available for some display cards and Windows drivers to manage them, Windows itself does not allow for high-color static bitmaps. As such, anything with more than 256 colors will be stored as a true-color bitmap.

As an aside, bitmapped graphics are usually stored in file formats that apply compression to them. This means that the image data itself is handled by an algorithm which "tokenizes" redundant data to make the files themselves smaller. The most commonly used PC image file formats, PCX and GIF, both employ compression.

When a compressed file is unpacked, its contents are read into memory as a conventional bitmap. As such, storing pictures as GIF files, for example, may save you some disk space, but it won't change the memory requirements of your software. The BMP format Windows uses to store bitmaps, discussed later in this chapter, uses no compression.

Another important thing to keep in mind about image compression is that it becomes decreasingly effective when confronted by images of increasing color depth and complexity. Drawn images compress fairly well, while scanned ones do not. Images with 256 colors can usually

be compressed to some extent. Scanned true-color images are usually so complex that applying a compression algorithm to one will so outrage it as to result in a disk file that's larger than it would have been had the image been left uncompressed.

As you might have gathered by now, a bitmap large enough to be useful and possessed of enough color depth to be interesting will typically be a somewhat voluminous object. While there was a time when 16 megabytes of memory was considered rather a lot, you can understand how quickly all this real estate could become full if your Windows applications were called upon to juggle several large bitmapped objects.

To further complicate this matter, some approaches to displaying bitmapped graphics under Windows require that Windows be allowed to create intermediate temporary bitmapped objects behind your back, further drawing on the available memory of your system.

Under Windows, applications rarely run out of memory. Confronted with a memory shortage, Windows will spill and spool and generally cheat to free up enough space to honor your memory requirements. However, all this takes time. Working with larger bitmapped elements under Windows is usually a tradeoff of functionality for time.

The other temporal element that will work itself into the discussion of Windows bitmapped graphics is the amount of time required by Windows to move a bitmap from where it lives in memory to your screen. This, as it turns out, can be almost instantaneous, even for fairly large bitmaps. The catch to allowing it to be so, however, can be a tremendous memory penalty.

⇨ Windows & color

Before you can begin to comprehend the real horror of working with bitmaps under Windows, you will have to come to grips with the nightmare of Windows' use of color. While there are probably more terrifying apparitions to be had in the video racks of most milk stores—and perhaps even in the refrigerator where they keep the milk, if it hasn't been cleaned out for a while—these are pretty nasty as such things go. They're worthy of an R rating at the very least.

In the previous section we discussed pictures having a finite number of colors. Pictures with 16 and 256 colors are said to be palette images. This means that each pixel in the bitmap in question is really not a color, but a number that represents an index into a lookup table of colors. The number of different colors that such a picture can contain will be determined by the size of the lookup table, or, if you prefer, the maximum number of permutations available for the numbers that hold indices into it.

A 256-color image uses one byte to store each pixel. A byte has eight bits, and eight bits can generate 256 distinct values.

In creating a theoretical 256-color image, you can actually choose from about 16 million possible colors, but you can use only 256 of them in one picture.

When Windows displays itself on a monitor, as mentioned earlier, it's effectively displaying a bitmap. Windows' display bitmap is constrained by the same conditions as other sorts of bitmaps. The number of colors Windows can display is determined by the Windows screen driver installed in your system. Windows drivers can support anywhere from 2 to 16 million colors. The most common Windows screen drivers are those that support 16 colors, as this is how Windows will be configured on a VGA system when it's first installed.

As explained in Chapter 1, Windows running a 16-color driver won't allow you to do much more than play Solitaire and leave yourself notes in Windows Write. Most serious Windows users will install a Super VGA screen driver supporting at least 256 colors before the shrink wrap from the Windows package has stopped crackling.

In a non-Windows environment, a 16-color bitmap can be comprised of any 16 colors you like. Under Windows, however, things are decidedly less flexible. Windows has a rather draconian view of palettes. The problem that Windows confronts in its use of color is that a typical Windows session may have multiple applications running at once. On a 16-color system, allowing each application to define which colors it wants to use would permit one application to shanghai the entire available hardware color palette for its own requirements. By nature, Windows likes to be able to pop up system

dialogs, switch between tasks, and generally integrate the multitude of discrete Windows programs into a single environment. Consider the problem this would cause if, for example, Windows found that the color it wants to use for printing text and the color it wants to use for the background of the dialog the text is to be printed on have already been defined speak, by the current application.

Windows deals with the problem of a finite color palette by not allowing applications to change the hardware color palette directly. Windows maintains an internal palette of 20 reserved colors. On a 16-color system this actually works out to 16 real colors and 4 additional colors generated by dithering with the first 16.

In this environment, if an application wants to draw something in green, for example, it would tell Windows which color it's after and Windows would locate the color in its reserved palette that's most like the requested color. This is a process called *remapping*.

Remapping colors like this means that—at least in a 16-color environment—most applications won't get precisely the colors they want, but no one will be confronted with wildly inappropriate colors.

On a system with a 256-color display, things will be quite a lot more flexible. Allowing that Windows will still allocate 20 colors for itself, there will be 236 colors free for use by the currently active application. For practical purposes, a 256-color graphic can usually be displayed under these conditions without any visible loss of color fidelity. Windows will juggle the color palette of the source image to allow for a minimum of color shifts.

What Windows palette management means to a 256-color display is that the current foreground application is allowed to modify 236 of the 256 available colors for its own use. It must do so through Windows, however, rather than by directly manipulating the palette registers of your display card.

One result of this arrangement is that, confronted with two applications, both of which would like to display different 256-color graphics having different palettes, the colors of the current foreground application will be correct and the colors of the

background application will be wildly inaccurate. In fact, the color palette of the foreground application will be imposed on the background application, with no thought as to how the results will look. This is illustrated in Fig. 4-2.

Figure 4-2

Two bitmapped graphics in separate windows with different palettes.

If your Windows system has a high-color or true-color driver, none of this will really matter, because for practical purposes displays with this much color depth can display an infinite number of colors with no palettes involved. Figure 4-3 illustrates what happens when the pictures in Fig. 4-2 are displayed on a system with a true-color display.

If you attempt to have Windows display a bitmap that has more colors than your display supports, the bitmap will be remapped to fit the available color palette. This means that 256-color bitmaps will be remapped to 16 colors on a 16-color display, something which is

 Figure 4-3

The bitmapped graphics from Fig. 4-2 displayed on a system with a true color driver.

rarely attractive. In addition to making your pictures ugly, remapping can be very time-consuming.

In creating software for displaying photo-realistic bitmaps, you'll be confronted with the problem of colors and color depth fairly early on. You can dither 256-color or true-color images down to 16 colors, and the results will offer the closest approximation of real color that a 16-color display can manage. Figure 4-4 shows an example of this. However, even at its best, color dithering loses a lot of detail and results in fairly unattractive graphics. There's not much that can be done about this for a 16-color system, but you could ask for something better on a system that supports a 256-color display.

Dithering, although by no means perfect, is decidedly preferable to allowing Windows to remap a bitmapped graphic.

To arrive at attractive, photo-realistic bitmapped graphics on systems with the hardware to display them (and dithered graphics should your software find itself running on a 16-color system), it's usually necessary to store two versions of each picture to be displayed and select one based on the color depth of the display on hand. There's a more detailed discussion of this technique in my book *Constructing Windows Dialogs*.

As an aside, if you'd like to work with dithered graphics of the sort illustrated in Fig. 4-4, you might want to investigate the Graphic Workshop for Windows package on the companion CD-ROM for this book. Among many other things, it can dither images down to 16 colors. In fact, it can create 16-color bitmaps that use the same color palette as Windows, thus eliminating any potential color shifts when they're displayed as well as the time-consuming process of having Windows remap them.

Figure 4-4

A full color image after dithering to sixteen colors. Not a pretty sight.

When you display a bitmap under Windows—and assuming that it embodies a color palette other than the one Windows is using at the moment—you must begin by realizing the palette of the new graphic. This, in effect, tells Windows what palette it's expected to accommodate and gives it the opportunity to fiddle with the existing colors to accomplish it. Having realized the palette for your bitmap, the graphic will display with the best possible color match based on Windows preexisting demands on the available color registers.

Realizing a palette actually involves having Windows do different things behind your back depending on the color depth of your display adapter. Realizing a palette on a 16-color display gives Windows the opportunity to decide which colors to remap the colors in the bitmap to; but as there are no free colors available on a 16-color display once Windows has taken its 20 reserved colors, this is as good as things get. On a 256-color display, Windows will most likely actually define up to 236 colors to accommodate the new bitmap being displayed. Because all the usual screen paraphernalia—window frames, menus, dialogs, and such—will have been drawn in colors from the 20 reserved colors of its fixed palette, defining the bitmap colors won't affect the colors of any existing objects on your screen.

If you're running on a system with a high-color or true-color display, realizing a palette doesn't really do anything.

Realizing a palette can be fairly time-consuming. If you realize a palette for one bitmap, other bitmaps with different palettes may not display correctly, or if they've previously been displayed, may suddenly exhibit some wildly incorrect colors. For this reason, as we'll see later on in this discussion of bitmaps, it's often convenient to create bitmapped graphics that only use the colors of the Windows reserved palette. By definition, these colors remain permanently realized. If you use bitmaps constrained to this color palette, there's no need to overtly realize their palettes before they're displayed. Furthermore, multiple bitmaps having the same palette can be displayed at one time without some of them changing color.

⇨ Storing bitmaps

Bitmapped graphics usually reside on disk and are loaded into memory to be displayed. In fact, as we'll discuss later on, it's possible to create them from scratch for situations in which images are to be generated algorithmically, rather than with a scanner or a paint package. We'll ignore this possibility for the sake of this discussion.

Bitmapped graphics stored as disk files can exist in two forms for a Windows application. The most commonly encountered bitmaps are those stored in discrete files. There are dozens of bitmapped graphic file formats, including BMP, GIF, PCX, TIFF, JPEG, and so on. An exhaustive discussion of them would easily double the size of this book, and would represent a digression of truly cosmic proportions. You will find such a discussion in my book *Windows Bitmapped Graphics*.

In this chapter, we'll assume that all bitmapped graphics are stored using the BMP format native to Windows. For graphics stored in other formats, you can use the Graphic Workshop for Windows package on the companion CD-ROM for this book to translate them into BMP files.

Even this degree of simplicity in file formats calls for a brief digression. There are two species of BMP files—to wit, Windows BMP files and OS/2 BMP files. They're similar, and some functions that work with BMP files will recognize and correctly deal with both types. Some won't. You can save yourself considerable additional confusion in an already confusing area of software design if you work exclusively with Windows BMP files.

If you're working with BMP files created by Windows Paintbrush, Corel Draw, or any other native Windows application, you can be fairly certain you'll have Windows BMP files, and all will be well. If you obtain BMP files from other sources, use the Get Info function of Graphic Workshop for Windows to determine their origins. Figure 4-5 illustrates Graphic Workshop's Get Info dialog for Windows and OS/2 BMP files.

Figure 4-5

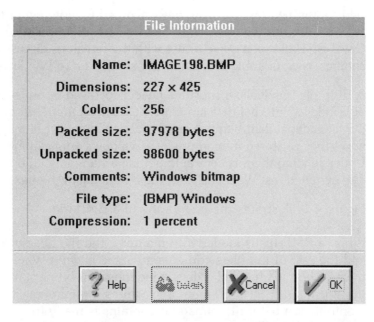

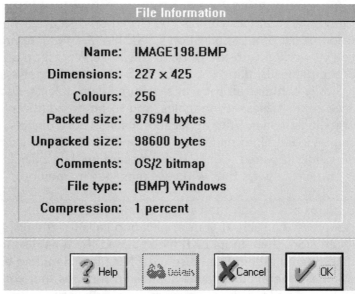

The Graphic Workshop Get Info dialogs for Windows and OS/2 BMP files.

While Graphic Workshop can be configured to write either type of BMP files, it will write Windows BMP files by default. If you encounter any OS/2 BMP files you'd like to use with the functions discussed in this chapter, have Graphic Workshop translate them to Windows BMP.

A BMP file is actually a short file header followed by a disk image of one of Windows' internal data structures, a *device-independent bitmap*. Device-independent bitmaps are the basic format for bitmapped images when they're stored in memory by a Windows application. Understanding them is central to getting a hammerlock on Windows' display functions. We'll deal with them in detail in the next section.

Figure 4-6 illustrates the geography of a BMP file.

When a BMP file is loaded into memory, the file header is discarded and the rest of the file's contents are exactly what Windows expects to see when it's handed a device-independent bitmap. This means that loading a BMP into memory requires a minimum of data manipulation before the image it contains is ready for use.

Bitmapped graphics can also be stored on disk as entries in the resource list of an application's EXE file. As you'll appreciate if you've worked with the Borland Resource Workshop application that accompanies Borland C++, the EXE file of a Windows application typically contains all sorts of structured data objects, such as menus, accelerator tables, string tables, and so on, in addition to the executable code of the application itself. These objects, or *resources*, can be loaded into memory, used, and finally discarded when they're no longer required. Loading and discarding data objects as resources is one of the ways that Windows manages its memory.

Bitmaps are among the various data objects that can be stored as resources. As such, if your application calls for the display of bitmaps, it can store them in its EXE file and load them as resources, rather than opening them from discrete BMP files. Handling bitmaps this way has several advantages: it's faster, requires that you write less dedicated code, reduces the number of ancillary files required by your application, and to some extent prevents users of your software from accidentally—or deliberately—modifying or deleting important graphics for your software.

Figure 4-6

Bitmapped
image data
(and caffeine)

*The structure of a BMP
file.*

Array of
RGBquad objects

Bitmapinfoheader

Bitmapfileheader

Using bitmap resources has turned up informally earlier in this
book—there's such a resource in the About dialog of every sample
application we've discussed.

You can include a bitmap in the resource script of a Windows
application with a line like this one:

```
AboutBitmap BITMAP ABOUT.BMP
```

The first item on this line is the name of the bitmap resource as it will be accessed from within your application. This can also be a number if you prefer. The second item defines this resource as a bitmap. The third item is the name of the BMP file containing the source graphic.

If a bitmap is stored as a resource in the EXE file of an application, it can be fetched in one of two ways. The first is with a call to LoadResource and the second is with a call to LoadBitmap. The distinction between these two calls and the circumstances under which they should be used may not be obvious.

A bitmap resource is really just a BMP file with its file header removed. If you call LoadResource to fetch it, the result will be a handle to a buffer containing your original BMP file. This is what Windows properly calls a device-independent bitmap.

If you call LoadBitmap, Windows will translate your device-independent bitmap into a BITMAP object and return an HBITMAP handle to that. A BITMAP object is a somewhat simpler structure— among other things, it doesn't contain any palette information. A BITMAP is assumed to refer to the currently realized palette.

Windows functions that work with bitmaps may want either sort of bitmap, depending on exactly what they're doing. This should become a bit clearer in a moment, when we deal with display contexts and such.

However you fetch a bitmap from the resource list of an application, the result will be a handle to a memory buffer. If you want to work directly with the contents of a loaded bitmap, you must lock this handle with LockResource and then unlock it when you're done with UnlockResource. These functions are analogous to the GlobalLock and GlobalUnlock calls used to handle global memory buffers, but they're not interchangeable.

Keep in mind that if you'll be working with bitmaps that fill a substantial portion of your screen, the resulting memory objects will be pretty large. A 256-color display with a resolution of 800 by 600 will require in excess of 480,000 bytes of memory to store its bitmap. Good memory management dictates that if you must lock a bitmap,

you should leave it locked for the shortest period of time, lest Windows comes to a wheezing, sputtering halt for lack of free memory. In addition, if you have cause to access the contents of a locked bitmap, make sure you do so with huge pointers if there's any likelihood of the image data requiring more than 64 kilobytes of memory.

For bitmaps of any worthwhile size, there's little likelihood of their image data *not* requiring more than 64 kilobytes of memory.

A device-independent bitmap object—what you'll get if you call LoadResource to fetch a bitmap—lends itself to being easily manipulated. You might have cause to do so if you want to find the dimensions of a bitmap, read its palette data, or read or modify its image information. The next example shows how you'd work with a locked bitmap. It assumes that the bitmap in question started life as a Windows BMP file rather than one for OS/2. If you're interested in dealing with both types, you might want to see the discussion of bitmaps in the companion volume to this one, *Multimedia Programming for Windows*.

The BITMAPINFOHEADER data structure defines the beginning of a device-independent bitmap. This is what it looks like:

```
typedef struct {
        DWORD biSize;
        DWORD biWidth;
        DWORD biHeight;
        WORD biPlanes;
        WORD biBitCount;
        DWORD biCompression;
        DWORD biSizeImage;
        DWORD biXPelsPerMeter;
        DWORD biYPelsPerMeter;
        DWORD biClrUsed;
        DWORD biClrImportant;
        } BITMAPINFOHEADER;
```

The biSize field defines the size of the header and will always be sizeof(BITMAPINFOHEADER). This may seem a bit redundant,

inasmuch as this value should be known simply by virtue of this being a device-independent bitmap. In fact, this number is extremely useful because it allows software capable of reading both Windows and OS/2 bitmaps to know which type it's looking at. The size of the header structure of an OS/2 bitmap is different.

The biWidth and biHeight values of a BITMAPINFOHEADER define the dimension of the bitmap in question in pixels. The biPlanes value defines the number of image planes in the bitmap. Since all device-independent bitmaps under Windows have only one plane, this field will always be set to one and can be ignored.

The biBitCount field defines the number of bits per pixel in the bitmap in question. Windows allows for only four possible color depths in a device-independent bitmap: 1, 4, 8, and 24 bits per pixel.

The biCompression field defines whether the bitmap in question has been compressed using Windows' simple run-length compression. If not, the field will be zero. For the sake of this discussion, we'll assume that all bitmaps are uncompressed.

The biSizeImage field of a BITMAPINFOHEADER object defines the number of bytes required for the image in question.

For this discussion, biXPelsPerMeter, biYPelsPerMeter, biClrUsed, and biClrImportant can be ignored. They're typically set to zero.

If handle represents the handle to a device-independent bitmap, as returned by LoadResource, this is how you'd deal with it to access its BITMAPINFOHEADER object:

```
LPBITMAPINFOHEADER lpbi;

if((lpbi=(LPBITMAPINFOHEADER)LockResource(handle)) != NULL) {

        /* some code goes here */

        UnlockResource(handle);
}
```

Having locked the bitmap, you could derive its dimensions, for example, as lpbi->biWidth and lpbi->biHeight.

Following the BITMAPINFOHEADER structure of a device-independent bitmap, you should find the color palette for the image, assuming there is one. Color palette entries are stored in RGBQUAD data structures, with one RGBQUAD per color. This is what they look like:

```
typedef struct {
        BYTE rgbBlue;
        BYTE rgbGreen;
        BYTE rgbRed;
        BYTE rgbReserved;
        } RGBQUAD;
```

The rgbBlue, rgbGreen, and rgbRed elements of an RGBQUAD object define the blue, green, and red indices of the color in question. Note that they're ordered differently from the way the rest of the known universe stores colors—that is, the more common red, green, and blue.

The number of RGBQUAD objects in a device-independent bitmap will be determined by the color depth of its image, as specified in its biBitCount field. There will be 1<<lpbi->biBitCount palette entries for bitmaps having up to 8 bits of color, and no entries at all for 24-bit bitmaps, as true-color images don't use palettes.

As an aside, Windows defines a somewhat confusing second version of a BITMAPINFOHEADER object called BITMAPINFO. A BITMAPINFO object is defined like this:

```
typedef struct {
        BITMAPINFOHEADER bmiHeader;
        RGBQUAD bmiColors[1];
        } BITMAPINFO;
```

A BITMAPINFO object is just a BITMAPINFOHEADER object with an array of one RGBQUAD object glued on afterwards. In fact, you can pretend that this array is of any size you like. As such, you could get at the RGBQUAD palette entries of a device-independent bitmap

fairly easily, as follows. This assumes that lpbi is an
LPBITMAPINFOHEADER pointer to a locked device-independent
bitmap:

```
LPBITMAPINFO lpbit;
unsigned int i,red,green,blue,colors;

lpbit=(LPBITMAPINFO)lpbi;

colors=1<<lpbi->biBitCount;

for(i=0;i<colors;++i) {
        red=lpbit->bmiColors[i].rgbRed;
        green=lpbit->bmiColors[i].rgbGreen;
        blue=lpbit->bmiColors[i].rgbBlue;
}
```

Make sure you don't interchange LPBITMAPINFOHEADER and
LPBITMAPINFO pointers when you're actually dealing with the image
data in a device-independent bitmap. The object pointed to by the
latter is four bytes larger than that of the former.

The image data in a device-independent bitmap is stored in raster
lines. The first raster line after the file header and palette is actually
the bottom of the image—the image in a device-independent bitmap
is stored upside down.

Images with two bits of color are stored as simple bit planes. Images
with eight bits of color are stored with one pixel per byte. True-color
images are stored with three bytes per pixel in the order blue, green,
red. Once again, note that this is the opposite of how true-color
pixels are stored in most other environments.

Images with four bits of color are stored using chunky pixels. This
means that each byte of a raster line contains two pixels—one in the
upper four bits and one in the lower four bits. Computer etymologists
will note that half a byte is called a *nibble* in this context. The term
for half a nibble is less easily defined, and of course, almost never
called for. I'm fond of *crumb*, myself.

Here's how you'd locate the image data for a device-independent bitmap. Once again, this assumes that lpbi points to a locked bitmap returned by LoadResource.

```
char huge *p;
unsigned int n;

n=1<<lpbi->biBitCount;

p=((char huge *)lpbi)+
    (long)sizeof(BITMAPINFOHEADER)+
    (long)(n*sizeof(RGBQUAD));
```

Note that if the bitmap in question has 24 bits of color, n should equal 2^{24}. However, shifting a 16-bit number to the right by 24 places will shift its contents right off the end of the dock and into the lake, leaving the actual value of this calculation as zero. This is, conveniently, the number of palette entries in a true-color, device-independent bitmap.

In working with the graphic code discussed in this chapter, you won't have to deal directly with the image data of a device-independent bitmap. You will, however, need access to some of the header fields. In fact, Windows offers a fairly elegant way to create device-independent bitmaps without having to actually get bytes under your fingernails. We'll look at that shortly as well.

Display surfaces & device contexts

One of the reasons there are so many ways to handle bitmaps under Windows is intimately connected with Windows' application of display surfaces. The other reason is generally poor planning, something that's beyond the scope of this book.

Windows regards the inside of your monitor as a display surface. A display surface can be thought of as a bitmap which has specific but largely ineffable characteristics. It's a device-dependent bitmap—that

is, it's peculiar to your particular display. Its dimensions, color depth, and display memory layout are things Windows knows about but you need never be troubled with.

When you want to draw something on your screen, Windows will provide you with an HDC object—that is, a handle to a device context. This is another ineffable phenomenon under Windows—it tells subsequent GDI calls about your monitor's characteristics, but you can't actually look at what it refers to and see what it says. For the sorts of applications discussed in this book, there's no need to do so.

Note that Windows sometimes describes an HDC as a handle to a device context and at other times as a handle to a display context. The former is probably somewhat more correct.

In order to be painted on your monitor, a bitmap must be in the same internal format as the virtual bitmap of your screen—or the image data must be translated on the fly. A device-independent bitmap, as we've seen, is structured in a fairly logical way for dealing with image data, but is largely meaningless to a display. As a simple example, a 16-color image will be stored using chunky pixels in a device-independent bitmap. Most display adapters actually use interleaved image planes for 16-color images. Both arrangements can contain the same image information, but you could not directly place a chunky-pixel bitmap on a planar screen.

Windows allows for a device-dependent bitmap to be created from a device-independent bitmap. It also offers an API call, BitBlt, to move rectangular areas between the internal bitmaps of compatible device contexts. The bitmaps in question can be actual bitmaps in memory, or they can be the virtual bitmap of your screen. Combining these functions—along with a few other bits required to make the whole juggling act work—will allow you to create a function that displays bitmaps. Here's an example of such a function—in the interest of simplicity, this one works with BITMAP objects rather than device-independent bitmaps:

```
void DrawDIB(HDC hdc,HBITMAP hBitmap)
{
```

```
        HDC hMemoryDC;
        HBITMAP hOldBitmap;

        if((hMemoryDC=CreateCompatibleDC(hdc)) != NULL) {
        hOldBitmap=SelectObject(hMemoryDC,hBitmap);
        if(hOldBitmap) {
          BitBlt(hdc,0,0,WIDE,DEEP,
            hMemoryDC,0,0,SRCCOPY);
          SelectObject(hMemoryDC,hOldBitmap);
        }
        DeleteDC(hMemoryDC);
      }
    }
```

This bit of code illustrates a lot about how device contexts work under Windows. The first argument to DrawDIB is the HDC of your display. It's typically provided by the BeginPaint call in the WM_PAINT case of the message handler for the window about to be updated. This object defines how the virtual bitmap of your screen is structured.

The CreateCompatibleDC call creates a new device context with the same display characteristics as your screen. However, it's not actually connected to your screen—for the moment, it's a sort of "monitorless monitor." It supports two colors and has the dimensions one by one pixel.

If a bitmap is selected into an HDC created by CreateCompatibleDC, the new device context will take on the dimensions and color depth of the bitmap—at least, it will do so as long as the bitmap doesn't support more colors than your screen does. The contents of the bitmap will be copied into the virtual bitmap of the new device context. The result will be a bitmap in the new device context that looks like the image in the original bitmap, but has the same physical structure as your screen. For example, if your screen is ordered in planes to handle 16-color graphics, the bitmap of the new device context will be ordered this way too, rather than being ordered as chunky pixels.

The BitBlt function is fairly complex, and some of its more exotic applications will turn up in detail in Chapter 5 when we discuss

animation. In its simplest form, however, BitBlt can copy a rectangular area of one bitmap into a rectangular area of another bitmap, so long as both bitmaps have the same internal structure. In this case, the two bitmaps are your screen and a memory device context which has been constructed to look just like your screen, having the dimensions, color depth, and contents of the bitmap to be displayed.

There are several good reasons for displaying bitmaps this way, and one good one for looking at an alternate approach. Using BitBlt is fast, flexible, and offers numerous ways to cheat if you have to display a limited number of smaller bitmapped elements quickly, as in creating animated elements in a larger graphic. The drawback to working with BitBlt is that it's fairly memory hungry. It must be allowed to create an intermediate object—the memory device context—at least as big as your source bitmap. If your source bitmap is relatively small, this is of little consequence. If your source bitmap is intended to fill your screen, memory might get a little scarce.

If you choose this approach to displaying bitmaps because it's fast, keep in mind that when Windows runs low on memory, it starts spilling objects in memory to disk. This is supremely time-consuming. The speed of BitBlt can be vastly dwarfed by the time it takes Windows to scare up a large temporary buffer if it is asked to display a large bitmap on a system with relatively little memory.

Keep in mind that the memory device context in this application of BitBlt is really an analog of the bitmap structure of your screen. This means that no matter what the color depth of your source bitmap, the bitmap represented by the memory device context will have the color depth of your screen. For example, a 16-color bitmap with the dimensions 640 by 480 would require something on the order of 150 kilobytes to be stored as a BITMAP object, versus 900 kilobytes in the memory device context to be painted on your screen, assuming your system is equipped with a true-color Windows screen driver.

The alternative to working with BitBlt is a call to SetDIBitsToDevice. Unlike BitBlt, this function can translate bitmaps on the fly between a device-independent bitmap and whatever a device context happens to be. It uses no extremely large intermediate objects. The catch, however, is that it's relatively slow.

The SetDIBitsToDevice function will turn up in action later in this chapter. Here's how it works:

```
SetDIBitsToDevice(    hdc,

                      xdest,
                      ydest,

                      width,
                      depth,

                      xsource,
                      ysource,

                      firstline,
                      linecount,

                      image,
                      bitmapinfo,
                      use);
```

The hdc argument to SetDIBitsToDevice is the HDC of the display surface that the bitmap is to be painted on. The xdest and ydest arguments indicate where the upper left corner of the bitmap will be relative to the upper left corner of the window it's to be painted in. The width and depth arguments specify the dimensions in pixels of the bitmap to be painted.

The xsource and ysource arguments to SetDIBitsToDevice define the upper left corner of the area of the source bitmap to be painted relative to the upper left corner of the bitmap. The firstline argument specifies the number of the first line in the source bitmap, and the linecount argument specifies the number of lines the bitmap contains.

The image argument is an LPSTR pointer to the actual image data of the bitmap. The bitmapinfo argument is a far pointer to a BITMAPINFO structure defining the source bitmap.

Finally, the use argument tells SetDIBitsToDevice how to handle the color in the bitmap being displayed. If it's set to

DIB_RGB_COLORS, the palette will be treated normally—that is, as a list of RGBQUAD objects. If it's set to RGB_PAL_COLORS, SetDIBitsToDevice will assume that the palette has been realized into the HDC in question, and that the list of RGBQUAD objects has been overwritten with a list of integers specifying the indices into the currently realized palette.

The latter application of the SetDIBitsToDevice palette management allows images to be displayed a lot quicker—in effect, it tells Windows not to worry about checking the color matching of the image to the currently realized palette.

Here's a final note about the DrawDIB function, and about working with bitmaps in general. In the foregoing function, the dimensions of the bitmap to be displayed were represented by two constants, WIDTH and DEPTH, without much explanation about how they got there. We've discussed how to determine the dimensions of a device-independent bitmap, but not of a BITMAP object—the structure that DrawDIB was interested in working with. Windows offers a way to do this, although it's less than obvious.

To begin with, this is a BITMAP object. While device-independent bitmaps are generally easier to work with in applications for which you'll be actively manipulating the data, this is how Windows expects bitmaps to be stored for its internal consumption:

```
typedef struct {
        int bmType;
        int bmWidth;
        int bmHeight;
        int bmWidthBytes;
        BYTE bmPlanes;
        BYTE bmBitsPixel;
        LPSTR bmBits;
        } BITMAP;
```

An HBITMAP handle is a handle to this data structure plus the actual bitmapped information for the image in question.

In a BITMAP object, the bmWidth and bmHeight elements contain the dimensions of the bitmap in question, and bmBitsPixel contains the color depth in pixels.

If you have a handle to a BITMAP object of undefined characteristics, in this case called hbitmap, you can fetch this data structure from it as follows:

```
BITMAP bitmap;

GetObject(hbitmap,sizeof(BITMAP),&bitmap);
```

With this bit of additional code, you can improve on the previous DrawDIB such that it can work out the dimensions of the bitmap it's asked to display:

```
void DrawDIB(HDC hdc,HBITMAP hBitmap)
{
        HDC hMemoryDC;
        HBITMAP hOldBitmap;
        BITMAP bitmap;

        GetObject(hbitmap,sizeof(BITMAP),&bitmap);

        if((hMemoryDC=CreateCompatibleDC(hdc)) != NULL) {
                hOldBitmap=SelectObject(hMemoryDC,hBitmap);
                if(hOldBitmap) {
                        BitBlt(hdc,0,0,bitmap.bmWidth,
                            bitmap.bmHeight,hMemoryDC,
                            0,0,SRCCOPY);
                        SelectObject(hMemoryDC,hOldBitmap);
                }
                DeleteDC(hMemoryDC);
        }
}
```

As a final note, keep in mind that the distinction between a bitmap defined by a BITMAP object and one defined by a BITMAPINFOHEADER object is somewhat historical—the former

dates back to Windows 2.0, while the latter appeared with Windows 3.0. Because a BITMAP object doesn't include a palette, but rather is assumed to refer to the currently realized palette, it's not a particularly portable way to store bitmaps. Both objects do represent device-independent bitmaps, however.

⇨ The lore of BitBlt

In order to really understand the bitmapped graphic application covered later in this chapter, you should have a very clear bead on what BitBlt is up to. Some of its capabilities are less than apparent, and its myriad arguments might not make immediate sense.

Here's a list of BitBlt arguments, followed by an explanation of what each one means:

```
BitBlt(desthdc,
       xdest,
       ydest,

       width,
       depth,

       sourcehdc,

       xsource,
       ysource,

       operation);
```

Honesty bids me to note that, even having used this thing for a while, I have a difficult time keeping these arguments straight, and as such I usually write calls to BitBlt with each argument on its own line, so that I can put notes to myself as comments after each one.

As mentioned earlier, BitBlt moves rectangular areas between two device contexts. The first argument is the HDC of the destination of the transfer. The xdest and ydest arguments specify where the transferred rectangle's upper left corner should appear in the

destination device context, relative to the device context's upper left corner. The width and depth arguments define the dimensions in pixels of the rectangular area to be transferred.

The sourcehdc argument defines the device context of the source bitmap. The xsource and ysource arguments define the upper left corner of the rectangular area to be transferred from the source bitmap, relative to the upper left corner of the bitmap.

The operation argument of BitBlt is one of the things that make it capable of so many impressive tricks. It defines how the source bitmap is to be combined with the destination bitmap's existing image information. The most common argument for this field will be SRCCOPY, which tells BitBlt to paint the source bitmap over the destination bitmap. Other choices for this argument include:

SRCAND   Perform a logical AND between the two bitmaps.
SRCINVERT   Perform a logical XOR between the two bitmaps.
SRCPAINT   Perform a logical OR between the two bitmaps.

The potential results of ANDing two color bitmaps together might not be immediately obvious. In ANDing two bitmaps, for example, what really happens is that the numerical value of each pixel in the source bitmap is logically ANDed with the numerical value of each corresponding pixel in the destination bitmap, with the results being written to the destination bitmap. Keeping in mind that since each pixel is really an index into the currently realized color palette for the device contexts in question, the result will be to change the color being displayed.

Here's an example of how this works. We'll assume that the color palette in question includes only eight colors to keep the numbers simple—something which would never actually occur under Windows:

Number	Color
0	Black
1	Red
2	Green
3	Yellow
4	Blue

Number	Color
5	Magenta
6	Cyan
7	White

Consider what would happen in ANDing two pixels together where one pixel is yellow and the other is magenta. These correspond to index values of three and five respectively. This would be expressed in binary notation as:

0011 Yellow
0101 Magenta

In performing a logical AND of two numbers, the resulting value will be a number in which only those bits that are set in *both* source numbers will be set in the destination number. As such, the result of ANDing these two values will be:

0001 Red

The result of ANDing two pixels makes sense numerically, but the actual colors that result from doing so won't bear any obvious relationship to the two source colors involved unless you consider the positions of the source colors in the palette being used.

We'll look at a practical application of bitwise operators for bitmaps in Chapter 5 of this book when we deal with animation.

Real-world bitmaps —something to look at

Displaying simple bitmaps from BMP files is discussed in detail in *Multimedia Programming for Windows*. It will turn up again in the sample application discussed in this section, although with considerable additional fanfare.

The fundamental problem with still graphics is that they're so . . . still. In the fairly lively world of most multimedia applications, a

picture that just hangs around in a window and looks content won't inspire much excitement among your users. While not all graphics lend themselves to animation, you can do a lot to make your pictures more noticeable by improving upon their entrances and exits.

The BMP-FX application discussed in this section is a collection of functions to do fancy transitions for bitmapped graphics. In fact, it embodies a simple image display function as well, although once you've seen a graphic tile or slide or raster or wipe or plummet onto your screen, simply having it appear probably won't seem wholly satisfying.

Figure 4-7 illustrates the principal window of the BMP-FX program. The list of check boxes along the right side specifies the effects it will inflict on the bitmaps it's asked to display.

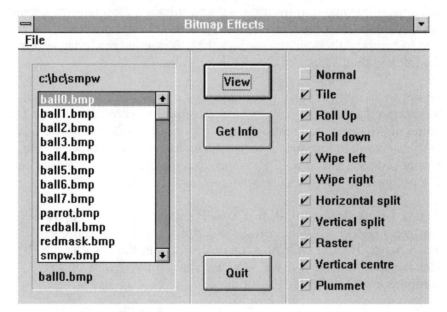

Figure 4-7

The BMP-FX application.

The BMP-FX application will open a BMP file and display it. In fact, it will display it multiple times—once for each of the effects you've enabled. When all the dancing pixels have finished their

performances, BMP-FX will return you to the principal window of the application to select another file.

In addition to working with BMP files read from your disk, BMP-FX illustrates how to apply these effects to bitmap resources read from the resource fork of your application's EXE file. We'll have a look at this shortly.

The BMP-FX application is a masterwork of poor program architecture: once it gets going on a list of effects, it's unstoppable. If you apply these functions to your own applications, you shouldn't run into this problem, as it's unlikely that you'll want to have the same picture appearing and disappearing over and over again with different effects.

As a final bit of preliminary discourse, the BMP-FX program illustrates each transition of images using a pair of effects. For example, an image will appear by wiping in from the left and then will disappear by wiping out to the left. In applying these functions to your applications, you're free to combine them in any way you like. A graphic might wipe in from the left and then vanish by dissolving into tiles.

To keep the code for BMP-FX simple, I've made the assumption that all the images it will work with will have dimensions evenly divisible by 16. Some of the effects may misbehave if this is not the case. As you'll probably come to appreciate when you've had a chance to look at the source code for BMP-FX.CPP, simplicity is a worthwhile consideration in this program. It's moderately huge even as it stands.

Figure 4-8 illustrates the BMP-FX.CPP source code file. Figure 4-9 illustrates BMP-FX.RC, its resource script. In addition to these files, you'll need PRJ and DEF files for BMP-FX, and the WAV and BMP files included in BMP-FX.RC. You will find all these files on the companion CD-ROM for this book.

Figure 4-8   *The BMP-FX.CPP source code.*

```
/*

        Bitmap Effects
        Copyright (c) 1993 Alchemy Mindworks Inc.
*/

#include <windows.h>
```

```c
#include <stdio.h>
#include <stdlib.h>
#include <dir.h>
#include <ctype.h>
#include <alloc.h>
#include <string.h>
#include <io.h>
#include <bwcc.h>
#include <dos.h>
#include <errno.h>
#include <math.h>
#include <mmsystem.h>
#include <commdlg.h>

#define say(s)      MessageBox(NULL,s,"Yo...",MB_OK | MB_ICONSTOP);
#define saynumber(f,s)     {char b[128]; sprintf((LPSTR)b,(LPSTR)f,s); \
     MessageBox(NULL,b,"Debug Message",MB_OK | MB_ICONSTOP); }

#define CheckOn(hwnd,item)              SendDlgItemMessage(hwnd,item,BM_SETCHECK,1,0L)

#define CheckOff(hwnd,item)             SendDlgItemMessage(hwnd,item,BM_SETCHECK,0,0L)

#define IsItemChecked(hwnd,item)    SendDlgItemMessage(hwnd,item,BM_GETCHECK,0,0L)

#defineItemName(item,string)           { dlgH=GetDlgItem(hwnd,item); \
                                        SetWindowText(dlgH,(LPSTR)string); \
                                        }

#defineItemOn(item)          { dlgH=GetDlgItem(hwnd,item); \
                               EnableWindow(dlgH,TRUE); \
                               EnableMenuItem(hmenu,item,MF_ENABLED);\
                               }

#defineItemOff(item)         { dlgH=GetDlgItem(hwnd,item); \
                               EnableWindow(dlgH,FALSE); \
                               EnableMenuItem(hmenu,item,MF_GRAYED);\
                               }

#defineDoMessage(hwnd,string) BWCCMessageBox(hwnd,string,"Message",\
                               MB_OK | MB_ICONINFORMATION)

#defineRoundUp(n,r)        (n+(n%r))

#defineWaitAfterDisplay()             { long t,l=ticks(); \
                                        while((t=ticks()) >= l && t < (l+(long)LONGWAIT));\
                                       }

#defineWaitForTick(twait)             {\
                                         while((t=ticks()) >= l && t < (l+(long)twait));\
                               }

#define SHORTWAIT       1
#define MEDIUMWAIT      10
```

133

Figure 4-8   *Continued.*

```
#define LONGWAIT        1000

#define TIMER_INTERVAL 1

// If it's defined, this macro will draw a black frame around each image
// after it's completed its effect. This is useful to make sure the image
// fragments are winding up where they're supposed to.
#if 0
#define CheckFrame(hdc,fi) { HBRUSH oldbrush; HPEN oldpen;\
                oldbrush=SelectObject(hdc,GetStockObject(NULL_BRUSH));\
                oldpen=SelectObject(hdc,GetStockObject(BLACK_PEN));\
                Rectangle(hdc,0,0,fi->width,fi->depth);\
                SelectObject(hdc,oldpen);\
                SelectObject(hdc,oldbrush);\
                }
#else
#defineCheckFrame(hdc,fi)
#endif

/* bad memory management techniques... conveniently packaged */
#define FixedGlobalAlloc(n)     MAKELONG(0,GlobalAlloc(GPTR,(DWORD)n))
#define FixedGlobalFree(p)      GlobalFree((GLOBALHANDLE)HIWORD((LONG)p));

#define STRINGSIZE      128         /* how big is a string? */
#define  pixels2bytes(n)  ((n+7)/8)

#define MAIN_LIST       201         /* objects in the main window */

#define MAIN_TITLE      301
#define MAIN_PATH       302

#define MAIN_VIEW       102
#define MAIN_GETINFO    103
#define MAIN_COLOUR     104
#define MAIN_ABOUT      105
#define MAIN_EXIT       107

#define MESSAGE_STRING  101         /* message box objects */

#define INFO_FILE       101         /* get info box objects */
#define INFO_COLOURS    102
#define INFO_DIMENSIONS 103
#define INFO_MEMORY     104

#define RGB_RED         0
#define RGB_GREEN       1
#define RGB_BLUE        2
#define RGB_SIZE        3

#define TILESIZE        8           /* size of display tiles */
#define ROLLSTEP        2           /* size of step for rolling effects */
```

```
#define RASTERBANDSIZE    8                    /* size of one band for rasters */
#define RASTERBANDSTEP    4                    /* size of one step for rasters */
#define BRICKSIZE         16                   /* size of plummetting tile */
#define BRICKDROP         1                    /* depth a tile can plummet in one cycle */

#define FX_NORMAL         400
#define FX_TILE           401
#define FX_ROLLUP         402
#define FX_ROLLDOWN       403
#define FX_WIPELEFT       404
#define FX_WIPERIGHT      405
#define FX_HSPLIT         406
#define FX_VSPLIT         407
#define FX_RASTER         408
#define FX_VCENTRE        409
#define FX_PLUMMET        410

#define FX_BASE           400
#define FX_COUNT          13

#ifndef max
#define max(a,b)               (((a)>(b))?(a):(b))
#endif
#ifndef min
#define min(a,b)               (((a)<(b))?(a):(b))
#endif

typedef struct {
        GLOBALHANDLE picture;
        char filename[16];
        unsigned int width;
        unsigned int depth;
        unsigned int bits;
        unsigned long memory;
        char palette[768];
        } FILEINFO;

typedef FILEINFO FAR *LPFILEINFO;

/* prototypes */
DWORD FAR PASCAL SelectProc(HWND hwnd,WORD message,WORD wParam,LONG lParam);
DWORD FAR PASCAL AboutDlgProc(HWND hwnd,WORD message,WORD wParam,LONG lParam);
DWORD FAR PASCAL InfoDlgProc(HWND hwnd,WORD message,WORD wParam,LONG lParam);
DWORD HandleCtlColour(HWND hwnd,WORD wParam,DWORD lParam);

HANDLE RealizePicturePalette(HDC hdc,LPFILEINFO fi);

long FAR PASCAL PictureProc(HWND hwnd,unsigned int message,
    unsigned int wParam,LONG lParam);
long ticks();

void ShowInfo(HWND hwnd,LPFILEINFO fi);
void ResetSelectorList(HWND hwnd);
```

Figure 4-8   *Continued.*

```
void CentreWindow(HWND hwnd);
void SaveConfig(HWND hwnd);
void LoadConfig(HWND hwnd);

unsigned int FindColourMatch(unsigned int r,unsigned int g,
    unsigned int b,LPSTR p,unsigned int n);

int BitmapToPicture(LPFILEINFO fi,HANDLE hpicture);
int testdisk(int n);
int GetInfo(LPFILEINFO fi,LPSTR path);
int ViewFile(HWND hwnd,LPSTR path);
int lmemcpy(LPSTR dest,LPSTR source,int n);

int SelectColour(HWND hwnd,COLORREF FAR *clr);
int DisplayPicture(HDC hdc,LPFILEINFO fi);
int TileFromPicture(HDC hdc,LPFILEINFO fi);
int TileToColour(HDC hdc,LPFILEINFO fi,COLORREF rgb);
int FadePictureToColour(HDC hdc,LPFILEINFO fi,COLORREF rgb);
int VerticalRollUpPicture(HDC hdc,LPFILEINFO fi);
int VerticalRollDownPicture(HDC hdc,LPFILEINFO fi);
int VerticalRollUpPictureAway(HDC hdc,LPFILEINFO fi,COLORREF rgb);
int VerticalRollDownPictureAway(HDC hdc,LPFILEINFO fi,COLORREF rgb);
int WipeInPictureFromLeft(HDC hdc,LPFILEINFO fi);
int WipeInPictureFromRight(HDC hdc,LPFILEINFO fi);
int WipeOutPictureFromLeft(HDC hdc,LPFILEINFO fi,COLORREF rgb);
int WipeOutPictureFromRight(HDC hdc,LPFILEINFO fi,COLORREF rgb);
int HorizontalSplitPictureIn(HDC hdc,LPFILEINFO fi);
int HorizontalSplitPictureOut(HDC hdc,LPFILEINFO fi,COLORREF rgb);
int VerticalSplitPictureIn(HDC hdc,LPFILEINFO fi);
int VerticalSplitPictureOut(HDC hdc,LPFILEINFO fi,COLORREF rgb);
int RasterPictureIn(HDC hdc,LPFILEINFO fi);
int RasterPictureOut(HDC hdc,LPFILEINFO fi,COLORREF rgb);
int VerticalCentrePictureIn(HDC hdc,LPFILEINFO fi);
int VerticalCentrePictureOut(HDC hdc,LPFILEINFO fi,COLORREF rgb);
int PlummetPictureIn(HDC hdc,LPFILEINFO fi);
int PlummetPictureOut(HDC hdc,LPFILEINFO fi,COLORREF rgb);

/* globals */
COLORREF background=RGB(64,64,64);

LPSTR messagehook;
char szAppName[]="BitmapEffects";

HANDLE hInst;

#pragma warn -par
int PASCAL WinMain(HANDLE hInstance,HANDLE hPrevInstance,
    LPSTR lpszCmdParam,int nCmdShow)
{
        FARPROC dlgProc;
        unsigned short r;
```

```
        BWCCGetVersion();

        if(lstrlen(lpszCmdParam)) messagehook=lpszCmdParam;
        else messagehook=NULL;

        hInst=hInstance;

        dlgProc=MakeProcInstance((FARPROC)SelectProc,hInst);
        r=DialogBox(hInst,"MainScreen",NULL,dlgProc);

        FreeProcInstance(dlgProc);

        return(r);
}

DWORD FAR PASCAL SelectProc(HWND hwnd,WORD message,WORD wParam,LONG lParam)
{
    FILEINFO fi;
    COLORREF rgb;
    PAINTSTRUCT ps;
    static HICON hIcon;
    HWND dlgH;
    HMENU hmenu;
    FARPROC lpfnDlgProc;
    char b[STRINGSIZE+1];
    long l;
    int i;

    switch(message) {
        case WM_CTLCOLOR:
            return(HandleCtlColour(hwnd,wParam,lParam));
        case WM_SYSCOMMAND:
            switch(wParam & 0xfff0) {
                case SC_CLOSE:
                    SendMessage(hwnd,WM_COMMAND,MAIN_EXIT,0L);
                    break;
            }
            break;
        case WM_INITDIALOG:
            hIcon=LoadIcon(hInst,szAppName);
            SetClassWord(hwnd,GCW_HICON,(WORD)hIcon);
            ResetSelectorList(hwnd);

            if((l=SendDlgItemMessage(hwnd,MAIN_LIST,
                LB_GETCURSEL,0,0L)) != LB_ERR) {
                SendDlgItemMessage(hwnd,MAIN_LIST,LB_GETTEXT,
                    (unsigned int)l,(long)b);
                if(b[0]=='[') {
                    ItemName(MAIN_TITLE," ");
                }
                else {
                    ItemName(MAIN_TITLE,b);
                }
```

Figure 4-8   *Continued.*

```
            hmenu=GetMenu(hwnd);
            if(b[0]=='[') {
                ItemOff(MAIN_VIEW);
                ItemOff(MAIN_GETINFO);
                EnableMenuItem(hmenu,MAIN_VIEW,MF_GRAYED);
                EnableMenuItem(hmenu,MAIN_GETINFO,MF_GRAYED);
            }
            else {
                ItemOn(MAIN_VIEW);
                ItemOn(MAIN_GETINFO);
                EnableMenuItem(hmenu,MAIN_VIEW,MF_ENABLED);
                EnableMenuItem(hmenu,MAIN_GETINFO,MF_ENABLED);
            }
        }

        CentreWindow(hwnd);

        LoadConfig(hwnd);

        if(messagehook != NULL) {
            if(SendDlgItemMessage(hwnd,MAIN_LIST,
              LB_SELECTSTRING,-1,(long)messagehook) != LB_ERR)
                PostMessagehwnd,WM_COMMAND,MAIN_VIEW,0L);
            else
                DoMessage(hwnd,"Error viewing file");
        }
        break;
    case WM_PAINT:
        BeginPaint(hwnd,&ps);
        EndPaint(hwnd,&ps);
        break;
    case WM_COMMAND:
        switch(wParam) {
            case MAIN_LIST:
                switch(HIWORD(lParam)) {
                    case LBN_DBLCLK:
                        if(DlgDirSelect(hwnd,b,MAIN_LIST)) {
                            i=lstrlen(b);
                            if(b[i-1]=='\\') {
                                b[i-1]=0;
                                chdir(b);
                            }
                            else {
                                if(!testdisk(b[0]-'A'))
                                    setdisk(toupper(b[0])-'A');
                                else
                                DoMessage(hwnd,"That drive is off line. "
                                        "Please check to see that "
                                        "there's a disk in it.");
```

```
                }
                ResetSelectorList(hwnd);
            }
            else PostMessage(hwnd,WM_COMMAND,MAIN_VIEW,0L);
    }
    if((l=SendDlgItemMessage(hwnd,MAIN_LIST,
        LB_GETCURSEL,0,0L)) != LB_ERR) {
        SendDlgItemMessage(hwnd,MAIN_LIST,
            LB_GETTEXT,(unsigned int)l,(long)b);
        if(b[0]=='[') {
            ItemName(MAIN_TITLE," ");
        }
        else {
            ItemName(MAIN_TITLE,b);
        }

        hmenu=GetMenu(hwnd);
        if(b[0]=='[') {
            ItemOff(MAIN_VIEW);
            ItemOff(MAIN_GETINFO);
            EnableMenuItem(hmenu,MAIN_VIEW,MF_GRAYED);
            EnableMenuItem(hmenu,MAIN_GETINFO,MF_GRAYED);
        }
        else {
            ItemOn(MAIN_VIEW);
            ItemOn(MAIN_GETINFO);
            EnableMenuItem(hmenu,MAIN_VIEW,MF_ENABLED);
            EnableMenuItem(hmenu,MAIN_GETINFO,MF_ENABLED);
        }
    }
    break;
case MAIN_COLOUR:
    rgb=background;
    if(SelectColour(hwnd,&rgb))
        background=rgb;
        break;
case MAIN_GETINFO:
    if((l=SendDlgItemMessage(hwnd,MAIN_LIST,
        LB_GETCURSEL,0,0L)) != LB_ERR) {
        SendDlgItemMessage(hwnd,MAIN_LIST,
            LB_GETTEXT,(unsigned int)l,(DWORD)b);
        if(GetInfo(&fi,b)) {
            ShowInfo(hwnd,&fi);
        } else DoMessage(hwnd,"Error getting information");
    }
    break;
case MAIN_VIEW:
    if((l=SendDlgItemMessage(hwnd,MAIN_LIST,
        LB_GETCURSEL,0,0L)) != LB_ERR) {
        SendDlgItemMessage(hwnd,MAIN_LIST,
            LB_GETTEXT,(unsigned int)l,(DWORD)b);
```

Figure 4-8   *Continued.*

```
                        ViewFile(hwnd,b);
                }
                break;
            case MAIN_ABOUT:
                if((lpfnDlgProc=MakeProcInstance((FARPROC)
                    AboutDlgProc,hInst)) != NULL) {
                    DialogBox(hInst,"AboutBox",hwnd,lpfnDlgProc);
                    FreeProcInstance(lpfnDlgProc);
                }
                break;
            case MAIN_EXIT:
                SaveConfig(hwnd);
                FreeResource(hIcon);
                PostQuitMessage(0);
                break;
        }
        break;

    }

    return(FALSE);
}

void SaveConfig(HWND hwnd)
{
    char b[STRINGSIZE+1];
    long l=0;
    unsigned int i;

    wsprintf(b,"%lu",(long)background);
    WriteProfileString(szAppName,"Background",b);

    for(i=0;i<FX_COUNT;++i) {
        if(IsItemChecked(hwnd,FX_BASE+i)) l |= (1L << i);
    }

    wsprintf(b,"%lu",(long)l);
    WriteProfileString(szAppName,"Functions",b);
}

void LoadConfig(HWND hwnd)
{
    char b[STRINGSIZE+1];
    long l;
    unsigned int i;

    GetProfileString(szAppName,"Background","~Unknown",b,STRINGSIZE);
    if(b[0] != '~') background=atol(b);

    GetProfileString(szAppName,"Functions","~Unknown",b,STRINGSIZE);
    if(b[0] != '~') l=atol(b);
```

```
                for(i=0;i<FX_COUNT;++i) {
                        if(l & (1L<<i)) CheckOn(hwnd,FX_BASE+i);
                }
        }

int BitmapToPicture(LPFILEINFO fi,HANDLE hpicture)
{
        LPBITMAPINFO bmp;
        LPSTR palette;
        char huge *source;
        char huge *dest;
        RGBQUAD rgb;
        unsigned long l,size;
        unsigned int i,j,n;

        if((bmp=(LPBITMAPINFO)LockResource(hpicture)) == NULL) return(FALSE);

        fi->width=(int)bmp->bmiHeader.biWidth;
        fi->depth=(int)bmp->bmiHeader.biHeight;
        fi->bits=bmp->bmiHeader.biBitCount;

        fi->memory=(long)pixels2bytes(fi->width)*(long)fi->bits*(long)fi->depth;

        n=1<<fi->bits;
        j=min(n,256);

        palette=(LPSTR)bmp+(unsigned int)bmp->bmiHeader.biSize;
        source=(LPSTR)bmp;

        size=fi->memory+(unsigned long)(bmp->bmiHeader.biSize+(j*sizeof(RGBQUAD)));

        if(fi->bits <= 8) {
                n=1<<fi->bits;

                for(i=0;i<n;++i) {
                        lmemcpy((LPSTR)&rgb,palette,sizeof(RGBQUAD));
                        palette+=sizeof(RGBQUAD);
                        fi->palette[i*RGB_SIZE+RGB_RED]=rgb.rgbRed;
                        fi->palette[i*RGB_SIZE+RGB_GREEN]=rgb.rgbGreen;
                        fi->palette[i*RGB_SIZE+RGB_BLUE]=rgb.rgbBlue;
                }
        }

        lstrcpy(fi->filename,"PICTURE.BMP");

        if((fi->picture=GlobalAlloc(GMEM_MOVEABLE,size))==NULL) {
                UnlockResource(hpicture);
                return(FALSE);
        }

        if((dest=(char huge *)GlobalLock(fi->picture))==NULL) {
                UnlockResource(hpicture);
                return(FALSE);
        }
```

Figure 4-8   *Continued.*

```
        for(l=0L;l<size;++l) *dest++=*source++;

        GlobalUnlock(fi->picture);

        UnlockResource(hpicture);
        return(TRUE);
}

DWORD FAR PASCAL AboutDlgProc(HWND hwnd,WORD message,WORD wParam,LONG lParam)
{
        FILEINFO fi;
        static HANDLE sound;
        static LPSTR psound;
        HDC hdc;
        PAINTSTRUCT ps;
        RECT rect;
        HANDLE handle,hPal;

        switch(message) {
                case WM_INITDIALOG:
                        if((handle=FindResource(hInst,
                            "AboutWave",RT_RCDATA)) != NULL) {
                                if((sound=LoadResource(hInst,handle)) != NULL) {
                                        if((psound=LockResource(sound)) != NULL)
                                                sndPlaySound(psound,SND_ASYNC |
                                                        SND_MEMORY | SND_NOSTOP);
                                }
                        }
                        CentreWindow(hwnd);
                        return(FALSE);
                case WM_PAINT:
                        hdc=BeginPaint(hwnd,&ps);
                        GetClientRect(hwnd,&rect);
                        timeBeginPeriod(TIMER_INTERVAL);
                        if((handle=LoadResource(hInst,FindResource(hInst,
                            MAKEINTRESOURCE(1801),RT_BITMAP))) != NULL) {
                                if(BitmapToPicture(&fi,handle)) {
                                        if((hPal=RealizePicturePalette(hdc,
                                            &fi)) != NULL) {
                                                SetWindowOrg(hdc,-(((rect.right-
                                                        rect.left)-fi.width)/2),-16);
                                                TileFromPicture(hdc,&fi);
                                                DeleteObject(hPal);
                                        }
                                }
                                FreeResource(handle);
                        }
                        timeEndPeriod(TIMER_INTERVAL);
                        EndPaint(hwnd,&ps);
                        return(FALSE);
                case WM_CTLCOLOR:
```

```
                                    return(HandleCtlColour(hwnd,wParam,lParam));
                    case WM_COMMAND:
                            switch(wParam) {
                                    case IDOK:
                                            sndPlaySound(NULL,SND_SYNC);
                                            if(psound != NULL) UnlockResource(sound);
                                            if(sound != NULL) FreeResource(sound);
                                            EndDialog(hwnd,wParam);
                                            return(FALSE);
                            }
                            break;
            }

        return(FALSE);
}

void ResetSelectorList(HWND hwnd)
{
        HWND dlgH;
        HCURSOR hSaveCursor,hHourGlass;
        char b[STRINGSIZE+1];

        hHourGlass=LoadCursor(NULL,IDC_WAIT);
        hSaveCursor=SetCursor(hHourGlass);

        dlgH=GetDlgItem(hwnd,MAIN_LIST);
        SendDlgItemMessage(hwnd,MAIN_LIST,LB_RESETCONTENT,0,0L);
        SendMessage(dlgH,WM_SETREDRAW,FALSE,0L);

        SendDlgItemMessage(hwnd,MAIN_LIST,LB_DIR,0x0000,(long )"*.BMP");

        SendDlgItemMessage(hwnd,MAIN_LIST,LB_DIR,0xc010,(long )"*.*");

        SendDlgItemMessage(hwnd,MAIN_LIST,LB_SETCURSEL,0,0L);
        SendDlgItemMessage(hwnd,MAIN_LIST,LB_GETTEXT,0,(long)b);

        SendMessage(dlgH,WM_SETREDRAW,TRUE,0L);

        ItemName(MAIN_TITLE,b);

        getcwd(b,STRINGSIZE);
        strlwr(b);
        ItemName(MAIN_PATH,b);

        SetCursor(hSaveCursor);
}

int testdisk(int n)
{
        FILE *fp;
        char b[32];
        int r;
```

143

Figure 4-8 *Continued.*

```
        SetErrorMode(1);
        sprintf(b,"%c:\\TEMP.DAT",n+'A');
        if((fp=fopen(b,"r")) != NULL) fclose(fp);

        if(_doserrno==ENOPATH) r=1;
        else r=0;

        SetErrorMode(0);
        return(r);
}

int GetInfo(LPFILEINFO fi,LPSTR path)
{
        RGBQUAD rgb;
        BITMAPFILEHEADER bmf;
        BITMAPINFOHEADER bmi;
        unsigned long l;
        int n,i,fh;

        lstrcpy(fi->filename,path);

        if((fh=_lopen(path,OF_READ))==-1) return(FALSE);

        if(_lread(fh,(LPSTR)&bmf,sizeof(BITMAPFILEHEADER))==sizeof(BITMAPFILEHEADER)) {
                if(!memcmp((char *)&bmf.bfType,"BM",2)) {
                        _lread(fh,(LPSTR)&l,sizeof(unsigned long));
                        _llseek(fh,-4L,SEEK_CUR);

                        if(l==12L) {
                                _lclose(fh);
                                return(FALSE);

                        }
                        if(_lread(fh,(LPSTR)&bmi,sizeof(BITMAPINFOHEADER)) !=
                           sizeof(BITMAPINFOHEADER)) {
                                _lclose(fh);
                                        return(FALSE);

                        }

                        fi->width=(int)bmi.biWidth;
                        fi->depth=(int)bmi.biHeight;
                        fi->bits=bmi.biBitCount;

                        fi->memory=(long)pixels2bytes(fi->width)*
                            (long)fi->bits*(long)fi->depth;

                        if(fi->bits <= 8) {
                                n=1<<fi->bits;

                                for(i=0;i<n;++i) {
```

```
                                     if(_lread(fh,(LPSTR)&rgb,
                                        sizeof(RGBQUAD)) != sizeof(RGBQUAD)) {
                                             _lclose(fh);
                                             return(FALSE);

                                     }
                                     fi->palette[i*RGB_SIZE+RGB_RED]=rgb.rgbRed;
                                     fi->palette[i*RGB_SIZE+RGB_GREEN]=rgb.rgbGreen;
                                     fi->palette[i*RGB_SIZE+RGB_BLUE]=rgb.rgbBlue;


                           }
                     }
                     _lclose(fh);
                     return(TRUE);
             }
             else {
                     _lclose(fh);
                     return(FALSE);
             }
    }
             else {
                     _lclose(fh);
                     return(FALSE);
             }
}


void ShowInfo(HWND hwnd,LPFILEINFO fi)
{
        FARPROC lpfnDlgProc;

        messagehook=(LPSTR)fi;
        if((lpfnDlgProc=MakeProcInstance((FARPROC)InfoDlgProc,hInst)) != NULL) {
                DialogBox(hInst,"InfoBox",hwnd,lpfnDlgProc);
                FreeProcInstance(lpfnDlgProc);
        }
}

DWORD FAR PASCAL InfoDlgProc(HWND hwnd,WORD message,WORD wParam,LONG lParam)
{
        static LPFILEINFO fi;
        HWND dlgH;
        PAINTSTRUCT ps;
        char b[STRINGSIZE+1];

        switch(message) {
                case WM_INITDIALOG:
                        fi=(LPFILEINFO )messagehook;
                        ItemName(INFO_FILE,fi->filename);

                        switch(fi->bits) {
                                case 1:
                                        ItemName(INFO_COLOURS,"Monochrome");
```

Figure 4-8   *Continued.*

```
                                            break;
                                 case 4:
                                            ItemName(INFO_COLOURS,"16 colours");
                                            break;
                                 case 8:
                                            ItemName(INFO_COLOURS,"256 colours");
                                            break;
                                 case 24:
                                            ItemName(INFO_COLOURS,"16,777,216 colours");
                                            break;
                        }

                        wsprintf(b,"%u x %u",fi->width,fi->depth);
                        ItemName(INFO_DIMENSIONS,(LPSTR)b)

                        wsprintf(b,"%lu bytes",(unsigned long)fi->memory);
                        ItemName(INFO_MEMORY,(LPSTR)b)

                        CentreWindow(hwnd);
                        return(TRUE);
                case WM_CTLCOLOR:
                        return(HandleCtlColour(hwnd,wParam,lParam));
                case WM_PAINT:
                        BeginPaint(hwnd,&ps);
                        EndPaint(hwnd,&ps);
                        break;
                case WM_COMMAND:
                        switch(wParam) {
                                case IDOK:
                                        EndDialog(hwnd,wParam);
                                        return(TRUE);
                        }
                        break;
        }

        return(FALSE);
}

int lmemcpy(LPSTR dest,LPSTR source,int n)
{
        int i;

        for(i=0;i<n;++i) dest[i]=source[i];
        return(n);
}

int SelectColour(HWND hwnd,COLORREF FAR *clr)
{
        CHOOSECOLOR cc;
        COLORREF pclr[16];
        int i,r;
```

```
        for(i=0;i<16;++i) pclr[i]=RGB(i<<4,i<<4,i<<4);

        memset((char *)&cc,0,sizeof(CHOOSECOLOR));

        cc.lStructSize=sizeof(CHOOSECOLOR);
        cc.hwndOwner=hwnd;
        cc.hInstance=hInst;
        cc.rgbResult=*clr;
        cc.lpCustColors=pclr;
        cc.Flags=CC_RGBINIT | CC_PREVENTFULLOPEN;;

        r=ChooseColor(&cc);

        *clr=cc.rgbResult;

        return(r);
}

int ViewFile(HWND hwnd,LPSTR path)
{
        BITMAPFILEHEADER bmf;
        FILEINFO fi;
        HBRUSH hbrush;
        HCURSOR hSaveCursor,hHourGlass;
        HWND childhwnd;
        MSG msg;
        WNDCLASS wndclass;
        char huge *p;
        unsigned long size;
        int fh;

        hHourGlass=LoadCursor(NULL,IDC_WAIT);
        hSaveCursor=SetCursor(hHourGlass);

        if(!GetInfo(&fi,path)) {
                SetCursor(hSaveCursor);
                DoMessage(hwnd,"Error getting information");
                return(0);
        }

        if(fi.bits > 8) {
                SetCursor(hSaveCursor);
                DoMessage(hwnd,"Too many colours");
                return(0);
        }

        if((fh=_lopen(path,OF_READ))==-1) {
                SetCursor(hSaveCursor);
                return(0);
        }

        if(_lread(fh,(char *)&bmf,sizeof(BITMAPFILEHEADER))!=
            sizeof(BITMAPFILEHEADER)) {
```

Figure 4-8   *Continued.*

```
                    SetCursor(hSaveCursor);
                    _lclose(fh);
                    DoMessage(hwnd,"Error reading file header");
                    return(0);
            }

            size=bmf.bfSize-(long)sizeof(BITMAPFILEHEADER);

            if((fi.picture=GlobalAlloc(GMEM_MOVEABLE,size))==NULL) {
                    SetCursor(hSaveCursor);
                    _lclose(fh);
                    DoMessage(hwnd,"Error allocating memory");
                    return(0);
            }

            if((p=(char huge *)GlobalLock(fi.picture))==NULL) {
                    GlobalFree(fi.picture);
                    SetCursor(hSaveCursor);
                    _lclose(fh);
                    DoMessage(hwnd,"Error locking memory");
                    return(0);
            }

            if(_hread(fh,p,size) != size) {
                    GlobalUnlock(fi.picture);
                    GlobalFree(fi.picture);
                    SetCursor(hSaveCursor);
                    _lclose(fh);
                    DoMessage(hwnd,"Error reading the file");
                    return(0);
            }

            _lclose(fh);

            GlobalUnlock(fi.picture);

            SetCursor(hSaveCursor);

            hbrush=CreateSolidBrush(background);

            messagehook=(LPSTR)&fi;
            wndclass.style=CS_HREDRAW | CS_VREDRAW;
            wndclass.lpfnWndProc=PictureProc;
            wndclass.cbClsExtra=0;
            wndclass.cbWndExtra=0;
            wndclass.hInstance=hInst;
            wndclass.hIcon=LoadIcon(NULL,IDI_APPLICATION);
            wndclass.hCursor=LoadCursor(NULL,IDC_ARROW);
            wndclass.hbrBackground=hbrush;
            wndclass.lpszMenuName=NULL;
            wndclass.lpszClassName=szAppName;
```

```
                RegisterClass(&wndclass);

                childhwnd = CreateWindow(szAppName,path,
                    WS_POPUP | WS_CAPTION | WS_SYSMENU ,
                    CW_USEDEFAULT,CW_USEDEFAULT,CW_USEDEFAULT,CW_USEDEFAULT,
                    hwnd,NULL,hInst,NULL);

                ShowWindow(childhwnd,SW_SHOWMAXIMIZED);
                UpdateWindow(childhwnd);

                while(GetMessage(&msg,NULL,0,0)) {
                        TranslateMessage(&msg);
                        DispatchMessage(&msg);
                }

                UnregisterClass(szAppName,hInst);

                DeleteObject(hbrush);

                GlobalFree(fi.picture);
                return(TRUE);
        }

HANDLE RealizePicturePalette(HDC hdc,LPFILEINFO fi)
{
        LPBITMAPINFO bmp;
        LOGPALETTE *pLogPal;
        HANDLE hPal=NULL;
        LPINT ip;
        int i,j,n;

        if((bmp=(LPBITMAPINFO)GlobalLock(fi->picture)) == NULL) return(NULL);

        n=1<<fi->bits;
        j=min(n,256);

        if((pLogPal=(LOGPALETTE *)malloc(sizeof(LOGPALETTE)+
            (j*sizeof(PALETTEENTRY)))) == NULL) {
                GlobalUnlock(fi->picture);
                return(NULL);
        }

        pLogPal->palVersion=0x0300;
        pLogPal->palNumEntries=j;

        for(i=0;i<j;i++) {
                pLogPal->palPalEntry[i].peRed=fi->palette[i*RGB_SIZE+RGB_RED];
                pLogPal->palPalEntry[i].peGreen=fi->palette[i*RGB_SIZE+RGB_GREEN];
                pLogPal->palPalEntry[i].peBlue=fi->palette[i*RGB_SIZE+RGB_BLUE];
                pLogPal->palPalEntry[i].peFlags=0;
        }

        hPal=CreatePalette(pLogPal);
```

149

Figure 4-8 *Continued.*

```
            SelectPalette(hdc,hPal,0);
            RealizePalette(hdc);

            ip=(LPINT)&bmp->bmiColors[0];
            for(i=0;i<j;++i) *ip++=i;

            free(pLogPal);

            GlobalUnlock(fi->picture);

            return(hPal);
}

#defineSetTitle(title)      { char bxx[STRINGSIZE+1]; \
                            wsprintf(bxx,"[ %s - %s ]",(LPSTR)fi->filename,\
                                (LPSTR)title);\
                            SetWindowText(hwnd,bxx);\
                            }

long FAR PASCAL PictureProc(HWND hwnd,unsigned int message,
    unsigned int wParam,LONG lParam)
{
            static LPFILEINFO fi;
            HANDLE hPal=NULL;
            HDC hdc;
            HWND dlgH;
            PAINTSTRUCT ps;
            RECT rect;
            int i,j;

            switch (message) {
                    case WM_CREATE:
                            fi=(LPFILEINFO)messagehook;
                            return(FALSE);
                    case WM_PAINT:
                            GetWindowRect(hwnd,&rect);
                            hdc=BeginPaint(hwnd,&ps);
                            timeBeginPeriod(TIMER_INTERVAL);

                            i=j=0;

                            if((rect.right-rect.left) > fi->width)
                                j=(rect.right-rect.left-fi->width)/2;
                            if((rect.bottom-rect.top) > fi->depth)
                                i=(rect.bottom-rect.top-fi->depth)/2;

                            SetWindowOrg(hdc,-j,-i);

                            if((hPal=RealizePicturePalette(hdc,fi))==NULL) {
                                    EndPaint(hwnd,&ps);
                                    return(FALSE);
                            }
```

```
dlgH=GetParent(hwnd);

if(IsItemChecked(dlgH,FX_NORMAL)) {
        SetTitle("Normal display");
        DisplayPicture(hdc,fi);
        WaitAfterDisplay();
}

if(IsItemChecked(dlgH,FX_TILE)) {
        SetTitle("Tile");
        TileFromPicture(hdc,fi);
        WaitAfterDisplay();
        TileToColour(hdc,fi,background);
}

if(IsItemChecked(dlgH,FX_ROLLUP)) {
        SetTitle("Roll up");
        VerticalRollUpPicture(hdc,fi);
        WaitAfterDisplay();
        VerticalRollDownPictureAway(hdc,fi,background);
}

if(IsItemChecked(dlgH,FX_ROLLDOWN)) {
        SetTitle("Roll down");
        VerticalRollDownPicture(hdc,fi);
        WaitAfterDisplay();
        VerticalRollUpPictureAway(hdc,fi,background);
}

if(IsItemChecked(dlgH,FX_WIPELEFT)) {
        SetTitle("Wipe left");
        WipeInPictureFromLeft(hdc,fi);
        WaitAfterDisplay();
        WipeOutPictureFromRight(hdc,fi,background);
}

if(IsItemChecked(dlgH,FX_WIPERIGHT)) {
        SetTitle("Wipe right");
        WipeInPictureFromRight(hdc,fi);
        WaitAfterDisplay();
        WipeOutPictureFromLeft(hdc,fi,background);
}

if(IsItemChecked(dlgH,FX_HSPLIT)) {
        SetTitle("Horizontal Split");
        HorizontalSplitPictureIn(hdc,fi);
        WaitAfterDisplay();
        HorizontalSplitPictureOut(hdc,fi,background);
}

if(IsItemChecked(dlgH,FX_VSPLIT)) {
        SetTitle("Vertical Split");
```

Figure 4-8 *Continued.*

```
                                VerticalSplitPictureIn(hdc,fi);
                                WaitAfterDisplay();
                                VerticalSplitPictureOut(hdc,fi,background);
                        }

                        if(IsItemChecked(dlgH,FX_RASTER)) {
                                SetTitle("Raster");
                                RasterPictureIn(hdc,fi);
                                WaitAfterDisplay();
                                RasterPictureOut(hdc,fi,background);
                        }

                        if(IsItemChecked(dlgH,FX_VCENTRE)) {
                                SetTitle("Vertical Centre");
                                VerticalCentrePictureIn(hdc,fi);
                                WaitAfterDisplay();
                                VerticalCentrePictureOut(hdc,fi,background);
                        }

                        if(IsItemChecked(dlgH,FX_PLUMMET)) {
                                SetTitle("Plummet");
                                PlummetPictureIn(hdc,fi);
                                WaitAfterDisplay();
                                PlummetPictureOut(hdc,fi,background);
                        }

                        DeleteObject(hPal);

                        timeEndPeriod(TIMER_INTERVAL);

                        EndPaint(hwnd,&ps);
                        PostMessage(hwnd,WM_SYSCOMMAND,SC_CLOSE,0L);
                        return(FALSE);
                case WM_DESTROY:
                        PostQuitMessage(0);
                        break;
                case WM_SYSCOMMAND:
                        switch(wParam & 0xfff0) {
                                case SC_CLOSE:
                                        SendMessage(hwnd,WM_DESTROY,0,0L);
                                        break;
                        }
                        break;

        }

        return(DefWindowProc(hwnd,message,wParam,lParam));
}

DWORD HandleCtlColour(HWND hwnd,WORD wParam,DWORD lParam)
{
```

```
                POINT point;
                HBRUSH hBrush;

                if(HIWORD(lParam)==CTLCOLOR_STATIC ||
                   HIWORD(lParam)==CTLCOLOR_DLG) {
                        hBrush=GetStockObject(LTGRAY_BRUSH);
                        SetBkColor(wParam,RGB(192,192,192));
                        SetTextColor(wParam,RGB(0,0,0));

                        ClientToScreen(hwnd,&point);
                        UnrealizeObject(hBrush);
                        SetBrushOrg(wParam,point.x,point.y);

                        return((DWORD)hBrush);

                }
                if(HIWORD(lParam)==CTLCOLOR_BTN) {
                        hBrush=GetStockObject(LTGRAY_BRUSH);
                        SetBkColor(wParam,RGB(192,192,192));
                        SetTextColor(wParam,RGB(0,0,0));

                        ClientToScreen(hwnd,&point);
                        UnrealizeObject(hBrush);
                        SetBrushOrg(wParam,point.x,point.y);

                        return((DWORD)hBrush);
                }
                return(FALSE);
        }

void CentreWindow(HWND hwnd)
{
        RECT rect;
        unsigned int x,y;

        GetWindowRect(hwnd,&rect);
        x=(GetSystemMetrics(SM_CXSCREEN)-(rect.right-rect.left))/2;
        y=(GetSystemMetrics(SM_CYSCREEN)-(rect.bottom-rect.top))/2;
        SetWindowPos(hwnd,NULL,x,y,rect.right-rect.left,
            rect.bottom-rect.top,SWP_NOSIZE);
}

int PlummetPictureOut(HDC hdc,LPFILEINFO fi,COLORREF rgb)
{
        HBRUSH hbrush,oldbrush;
        HPEN oldpen;
        LPPOINT point;
        unsigned long l,t;
        unsigned int tiles,i,n,x,y;

        hbrush=CreateSolidBrush(rgb);
        oldbrush=SelectObject(hdc,hbrush);
        oldpen=SelectObject(hdc,GetStockObject(NULL_PEN));
```

Figure 4-8   *Continued.*

```
tiles=(fi->width/BRICKSIZE);

if((point=(LPPOINT)FixedGlobalAlloc((long)tiles*(long)sizeof(POINT)))== NULL)
      return(FALSE);

for(i=0;i<tiles;++i) {
        point[i].x=i*BRICKSIZE;
        point[i].y=0;

}

randomize();

for(;tiles > 0;—tiles) {
        n=random(tiles);
        x=point[n].x;
        y=point[n].y;

        for(i=0;i<fi->depth;i+=BRICKDROP) {
                l=ticks();

                BitBlt(hdc,

                        x,                              //x dest
                        i+BRICKDROP,                    //y dest

                        BRICKSIZE,                      //width
                        fi->depth-i-BRICKDROP,          //depth

                        hdc,

                        x,                              //x source
                        i,                              //y source
                        SRCCOPY);

                Rectangle(hdc,x,i,x+BRICKSIZE+1,i+BRICKDROP+1);

                WaitForTick(SHORTWAIT);
        }
        x=point[tiles-1].x;
        y=point[tiles-1].y;

        point[n].x=x;
        point[n].y=y;
}

FixedGlobalFree(point);

SelectObject(hdc,oldbrush);
SelectObject(hdc,oldpen);
```

```
            DeleteObject(hbrush);
            return(TRUE);
}


int PlummetPictureIn(HDC hdc,LPFILEINFO fi)
{
            LPSTR image;
            LPBITMAPINFO bmp;
            LPPOINT point;
            unsigned long l,t;
            unsigned int tiles,i,j,n;
            unsigned int x=0,y=0;

            tiles=(fi->width/BRICKSIZE);

            if((point=(LPPOINT)FixedGlobalAlloc((long)tiles*(long)sizeof(POINT)))== NULL)
                return(FALSE);

            for(i=0;i<tiles;++i) {
                    point[i].x=i*BRICKSIZE;
                    point[i].y=0;

            }

            randomize();

            if((bmp=(LPBITMAPINFO)GlobalLock(fi->picture))== NULL) {
                    FixedGlobalFree(point);
                    return(FALSE);
            }

            n=1<<fi->bits;
            j=min(n,256);

            image=(LPSTR)bmp+(unsigned int)bmp->bmiHeader.biSize+(j*sizeof(RGBQUAD));

            for(;tiles > 0;–tiles) {
                    n=random(tiles);
                    x=point[n].x;
                    y=point[n].y;

                    for(i=0;i<fi->depth;i+=BRICKDROP) {
                            l=ticks();
                            BitBlt(hdc,

                                    x,                      //x dest
                                    BRICKDROP,              //y dest

                                    BRICKSIZE,              //width
                                    i,                      //depth

                                    hdc,
```

Figure 4-8   *Continued.*

```
                                x,                      //x source
                                0,                      //y source
                                SRCCOPY);


                    SetDIBitsToDevice(hdc,
                                x,                      //x dest
                                0,                      //y dest

                                BRICKSIZE,              //x extent
                                BRICKDROP,              //y extent

                                x,                      //x source
                                i,                      //y source

                                0,                      //first scan line
                                fi->depth,              //number of scan lines
                                image,
                                bmp,
                                DIB_PAL_COLORS);

                    WaitForTick(SHORTWAIT);
            }
            x=point[tiles-1].x;
            y=point[tiles-1].y;

            point[n].x=x;
            point[n].y=y;
        }

        GlobalUnlock(fi->picture);

        FixedGlobalFree(point);

        CheckFrame(hdc,fi);

        return(TRUE);
}

int VerticalCentrePictureOut(HDC hdc,LPFILEINFO fi,COLORREF rgb)
{
        HBRUSH hbrush,oldbrush;
        HPEN oldpen;
        unsigned long l,t;
        unsigned int i,n;

        hbrush=CreateSolidBrush(rgb);
        oldbrush=SelectObject(hdc,hbrush);
        oldpen=SelectObject(hdc,GetStockObject(NULL_PEN));

        n=fi->depth/2;
```

```
        for(i=0;i<=n;i+=ROLLSTEP) {
                l=ticks();

                BitBlt(hdc,
                        0,                      //x dest
                        i+ROLLSTEP,             //y dest

                        fi->width,              //width
                        n-i,                    //depth

                        hdc,

                        0,                      //x source
                        i,                      //y source
                        SRCCOPY);

                Rectangle(hdc,0,i,fi->width+1,i+ROLLSTEP+1);

                if(i >= (n-1)) break;

                BitBlt(hdc,
                        0,                      //x dest
                        n,                      //y dest

                        fi->width,              //width
                        n-i,                    //depth

                        hdc,

                        0,                      //x source
                        n+ROLLSTEP,             //y source
                        SRCCOPY);

                Rectangle(hdc,0,fi->depth-i-ROLLSTEP,fi->width+1,fi->depth-i+1);

                WaitForTick(MEDIUMWAIT);
        }

        SelectObject(hdc,oldbrush);
        SelectObject(hdc,oldpen);
        DeleteObject(hbrush);
        return(TRUE);
}

int VerticalCentrePictureIn(HDC hdc,LPFILEINFO fi)
{
        LPSTR image;
        LPBITMAPINFO bmp;
        unsigned long l,t;
        unsigned int i,j,n;

        if((bmp=(LPBITMAPINFO)GlobalLock(fi->picture))== NULL) return(FALSE);
```

Figure 4-8 *Continued.*

```
n=1<<fi->bits;
j=min(n,256);

image=(LPSTR)bmp+(unsigned int)bmp->bmiHeader.biSize+(j*sizeof(RGBQUAD));

n=fi->depth/2;
for(i=0;i<=n;i+=ROLLSTEP) {
        l=ticks();

        BitBlt(hdc,

                0,                      //x dest
                n-i-ROLLSTEP,           //y dest

                fi->width,              //width
                i,                      //depth

                hdc,

                0,                      //x source
                n-i,                    //y source
                SRCCOPY);


        SetDIBitsToDevice(hdc,
                        0,              //x dest
                        n-ROLLSTEP,     //y dest

                        fi->width,      //x extent
                        ROLLSTEP,       //y extent

                        0,              //x source
                        fi->depth-i,    //y source

                        0,              //first scan line
                        fi->depth,      //number of scan lines
                        image,
                        bmp,
                        DIB_PAL_COLORS);

        if(i >= (n-1)) break;

        BitBlt(hdc,

                0,                      //x dest
                n+ROLLSTEP,             //y dest

                fi->width,              //width
                i,                      //depth

                hdc,
```

```
                                 0,                     //x source
                                 n,                     //y source
                                 SRCCOPY);

                SetDIBitsToDevice(hdc,
                                 0,                     //x dest
                                 n,                     //y dest

                                 fi->width,             //x extent
                                 ROLLSTEP,              //y extent

                                 0,                     //x source
                                 i,                     //y source

                                 0,                     //first scan line
                                 fi->depth,             //number of scan lines
                                 image,
                                 bmp,
                                 DIB_PAL_COLORS);

                WaitForTick(MEDIUMWAIT);
        }

        CheckFrame(hdc,fi);

        GlobalUnlock(fi->picture);
        return(TRUE);
}

int RasterPictureOut(HDC hdc,LPFILEINFO fi,COLORREF rgb)
{
        HBRUSH hbrush,oldbrush;
        HPEN oldpen;
        unsigned long l,t;
        unsigned int i,j;

        hbrush=CreateSolidBrush(rgb);
        oldbrush=SelectObject(hdc,hbrush);
        oldpen=SelectObject(hdc,GetStockObject(NULL_PEN));

        for(i=0;i<fi->width;i+=RASTERBANDSTEP) {
                l=ticks();
                for(j=0;j<fi->depth;) {

                        BitBlt(hdc,
                                0,                      //x dest
                                j,                      //y dest

                                fi->width-i,            //width
                                RASTERBANDSIZE,         //depth

                                hdc,
```

Figure 4-8   *Continued.*

```
                                 RASTERBANDSTEP,     //x source
                                 j,                  //y source
                                 SRCCOPY);

                        Rectangle(hdc,fi->width-i,j,fi->width-i+RASTERBANDSTEP+1,
                            j+RASTERBANDSIZE+1);
                        j+=RASTERBANDSIZE;

                        BitBlt(hdc,
                                 i+RASTERBANDSTEP,   //x dest
                                 j,                  //y dest

                                 fi->width-i,        //width
                                 RASTERBANDSIZE,     //depth

                                 hdc,

                                 i,                  //x source
                                 j,                  //y source
                                 SRCCOPY);

                        Rectangle(hdc,i-RASTERBANDSTEP,j,i+(RASTERBANDSTEP*2),
                            j+RASTERBANDSIZE+1);

                        j+=RASTERBANDSIZE;

                }

                WaitForTick(MEDIUMWAIT);
        }

        for(j=0;j<fi->depth;) {
                Rectangle(hdc,0,j,RASTERBANDSTEP*2,j+RASTERBANDSIZE+1);
                j+=RASTERBANDSIZE;
                Rectangle(hdc,fi->width-RASTERBANDSTEP,j,fi->width+RASTERBANDSTEP*2,
                    j+RASTERBANDSIZE+1);
                j+=RASTERBANDSIZE;
        }

        SelectObject(hdc,oldbrush);
        SelectObject(hdc,oldpen);
        DeleteObject(hbrush);
        return(TRUE);
}

int RasterPictureIn(HDC hdc,LPFILEINFO fi)
{
        LPSTR image;
        LPBITMAPINFO bmp;
        unsigned long l,t;
        unsigned int i,j,n;
```

```
if((bmp=(LPBITMAPINFO)GlobalLock(fi->picture))== NULL) return(FALSE);

n=1<<fi->bits;
j=min(n,256);

image=(LPSTR)bmp+(unsigned int)bmp->bmiHeader.biSize+(j*sizeof(RGBQUAD));

for(i=0;i<fi->width;i+=RASTERBANDSTEP) {
        l=ticks();

        for(j=0;j<fi->depth;) {
                BitBlt(hdc,

                        fi->width-i-RASTERBANDSTEP,        //x dest
                        fi->depth-j-RASTERBANDSIZE,        //y dest

                        i,                                 //width
                        RASTERBANDSIZE,                    //depth

                        hdc,

                        fi->width-i,                       //x source
                        fi->depth-j-RASTERBANDSIZE,        //y source
                        SRCCOPY);

                SetDIBitsToDevice(hdc,
                        fi->width-RASTERBANDSTEP,     //x dest
                        fi->depth-j-RASTERBANDSIZE,   //y dest

                        RASTERBANDSTEP,               //x extent
                        RASTERBANDSIZE,               //y extent

                        i,                            //x source
                        j,                            //y source

                        0,                 //first scan line
                        fi->depth,         //number of scan lines
                        image,
                        bmp,
                        DIB_PAL_COLORS);

                j+=RASTERBANDSIZE;

                BitBlt(hdc,

                        RASTERBANDSTEP,                    //x dest
                        fi->depth-j-RASTERBANDSIZE,        //y dest

                        i,                                 //width
                        RASTERBANDSIZE,                    //depth

                        hdc,
```

161

Figure 4-8   *Continued.*

```
                              0,                              //x source
                              fi->depth-j-RASTERBANDSIZE,      //y source
                              SRCCOPY);
                    SetDIBitsToDevice(hdc,
                              0,                              //x dest
                              fi->depth-j-RASTERBANDSIZE,   //y dest

                              RASTERBANDSTEP,                 //x extent
                              RASTERBANDSIZE,                 //y extent

                              fi->width-i-RASTERBANDSTEP,   //x source
                              j,                              //y source

                              0,                      //first scan line
                              fi->depth,          //number of scan lines
                              image,
                              bmp,
                              DIB_PAL_COLORS);

                    j+=RASTERBANDSIZE;
                }

                WaitForTick(MEDIUMWAIT);

        }

        CheckFrame(hdc,fi);

        GlobalUnlock(fi->picture);
        return(TRUE);
}

int VerticalSplitPictureOut(HDC hdc,LPFILEINFO fi,COLORREF rgb)
{
        HBRUSH hbrush,oldbrush;
        HPEN oldpen;
        unsigned long l,t;
        unsigned int i;

        hbrush=CreateSolidBrush(rgb);
        oldbrush=SelectObject(hdc,hbrush);
        oldpen=SelectObject(hdc,GetStockObject(NULL_PEN));

        for(i=0;i<fi->depth;i+=ROLLSTEP) {
                l=ticks();
                BitBlt(hdc,
                        0,                      //x dest
                        i+ROLLSTEP,             //y dest

                        fi->width/2,            //width
                        fi->depth-i,            //depth
```

```
                                hdc,

                                0,                      //x source
                                i,                      //y source
                                SRCCOPY);

                    Rectangle(hdc,0,i-ROLLSTEP,fi->width/2+1,i+(ROLLSTEP*2)+1);

                    BitBlt(hdc,
                            fi->width/2,                //x dest
                            0,                          //y dest

                            fi->width/2,                //width
                            fi->depth-i,                //depth

                            hdc,

                            fi->width/2,                //x source
                            ROLLSTEP,                   //y source
                            SRCCOPY);

                    Rectangle(hdc,fi->width/2,fi->depth-i-ROLLSTEP,fi->width+1,
                        fi->depth-i+(ROLLSTEP*2));

                    WaitForTick(MEDIUMWAIT);
            }

        SelectObject(hdc,oldbrush);
        SelectObject(hdc,oldpen);
        DeleteObject(hbrush);
        return(TRUE);
}

int VerticalSplitPictureIn(HDC hdc,LPFILEINFO fi)
{
        LPSTR image;
        LPBITMAPINFO bmp;
        unsigned long l,t;
        unsigned int i,j,n;

        if((bmp=(LPBITMAPINFO)GlobalLock(fi->picture))== NULL) return(FALSE);

        n=1<<fi->bits;
        j=min(n,256);

        image=(LPSTR)bmp+(unsigned int)bmp->bmiHeader.biSize+(j*sizeof(RGBQUAD));

        for(i=0;i<fi->depth;i+=ROLLSTEP) {
                l=ticks();
                SetDIBitsToDevice(hdc,
                                    0,                      //x dest
                                    fi->depth-ROLLSTEP,     //y dest
```

Figure 4-8   *Continued.*

```
                              fi->width/2,              //x extent
                              ROLLSTEP,                 //y extent

                              0,                        //x source
                              fi->depth-i,              //y source

                              0,                        //first scan line
                              fi->depth,                //number of scan lines
                              image,
                              bmp,
                              DIB_PAL_COLORS);

        BitBlt(hdc,

                0,                        //x dest
                fi->depth-i-ROLLSTEP,     //y dest

                fi->width/2,              //width
                i,                        //depth

                hdc,

                0,                        //x source
                fi->depth-i,              //y source
                SRCCOPY);

        SetDIBitsToDevice(hdc,
                              fi->width/2,              //x dest
                              0,                        //y dest

                              fi->width/2,              //x extent
                              ROLLSTEP,                 //y extent

                              fi->width/2,              //x source
                              i-ROLLSTEP,               //y source

                              0,                        //first scan line
                              fi->depth,                //number of scan lines
                              image,
                              bmp,
                              DIB_PAL_COLORS);

        BitBlt(hdc,

                fi->width/2,              //x dest
                ROLLSTEP,                 //y dest

                fi->width,                //width
                i,                        //depth

                hdc,
```

```
                            fi->width/2,           //x source
                            0,                     //y source
                            SRCCOPY);

                    WaitForTick(MEDIUMWAIT);

            }

        SetDIBitsToDevice(hdc,
                            0,                          //x dest
                            fi->depth-ROLLSTEP,         //y dest

                            fi->width/2,                //x extent
                            ROLLSTEP,                   //y extent

                            0,                          //x source
                            0,                          //y source

                            0,                          //first scan line
                            fi->depth,                  //number of scan lines
                            image,
                            bmp,
                            DIB_PAL_COLORS);

        SetDIBitsToDevice(hdc,
                            fi->width/2,           //x dest
                            0,                     //y dest

                            fi->width/2,           //x extent
                            ROLLSTEP,              //y extent

                            fi->width/2,           //x source
                            fi->depth-ROLLSTEP,    //y source

                            0,                     //first scan line
                            fi->depth,             //number of scan lines

                            image,
                            bmp,
                            DIB_PAL_COLORS);

        CheckFrame(hdc,fi);

        GlobalUnlock(fi->picture);
        return(TRUE);
}

int HorizontalSplitPictureOut(HDC hdc,LPFILEINFO fi,COLORREF rgb)
{
        HBRUSH hbrush,oldbrush;
        HPEN oldpen;
        unsigned long l,t;
        unsigned int i;
```

Figure 4-8 *Continued.*

```
                hbrush=CreateSolidBrush(rgb);
                oldbrush=SelectObject(hdc,hbrush);
                oldpen=SelectObject(hdc,GetStockObject(NULL_PEN));

                for(i=0;i<fi->width;i+=ROLLSTEP) {
                        l=ticks();
                        BitBlt(hdc,
                                0,                      //x dest
                                0,                      //y dest

                                fi->width-i,            //width
                                fi->depth/2,            //depth

                                hdc,

                                ROLLSTEP,               //x source
                                0,                      //y source
                                SRCCOPY);

                        Rectangle(hdc,fi->width-i,0,fi->width-i+(ROLLSTEP*2),fi->depth/2+1);

                        BitBlt(hdc,
                                i+ROLLSTEP,             //x dest
                                fi->depth/2,            //y dest

                                fi->width-i,            //width
                                fi->depth/2,            //depth

                                hdc,

                                i,                      //x source
                                fi->depth/2,            //y source
                                SRCCOPY);

                        Rectangle(hdc,i-ROLLSTEP,fi->depth/2,i+(ROLLSTEP*2),fi->depth+1);

                        WaitForTick(MEDIUMWAIT);
                }

                Rectangle(hdc,0,0,ROLLSTEP*2,fi->depth/2+1);
                Rectangle(hdc,fi->width,fi->depth/2,fi->width+ROLLSTEP+1,fi->depth+1);

                SelectObject(hdc,oldbrush);
                SelectObject(hdc,oldpen);
                DeleteObject(hbrush);
                return(TRUE);
        }

        int HorizontalSplitPictureIn(HDC hdc,LPFILEINFO fi)
        {
                LPSTR image;
```

```
LPBITMAPINFO bmp;
unsigned long l,t;
unsigned int i,j,n;

if((bmp=(LPBITMAPINFO)GlobalLock(fi->picture))== NULL) return(FALSE);

n=1<<fi->bits;
j=min(n,256);

image=(LPSTR)bmp+(unsigned int)bmp->bmiHeader.biSize+(j*sizeof(RGBQUAD));

for(i=0;i<fi->width;i+=ROLLSTEP) {
        l=ticks();

        BitBlt(hdc,

                fi->width-i-ROLLSTEP,               //x dest
                0,                                  //y dest

                i,                                  //width
                fi->depth/2,                        //depth

                hdc,

                fi->width-i,                        //x source
                0,                                  //y source
                SRCCOPY);

        SetDIBitsToDevice(hdc,
                        fi->width-ROLLSTEP,   //x dest
                        0,                    //y dest

                        ROLLSTEP,             //x extent
                        fi->depth/2,          //y extent

                        i,                    //x source
                        fi->depth/2,          //y source

                        0,                    //first scan line
                        fi->depth,            //number of scan lines
                        image,
                        bmp,
                        DIB_PAL_COLORS);

        BitBlt(hdc,

                ROLLSTEP,             //x dest
                fi->depth/2,          //y dest

                i,                    //width
                fi->depth/2,          //depth

                hdc,
```

Figure 4-8   *Continued.*

```
                                0,                      //x source
                                fi->depth/2,            //y source
                                SRCCOPY);

                SetDIBitsToDevice(hdc,
                                0,                      //x dest
                                fi->depth/2,            //y dest

                                ROLLSTEP,               //x extent
                                fi->depth/2,            //y extent

                                fi->width-i-ROLLSTEP,   //x source
                                0,                      //y source

                                0,                      //first scan line
                                fi->depth,              //number of scan lines
                                image,
                                bmp,
                                DIB_PAL_COLORS);


                WaitForTick(MEDIUMWAIT);

        }

        CheckFrame(hdc,fi);

        GlobalUnlock(fi->picture);
        return(TRUE);
}

int WipeOutPictureFromRight(HDC hdc,LPFILEINFO fi,COLORREF rgb)
{
        HBRUSH hbrush,oldbrush;
        HPEN oldpen;
        unsigned long l,t;
        unsigned int i;

        hbrush=CreateSolidBrush(rgb);
        oldbrush=SelectObject(hdc,hbrush);
        oldpen=SelectObject(hdc,GetStockObject(NULL_PEN));

        for(i=0;i<fi->width;i+=ROLLSTEP) {
                l=ticks();
                BitBlt(hdc,
                        0,              //x dest
                        0,              //y dest

                        fi->width-i,    //width
                        fi->depth,      //depth
                        hdc,
```

```
                        ROLLSTEP,            //x source
                        0,                   //y source
                        SRCCOPY);

                Rectangle(hdc,fi->width-i,0,fi->width-i+(ROLLSTEP*2),fi->depth+1);
                WaitForTick(MEDIUMWAIT);
        }

        Rectangle(hdc,0,0,(ROLLSTEP*2),fi->depth+1);

        SelectObject(hdc,oldbrush);
        SelectObject(hdc,oldpen);
        DeleteObject(hbrush);
        return(TRUE);
}

int WipeOutPictureFromLeft(HDC hdc,LPFILEINFO fi,COLORREF rgb)
{
        HBRUSH hbrush,oldbrush;
        HPEN oldpen;
        unsigned long l,t;
        unsigned int i;

        hbrush=CreateSolidBrush(rgb);
        oldbrush=SelectObject(hdc,hbrush);
        oldpen=SelectObject(hdc,GetStockObject(NULL_PEN));

        for(i=0;i<fi->width;i+=ROLLSTEP) {
                l=ticks();
                BitBlt(hdc,
                        i+ROLLSTEP,          //x dest
                        0,                   //y dest

                        fi->width-i,         //width
                        fi->depth,           //depth

                        hdc,

                        i,                   //x source
                        0,                   //y source
                        SRCCOPY);

                Rectangle(hdc,i-ROLLSTEP,0,i+ROLLSTEP+1,fi->depth+1);
                WaitForTick(MEDIUMWAIT);
        }

        Rectangle(hdc,fi->width,0,fi->width+ROLLSTEP+1,fi->depth+1);

        SelectObject(hdc,oldbrush);
        SelectObject(hdc,oldpen);
        DeleteObject(hbrush);
        return(TRUE);
}
```

Figure 4-8 *Continued.*

```
int WipeInPictureFromRight(HDC hdc,LPFILEINFO fi)
{
        LPSTR image;
        LPBITMAPINFO bmp;
        unsigned long l,t;
        unsigned int i,j,n;

        if((bmp=(LPBITMAPINFO)GlobalLock(fi->picture))== NULL) return(FALSE);

        n=1<<fi->bits;
        j=min(n,256);

        image=(LPSTR)bmp+(unsigned int)bmp->bmiHeader.biSize+(j*sizeof(RGBQUAD));

        for(i=0;i<fi->width;i+=ROLLSTEP) {
                l=ticks();

                BitBlt(hdc,

                        fi->width-i-ROLLSTEP,          //x dest
                        0,                             //y dest

                        i,                             //width
                        fi->depth,                     //depth

                        hdc,

                        fi->width-i,                   //x source
                        0,                             //y source
                        SRCCOPY);

                SetDIBitsToDevice(hdc,
                                fi->width-ROLLSTEP,   //x dest
                                0,                    //y dest

                                ROLLSTEP,             //x extent
                                fi->depth,            //y extent

                                i,                    //x source
                                0,                    //y source

                                0,                    //first scan line
                                fi->depth,            //number of scan lines
                                image,
                                bmp,
                                DIB_PAL_COLORS);

                WaitForTick(MEDIUMWAIT);

        }
```

```
                CheckFrame(hdc,fi);

                GlobalUnlock(fi->picture);
                return(TRUE);
        }

        int WipeInPictureFromLeft(HDC hdc,LPFILEINFO fi)
        {
                LPSTR image;
                LPBITMAPINFO bmp;
                unsigned long l,t;
                unsigned int i,j,n;

                if((bmp=(LPBITMAPINFO)GlobalLock(fi->picture))== NULL) return(FALSE);

                n=1<<fi->bits;
                j=min(n,256);

                image=(LPSTR)bmp+(unsigned int)bmp->bmiHeader.biSize+(j*sizeof(RGBQUAD));

                for(i=0;i<fi->width;i+=ROLLSTEP) {
                        l=ticks();

                        BitBlt(hdc,

                                ROLLSTEP,           //x dest
                                0,                  //y dest

                                i,                  //width
                                fi->depth,          //depth

                                hdc,

                                0,                  //x source
                                0,                  //y source
                                SRCCOPY);

                        SetDIBitsToDevice(hdc,
                                        0,                          //x dest
                                        0,                          //y dest

                                        ROLLSTEP,                   //x extent
                                        fi->depth,                  //y extent

                                        fi->width-i-ROLLSTEP,       //x source
                                        0,                          //y source

                                        0,                          //first scan line
                                        fi->depth,                  //number of scan lines
                                        image,
                                        bmp,
                                        DIB_PAL_COLORS);
```

Figure 4-8   *Continued.*

```
                WaitForTick(MEDIUMWAIT);

        }

        CheckFrame(hdc,fi);

        GlobalUnlock(fi->picture);
        return(TRUE);
}

int VerticalRollDownPictureAway(HDC hdc,LPFILEINFO fi,COLORREF rgb)
{
        HBRUSH hbrush,oldbrush;
        HPEN oldpen;
        unsigned long l,t;
        unsigned int i;

        hbrush=CreateSolidBrush(rgb);
        oldbrush=SelectObject(hdc,hbrush);
        oldpen=SelectObject(hdc,GetStockObject(NULL_PEN));

        for(i=0;i<fi->depth;i+=ROLLSTEP) {
                l=ticks();
                BitBlt(hdc,
                        0,                   //x dest
                        i+ROLLSTEP,          //y dest

                        fi->width,           //width
                        fi->depth-i,         //depth

                        hdc,

                        0,                   //x source
                        i,                   //y source
                        SRCCOPY);

                Rectangle(hdc,0,i-ROLLSTEP,fi->width+1,i+(ROLLSTEP*2)+1);
                WaitForTick(MEDIUMWAIT);
        }

        SelectObject(hdc,oldbrush);
        SelectObject(hdc,oldpen);
        DeleteObject(hbrush);
        return(TRUE);
}

int VerticalRollUpPictureAway(HDC hdc,LPFILEINFO fi,COLORREF rgb)
{
        HBRUSH hbrush,oldbrush;
        HPEN oldpen;
        unsigned long l,t;
        unsigned int i;
```

```
        hbrush=CreateSolidBrush(rgb);
        oldbrush=SelectObject(hdc,hbrush);
        oldpen=SelectObject(hdc,GetStockObject(NULL_PEN));

        for(i=0;i<fi->depth;i+=ROLLSTEP) {
                l=ticks();
                BitBlt(hdc,
                        0,                      //x dest
                        0,                      //y dest

                        fi->width,              //width
                        fi->depth-i,            //depth

                        hdc,

                        0,                      //x source
                        ROLLSTEP,               //y source
                        SRCCOPY);

                Rectangle(hdc,0,fi->depth-i-ROLLSTEP,fi->width+1,
                        fi->depth-i+(ROLLSTEP*2));
                WaitForTick(MEDIUMWAIT);
        }

        SelectObject(hdc,oldbrush);
        SelectObject(hdc,oldpen);
        DeleteObject(hbrush);
        return(TRUE);
}

int VerticalRollUpPicture(HDC hdc,LPFILEINFO fi)
{
        LPSTR image;
        LPBITMAPINFO bmp;
        unsigned long l,t;
        unsigned int i,j,n;

        if((bmp=(LPBITMAPINFO)GlobalLock(fi->picture))== NULL)
          return(FALSE);

        n=1<<fi->bits;
        j=min(n,256);

        image=(LPSTR)bmp+(unsigned int)bmp->bmiHeader.biSize+
          (j*sizeof(RGBQUAD));

        for(i=0;i<fi->depth;i+=ROLLSTEP) {
                l=ticks();
                SetDIBitsToDevice(hdc,
                                0,                      //x dest
                                fi->depth-ROLLSTEP,     //y dest

                                fi->width,              //x extent
                                ROLLSTEP,               //y extent
```

173

Figure 4-8   *Continued.*

```
                                        0,                      //x source
                                        fi->depth-i,            //y source

                                        0,                      //first scan line
                                        fi->depth,              //number of scan lines
                                        image,
                                        bmp,
                                        DIB_PAL_COLORS);

                 BitBlt(hdc,

                        0,                              //x dest
                        fi->depth-i-ROLLSTEP,           //y dest

                        fi->width,              //width
                        i,                      //depth

                        hdc,

                        0,                      //x source
                        fi->depth-i,            //y source
                        SRCCOPY);

                 WaitForTick(MEDIUMWAIT);

            }

            SetDIBitsToDevice(hdc,
                        0,                      //x dest
                        fi->depth-ROLLSTEP,     //y dest

                        fi->width,              //x extent
                        ROLLSTEP,               //y extent

                        0,                      //x source
                        0,                      //y source

                        0,                      //first scan line
                        fi->depth,              //number of scan lines
                        image,
                        bmp,
                        DIB_PAL_COLORS);


            CheckFrame(hdc,fi);

            GlobalUnlock(fi->picture);
            return(TRUE);
}
int VerticalRollDownPicture(HDC hdc,LPFILEINFO fi)
{
```

```
LPSTR image;
LPBITMAPINFO bmp;
unsigned long l,t;
unsigned int i,j,n;

if((bmp=(LPBITMAPINFO)GlobalLock(fi->picture))== NULL) return(FALSE);

n=1<<fi->bits;
j=min(n,256);

image=(LPSTR)bmp+(unsigned int)bmp->bmiHeader.biSize+(j*sizeof(RGBQUAD));

for(i=0;i<fi->depth;i+=ROLLSTEP) {
        l=ticks();
        SetDIBitsToDevice(hdc,
                            0,                  //x dest
                            0,                  //y dest

                            fi->width,          //x extent
                            ROLLSTEP,           //y extent

                            0,                  //x source
                            i-ROLLSTEP,         //y source

                            0,                  //first scan line
                            fi->depth,          //number of scan lines
                            image,
                            bmp,
                            DIB_PAL_COLORS);

        BitBlt(hdc,

                0,                  //x dest
                ROLLSTEP,           //y dest

                fi->width,          //width
                i,                  //depth

                hdc,

                0,                  //x source
                0,                  //y source
                SRCCOPY);

        WaitForTick(MEDIUMWAIT);

}

SetDIBitsToDevice(hdc,
        0,
        0,

        fi->width,
        ROLLSTEP,
```

Figure 4-8 *Continued.*

```
                0,
                fi->depth-ROLLSTEP,

                fi->depth,

                image,
                bmp,
                DIB_PAL_COLORS);

        CheckFrame(hdc,fi);

        GlobalUnlock(fi->picture);
        return(TRUE);
}

#define         AdjustValue(t,c)        { if(t > c) \
                                            { —t; flag=1;}\
                                        else if(t < c)\
                                            { ++t; flag=1;}\
                                        }
int FadePictureToColour(HDC hdc,LPFILEINFO fi,COLORREF rgb)
{
        LOGPALETTE *pLogPal;
        HANDLE hPal=NULL;
        LPSTR image;
        LPBITMAPINFO bmp;
        unsigned long l,t;
        char palette[768];
        unsigned int i,j,n,r,g,b,tr,tg,tb,flag;

        r=GetRValue(rgb);
        g=GetGValue(rgb);
        b=GetBValue(rgb);

        if((bmp=(LPBITMAPINFO)GlobalLock(fi->picture))== NULL) return(FALSE);

        n=1<<fi->bits;
        j=min(n,256);

        image=(LPSTR)bmp+(unsigned int)bmp->bmiHeader.biSize+(j*sizeof(RGBQUAD));

        if((pLogPal=(LOGPALETTE *)malloc(sizeof(LOGPALETTE)+
            (j*sizeof(PALETTEENTRY)))) == NULL) {
                GlobalUnlock(fi->picture);
                return(FALSE);
        }

        pLogPal->palVersion=0x0300;
        pLogPal->palNumEntries=j;

        for(i=0;i<j;i++) {
```

```
                pLogPal->palPalEntry[i].peRed=fi->palette[i*RGB_SIZE+RGB_RED];
                pLogPal->palPalEntry[i].peGreen=fi->palette[i*RGB_SIZE+RGB_GREEN];
                pLogPal->palPalEntry[i].peBlue=fi->palette[i*RGB_SIZE+RGB_BLUE];
                pLogPal->palPalEntry[i].peFlags=0;
        }

        hPal=CreatePalette(pLogPal);

        SelectPalette(hdc,hPal,0);
        RealizePalette(hdc);

        SetDIBitsToDevice(hdc,0,0,fi->width,fi->depth,
            0,0,0,fi->depth,image,bmp,DIB_PAL_COLORS);

        lmemcpy(palette,fi->palette,768);

        do {
                l=ticks();
                flag=0;
                for(i=0;i<j;++i) {
                        tr=fi->palette[i*RGB_SIZE+RGB_RED];
                        tg=fi->palette[i*RGB_SIZE+RGB_GREEN];
                        tb=fi->palette[i*RGB_SIZE+RGB_BLUE];

                        AdjustValue(tr,r);
                        AdjustValue(tg,g);
                        AdjustValue(tb,b);

                        fi->palette[i*RGB_SIZE+RGB_RED]=tr;
                        fi->palette[i*RGB_SIZE+RGB_GREEN]=tg;
                        fi->palette[i*RGB_SIZE+RGB_BLUE]=tb;

                        pLogPal->palPalEntry[i].peRed=tr;
                        pLogPal->palPalEntry[i].peGreen=tg;
                        pLogPal->palPalEntry[i].peBlue=tb;
                        pLogPal->palPalEntry[i].peFlags=0;
                }
                SelectPalette(hdc,hPal,0);
                RealizePalette(hdc);
                WaitForTick(MEDIUMWAIT);
        } while(flag);

        if(hPal != NULL) DeleteObject(hPal);
        free(pLogPal);

        GlobalUnlock(fi->picture);

        CheckFrame(hdc,fi);

        return(TRUE);
}
#undef AdjustColour
```

Figure 4-8 *Continued.*

```
int DisplayPicture(HDC hdc,LPFILEINFO fi)
{
        LPSTR image;
        LPBITMAPINFO bmp;
        unsigned int j,n;

        if((bmp=(LPBITMAPINFO)GlobalLock(fi->picture))== NULL) return(FALSE);

        n=1<<fi->bits;
        j=min(n,256);

        image=(LPSTR)bmp+(unsigned int)bmp->bmiHeader.biSize+(j*sizeof(RGBQUAD));

        SetDIBitsToDevice(hdc,0,0,fi->width,fi->depth,
            0,0,0,fi->depth,image,bmp,DIB_PAL_COLORS);

        GlobalUnlock(fi->picture);

        CheckFrame(hdc,fi);

        return(TRUE);
}

int TileFromPicture(HDC hdc,LPFILEINFO fi)
{
        HANDLE hPal=NULL;
        LPSTR image;
        LPBITMAPINFO bmp;
        POINT huge *point;
        unsigned long l,t;
        unsigned int tiles,i,j,n;
        unsigned int x=0,y=0;

        /* count the number of tiles */
        tiles=(fi->width/TILESIZE)*(fi->depth/TILESIZE);

        /* allocate somewhere to put them */
        if((point=(POINT huge *)FixedGlobalAlloc((long)tiles*
            (long)sizeof(POINT)))== NULL) return(FALSE);

        /* initialize the tile array */
        for(i=0;i<tiles;++i) {
                point[i].x=x;
                point[i].y=y;

                x+=TILESIZE;
                if(x >= fi->width) {
                        x=0;
                        y+=TILESIZE;
                }
        }
```

```
        randomize();

        /* now draw the tiles */
        if((bmp=(LPBITMAPINFO)GlobalLock(fi->picture))== NULL) {
                FixedGlobalFree(point);
                return(FALSE);
        }

        n=1<<fi->bits;
        j=min(n,256);

        image=(LPSTR)bmp+(unsigned int)bmp->bmiHeader.biSize+(j*sizeof(RGBQUAD));

        for(;tiles > 0;—tiles) {
                l=ticks();
                n=random(tiles);
                x=point[n].x;
                y=point[n].y;

                SetDIBitsToDevice(hdc,
                                  x,
                                  fi->depth-y-TILESIZE,
                                  TILESIZE,
                                  TILESIZE,
                                  x,
                                  y,
                                  0,
                                  fi->depth,
                                  image,
                                  bmp,
                                  DIB_PAL_COLORS);

                x=point[tiles-1].x;
                y=point[tiles-1].y;

                point[n].x=x;
                point[n].y=y;
                WaitForTick(SHORTWAIT);
        }

        if(hPal != NULL) DeleteObject(hPal);
        GlobalUnlock(fi->picture);

        FixedGlobalFree(point);

        CheckFrame(hdc,fi);

        return(TRUE);
}

int TileToColour(HDC hdc,LPFILEINFO fi,COLORREF rgb)
{
        HBRUSH hbrush,oldbrush;
```

Figure 4-8   *Continued.*

```
HPEN oldpen;
POINT huge *point;
unsigned long l,t;
unsigned int tiles,i,n;
unsigned int x=0,y=0,width,depth;

width=RoundUp(fi->width,TILESIZE);
depth=RoundUp(fi->depth,TILESIZE);

/* count the number of tiles */
tiles=(width/TILESIZE)*(depth/TILESIZE);

/* allocate somewhere to put them */
if((point=(POINT huge *)FixedGlobalAlloc((long)tiles*
    (long)sizeof(POINT)))== NULL) return(FALSE);

/* initialize the tile array */
for(i=0;i<tiles;++i) {
        point[i].x=x;
        point[i].y=y;

        x+=TILESIZE;
        if(x >= width) {
                x=0;
                y+=TILESIZE;
        }
}

randomize();

/* now draw the tiles */
hbrush=CreateSolidBrush(rgb);
oldbrush=SelectObject(hdc,hbrush);
oldpen=SelectObject(hdc,GetStockObject(NULL_PEN));

for(;tiles > 0;--tiles) {
        l=ticks();
        n=random(tiles);
        Rectangle(hdc,point[n].x,point[n].y,point[n].x+TILESIZE+1,
            point[n].y+TILESIZE+1);

        x=point[tiles-1].x;
        y=point[tiles-1].y;

        point[n].x=x;
        point[n].y=y;

        WaitForTick(SHORTWAIT);

}
```

```
        SelectObject(hdc,oldpen);
        SelectObject(hdc,oldbrush);

        DeleteObject(hbrush);

        FixedGlobalFree(point);

        return(TRUE);
}

long ticks()
{
        timeGetTime();
}
```

The BMP-FX.RC resource script.   Figure 4-9

```
MainScreen DIALOG 49, 48, 240, 144
STYLE WS_POPUP | WS_CAPTION | WS_SYSMENU | WS_MINIMIZEBOX
CAPTION "Bitmap Effects"
MENU MainMenu
BEGIN
        CONTROL "", 201, "LISTBOX", LBS_STANDARD | WS_CHILD | WS_VISIBLE,
            12, 24, 76, 100
        LTEXT "", 301, 12, 124, 76, 8, WS_CHILD | WS_VISIBLE | WS_GROUP
        CONTROL "", -1, "BorShade", BSS_GROUP | WS_CHILD | WS_VISIBLE, 8, 8, 84, 128
        DEFPUSHBUTTON "View", 102, 108, 8, 40, 20, WS_CHILD | WS_VISIBLE | WS_TABSTOP
        PUSHBUTTON "Get Info", 103, 108, 36, 40, 20, WS_CHILD | WS_VISIBLE | WS_TABSTOP
        PUSHBUTTON "Quit", 107, 108, 116, 40, 20, WS_CHILD | WS_VISIBLE | WS_TABSTOP
        CONTROL "", -1, "BorShade", BSS_VDIP | WS_CHILD | WS_VISIBLE, 100, 0, 1, 144
        LTEXT "", 302, 12, 12, 76, 8, WS_CHILD | WS_VISIBLE | WS_GROUP
        CONTROL "", 104, "BorShade", 3 | WS_CHILD | WS_VISIBLE, 156, 0, 1, 144
        CONTROL "Normal", 400, "BorCheck", BS_AUTOCHECKBOX | WS_CHILD | WS_VISIBLE |
            WS_TABSTOP, 164, 9, 68, 10
        CONTROL "Tile", 401, "BorCheck", BS_AUTOCHECKBOX | WS_CHILD | WS_VISIBLE |
            WS_TABSTOP, 164, 20, 68, 10
        CONTROL "Roll Up", 402, "BorCheck", BS_AUTOCHECKBOX | WS_CHILD | WS_VISIBLE |
            WS_TABSTOP, 164, 32, 68, 10
        CONTROL "Roll down", 403, "BorCheck", BS_AUTOCHECKBOX | WS_CHILD | WS_VISIBLE |
            WS_TABSTOP, 164, 44, 68, 10
        CONTROL "Wipe right", 405, "BorCheck", BS_AUTOCHECKBOX | WS_CHILD | WS_VISIBLE |
            WS_TABSTOP, 164, 68, 68, 10
        CONTROL "Wipe left", 404, "BorCheck", BS_AUTOCHECKBOX | WS_CHILD | WS_VISIBLE |
            WS_TABSTOP, 164, 56, 68, 10
        CONTROL "Horizontal split", 406, "BorCheck", BS_AUTOCHECKBOX | WS_CHILD | WS_VISIBLE |
            WS_TABSTOP, 164, 80, 68, 10
        CONTROL "Vertical split", 407, "BorCheck", BS_AUTOCHECKBOX | WS_CHILD | WS_VISIBLE |
            WS_TABSTOP, 164, 92, 68, 10
        CONTROL "Raster", 408, "BorCheck", BS_AUTOCHECKBOX | WS_CHILD | WS_VISIBLE |
            WS_TABSTOP, 164, 104, 68, 10
        CONTROL "Vertical centre", 409, "BorCheck", BS_AUTOCHECKBOX | WS_CHILD | WS_VISIBLE |
            WS_TABSTOP, 164, 116, 68, 10
```

Figure 4-9 *Continued.*

```
            CONTROL "Plummet", 410, "BorCheck", BS_AUTOCHECKBOX | WS_CHILD | WS_VISIBLE |
                WS_TABSTOP, 164, 128, 68, 10
END

MainMenu MENU
BEGIN
        POPUP "&File"
        BEGIN
                MENUITEM "&View", 102
                MENUITEM "&Get Info", 103
                MENUITEM "&Colour", 104
                MENUITEM "&About", 105
                MENUITEM SEPARATOR
                MENUITEM "E&xit", 107
        END

END

AboutBox DIALOG 18, 18, 184, 180
STYLE WS_POPUP | WS_CAPTION
CAPTION "About..."
BEGIN
        CONTROL "", 102, "BorShade", BSS_GROUP | WS_CHILD | WS_VISIBLE |
            WS_TABSTOP, 8, 68, 168, 76
        CTEXT "Bitmap Effects 1.0\n\nCopyright © 1994 Alchemy Mindworks Inc.\n\n
            This program is part of the book Advanced Multimedia Programming for
            Windows by Steven William Rimmer, published by Windcrest/McGraw Hill.",
            -1, 12, 72, 160, 68, WS_CHILD | WS_VISIBLE | WS_GROUP
        CONTROL "Button", IDOK, "BorBtn", BS_DEFPUSHBUTTON | WS_CHILD |
            WS_VISIBLE | WS_TABSTOP, 74, 152, 32, 20
END

1801 BITMAP "smpw.bmp"

AboutWave RCDATA "ABOUT.WAV"

InfoBox DIALOG 6, -11, 180, 92
STYLE DS_MODALFRAME | WS_POPUP | WS_CAPTION
CAPTION "Get Info"
BEGIN
        DEFPUSHBUTTON "Ok", IDOK, 140, 64, 32, 20, WS_CHILD | WS_VISIBLE | WS_TABSTOP
        RTEXT "File:", -1, 8, 12, 44, 8, SS_RIGHT | WS_CHILD | WS_VISIBLE | WS_GROUP
        RTEXT "Colours:", -1, 8, 24, 44, 8, SS_RIGHT | WS_CHILD | WS_VISIBLE | WS_GROUP
        RTEXT "Dimensions:", -1, 8, 36, 44, 8, SS_RIGHT | WS_CHILD |
            WS_VISIBLE | WS_GROUP
        RTEXT "Memory:", -1, 8, 48, 44, 8, SS_RIGHT | WS_CHILD | WS_VISIBLE | WS_GROUP
        LTEXT "", 101, 60, 12, 60, 8, WS_CHILD | WS_VISIBLE | WS_GROUP
        LTEXT "", 102, 60, 24, 60, 8, WS_CHILD | WS_VISIBLE | WS_GROUP
        LTEXT "", 103, 60, 36, 60, 8, WS_CHILD | WS_VISIBLE | WS_GROUP
        LTEXT "", 104, 60, 48, 60, 8, WS_CHILD | WS_VISIBLE | WS_GROUP
END
BitmapEffects ICON
```

```
BEGIN
    '00 00 01 00 01 00 20 20 10 00 00 00 00 00 E8 02'
    '00 00 16 00 00 00 28 00 00 00 20 00 00 00 40 00'
    '00 00 01 00 04 00 00 00 00 00 80 02 00 00 00 00'
    '00 00 00 00 00 00 00 10 00 00 00 00 00 00 00 00'
    '00 00 00 00 BF 00 00 BF 00 00 00 BF BF 00 BF 00'
    '00 00 BF 00 BF 00 BF BF 00 00 C0 C0 C0 00 80 80'
    '80 00 00 00 FF 00 00 FF 00 00 00 FF FF 00 FF 00'
    '00 00 FF 00 FF 00 FF FF 00 00 FF FF FF 00 77 77'
    '77 77 77 77 77 77 77 77 77 77 77 77 77 77 7F 88'
    '88 88 88 88 88 88 88 88 88 88 88 88 88 87 7F F8'
    '88 88 88 88 88 88 88 88 88 88 88 88 88 87 7F F7'
    '77 77 77 77 77 77 77 77 77 77 77 77 78 87 7F F7'
    '77 77 77 77 77 77 77 77 77 77 77 77 78 87 7F F7'
    '77 77 FF 77 77 77 77 FF 77 77 FF 77 78 87 7F F7'
    '77 78 8F 77 77 77 78 8F 77 78 8F 77 78 87 7F F7'
    '77 78 8F 77 77 77 78 8F F7 78 87 77 78 87 7F F7'
    '77 78 8F 77 77 77 77 88 F7 88 F7 77 78 87 7F F7'
    '77 78 8F 77 77 77 77 88 FF 88 77 77 78 87 7F F7'
    '77 78 8F FF FF 77 77 78 88 87 77 77 78 87 7F F7'
    '77 78 88 88 8F 77 77 77 88 F7 77 77 78 87 7F F7'
    '77 78 88 88 87 77 77 77 88 FF 77 77 78 87 7F F7'
    '77 78 8F 77 77 77 77 78 88 8F F7 77 78 87 7F F7'
    '77 78 8F 77 77 77 77 88 F7 88 F7 77 78 87 7F F7'
    '77 78 8F FF FF FF 77 88 77 88 FF 77 78 87 7F F7'
    '77 78 88 88 88 8F 78 88 F7 78 8F 77 78 87 7F F7'
    '77 78 88 88 88 87 78 87 77 78 87 77 78 87 7F F7'
    '77 77 77 77 77 77 77 77 77 77 77 77 78 87 7F F7'
    '77 77 77 77 77 77 77 77 77 77 7F 77 78 87 7F F7'
    '77 77 77 77 77 77 77 77 77 77 8F 77 78 87 7F F7'
    'FF FF 77 F7 7F 7F 7F 7F 77 FF 8F FF 78 87 7F F8'
    '88 87 F8 F7 87 8F 8F 8F 78 8F 88 87 F8 87 7F F8'
    'F7 78 F8 F8 F7 8F 8F 8F 87 8F 8F 78 F8 87 7F F8'
    'FF F8 78 F8 FF 8F 8F 87 7F 87 8F F8 78 87 7F F8'
    '88 87 F8 78 87 88 88 77 88 77 88 87 78 87 7F F8'
    'FF F8 77 F8 77 77 77 77 77 77 77 77 78 87 7F F8'
    '88 87 78 77 77 77 77 77 77 77 77 77 78 87 7F F7'
    '77 77 77 77 77 77 77 77 77 77 77 77 78 87 7F FF'
    'FF FF FF FF FF FF FF FF FF FF FF FF F8 87 7F FF'
    'FF FF FF FF FF FF FF FF FF FF FF FF 87 77 77'
    '77 77 77 77 77 77 77 77 77 77 77 77 77 00 00'
    '00 00 00 00 00 00 00 00 00 00 00 00 00 00 00 00'
    '00 00 00 00 00 00 00 00 00 00 00 00 00 00 00 00'
    '00 00 00 00 00 00 00 00 00 00 00 00 00 00 00 00'
    '00 00 00 00 00 00 00 00 00 00 00 00 00 00 00 00'
    '00 00 00 00 00 00 00 00 00 00 00 00 00 00 00 00'
    '00 00 00 00 00 00 00 00 00 00 00 00 00 00 00 00'
    '00 00 00 00 00 00 00 00 00 00 00 00 00 00 00 00'
    '00 00 00 00 00 00 00 00 00 00 00 00 00 00 00'
END
```

There's quite a bit going on in BMP-FX. The main window of the BMP-FX application is essentially a list box and some additional controls. If you've previously had a look at the sample applications in *Windows Multimedia Programming*, this will no doubt be quite familiar. The list box contains the names of the BMP files in the current directory, as well as entries for any visible subdirectories and the system drive letters. You can use the latter elements to navigate to other subdirectories in search of BMP files if you like. Click on a file name in the list box and click on View—or just double click on a file name—to view the selected image.

The SelectProc function handles messages for the main window of BMP-FX. The most important bit at the moment is the code that handles a WM_COMMAND message with MAIN_VIEW as its wParam argument. This will locate the currently selected entry in the list box and pass it as a file name to ViewFile.

The ViewFile function will load a BMP file into memory, open a window the size of your screen, and display the image using the appropriate special effects. It begins by calling the GetInfo function. The GetInfo call will read the header of a BMP file and fill in the fields of a FILEINFO object, as defined at the top of BMP-FX.CPP. This tells ViewFile the dimensions and color depth of the image to be viewed, among other things. Note that ViewFile will refuse to display BMP files having more than eight bits of color. The system requirements for handling true-color images with some of the special effects would become prohibitive.

The GetInfo function will return FALSE if the file it is given to read cannot be opened or isn't actually a BMP file.

A FILEINFO object looks like this:

```
typedef struct {
        GLOBALHANDLE picture;
        char filename[16];
        unsigned int width;
        unsigned int depth;
        unsigned int bits;
        unsigned long memory;
        char palette[768];
        } FILEINFO;
```

The BMP-FX application uses FILEINFO objects to keep track of the pictures it's working with. The FILEINFO for a picture is partially filled in by GetInfo—it also serves to contain the handle of the memory buffer that will ultimately contain the device-independent bitmap for an image loaded into memory.

Having ascertained that the BMP file in question isn't actually a list of infamous renaissance courtesans cunningly renamed with the extension BMP to disguise its true nature, the ViewFile function will read the first bit of the BMP file, the BITMAPFILEHEADER object. Doing so tells it how much memory will be required for the rest of the image and also serves to seek past this object, which isn't required in the structure of a device-independent bitmap.

The next bit of ViewFile allocates a buffer to store the image, locks it, and reads the rest of the BMP file in question into it. Note that the _hread rather than _lread call is used to load the image, to allow for bitmaps larger than 64 kilobytes. The _hread function is actually part of the multimedia extensions.

Once a BMP file has been loaded into memory, ViewFile can open a window to display it in. This version of the function uses a full-screen window. It creates a brush with which to paint its background, based on the color defined by the global object background. We'll look at how the background color is managed later in this section.

Messages for the image window created by ViewFile are handled by the PictureProc function. Most of it is concerned with what happens when a WM_PAINT message shows up, as this is where all the work is done. It will display the image pointed to by the FILEINFO pointer fi. The effects it chooses will be based on the state of the check boxes in the main window of BMP-FX, as ascertained by calling GetParent to find the main window handle, and then using the IsItemChecked macro to test each of the check boxes.

When BMP-FX displays a picture, it centers it in the large display window. There are a number of ways to arrange this—it's handled in PictureProc by working out the displacement required to center the picture and then using SetWindowOrg to shift the origin of the

window down and to the right relative to the physical upper left corner of the window as it's drawn on your screen.

The RealizePicturePalette function, as it's called from PictureProc, realizes the palette of the picture specified by its fi argument into the HDC specified by its hdc argument. It returns a handle to a palette, which must be destroyed when it's no longer required.

Displaying bitmaps without effects

The DisplayPicture function in BMP-FX.CPP is the simplest of the graphic display calls. It displays a bitmap specified by a FILEINFO object with no special effects. Basically, it implements the SetDIBitsToDevice call to do all the work. While not particularly exciting, this function illustrates the basic structure of all the display functions. Specifically, it locks the image specified by fi->picture and calculates the location of its image data based on the number of colors—and hence the number of RGBQUAD objects—it contains.

Note that SetDIBitsToDevice uses the DIB_PAL_COLORS constant as its final argument. The palette for the bitmap will have been displayed and its palette information overwritten with a list of palette indices before any of the display functions are called, as discussed earlier in this chapter.

The CheckFrame call in DisplayPicture is actually a macro call, and if you skip back up to the beginning of BMP-FX.CPP, you'll notice that by default, it expands out to nothing. This is a debugging gadget you might find handy if you decide to write additional effects functions. If you define this macro, it draws a black frame around a bitmap once it has been displayed. Rather, it draws a black frame around where the bitmap should have been displayed.

The CheckFrame macro is useful because more complex display functions usually involve moving fragments of the image being displayed. Without a reference as to where they should ultimately be when they stop moving, it might not be obvious whether your new effects are behaving exactly as they should.

Displaying bitmaps with tiling

Figure 4-10 illustrates a bitmap being tiled onto the screen. When a picture is tiled, the source image is broken up into a matrix of squares. The squares are painted into the destination window in a random order.

The TileFromPicture function in BMP-FX.CPP handles tiling a bitmap onto the screen, and the TileToColour function handles tiling it off again. In fact, TileToColour tiles over the previously displayed bitmap with squares of the background color.

There are two distinct problems to be solved in writing the TileFromPicture function. The first involves finding a workable approach to randomizing the sequence of tiles to be drawn. The second—and very much simpler—problem is figuring out how to extract rectangular sections from the source bitmap and paint them on the screen.

In this function, the constant TILESIZE defines the number of pixels along one edge of a tile. As such, the number of tiles in an image can be calculated as:

```
(fi->width/TILESIZE)*(fi->depth/TILESIZE)
```

In fact, the fi->width and fi->depth values are rounded up to the nearest even tile.

The upper left corner of each tile can be defined as a point—keep in mind that prior to calling a display function, the origin of the window into which the picture in question will be displayed has been adjusted so that its effective upper left corner will be the same as that of the bitmap. The first step in working out how to display the tiles, then, is to create an array of POINT objects and initialize it such that each point specifies the origin of one tile.

If the tiles defined by the points in the array of POINT objects were to be painted in the order in which they appear when the array has just been initialized, the tiles would be painted in order, starting with the upper left tile and ending with the upper right tile.

Figure 4-10

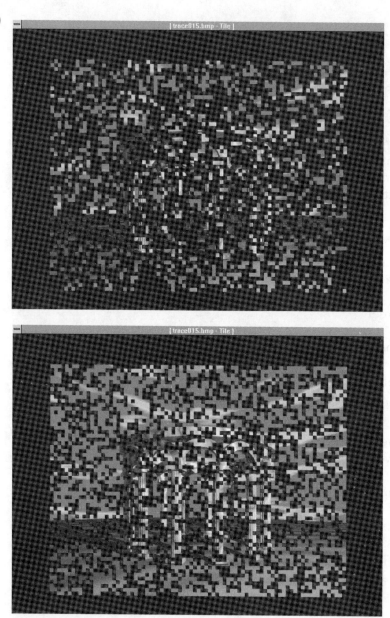

A bitmap being tiled into a window.

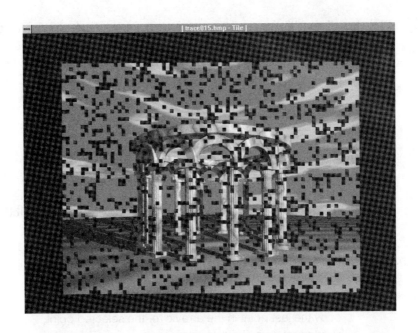

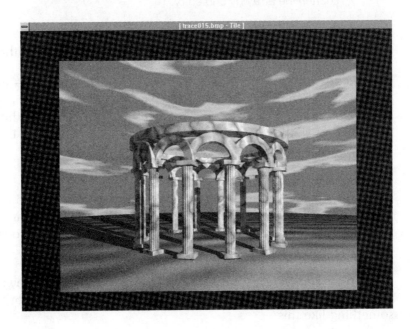

Clearly, all that's required is a way to randomize the order of the POINT objects in the array of points, and then paint the tiles. Unfortunately, this isn't particularly easy to accomplish. At least, it isn't particularly easy to accomplish in a reasonable time. Doing so would involve a noticeable wait before the TileFromPicture actually displayed anything.

In fact, the TileFromPicture function handles the problem a bit differently. The approach it uses is both faster than an algorithm to randomize the array of points, and it allows TileFromPicture to paint tiles as it manipulates its array. You can see it at work in the somewhat unconventional for loop at the bottom of the function.

Here's what this loop is doing in pseudocode:

```
for(as long as there are points in the array) {
        randomly choose one point in the array;
        display the tile it represents;
        copy the last point in the array over the selected point;
        shorten the array by one entry;
}
```

The SetDIBitsToDevice function is used to actually display the tiles.

There's one other element of import in the TileFromPicture function. You'll notice two functions in the for loop that draw the tiles—ticks and WaitForTick. The latter is actually a macro, defined at the beginning of BMP-FX.CPP. These bits of code use some of the timer facilities discussed in Chapter 3.

If you write the for loop in a function like TileFromPicture to run at its maximum speed, it will take a variable amount of time to complete its task—it will take a lot longer to run on an old 80286 machine than on a very much faster 80486 system. In fact, it will probably run much too fast on any system.

Back in the dark ages, the problem of slowing down the drawing code would have been solved by building a delay loop into the works— something like this:

```
for(n=0;n<10000;++n);
```

This loop doesn't do anything, but it kills some time while it's not doing it. Unfortunately, the speed of this loop would also be machine-dependent.

What's really needed in this application is a way to wait for a specific period, regardless of the machine speed, and to have the period begin before the drawing operation does. As such, if the drawing operation takes longer than the defined period, no additional delay will be added to the time it requires.

The ticks function, defined at the very bottom of BMP-FX.CPP, fetches the current timer count in milliseconds. The WaitForTick macro will then repeatedly fetch the time count until it's greater than the original time count plus a fixed delay value—in this case, SHORTWAIT, or one millisecond. This is what WaitForTick looks like:

```
#defineWaitForTick(twait) {\
        while((t=ticks()) >= l && t < (l+(long)twait));\
                        }
```

WaitForTick also checks for the relatively unlikely prospect that the timer count might have rolled over past zero between calls to ticks. This will only happen if Windows has been running continuously for about a month and a half.

As it stands, the tile functions work well for bitmaps of varying dimensions on a pretty good range of machines. If you plan on displaying exceedingly small or exceedingly large pictures, you might want to modify the code a bit to calibrate the delays based on the image dimensions.

Note that back in PictureProc, where TileFromPicture is actually called, there's another delay macro. The WaitAfterDisplay call is also defined at the top of BMP-FX.CPP, and introduces a brief pause between the appearance of a graphic and its dissolution.

⇨ Rolls & wipes

Four effects involve having a graphic appear to roll or wipe onto the screen—to wit, VerticalRollUpPicture, VerticalRollDownPicture,

WipeInPictureFromLeft, and WipeInPictureFromRight. Four corresponding functions handle removing pictures with corresponding effects: VerticalRollUpPictureAway, VerticalRollDownPictureAway, WipeOutPictureFromLeft, and WipeOutPictureFromRight.

Each of the first four functions is based on essentially the same bit of animation. Here's what it looks like in pseudocode:

```
for(as long as the whole graphic isn't visible) {
        paint a small section of the graphic;
        delay for a short time;
        move the visible part of the graphic over slightly;
}
```

In fact, the order of the operations in the for loop is reversed in the actual implementations of these functions. The visible part of the graphic is moved first—on the first pass through the loop there will be no visible part of the graphic.

The WipeInPictureFromRight function in BMP-FX.CPP is an example of this process in real code. It displays the graphic in question in increments of ROLLSTEP, a constant defined at the top of the source file. For each iteration of its principal for loop, the function begins by using BitBlt to move the visible part of the graphic to the left by ROLLSTEP pixels. It then paints over the rightmost band of the visible part of the bitmap with a call to SetDIBitsToDevice.

You might well ask why this effect isn't created by simply calling SetDIBitsToDevice multiple times, allowing it to paint a slightly larger section of the source bitmap each time. While you could do it this way, the speed at which the graphic appeared to roll onto the screen would decrease noticeably as more and more of the graphic became visible. The SetDIBitsToDevice function is relatively slow, and it gets slower as it's asked to paint larger areas to the screen. By comparison, calling BitBlt to move areas between identical device contexts— in this case from the screen to the screen—is blindingly fast.

The WipeInPictureFromRight function repeatedly calls SetDIBitsToDevice to draw a band of the source image—the dimensions of the band will be the same with each call, and as such, so will be the time required to paint it. The time required by BitBlt

will increase as more of the picture becomes visible; but even on fairly large bitmaps, this will still be less than one delay interval, as set by WaitForTick. One delay interval is defined by the constant MEDIUMWAIT at the top of BMP-FX.CPP—10 milliseconds here. You can increase this value to slow down the effect.

You can also decrease this value to speed up the effect, but keep in mind that doing so may not work well for large bitmaps displayed on slower computers. If one call to BitBlt and one call to SetDIBitsToDevice require more than the time specified by MEDIUMWAIT, the graphic being displayed will appear to slow down in its transit across the screen as more of it becomes visible.

The WipeOutPictureFromLeft is called by PictureProc to clear the display window after a graphic has been wiped in from the right. It works very much like WipeInPictureFromRight, except that rather than calling SetDIBitsToDevice to paint part of a bitmap on your screen, it calls Rectangle to paint a solid area.

⇨ Complex effects

The remaining effects in BMP-FX.CPP are really just variations on the rolls and wipes discussed in the previous section. The HorizontalSplitPictureIn effect, for example, is created by performing WipeInPictureFromLeft on half the picture and WipeInPictureFromRight on the other half. The RasterPictureIn function involves splitting the picture to be displayed into multiple horizontal bands, rather than just two. It can be seen in Fig. 4-11.

The VerticalCentre effect is a variation on the vertical roll functions. It rolls in two sections from the center outwards, looking a bit like the Thames Television logo.

The PlummetPictureIn effect is the most complicated of the lot. It embodies elements from all of the foregoing effects functions. It splits the graphic to be displayed into vertical bands and appears to drop them into the image area in random order. The corresponding PlummetPictureOut function makes the vertical sections appear to drop out the bottom of the window. You can see the plummet effect in action in Fig. 4-12.

Figure 4-11

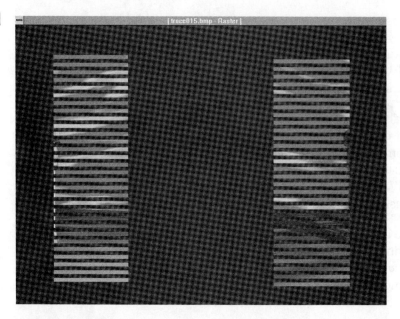

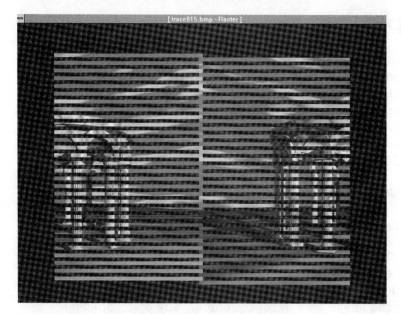

A bitmap being displayed with the raster effect.

Figure 4-11

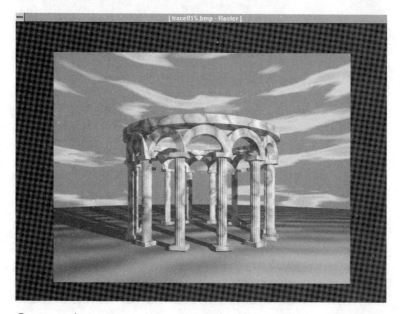

Continued.

Figure 4-12

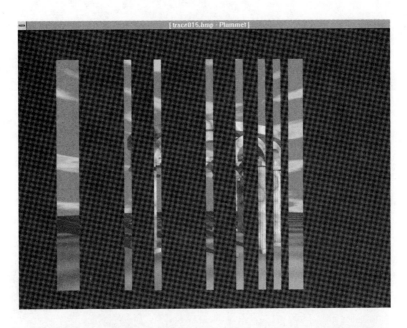

A plummeting bitmap.

Figure 4-12

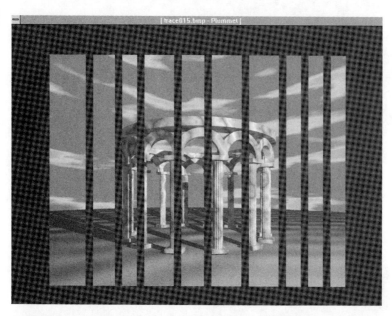

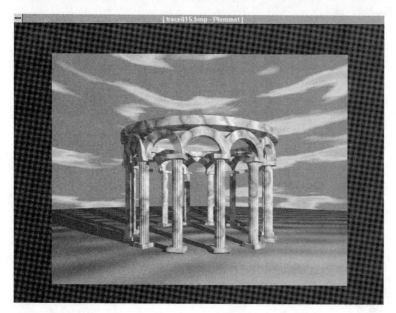

Continued.

The PlummetPictureIn function uses the same arrangement of BitBlt to move previously displayed image fragments and SetDIBitsToDevice to paint new ones. However, it also uses the random point array selection technique discussed in the section on tiling effects. The tiles will be BRICKSIZE wide and will fall in increments of BRICKDROP, as defined at the top of BMP-FX.CPP. The sections will appear in random order as they're selected from an array of points.

Using special effects with bitmap resources

If you open the About dialog of the BMP-FX application, you'll find that it ultimately comes to look just like the About dialogs in the earlier applications discussed in this book, but it takes a moment getting that way. Unlike the About dialogs in the wave file programs from Chapter 2, the graphic isn't handled as a Borland bitmap. Rather, it tiles itself into the window, clearly implementing a call to TileFromPicture.

While BMP-FX primarily illustrates its special effects as they're applied to BMP files loaded from disk, you'll probably want to use these effects on bitmap resources stored in the EXE files of your applications. You can see how this is handled if you look at the AboutDlgProc function in BMP-FX.CPP.

The WM_PAINT handler in AboutDlgProc is charged with the task of loading the About dialog graphic into memory and displaying it through a call to TileFromPicture. Because all the special effects in this application work with device-independent bitmaps stored with BITMAPINFO structures, rather than as BITMAP objects, it uses LoadResource rather than LoadBitmap to fetch the graphic. Because the About dialog graphic is stored as a numbered resource, rather than a named one, the MAKINTRESOURCE macro must be used to specify it.

The BitmapToPicture function, as declared in BMP-FX.CPP, fills in a FILEINFO object based on the bitmap resource returned by

199

LoadResource. There's nothing particularly sneaky about it—it just copies the appropriate data from the BITMAPINFO header of the resource and initializes the FILEINFO object under construction. The result is something that TileFromPicture can make sense of.

You can replace TileFromPicture with any other effects call you like the look of.

Other features

You might have noticed two additional elements of BMP-FX while perusing the code. The first involves the LoadConfig and SaveConfig functions. These preserve the state of two elements of BMP-FX between sessions by storing them as entries in your \WINDOWS\WIN.INI file. Specifically, they preserve the state of the check boxes in the main window and the current background color as stored in the object background.

The state of the check boxes is stored by setting bits in a long integer. The value of the long integer is saved as a number—which won't appear to mean very much because it's really just a collection of bit fields. Up to 32 check boxes can be kept track of this way.

The background color value is also stored as a long integer. While background is declared as a COLORREF object, some perusing through the WINDOWS.H header file will reveal that this is really just a long integer with one byte unused. Again, this number won't appear to mean very much if you locate the entries for BMP-FX in your WIN.INI file.

The other element of BMP-FX worth noting is the SelectColour function, as called from the MAIN_COLOUR handler of SelectProc. This function uses the Choose Color common dialog to allow you to define the background color to be used in BMP-FX's display window. Dealing with the Windows common dialogs in detail is beyond the scope of this book—there's a very thorough treatment of them in *Constructing Windows Dialogs*.

The modular nature of the effects functions in BMP-FX should make it fairly simple to extract functions from it to use in your own software. If you'll be presenting pictures in your multimedia applications, doing so with some animated transitions will go a long way toward preventing your static graphics from merely sitting there.

The monitor that wasn't there —working with DIB.DRV

Windows provides a pretty respectable range of GDI calls to manage graphics on your screen—the bitmap display functions in the first portion of this chapter were among them. In addition to these, there are calls to draw lines, rectangles, and more complex shapes; to manage regions, to manage drawing objects; and finally, to manage collections of calls to the simpler drawing functions as metafiles.

We'll get back to metafiles shortly.

The potential drawback to using a lot of GDI drawing calls is that they require a finite time to draw. In some applications, having a screen drawn and redrawn before your users' eyes can be fairly unprofessional looking. It would be useful if you could do all the drawing out of sight—perhaps on a hidden bitmap of some sort—and then paint the results to your application's window with BitBlt or SetDIBitsToDevice.

In fact, this can be handled reasonably well by creating a synthetic HDC, like this:

```
HDC hdc;

hdc=GetDC(NULL);
```

This call will create a device context with the characteristics of your monitor, but without actually being connected to it. If you subsequently create a bitmap and select it into this device context, the device it represents will acquire the dimensions and color depth of the bitmap, and you'll be able to draw on it.

In practice, there are several drawbacks to this technique. One of the easiest ones to spot is that while a device context created this way won't be connected to your screen, it will have your screen's characteristics. For example, if your screen can support no more than 16 colors, the device context you create this way will have the same limitation. This can complicate applications that use synthetic device contexts to print with or to create exportable bitmaps. It can also be somewhat restricting even if you simply want to display the contents of a synthetic device in a window.

The Windows Multimedia Development Kit offers an alternative for creating synthetic devices. The DIB.DRV driver can be used to create a synthetic device context that isn't derived from or connected to anything. It can have any color depth you like—up to eight bits, or 256 colors—regardless of the display characteristics of your current Windows screen driver.

There are two very small catches inherent in using DIB.DRV. First, it doesn't allow for 24-bit device contexts. Second, the DIB.DRV file itself must be accessible to applications that want to use it. Specifically, it should be somewhere on your DOS path, in your \WINDOWS directory, in your \WINDOWS\SYSTEM directory, or in the same directory as your application's EXE files.

Creating a device context with DIB.DRV is fairly simple. Here's the call to summon one into existence:

```
HDC hdc;

hdc=CreateDC("DIB",NULL,NULL,(LPSTR)lpbi);
```

The first argument to CreateDC is the name of the driver to be used in the incantation. The fourth argument is a pointer to a device-independent bitmap. The device-independent bitmap should begin with a BITMAPINFOHEADER object—this is assumed to be an LPBITMAPINFOHEADER pointer.

The synthetic device created this way will have the dimensions and color depth of the bitmap defined by the fourth argument to CreateDC. In effect, it will behave like a screen window, except that whatever you draw on it won't be immediately visible.

If you subsequently draw on the HDC thus created, the lines and shapes and other drawing elements in question will be rendered in the bitmap originally passed to CreateDC.

You should consider applying DIB.DRV to your applications whenever you require a lot of drawing operations to create the contents of a window. Especially for users with nonaccelerated display cards, rendering graphics on a hidden bitmap will reduce the time it takes to generate a complex drawing.

 Metafiles

I mentioned that I'd get back to the issue of metafiles. While they don't have anything to do with the DIB.DRV driver per se, they can be a very useful element in creating graphics for multimedia software. You can use metafiles to automate the drawing of complex graphics in a window—or in a device context created with DIB.DRV, if you like.

Whenever something is drawn under Windows—whether it's a window frame or a complex line drawing—multiple calls are made to Windows' GDI drawing engine. If you were to record each call and its parameters, the same drawing could be recreated by "playing back" the record of calls. Windows provides a mechanism to handle this. Such a record is called a metafile.

Because Windows offers a fairly rich palette of drawing objects, metafiles can be used to store exceedingly complex graphics. Figure 4-13, for example, was stored as a Windows metafile. Windows metafiles have the extension WMF when they appear on disk.

A Windows metafile can be thought of as analogous to other sorts of drawing file formats, such as CDR or DXF files. In fact, this isn't a wholly flawless analogy—CDR files offer a far better range of drawing objects and facilities, and DXF files can define objects with vastly more precision than metafiles can. Because they're really intended to define drawing on a Windows display, metafiles are relatively modest souls.

Figure 4-13

A Windows metafile.

Metafiles are also disturbingly large when they're asked to contain complex graphics like the one in Fig. 4-13. The structure under which drawing calls are stored in a metafile isn't terribly efficient.

While there certainly are reasons for recording metafiles under Windows and then replaying them, a far more useful application for this facility is to create them in a drawing package. I used Corel Draw to generate and export the metafiles used in this chapter. You can create sophisticated graphics this way and have them appear in your applications.

Unlike a bitmap, metafiles are infinitely scaleable. This means that you could, for example, create a graphic which would adjust itself automatically to suit the size of the window it appears in—all without the scaling aberrations that appear if a bitmap is stretched to fit somewhere it doesn't really want to go.

Metafiles can be stored as elements in the resource list of an application, just like bitmaps.

The only potential catch to using metafiles this way is that Windows treats the output of a metafile being played back as it would any other

GDI calls. Specifically, if asked to draw in colors that don't exist in the palette currently selected into the HDC in question, Windows will dither. If you create drawing objects in Corel Draw and export them to WMF files, you must be careful to choose colors that will exist in the palette of the device context the metafiles will ultimately be played back into in order to avoid dithering.

Windows' screen dithering isn't particularly attractive when it appears in complex drawings.

As an aside, there are several flavors of Windows metafiles. In addition to the ones defined by Windows, Aldus created *placeable* metafiles for use with its PageMaker desktop publishing software. A placeable metafile contains a header before the metafile information telling PageMaker the dimensions of the rectangle the metafile should be rendered in to preserve its aspect ratio.

The Windows metafile functions won't deal with placeable metafiles correctly. If you're generating metafiles with a package like Corel Draw—which will optionally add the placeable header—make sure you have it create basic Windows metafiles, with the header disabled.

The Graphic Workshop for Windows package on the companion CD-ROM for this book will tell you whether a metafile is placeable or not through its Get Info function. The Comments field of its File Information dialog will specify the number of drawing objects in a nonplaceable file and will contain the phrase "Placeable metafile" otherwise.

The CLP files created by the Windows Clipboard application are also metafiles, or perhaps more correctly, they contain metafiles in a more complex structure. You can't use these as metafiles in the context of this chapter, however.

The DIBDEMO application

Figure 4-14 illustrates the main window of the DIBDEMO application. Like all really good demonstration software, this program does nothing of any practical use, but it does so in the most elegant way possible.

Figure 4-14

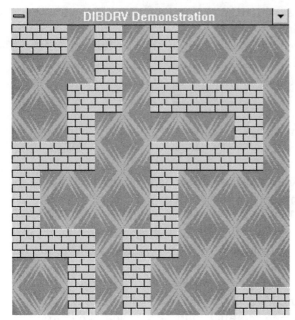

The DIBDEMO application.

The DIBDEMO program creates a large virtual landscape and allows you to pan over it. Click near the right edge of the display window to pan right, near the bottom edge to pan down, and so on. Double click in the system menu icon when the novelty of this begins to wear thin.

As you might imagine, based on the foregoing discussions of virtual device contexts and metafiles, the landscape image for DIBDEMO is created as a large bitmap, sections of which are painted to the display window of DIBDEMO as you pan around. What might be less than apparent is that the square tiles that form the landscape are actually metafiles. They were created in Corel Draw, exported as discrete WMF files, and stored as resource objects in DIBDEMO.EXE. The arrangement of tiles was defined as a matrix of indices into a list of metafile resources.

This approach to creating graphics like this one is agreeably flexible, although it can be a bit time-consuming for complex screens. There are those who would argue that this isn't an unreasonable situation—

one recent shareware game I encountered, for example, was averaging about 20 seconds per level to assemble its graphics. If the aliens to be killed are venomous enough, the phasor blasts lethal enough, and the opportunities for sudden, terrifying death awesome enough, most users will accept a bit of a wait before the green blood starts flowing.

Figure 4-15 illustrates the DIBDEMO.CPP source code. Figure 4-16 is its accompanying DIBDEMO.RC file. In addition to these, you'll need PRJ and DEF files, plus the requisite WAV, BMP, and WMF files for this application. All of these files can be found on the companion CD-ROM for this book. You'll also find a file called TILES.CDR, the original Corel Draw file I used to create the metafile tiles for this application, should you wish to meddle with them further.

The DIBDEMO.CPP source code.   Figure 4-15

```
/*
        DIBDRV Demonstration
        Copyright (c) 1994 Alchemy Mindworks Inc.
*/

#include <windows.h>
#include <stdio.h>
#include <bwcc.h>
#include <mmsystem.h>

#define say(s)      MessageBox(NULL,s,"Yo...",MB_OK | MB_ICONSTOP);
#define saynumber(f,s)    {char b[128]; sprintf((LPSTR)b,(LPSTR)f,s); \
                    MessageBox(NULL,b,"Debug Message",MB_OK | MB_ICONSTOP); \
                    }

#define DoMessage(hwnd,string) BWCCMessageBox(hwnd,string,"Message",\
                    MB_OK | MB_ICONINFORMATION)

#define STRINGSIZE      128              /* how big is a string? */

#define MAIN_ABOUT      102
#define MAIN_EXIT       199

#define RGB_RED         0
#define RGB_GREEN       1
#define RGB_BLUE        2
#define RGB_SIZE        3

#define MAXTILES        9

#define TILEWIDE        32
#define TILEDEEP        32
```

Figure 4-15 *Continued.*

```
#define MATRIXWIDE          20
#define MATRIXDEEP          20

#define SCENEWIDE           (TILEWIDE*MATRIXWIDE)
#define SCENEDEEP           (TILEDEEP*MATRIXDEEP)
#define SCENEBITS           4

#define WINDOWWIDE          (SCENEWIDE/2)
#define WINDOWDEEP          (SCENEDEEP/2)

#ifndef max
#define max(a,b)            (((a)>(b))?(a):(b))
#endif
#ifndef min
#define min(a,b)            (((a)<(b))?(a):(b))
#endif

/* prototypes */
DWORD FAR PASCAL SelectProc(HWND hwnd,WORD message,WORD wParam,LONG lParam);
DWORD FAR PASCAL AboutDlgProc(HWND hwnd,WORD message,WORD wParam,LONG lParam);

GLOBALHANDLE RasterizeMetafile();
HANDLE CreateDib(int dx,int dy,LPSTR palette,int bits);

void lmemset(LPSTR s,int n,unsigned int size);
void CentreWindow(HWND hwnd);
void FreeAllTiles();

unsigned int lmemcpy(LPSTR dest,LPSTR source,unsigned int n);

int DrawDIB(HWND hwnd,HDC hdc,WORD x,WORD y,HBITMAP hBitmap);
int LoadAllTiles();

/* globals */
char matrix[MATRIXDEEP][MATRIXWIDE]= {
        6,4,6,6,6,6,6,6,6,6,6,6,6,6,6,6,6,6,6,6,
        6,4,4,4,2,3,2,4,2,3,2,3,2,3,2,3,2,3,2,6,
        6,1,0,4,0,4,4,4,0,1,0,1,4,4,4,4,4,0,0,6,
        6,3,2,4,2,4,2,4,2,4,4,4,4,7,2,3,2,4,2,6,
        6,1,0,4,4,4,0,4,0,4,0,1,0,1,0,1,0,4,0,6,
        6,3,2,3,2,3,2,4,2,4,2,3,2,3,4,4,2,4,2,6,
        6,1,0,1,0,1,4,4,0,4,4,4,4,1,4,4,4,4,5,6,
        6,3,2,3,2,3,4,3,2,3,2,3,4,3,4,3,2,3,4,6,
        6,1,0,1,4,4,4,1,0,4,4,4,4,1,4,1,0,1,4,6,
        6,3,2,3,4,3,2,3,2,4,2,3,2,3,4,3,2,3,4,6,
        6,1,0,4,4,1,0,1,0,4,0,1,0,1,4,4,4,4,4,6,
        6,3,2,3,4,4,4,3,4,4,2,3,2,3,2,3,2,4,4,6,
        6,1,0,1,0,1,4,1,4,1,0,1,0,1,0,1,0,4,4,6,
        6,3,2,3,2,3,4,3,4,3,2,3,4,4,4,4,2,4,4,6,
        6,1,4,4,4,4,4,1,4,1,0,1,4,1,0,4,4,4,4,6,
        6,3,4,3,2,3,2,3,4,3,2,3,4,3,2,3,2,3,4,6,
```

```
                6,1,4,1,0,4,4,4,4,1,0,1,4,1,4,4,4,4,4,6,
                6,3,4,4,4,4,2,3,2,3,2,3,4,3,4,3,2,3,4,6,
                6,1,0,8,0,1,0,1,0,1,0,1,4,4,4,1,0,1,4,6,
                6,6,6,6,6,6,6,6,6,6,6,6,6,6,6,6,6,4,6,
                };

char palette[48]= {
                0x00,0x00,0x00,0x80,0x00,0x00,
                0x00,0x80,0x00,0x80,0x80,0x00,
                0x00,0x00,0x80,0x80,0x00,0x80,
                0x00,0x80,0x80,0x80,0x80,0x80,
                0xC0,0xC0,0xC0,0xFF,0x00,0x00,
                0x00,0xFF,0x00,0xFF,0xFF,0x00,
                0x00,0x00,0xFF,0xFF,0x00,0xFF,
                0x00,0xFF,0xFF,0xFF,0xFF,0xFF
                };

char szAppName[] = "DIBDRVDemo";
HANDLE hInst;

HANDLE tile[MAXTILES];

#pragma warn -par
int PASCAL WinMain(HANDLE hInstance,HANDLE hPrevInstance,
                LPSTR lpszCmdParam,int nCmdShow)
{
        FARPROC dlgProc;
        int r=0;

        BWCCGetVersion();

        hInst=hInstance;

        dlgProc=MakeProcInstance((FARPROC)SelectProc,hInst);
        r=DialogBox(hInst,"MainScreen",NULL,dlgProc);

        FreeProcInstance(dlgProc);

        return(r);
}

DWORD FAR PASCAL SelectProc(HWND hwnd,WORD message,WORD wParam,LONG lParam)
{
        PAINTSTRUCT ps;
        static HICON hIcon;
        static GLOBALHANDLE hdib;
        static HBITMAP hBitmap;
        LPBITMAPINFOHEADER lpbi;
        static unsigned int x,y;
        FARPROC lpfnDlgProc;
        RECT rect;
        HDC hdc;
        HMENU hmenu;
```

Figure 4-15 *Continued.*

```
LPSTR p;
unsigned int mx,my,xlimit,ylimit;

switch(message) {
        case WM_SYSCOMMAND:
                switch(wParam & 0xfff0) {
                        case SC_CLOSE:
                                SendMessage(hwnd,WM_COMMAND,MAIN_EXIT,0L);
                                break;
                }
                switch(wParam) {
                        case MAIN_ABOUT:
                                if((lpfnDlgProc=MakeProcInstance((FARPROC)
                                    AboutDlgProc,hInst)) != NULL) {
                                        DialogBox(hInst,"AboutBox",
                                            hwnd,lpfnDlgProc);
                                        FreeProcInstance(lpfnDlgProc);
                                }
                                break;
                }
                break;
        case WM_INITDIALOG:
                hdib=hBitmap=NULL;

                hIcon=LoadIcon(hInst,szAppName);
                SetClassWord(hwnd,GCW_HICON,(WORD)hIcon);
                CentreWindow(hwnd);

                hmenu=GetSystemMenu(hwnd,FALSE);
                AppendMenu(hmenu,MF_STRING,MAIN_ABOUT,"About");

                if(!LoadAllTiles()) {
                        DoMessage(hwnd,"Error loading tiles");
                        PostMessage(hwnd,WM_COMMAND,MAIN_EXIT,0L);
                }

                if((hdib=RasterizeMetafile())==NULL) {
                        DoMessage(hwnd,"Error creating scene");
                        PostMessage(hwnd,WM_COMMAND,MAIN_EXIT,0L);
                }

                hdc=GetDC(hwnd);

                if((lpbi=(LPBITMAPINFOHEADER)GlobalLock(hdib)) != NULL) {

                        p=(LPSTR)lpbi+sizeof(BITMAPINFOHEADER)+
                            (1<<lpbi->biBitCount)*sizeof(RGBQUAD);

                        hBitmap=CreateDIBitmap(hdc,lpbi,CBM_INIT,p,
                            (LPBITMAPINFO)lpbi,DIB_RGB_COLORS);
```

```
                                GlobalUnlock(hdib);
                }
                else {
                        DoMessage(hwnd,"Error creating bitmap");
                        PostMessage(hwnd,WM_COMMAND,MAIN_EXIT,0L);
                }

                ReleaseDC(hwnd,hdc);

                SetWindowPos(hwnd,NULL,0,0,WINDOWWIDE,
                    WINDOWDEEP+GetSystemMetrics(SM_CYCAPTION),SWP_NOMOVE);
                CentreWindow(hwnd);

                x=y=0;
                break;
        case WM_LBUTTONDOWN:
                GetClientRect(hwnd,&rect);
                xlimit=(rect.right-rect.left)/TILEWIDE;
                ylimit=(rect.bottom-rect.top)/TILEDEEP;

                mx=LOWORD(lParam)/TILEWIDE;
                my=HIWORD(lParam)/TILEDEEP;

                if(mx < (xlimit/4)) {
                        if(x > 0)—x;
                        InvalidateRect(hwnd,NULL,FALSE);
                }
                else if(mx > ((xlimit*3)/4)) {
                        if(x <= xlimit) ++x;
                        InvalidateRect(hwnd,NULL,FALSE);
                }

                if(my < (ylimit/2)) {
                        if(y > 0)—y;
                        InvalidateRect(hwnd,NULL,FALSE);
                }
                else if(my > ((ylimit*3)/4)) {
                        if(y <= ylimit) ++y;
                        InvalidateRect(hwnd,NULL,FALSE);
                }
                break;
        case WM_SIZE:
                InvalidateRect(hwnd,NULL,TRUE);
                break;
        case WM_PAINT:
                hdc=BeginPaint(hwnd,&ps);
                DrawDIB(hwnd,hdc,x*TILEWIDE,y*TILEDEEP,hBitmap);
                EndPaint(hwnd,&ps);
                break;
        case WM_COMMAND:
                switch(wParam) {
                        case MAIN_EXIT:
                                FreeAllTiles();
```

Figure 4-15 *Continued.*

```
                                              if(hdib != NULL) GlobalFree(hdib);
                                              if(hBitmap != NULL) DeleteObject(hBitmap);
                                              FreeResource(hIcon);
                                              PostQuitMessage(0);
                                              break;
                            }
                            break;

              }

              return(FALSE);
}

DWORD FAR PASCAL AboutDlgProc(HWND hwnd,WORD message,WORD wParam,LONG lParam)
{
              static HANDLE sound;
              static LPSTR psound;
              HANDLE handle;
              POINT point;

              switch(message) {
                    case WM_INITDIALOG:
                            if((handle=FindResource(hInst,"AboutWave",
                                RT_RCDATA)) != NULL) {
                                    if((sound=LoadResource(hInst,handle)) != NULL) {
                                              if((psound=LockResource(sound)) != NULL)
                                                    sndPlaySound(psound,SND_ASYNC |
                                                          SND_MEMORY | SND_NOSTOP);
                                    }
                            }
                            CentreWindow(hwnd);
                            return(FALSE);
                    case WM_CTLCOLOR:
                            if(HIWORD(lParam)==CTLCOLOR_STATIC ||
                                HIWORD(lParam)==CTLCOLOR_DLG) {
                                    SetBkColor(wParam,RGB(192,192,192));
                                    SetTextColor(wParam,RGB(0,0,0));

                                    ClientToScreen(hwnd,&point);
                                    UnrealizeObject(GetStockObject(LTGRAY_BRUSH));
                                    SetBrushOrg(wParam,point.x,point.y);

                                    return((DWORD)GetStockObject(LTGRAY_BRUSH));

                            }
                            if(HIWORD(lParam)==CTLCOLOR_BTN) {
                                    SetBkColor(wParam,RGB(192,192,192));
                                    SetTextColor(wParam,RGB(0,0,0));

                                    ClientToScreen(hwnd,&point);
                                    UnrealizeObject(GetStockObject(BLACK_BRUSH));
                                    SetBrushOrg(wParam,point.x,point.y);
```

```
                                return((DWORD)GetStockObject(BLACK_BRUSH));
                        }
                        break;
                case WM_COMMAND:
                        switch(wParam) {
                                case IDOK:
                                        sndPlaySound(NULL,SND_SYNC);
                                        if(psound != NULL) UnlockResource(sound);
                                        if(sound != NULL) FreeResource(sound);
                                        EndDialog(hwnd,wParam);
                                        return(FALSE);
                                }
                                break;
                }

        return(FALSE);
}

void lmemset(LPSTR s,int n,unsigned int size)
{
        unsigned int i;

        for(i=0;i<size;++i) *s++=n;
}



void CentreWindow(HWND hwnd)
{
        RECT rect;
        unsigned int x,y;

        GetWindowRect(hwnd,&rect);
        x=(GetSystemMetrics(SM_CXSCREEN)-(rect.right-rect.left))/2;
        y=(GetSystemMetrics(SM_CYSCREEN)-(rect.bottom-rect.top))/2;
        SetWindowPos(hwnd,NULL,x,y,rect.right-rect.left,
            rect.bottom-rect.top,SWP_NOSIZE);
}

#define FreeAllObjects()            {          \
                                    if(lpbiNew != NULL) GlobalUnlock(hdib); \
                                    if(hdib != NULL) GlobalFree(hdib);\
                                    if(hdc != NULL) DeleteDC(hdc); \
                                    SetCursor(hSaveCursor);\
                                    }
GLOBALHANDLE RasterizeMetafile()
{
        HCURSOR hSaveCursor,hHourGlass;
        LPBITMAPINFOHEADER lpbiNew=NULL;
        GLOBALHANDLE hdib;
        HDC hdc=NULL;
        HBRUSH oldbrush;
        HPEN oldpen;
        unsigned int i,j;
```

Figure 4-15 *Continued.*

```
                    hHourGlass=LoadCursor(NULL,IDC_WAIT);
                    hSaveCursor=SetCursor(hHourGlass);

                    if((hdib=CreateDib(SCENEWIDE,SCENEDEEP,palette,SCENEBITS))==NULL) {
                            FreeAllObjects();
                            return(NULL);
                    }

                    if((lpbiNew=(LPBITMAPINFOHEADER)GlobalLock(hdib))==NULL) {
                            FreeAllObjects();
                            return(NULL);
                    }

                    if((hdc=CreateDC("DIB",NULL,NULL,(LPSTR)lpbiNew))==NULL) {
                            FreeAllObjects();
                            return(NULL);
                    }

                    SetMapMode(hdc,MM_ANISOTROPIC);
                    SetWindowExt(hdc,SCENEWIDE,SCENEDEEP);
                    SetViewportExt(hdc,SCENEWIDE,SCENEDEEP);

                    oldpen=SelectObject(hdc,GetStockObject(NULL_PEN));
                    oldbrush=SelectObject(hdc,GetStockObject(LTGRAY_BRUSH));
                    Rectangle(hdc,0,0,SCENEWIDE+1,SCENEDEEP+1);
                    SelectObject(hdc,oldbrush);
                    SelectObject(hdc,oldpen);


                    for(i=0;i<MATRIXDEEP;++i) {
                            for(j=0;j<MATRIXWIDE;++j) {
                                    SaveDC(hdc);
                                    SetViewportOrg(hdc,j*TILEWIDE,i*TILEDEEP);
                                    SetWindowExt(hdc,TILEWIDE,TILEDEEP);
                                    SetViewportExt(hdc,TILEWIDE,TILEDEEP);

                                    if(!PlayMetaFile(hdc,tile[matrix[i][j]])) {
                                            FreeAllObjects();
                                            return(NULL);
                                    }
                                    RestoreDC(hdc,-1);
                            }
                    }

                    DeleteDC(hdc);

                    GlobalUnlock(hdib);
                    SetCursor(hSaveCursor);
                    return(hdib);
            }
            #undef FreeAllObjects()
```

```
#define WIDTHBYTES(i)    ((i+31)/32*4)
HANDLE CreateDib(int dx,int dy,LPSTR palette,int bits)
{
        HANDLE hdibN;
        BITMAPINFOHEADER bi;
        LPBITMAPINFOHEADER lpbi;
        RGBQUAD FAR *pRgb;
        int i;

        bi.biSize           = sizeof(BITMAPINFOHEADER);
        bi.biPlanes         = 1;
        bi.biBitCount       = bits;
        bi.biWidth          = (long)dx;
        bi.biHeight         = (long)dy;
        bi.biCompression    = BI_RGB;
        bi.biSizeImage      = 0;
        bi.biXPelsPerMeter  = 0;
        bi.biYPelsPerMeter  = 0;
        bi.biClrUsed        = 1<<bits;
        bi.biClrImportant   = 0;

        bi.biSizeImage=WIDTHBYTES(bi.biWidth*bi.biBitCount)*(long)dy;

        if((hdibN=GlobalAlloc(GMEM_MOVEABLE,sizeof(BITMAPINFOHEADER) +
                + (long)bi.biClrUsed * sizeof(RGBQUAD) + bi.biSizeImage))==NULL)
                    return(NULL);

        if((lpbi=(LPBITMAPINFOHEADER)GlobalLock(hdibN)) == NULL) {
                GlobalFree(hdibN);
                return(NULL);
        }

        lmemcpy((LPSTR)lpbi,(LPSTR)&bi,sizeof(BITMAPINFOHEADER));

        pRgb = (RGBQUAD FAR *)((LPSTR)lpbi+(unsigned int)lpbi->biSize);

        for(i=0;i<bi.biClrUsed;++i) {
                pRgb[i].rgbRed=palette[i*RGB_SIZE+RGB_RED];
                pRgb[i].rgbGreen=palette[i*RGB_SIZE+RGB_GREEN];
                pRgb[i].rgbBlue=palette[i*RGB_SIZE+RGB_BLUE];
                pRgb[i].rgbReserved=0;
        }

        GlobalUnlock(hdibN);
        return(hdibN);
}

unsigned int lmemcpy(LPSTR dest,LPSTR source,unsigned int n)
{
        unsigned int i;

        for(i=0;i<n;++i) dest[i]=source[i];
}
```

Figure 4-15 *Continued.*

```
int DrawDIB(HWND hwnd,HDC hdc,WORD x,WORD y,HBITMAP hBitmap)
{
        HCURSOR hSaveCursor,hHourGlass;
        HDC hMemoryDC;
        HBITMAP hOldBitmap;
        int r=FALSE;

        hHourGlass=LoadCursor(NULL,IDC_WAIT);
        hSaveCursor=SetCursor(hHourGlass);

        if((hMemoryDC=CreateCompatibleDC(hdc)) != NULL) {
                hOldBitmap=SelectObject(hMemoryDC,hBitmap);
                if(hOldBitmap) {
                        BitBlt(hdc,0,0,SCENEWIDE,SCENEDEEP,hMemoryDC,x,y,SRCCOPY);
                        SelectObject(hMemoryDC,hOldBitmap);
                        r=TRUE;
                }
                DeleteDC(hMemoryDC);
        }

        SetCursor(hSaveCursor);
        return(r);
}

int LoadAllTiles()
{
        int i,r=TRUE;
        char b[STRINGSIZE+1];

        for(i=0;i<MAXTILES;++i) {
                wsprintf(b,"Tile%u",i);
                tile[i]=LoadResource(hInst,FindResource(hInst,b,RT_RCDATA));
                if(tile[i]==NULL) r=FALSE;
        }
        return(r);
}

void FreeAllTiles()
{
        int i;

        for(i=0;i<MAXTILES;++i) {
                if(tile[i] != NULL) FreeResource(tile[i]);
        }
}
```

The DIBDEMO.RC resource script.

Figure 4-16

```
MainScreen DIALOG 12, 24, 184, 184
STYLE WS_POPUP | WS_CAPTION | WS_SYSMENU | WS_MINIMIZEBOX
CAPTION "DIBDRV Demonstration"
BEGIN
END


AboutBox DIALOG 18, 18, 184, 180
STYLE WS_POPUP | WS_CAPTION
CAPTION "About..."
BEGIN
        CONTROL "", 102, "BorShade", BSS_GROUP | WS_CHILD | WS_VISIBLE | WS_TABSTOP,
            8, 68, 168, 76
        CTEXT "DIBDRV Demonstration 1.0\n\nCopyright (c) 1994 Alchemy Mindworks Inc.\n\n
            This program is part of the book Advanced Multimedia Programming for
            Windows by Steven William Rimmer, published by Windcrest/McGraw Hill.",
            -1, 12, 72, 160, 68 WS_CHILD | WS_VISIBLE | WS_GROUP
        CONTROL "Button", IDOK, "BorBtn", BS_DEFPUSHBUTTON | WS_CHILD | WS_VISIBLE |
            WS_TABSTOP, 74, 152, 32, 20
        CONTROL "Button", 801, "BorBtn", BS_PUSHBUTTON | WS_CHILD | WS_VISIBLE |
            WS_TABSTOP, 36, 8, 32, 20
END

1801 BITMAP "smpw.bmp"

AboutWave RCDATA "ABOUT.WAV"

Tile0 RCDATA "tile0000.wmf"
Tile1 RCDATA "tile0001.wmf"
Tile2 RCDATA "tile0002.wmf"
Tile3 RCDATA "tile0003.wmf"
Tile4 RCDATA "tile0004.wmf"
Tile5 RCDATA "tile0005.wmf"
Tile6 RCDATA "tile0006.wmf"
Tile7 RCDATA "tile0007.wmf"
Tile8 RCDATA "tile0008.wmf"

DIBDemo ICON
BEGIN
        '00 00 01 00 01 00 20 20 10 00 00 00 00 00 E8 02'
        '00 00 16 00 00 00 28 00 00 00 20 00 00 00 40 00'
        '00 00 01 00 04 00 00 00 00 00 80 02 00 00 00 00'
        '00 00 00 00 00 00 10 00 00 00 00 00 00 00 00 00'
        '00 00 00 00 BF 00 00 BF 00 00 00 BF BF 00 BF 00'
        '00 00 BF 00 BF 00 BF BF 00 00 C0 C0 C0 00 80 80'
        '80 00 00 00 FF 00 00 FF 00 00 00 FF FF 00 FF 00'
        '00 00 FF 00 FF 00 FF FF 00 00 FF FF FF 00 77 77'
        '77 77 77 77 77 77 77 77 77 77 77 77 77 77 7F 88'
        '88 88 88 88 88 88 88 88 88 88 88 88 87 7F F8'
        '88 88 88 88 88 88 88 88 88 88 88 88 87 7F F7'
        '77 77 77 77 77 77 77 77 77 77 77 77 78 87 7F F7'
```

Figure 4-16 *Continued.*

```
'77 77 77 77 77 77 77 77 77 77 77 77 78 87 7F F7'
'77 77 77 77 77 77 77 77 77 77 77 77 78 87 7F F7'
'77 77 77 77 77 77 77 77 77 77 77 77 78 87 7F F7'
'77 77 70 00 07 77 77 77 77 77 77 77 78 87 7F F7'
'77 70 99 99 00 07 77 77 77 77 77 77 78 87 7F F7'
'77 99 99 99 99 00 77 77 77 77 77 77 78 87 7F F7'
'79 99 99 99 99 90 77 77 77 77 77 77 78 87 7F F7'
'79 99 99 99 99 90 07 77 77 77 77 77 78 87 7F F7'
'99 99 99 99 99 99 07 77 77 77 77 77 78 87 7F F7'
'99 99 99 99 99 99 07 77 77 77 77 77 78 87 7F F7'
'99 99 99 99 99 99 07 77 77 77 77 77 78 87 7F F7'
'99 9F 99 99 99 99 07 77 70 77 77 77 78 87 7F F7'
'99 F9 F9 99 99 99 77 77 90 77 07 77 78 87 7F F7'
'79 9F 9F 99 99 90 77 77 90 79 07 70 08 87 7F F7'
'77 99 F9 99 99 97 77 77 B7 09 70 99 78 87 7F F7'
'77 79 99 99 97 77 77 77 0B B0 BB 77 78 87 7F F7'
'77 77 11 11 07 77 77 09 9B B7 70 07 78 87 7F F7'
'77 77 11 11 77 77 79 97 70 77 BB 77 78 87 7F F7'
'77 77 77 90 77 77 70 99 77 B7 7B 70 77 78 87 7F F7'
'77 77 77 97 00 99 77 7B 77 B0 B7 07 78 87 7F F7'
'77 77 77 79 99 97 77 97 77 90 79 90 78 87 7F F7'
'77 77 77 77 77 77 79 77 77 97 77 C7 78 87 7F F7'
'77 77 77 77 77 77 77 77 77 77 77 77 78 87 7F F7'
'77 77 77 77 77 77 77 77 77 77 77 77 78 87 7F F7'
'77 77 77 77 77 77 77 77 77 77 77 77 78 87 7F FF'
'FF FF FF FF FF FF FF FF FF FF FF FF F8 87 7F FF'
'FF FF FF FF FF FF FF FF FF FF FF FF FF 87 77 77'
'77 77 77 77 77 77 77 77 77 77 77 77 77 77 00 00'
'00 00 00 00 00 00 00 00 00 00 00 00 00 00 00 00'
'00 00 00 00 00 00 00 00 00 00 00 00 00 00 00 00'
'00 00 00 00 00 00 00 00 00 00 00 00 00 00 00 00'
'00 00 00 00 00 00 00 00 00 00 00 00 00 00 00 00'
'00 00 00 00 00 00 00 00 00 00 00 00 00 00 00 00'
'00 00 00 00 00 00 00 00 00 00 00 00 00 00 00 00'
'00 00 00 00 00 00 00 00 00 00 00 00 00 00 00 00'
'00 00 00 00 00 00 00 00 00 00 00 00 00 00 00'
END
```

The structure of DIBDEMO is superficially like that of the BMP-FX application in the first half of this chapter. The interesting elements of DIBDEMO.CPP are the functions that deal with creating a synthetic device context and then filling it with metafile graphics.

Figure 4-17 illustrates the tiles used to create the landscape graphic for DIBDEMO, and the complete graphic that the application pans over. Mind the camels and time bombs.

Figure 4-17

 Tile 0

 Tile 1

 Tile 2

 Tile 3

 Tile 4

The tiles used to create DIBDEMO.

 Tile 5

 Tile 6

 Tile 7

 Tile 8

If you look at the top of DIBDEMO.CPP, you'll find an object called matrix. This is an array of numbers corresponding to the tiles found in Fig. 4-17. In creating the large landscape bitmap, DIBDEMO will actually generate a bitmap divided into grid elements and place a tile corresponding to the number in each element of matrix in a grid square of the bitmap. Among other things, this makes changing the landscape graphic fairly effortless—all you need do is change the numbers. In more complex applications of this technique, you'd probably want to write a matrix editor of some sort—it's a bit hard to visualize a graphic by looking at a matrix of integers.

Note that the bitmap created by DIBDEMO is based on the Windows reserved color palette. Because this palette is automatically selected into any display context unless you explicitly select a different one, it's not necessary to realize the bitmap palette when the graphic is painted on your screen. However, this means that you can't draw with any colors in the metafiles used to create the bitmap that don't exist in the Windows reserved palette, unless you're prepared to have them dithered.

The first important element of DIBDEMO.CPP is the call to LoadAllTiles in the WM_INITDIALOG handler of SelectProc. As you might expect, this fetches the metafile tile objects from the resource list of DIBDEMO.EXE. You'll find the declaration for LoadAllTiles near the bottom of DIBDEMO.CPP. In fact, all it really does is call LoadResource once for each tile in the list and assign the resource handle it returns to an element of the array tile.

The Windows Software Development Kit documentation speaks of metafile handles as some sort of unique entity. In fact, they're just handles to a list of drawing instructions stored in a global buffer.

Having loaded all the tiles back in SelectProc, the RasterizeMetafile function is called to actually generate a large bitmap of the landscape. It begins by calling CreateDib, also defined in DIBDEMO.CPP, which creates a device-independent bitmap of specific dimensions suitable for use with CreateDC, as discussed earlier in this section. The return value of CreateDib is a handle to a bitmap, rather than a pointer. It must be locked before it can be used.

While it's not actually necessary in this application—as tiles will be used to cover the entire area of the bitmap used by the synthetic device context—you should initialize the bitmap originally passed to CreateDC to a suitable background color. The easiest way to do this is to select a brush of the background color you'd like to use into the HDC returned by CreateDC, and then call Rectangle to paint the entire area of the virtual display with it. That's what RasterizeMetafile does after it calls CreateDC.

The for loop in RasterizeMetafile steps through each of the elements in matrix and places the appropriate tile in the synthetic device context. Drawing a metafile in a device context is dead easy— Windows provides the PlayMetaFile function to handle it. PlayMetaFile will draw a metafile to fill the display in question by default—the SetViewportOrg, SetWindowExt, and SetViewportExt calls serve to lie to it, making PlayMetaFile think that the synthetic window it's drawing in has the dimensions of one tile and the location specified by the current matrix position.

In a real-world implementation of this technique, you could speed up the generation of the landscape bitmap by creating one small bitmap for each tile in the tile array, calling PlayMetaFile once to draw each metafile in its corresponding tile and then painting the small tile bitmaps into the larger landscape bitmap.

Note the use of the FreeAllObjects macro in RasterizeMetafile. In many complex functions it's necessary to keep track of a number of allocated objects that must subsequently be freed or destroyed before the function terminates. You can do this by simply nesting all the conditional function calls, but this usually results in the working part of a function like RasterizeMetafile resting 10 columns beyond the right edge of your screen.

Creating a temporary macro to free all the allocated objects provides a convenient way around this problem. If you find you have to add a new object to your function, you can add the code to delete it to the macro, rather than having to add it to each condition under which the function might terminate prematurely. This is a wonderful time saver, as well as a way to eliminate whole phyla of bugs.

The rest of DIBDEMO is pretty unadventurous. It calls the DrawDIB function from the WM_PAINT handler of electProc to paint the landscape bitmap in the DIBDEMO main window. The DrawDIB function is an implementation of the BitBlt function discussed at length earlier in this chapter. This is an application for which a reasonable argument could be made for using BitBlt or SetDIBitsToDevice. The former makes the changes to the display appear instantly, but there's a brief pause for BitBlt internal housekeeping after each update.

In fact, in a more sophisticated display system, you'd probably want to use BitBlt to move the existing screen contents around and only repaint a strip of the image to display the area panned onto.

The WM_LBUTTONDOWN handler in SelectProc takes care of calculating the new area of the landscape bitmap to be displayed when a mouse click occurs in the display window.

 # Animation
—the undiscovered country

The main drawback to the graphics discussed in this chapter is that they're all static. While still pictures have their places in multimedia applications, having things move is a lot more interesting. In the next chapter we'll look at animation under Windows. This is not a matter to be trifled with—Windows does not include a workable animation protocol, and anything that moves in a Windows application must do so under its own steam.

I suspect that Windows was not amusing to write, and as a result its creators were not disposed to make it amusing to use.

Animation, joysticks, & screen savers

C H A P T E R 5

"Choose the right costume and the part will play itself."
—Graffiti

MAKING graphics move is considerably more involved than simply making them appear. While some of the special effects in Chapter 4 might qualify as animation, they represent animation at its tamest and least diabolical. Real-time animation, in which figures actually move about in a window, is considerably more involved.

If you could spend a year devising a user interface and application environment specifically designed to make animation singularly awkward to implement, it would probably wind up looking a lot like Windows.

There are a number of elements that gang up on a Windows application seeking to make its graphics move. To begin with, even the relatively fast Windows bitmapped functions, such as BitBlt, are only fast in a relative sense. Fairly sloppy dedicated code under DOS can easily outperform anything BitBlt can manage on its best day—by several warp factors. The price of Windows' device-independence is a pretty thick layer of padding between your application and the inner surface of your monitor. Simple graphic operations require a substantial amount of time to perform.

In addition to this, there are some functions you simply can't do, or can't do in an elegant way, because Windows does not allow you direct access to a device surface. Software authors who write animated games and other graphic applications to run under DOS have infinitely more control over the display hardware of the systems their software will run on than do those who create Windows software.

Despite all these potential restrictions, Windows animation is possible. A very simple example is presented in the companion volume to this one, *Multimedia Programming for Windows*. We'll look at two somewhat more sophisticated applications of animation in this chapter.

In addition to the actual mechanics of handling animation, this chapter will deal with two somewhat more specialized bits of

multimedia: interfacing to a joystick and creating a screen saver. The latter has become a high art form in some circles.

⇨ Beach ball in cheap sunglasses

Figure 5-1 illustrates a fairly typical street scene from the sort of alternate virtual reality universe that seems to be popular in science fiction novels at the moment. This is, of course, a beach ball wearing cheap sunglasses.

The graphic illustrated in Fig. 5-1 is actually the main window of the first of two applications discussed in this chapter. Once again, in the grand tradition of demonstration software, it doesn't do much of anything. The bespectacled beach ball will dart about the window it finds itself in based on movements of a joystick. However, before it can so much as show itself, it must come to terms with the basic elements of animation under Windows.

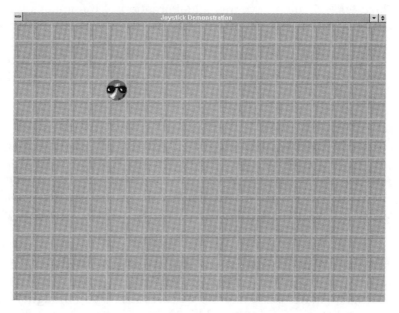

Figure 5-1

A beach ball in cheap sunglasses—the JOYDEMO application.

Animation predates computers, of course. Conventional paper animation is often referred to as Disney animation, after Walt Disney, who more or less created it. In fact, animation existed in still earlier forms as nickelodeons, for example, but these were more like novelties rather than a real application of the technique. It might well be argued that later practitioners of the art form introduced more content than Walt managed in most of his films—it's difficult to become wholly captivated by a three-fingered mouse with a speech problem.

In its simplest form, Disney animation synthesizes the individual frames of motion picture film with individual drawings. Objects appear to move in an animated film for the same reason they appear to move in a conventional real-life film.

Computer animation works in somewhat the same way, although with different constraints than film animation. The reality of film animation is that while it might take Mickey Mouse 15 seconds to walk across the screen or Wiley Coyote a small fraction of this time to blow his face off . . . again . . ., the actual creation of the images that make animated films work can represent weeks of drawing. However, because each frame of the film is exposed individually—and the camera involved doesn't care whether its operator takes a coffee break between frames—the whole image comes off in real time even if it couldn't possibly be created that way.

In reality, most film animation doesn't involve drawing an entire cell for each frame of the final film. Rather, a background image is drawn on paper and then the characters that move are drawn on acetate. As such, the background need only be drawn once. This is fairly easy to see in some animated films, such as Ralph Bakshi's *Cool World*, in which the backgrounds are a montage of graphics, rather than simple drawings.

Now available on video tape, *Cool World* is a worthwhile study in animation techniques. It's also a splendid example of the notion that not all animated films have to be cartoons. If you thought *Who Framed Roger Rabbit?* would have been better without the rabbit, you'll certainly enjoy it.

Real-time computer animation doesn't have the same luxury of time that film animation does. Although it can involve graphics that require quite a while to create, they must be realized as they're viewed. This is analogous to an animation camera operator shooting film in real time at 24 frames a second—you have to drink a great deal of coffee to be able to keep this up all day.

In real-time computer animation, it's necessary to paint bitmaps on your screen at a rate sufficient to make it look like the objects in question are moving, rather than being updated in discrete steps. As you'll probably have noticed in the graphic applications covered in previous chapters, larger bitmaps require more time to paint in a window than smaller ones do.

The running dog application in *Multimedia Programming for Windows* is a very simple illustration of cell animation in a Windows application. It gets away with using relatively large cells, too, because it succeeds in ignoring most of the really unpleasant elements of creating animated graphics in a window. As illustrated in Fig. 5-2, the image consists of a black and white line drawing against a white background.

Figure 5-2

The running dog demo from Multimedia Programming for Windows, *a simple example of animation.*

Animation on a computer consists of displaying one cell of the animated sequence, erasing it with the former background contents, and then displaying the next cell. In the case of the running dog, this is fairly easy, because the background can be counted on to be consistently white. Erasing the background only involved painting a white rectangle over the previously drawn cell.

The beach ball in cheap sunglasses graphic in Fig. 5-1 has been deliberately created to make the problem of animation rather more difficult. The background is not solid, and as such can't be replaced

by simple drawing. As the beach ball moves, the background where it's about to appear must be copied into a buffer, the beach ball drawn, and then the background copied from the buffer back to the screen when it's time for the ball to move again.

Actually, it's more complicated still. Like beach balls everywhere, this ball is spherical. Bitmaps are always rectangular. Simply painting the beach ball bitmap over the background would leave it inset in a black rectangle wherever it travelled—hardly a convincing application of animated graphics. What's called for here is a way to paint only part of a bitmap on your screen—the interesting bits must appear solid, and the rest transparent. The transparent portion in this case is the area outside the circle of the ball but inside the rectangle that encloses it.

Perhaps not surprisingly, Windows does not provide a function to achieve this directly. It doesn't really allow for transparent bitmaps per se, even though they do turn up in other contexts. There, as here, the effect of transparency must be created synthetically.

It must also be created very quickly if the animated beach ball is really to appear to be moving.

The animated beach ball graphic is actually two images. They're illustrated in Fig. 5-3. These two graphics are called a figure and a mask.

Figure 5-3

The figure and mask of the beach ball graphic.

The only reasonably fast function available to paint bitmaps in a window is BitBlt, as discussed in Chapter 4. While BitBlt can't paint transparent bitmaps, it can paint using a variety of bitwise operators. These—along with the two graphics in Fig. 5-3—can be used to achieve a sort of transparency.

Let's begin with the mask graphic. If this graphic is copied to the screen with BitBlt using the SRCCOPY operator that turned up in the previous chapter, it will appear just as it looks here. However, consider what will happen if it were to be copied using the SRCAND operator. This will cause the pixels in the destination device context—your screen—to be ANDed with the pixels in the source bitmap over the area of the source bitmap. The source bitmap consists of black areas and white areas, colors 0 and 15 respectively. These are 0000 and 1111 binary. ANDing 0000 with any other value will result in a value of 0000, as there are no bits common to both numbers. ANDing 1111 with any other number will result in whatever the other number is.

Copying the mask bitmap to the screen with the SRCAND operator will knock a black circle out of the background. The area beyond the circle but within its bounding rectangle won't be affected, because these pixels will have been ANDed with a value that won't alter any of their bits.

Turning to the figure graphic in Fig. 5-3, you can't just paint the figure onto the destination window. However, consider what would happen if it were painted with the SRCINVERT operator. This causes each pixel in the destination to be XORed with the pixels in the source bitmap. The XOR function will invert the bits in the destination value that have corresponding bits in the source value. The pixels outside the circle in the graphic are black, or 0000 binary. They have no bits set, and as such will have no effect on anything they're XORed with. The pixels inside the circle do have some bits set—they're a variety of colors. However, the corresponding pixels on the screen are all black, with no bits set, because they were all set that way when the mask was ANDed with them. Zero XORed with any value will become the value XORed with it.

Only the area inside the circle will be painted on the destination device.

This approach to painting transparent bitmaps is somewhat complex, requiring a mask and a figure for anything you want to display this way. It also imposes some meaningful restrictions on what you can animate.

Because it takes a measurable time to paint a bitmap to the screen—
and somewhat more time still to mask one and then paint it—
animated figures in a Windows application can't be very large.
Objects requiring bitmaps significantly bigger than the beach ball
graphic will exhibit noticeable flickering when they move, as the mask
and then the figure are repeatedly painted on your screen.

⇨ Animation functions

The code to handle the animation of small objects like the beach ball
is relatively simple—it uses a few obscure options of some of the GDI
calls. To begin with, we'll need a place to store the area behind the
animated graphic while it's visible. Here's the code to create a
temporary bitmap:

```
HDC hdc;
HBITMAP hback;

hdc=GetDC(hwnd);

if((hback=CreateCompatibleBitmap(hdc,ballwide,balldeep))==NULL) {
        /* there was a problem */
}

ReleaseDC(hwnd,hdc);
```

In this code fragment, the ballwide and balldeep values are assumed
to contain the dimensions of the bitmap to be animated. The bitmap
thus created will be in the same format as the virtual bitmap of your
screen. Such a bitmap is useless for anything other than storing
screen fragments, but that's all it will be called upon to do in this
application. Because the structure of the bitmap and that of your
screen will be the same, copying image information between them
can be handled fairly quickly.

To reduce the time required to draw one iteration of the animated
graphic, we will allocate this bitmap once and keep it around
thereafter, rather than allocating it and freeing it with each iteration
of the image.

Having created a place to store the divot behind the animated cell, we'll need a function to fetch the screen area in question into the background bitmap:

```
void GetBackground(HDC hdc,HDC hMemoryDC,
     HBITMAP hback,WORD xpos,WORD ypos)
{
     HBITMAP oldbitmap;

     if((oldbitmap=SelectObject(hMemoryDC,hback)) != NULL) {
          BitBlt(hMemoryDC,

                    0,
                    0,
                    ballwide,
                    balldeep,
                    hdc,
                    xpos,
                    ypos,
                    SRCCOPY);

          SelectObject(hMemoryDC,oldbitmap);
     }
}
```

The GetBackground function is an implementation of the BitBlt function. It copies from the screen to the hback bitmap.

The function to actually draw one cell is somewhat more complicated, as it must manage both the mask and the figure bitmaps:

```
void DrawCell(HDC hdc,HDC hMemoryDC,HBITMAP hball,
     HBITMAP hback,WORD xpos,WORD ypos)
{
     HBITMAP oldbitmap;

     if((oldbitmap=SelectObject(hMemoryDC,hmask)) != NULL) {
          BitBlt(hdc,
                    xpos,
                    ypos,
```

```
                ballwide,
                balldeep,
                hMemoryDC,
                0,
                0,
                SRCAND);
        SelectObject(hMemoryDC,oldbitmap);
    }

    if((oldbitmap=SelectObject(hMemoryDC,hball)) != NULL) {
        BitBlt(hdc,
                xpos,
                ypos,
                ballwide,
                balldeep,
                hMemoryDC,
                0,
                0,
                SRCINVERT);
        SelectObject(hMemoryDC,oldbitmap);
    }
}
```

Finally, once the ball has been drawn and is ready to move again, its former self must be erased. This really means that the screen divot previously fetched by GetBackground must be replaced:

```
void HideCell(HDC hdc,HDC hMemoryDC,
    HBITMAP hback,WORD xpos,WORD ypos)
{
        HBITMAP oldbitmap;

        if((oldbitmap=SelectObject(hMemoryDC,hback)) != NULL) {
            BitBlt(hdc,
                    xpos,
                    ypos,
                    ballwide,
                    balldeep,
                    hMemoryDC,
                    0,
```

```
                        0,
                        SRCCOPY);
            SelectObject(hMemoryDC,oldbitmap);
    }
}
```

The HideCell function copies the hback bitmap back to the screen, obscuring the cell that was previously painted with DrawCell.

Joysticks—the most suggestive peripheral

The origin of the word *joystick* isn't what you might think. A joystick was originally the control stick of an airplane, back when airplanes were made of wood and canvas and carried no onboard computers. The name has survived much longer than most of the planes, although out where we live biplanes can still be seen dotting the skies in the summer. The local farmers maintain they're required for dusting crops, but as most of these farmers grow sod, the assertion is a bit questionable.

Every Friday afternoon, from March until the snow flies, people swarm out of the city up north to cottage country. The roads become impassable with "lemmings." The sod farmers seem to pick the times of these migrations to venture into the skies. For the most part, they hang in the air above the larger highways and occasionally buzz the traffic.

Computer joysticks bear only a passing resemblance to the joysticks of biplanes—for one thing, the joysticks on planes don't have fire buttons, although I suspect that some of the sod farmers wish they did.

The Windows multimedia extensions include support for joysticks. The joystick interface is flexible, relatively easy to implement, and works with a surprising range of joystick hardware. The one I used to develop the sample joystick application in this chapter was made by Gravis.

233

Joysticks, like mice, represent a fairly nettlesome problem for software. It's impossible for an application to know when a joystick will move. Joystick movement—and banging on a joystick's fire buttons—are considered to be asynchronous events.

There are two ways to manage a joystick, and the multimedia joystick interface supports both. The most obvious is to poll the joystick—that is, to wait in a loop that periodically checks the joystick's status. Windows loathes this sort of thing, as it ties up a lot of processor time doing practically nothing.

A better joystick interface is one that is message driven. You can configure the Windows joystick interface to send a message to the window of your choice every time the joystick moves or a fire button is hit. This allows an application wanting to interface to a joystick to ignore its presence until something actually happens, respond to the joystick message, and then go back to doing something else.

Windows calls this approach *capturing* a joystick. Clearly, someone was thinking about computer games while all this was going together.

There is one potential catch in using the Windows joystick interface. It requires that a joystick driver be loaded before any communication with the joystick is undertaken. The usual driver for this is IBMJOY.DRV, which is included on the Windows Multimedia Development Kit CD-ROM. The driver package includes the driver itself and the JOYSTICK.CPL file.

To install the driver, copy IBMJOY.DRV to your \WINDOWS\SYSTEM directory and JOYSTICK.CPL to your \WINDOWS directory. Open your SYSTEM.INI file with the Windows Notepad application and locate the section headed [Drivers] . Add the following line:

```
joystick=ibmjoy.drv
```

Save the changes to SYSTEM.INI and restart Windows.

If you open the Windows Control Panel, you'll find a new applet icon, called Joystick. It's shown in Fig. 5-4. The Joystick Control Panel applet allows you to calibrate your joystick.

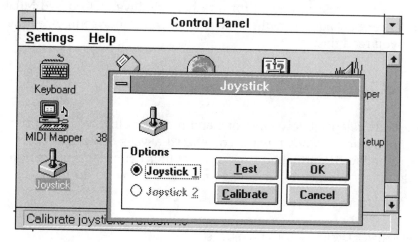

Figure 5-4

The Windows control panel with the Joystick applet installed.

The catch is that some versions of the IBMJOY.DRV driver don't work correctly with some joystick hardware. The problem manifests itself as the joystick telling your applications that it has only travelled half as far as it really has. This problem will persist until you open the Joystick applet in the Control Panel. The joystick will then behave correctly for the rest of your current Windows session.

If you encounter this problem, you should find a newer joystick driver, or one written specifically for your joystick.

Another bit of joystick lore you might not be aware of has to do with where the beast plugs in. Some systems have hardware joystick ports—if your computer is so equipped you need read no further. If you're lacking a joystick port, be aware that most sound cards include onboard joystick ports. They're brought off the card in a complex connector, which also provides access to the MIDI ports. Among the sound cards that handle the joystick port this way are the AdLib, SoundBlaster, and MediaMaster cards, and their clones.

235

To connect a joystick to the joystick port on a sound card, you'll need an adapter cable. The cable also provides MIDI connectors. I found such a cable as part of the SoundBlaster MIDI Kit, from Creative Labs. This is a somewhat expensive way to acquire it, however, because you are also paying for a rather primitive DOS-based MIDI sequencer package. It might be available from other sources by the time you read this.

The joystick interface

There are relatively few functions and messages involved in working with a joystick. To begin with, you should always make sure there's at least one joystick attached to your computer before an application that expects joystick input gets going. Here's how to do this:

```
WORD NumberOfJoysticks;

NumberOfJoysticks=joyGetNumDevs();
```

If the value returned by joyGetNumDevs is zero, no joysticks were found. Keep in mind that this result could also indicate a problem with IBMJOY.DRV.

Once you've determined that at least one joystick device is present in software, you can make sure there's a physical joystick connected to it like this:

```
JOYINFO joyinfo;

if(joyGetPos(JOYSTICKID1,&joyinfo)==JOYERR_UNPLUGGED) {
        /* the joystick isn't connected */
}
```

The joyGetPos function returns the current joystick position. Its first argument should be either JOYSTICKID1 or JOYSTICKID2—in most cases it will be the former, indicating the first joystick in the system. The JOYINFO object passed to the joyGetPos function looks like this:

```
typedef struct {
        WORD wXpos;
        WORD wYpos;
        WORD wZpos;
        WORD wButtons;
        } JOYINFO;
```

The first three elements in a JOYINFO object will be filled in with the location of the joystick at the time joyGetPos was called. The multimedia extensions support three-dimensional joysticks, should you think of an application for one. The wButtons element is a set of flags. You can test the button state by ANDing this value with the constants JOY_BUTTON1 through JOY_BUTTON4.

It's not a good idea to interface to a joystick by repeatedly calling joyGetPos in a loop. In most applications you'd use joySetCapture to direct joystick messages to a window message handler, like this:

```
joySetCapture(hwnd,JOYSTICKID1,JOYINTERVAL,FALSE);
```

The first argument to joySetCapture is the HWND window handle for the window to which the joystick messages are to be sent. The second is a joystick ID constant. The third is the frequency with which Windows is to check the status of the joystick, measured in milliseconds. The fourth argument is a flag—if it's set true, joystick messages will appear only if the joystick has moved by a predetermined amount since the last sample.

The joyReleaseCapture function will stop joystick messages being sent to a window. It should be called before the termination of an application called by joySetCapture.

The relevant messages generated by joystick activity are MM_JOY1MOVE and MM_JOY1BUTTONDOWN—the former will appear when the joystick has moved and the latter when the first button on the joystick has been hit. By convention, the first button is usually the fire button on the end of the joystick. There are separate messages for a second joystick and for the remaining buttons.

When an MM_JOY1MOVE message appears, its wParam argument will contain a set of flags to indicate which buttons, if any, are down. You can AND wParam with JOY_BUTTON1 through JOY_BUTTON4 to test the button states. The lParam argument will contain the current joystick position, with the horizontal coordinates in the low-order word and the vertical coordinates in the high-order word.

Joystick coordinates don't appear in a particularly useful form. They're based on the arbitrary matrix that the joystick moves in, which can be of any size. An application can determine the limits of the matrix by calling joyGetDevCaps. This function will fill in a JOYCAPS object, as follows:

```
typedef struct {
        UINT wMid;                      /* manufacturer ID */
        UINT wPid;                      /* product ID */
        char szPname[MAXPNAMELEN];      /* product name */
        UINT wXmin;                     /* minimum x position value */
        UINT wXmax;                     /* maximum x position value */
        UINT wYmin;                     /* minimum y position value */
        UINT wYmax;                     /* maximum y position value */
        UINT wZmin;                     /* minimum z position value */
        UINT wZmax;                     /* maximum z position value */
        UINT wNumButtons;               /* number of buttons */
        UINT wPeriodMin;                /* minimum message period */
        UINT wPeriodMax;                /* maximum message period */
        } JOYCAPS;
```

Not all of the information in a JOYCAPS object is particularly useful. However, you can use the minimum and maximum coordinate values to scale the joystick position values that turn up when an MM_JOY1MOVE message appears to suit your application.

IBMJOY.DRV usually works with a matrix that runs from 0 through 65,535 in both dimensions. In scaling these values, make sure you use unsigned integers, or very odd things will happen.

The JOYDEMO application

The window illustrated in Fig. 5-1 at the beginning of this chapter is the main screen of JOYDEMO, a Windows application designed to explore the multimedia joystick interface and to illustrate real-world animation under Windows. JOYDEMO draws a green background with a grid over it and then animates the oft-mentioned beach ball with sunglasses. Moving your joystick will move the beach ball. Hitting the fire button on your joystick will cause your sound card to make some noise. By convention, the sound generated by hitting the fire button on a joystick should be a phasor blast or an explosion— but I couldn't quite imagine a lethal beach ball. Consequently, this application makes a loud springing sound when you hit the fire button of your joystick.

Despite its not actually doing anything worthwhile, the JOYDEMO application can be fairly satisfying to play with. You might want to look at expanding it a bit so that the ambulatory beach ball can bounce into things—sunbathers, perhaps.

Figure 5-5 illustrates the JOYDEMO.CPP source code file. Figure 5-6 illustrates JOYDEMO.RC, its resource script. In addition to these files, you'll need PRJ and DEF files for JOYDEMO, and the WAV and BMP files included in JOYDEMO.RC. You'll find all these files on the companion CD-ROM for this book.

The JOYDEMO.CPP source code.

Figure 5-5

```
/*
        Joystick Demonstration
        Copyright (c) 1993 Alchemy Mindworks Inc.
*/
#include <windows.h>
#include <stdio.h>
#include <stdlib.h>
#include <dir.h>
#include <ctype.h>
#include <alloc.h>
#include <string.h>
#include <io.h>
#include <bwcc.h>
#include <dos.h>
#include <errno.h>
```

Figure 5-5   *Continued.*

```
#include <math.h>
#include <commdlg.h>
#include <mmsystem.h>

#define say(s)      MessageBox(NULL,s,"Yo...",MB_OK | MB_ICONSTOP);
#define saynumber(f,s)    {char b[128]; sprintf((LPSTR)b,(LPSTR)f,s); \
                    MessageBox(NULL,b,"Debug Message",MB_OK | MB_ICONSTOP); \
                    }

#define ItemName(item,string)    { dlgH=GetDlgItem(hwnd,item); \
                        SetWindowText(dlgH,(LPSTR)string); \
                        }

#define ItemOn(item)      { dlgH=GetDlgItem(hwnd,item); \
                    EnableWindow(dlgH,TRUE); \
                    EnableMenuItem(hmenu,item,MF_ENABLED);\
                    }

#define ItemOff(item)     { dlgH=GetDlgItem(hwnd,item); \
                    EnableWindow(dlgH,FALSE); \
                    EnableMenuItem(hmenu,item,MF_GRAYED);\
                    }

#define DoMessage(hwnd,string) BWCCMessageBox(hwnd,string,"Message",\
                        MB_OK | MB_ICONINFORMATION)

#define STRINGSIZE      128              /* how big is a string? */

#define MAIN_ABOUT      102
#define MAIN_EXIT       199

#define BACKGROUND      RGB(0,192,0)
#define SHADOWS         RGB(0,64,0)
#define LINES           RGB(0,255,0)
#define GRIDSIZE        40
#define GRIDOFF         8
#define GRIDLINESIZE    3

#define JOYINTERVAL     5

#define JITTER          8

#ifndef max
#define max(a,b)            (((a)>(b))?(a):(b))
#endif
#ifndef min
#define min(a,b)            (((a)<(b))?(a):(b))
#endif

#define ROUNDUP(n,r)        (n+(r-(n%r)))
```

```
/* prototypes */
DWORD FAR PASCAL SelectProc(HWND hwnd,WORD message,WORD wParam,LONG lParam);
DWORD FAR PASCAL AboutDlgProc(HWND hwnd,WORD message,WORD wParam,LONG lParam);

void lmemset(LPSTR s,int n,unsigned int size);
void CentreWindow(HWND hwnd);

void GetBackground(HDC hdc,HDC hMemoryDC,HBITMAP hback,WORD xpos,WORD ypos);
void DrawCell(HDC hdc,HDC hMemoryDC,HBITMAP hball,HBITMAP hback,WORD xpos,WORD ypos);
void HideCell(HDC hdc,HDC hMemoryDC,HBITMAP hback,WORD xpos,WORD ypos);
WORD AdjustJoyXPOS(WORD n,LPRECT rect);
WORD AdjustJoyYPOS(WORD n,LPRECT rect);

/* globals */
char szAppName[] = "JoystickDemo";
GLOBALHANDLE blasthandle;
LPSTR blast;
HANDLE hInst;
WORD xpos,ypos,oldxpos,oldypos,ballwide,balldeep;
int firstpass=TRUE;
HBITMAP hball,hmask,hback;
JOYCAPS joycaps;

#pragma warn -par
int PASCAL WinMain(HANDLE hInstance,HANDLE hPrevInstance,
             LPSTR lpszCmdParam,int nCmdShow)
{
        FARPROC dlgProc;
        int r=0;

        BWCCGetVersion();

        hInst=hInstance;

        dlgProc=MakeProcInstance((FARPROC)SelectProc,hInst);
        r=DialogBox(hInst,"MainScreen",NULL,dlgProc);

        FreeProcInstance(dlgProc);

        return(r);
}

DWORD FAR PASCAL SelectProc(HWND hwnd,WORD message,WORD wParam,LONG lParam)
{
        PAINTSTRUCT ps;
        static HICON hIcon;
        BITMAP bitmap;
        FARPROC lpfnDlgProc;
        RECT rect;
        HDC hdc,hMemoryDC;
        HBRUSH hbrush,oldbrush;
        HPEN hpen,oldpen;
        HMENU hmenu;
        WORD i,x,y;
```

Figure 5-5   *Continued.*

```
switch(message) {
        case MM_JOY1BUTTONDOWN:
                if(blast != NULL)
                        sndPlaySound(blast,SND_ASYNC | SND_MEMORY);
                break;
        case MM_JOY1MOVE:
                if(!IsWindowEnabled(hwnd)) return(FALSE);
                GetClientRect(hwnd,&rect);

                x=oldxpos;
                y=oldypos;

                xpos=AdjustJoyXPOS(LOWORD(lParam),&rect);
                ypos=AdjustJoyYPOS(HIWORD(lParam),&rect);

                if(ROUNDUP(oldxpos,JITTER) != ROUNDUP(xpos,JITTER) ||
                   ROUNDUP(oldypos,JITTER) != ROUNDUP(ypos,JITTER)) {

                        hdc=GetDC(hwnd);
                        if((hMemoryDC=CreateCompatibleDC(hdc)) != NULL) {

                                oldxpos=xpos;
                                oldypos=ypos;

                                if(!firstpass)
                                        HideCell(hdc,hMemoryDC,hback,x,y);

                                firstpass=FALSE;

                                GetBackground(hdc,hMemoryDC,hback,xpos,ypos);

                                DrawCell(hdc,hMemoryDC,hball,hback,xpos,ypos);
                                DeleteDC(hMemoryDC);
                        }
                        ReleaseDC(hwnd,hdc);
                }
                break;
        case WM_SYSCOMMAND:
                switch(wParam & 0xfff0) {
                        case SC_CLOSE:
                                SendMessage(hwnd,WM_COMMAND,MAIN_EXIT,0L);
                                break;
                }
                switch(wParam) {
                        case MAIN_ABOUT:
                                if((lpfnDlgProc=MakeProcInstance((FARPROC)
                                   AboutDlgProc,hInst)) != NULL) {
                                        DialogBox(hInst,"AboutBox",
                                            hwnd,lpfnDlgProc);
                                        FreeProcInstance(lpfnDlgProc);
                                }
```

```
                                     break;
              }
              break;
      case WM_INITDIALOG:
              hIcon=LoadIcon(hInst,szAppName);
              SetClassWord(hwnd,GCW_HICON,(WORD)hIcon);
              CentreWindow(hwnd);
              SendMessage(hwnd,WM_SYSCOMMAND,SC_MAXIMIZE,0L);

              hmenu=GetSystemMenu(hwnd,FALSE);
              AppendMenu(hmenu,MF_STRING,MAIN_ABOUT,"About");

              if((blasthandle=LoadResource(hInst,
                  FindResource(hInst,"BlastWave",RT_RCDATA))) != NULL) {
                      blast=LockResource(blasthandle);

              }

              GetClientRect(hwnd,&rect);
              if((hball=LoadBitmap(hInst,"RedBall")) == NULL ¦¦
                 (hmask=LoadBitmap(hInst,"RedMask")) == NULL) {
                      DoMessage(hwnd,"Error loading bitmap resources");
                       PostMessage(hwnd,WM_COMMAND,MAIN_EXIT,0L);
              }

              GetObject(hball,sizeof(BITMAP),(LPSTR)&bitmap);

              ballwide=bitmap.bmWidth;
              balldeep=bitmap.bmHeight;

              GetClientRect(hwnd,&rect);

              xpos=(rect.right-rect.left-ballwide)/2;
              ypos=(rect.bottom-rect.top-balldeep)/2;

              hdc=GetDC(hwnd);

              if((hback=CreateCompatibleBitmap(hdc,ballwide,balldeep))==NULL) {
                      DoMessage(hwnd,"Error creating bitmap");
                       PostMessage(hwnd,WM_COMMAND,MAIN_EXIT,0L);
              }

              ReleaseDC(hwnd,hdc);

              if(!joyGetNumDevs()) {
                      DoMessage(hwnd,"No joystick is present in your system");
                       PostMessage(hwnd,WM_COMMAND,MAIN_EXIT,0L);
              }

              if(joySetCapture(hwnd,JOYSTICKID1,JOYINTERVAL,FALSE) !=
                 JOYERR_NOERROR) {
                      DoMessage(hwnd,"Error initializing the joystick");
                       PostMessage(hwnd,WM_COMMAND,MAIN_EXIT,0L);
              }
```

Figure 5-5   *Continued.*

```
                    joyGetDevCaps(JOYSTICKID1,&joycaps,sizeof(JOYCAPS));

                    firstpass=TRUE;
                    break;
            case WM_SIZE:
                    InvalidateRect(hwnd,NULL,TRUE);
                    break;
            case WM_PAINT:
                    hdc=BeginPaint(hwnd,&ps);
                    GetClientRect(hwnd,&rect);

                    hbrush=CreateSolidBrush(BACKGROUND);
                    oldbrush=SelectObject(hdc,hbrush);
                    oldpen=SelectObject(hdc,GetStockObject(NULL_PEN));
                    Rectangle(hdc,rect.left,rect.top,rect.right+1,rect.bottom+1);
                    SelectObject(hdc,oldpen);
                    SelectObject(hdc,oldbrush);

                    hpen=CreatePen(PS_SOLID,GRIDLINESIZE,SHADOWS);
                    oldpen=SelectObject(hdc,hpen);

                    for(i=rect.left;i<=rect.right;i+=GRIDSIZE) {
                            MoveTo(hdc,i+GRIDOFF,rect.top+GRIDOFF);
                            LineTo(hdc,i+GRIDOFF,rect.bottom+1+GRIDOFF);
                    }

                    for(i=rect.top;i<=rect.bottom;i+=GRIDSIZE) {
                            MoveTo(hdc,rect.left+GRIDOFF,i+GRIDOFF);
                            LineTo(hdc,rect.right+1+GRIDOFF,i+GRIDOFF);
                    }

                    SelectObject(hdc,oldpen);
                    DeleteObject(hpen);

                    hpen=CreatePen(PS_SOLID,GRIDLINESIZE,LINES);
                    oldpen=SelectObject(hdc,hpen);

                    for(i=rect.left;i<=rect.right;i+=GRIDSIZE) {
                            MoveTo(hdc,i,rect.top);
                            LineTo(hdc,i,rect.bottom+1);
                    }

                    for(i=rect.top;i<=rect.bottom;i+=GRIDSIZE) {
                            MoveTo(hdc,rect.left,i);
                            LineTo(hdc,rect.right+1,i);
                    }

                    SelectObject(hdc,oldpen);
                    DeleteObject(hpen);

                    if(!firstpass && (hMemoryDC=CreateCompatibleDC(hdc)) != NULL) {
```

```
                              oldxpos=xpos;
                              oldypos=ypos;

                              GetBackground(hdc,hMemoryDC,hback,xpos,ypos);

                              DrawCell(hdc,hMemoryDC,hball,hback,xpos,ypos);
                              DeleteDC(hMemoryDC);
                      }

                      EndPaint(hwnd,&ps);
                      break;
              case WM_COMMAND:
                      switch(wParam) {
                              case MAIN_EXIT:
                                      sndPlaySound(NULL,SND_SYNC);
                                      if(blast != NULL) UnlockResource(blasthandle);
                                      if(blasthandle != NULL)
                                          FreeResource(blasthandle);
                                      joyReleaseCapture(JOYSTICKID1);
                                      if(hback != NULL) DeleteObject(hback);
                                      if(hmask != NULL) DeleteObject(hmask);
                                      if(hball != NULL) DeleteObject(hball);
                                      FreeResource(hIcon);
                                      PostQuitMessage(0);
                                      break;
                      }
                      break;

      }

      return(FALSE);
}

void HideCell(HDC hdc,HDC hMemoryDC,HBITMAP hback,WORD xpos,WORD ypos)
{
      HBITMAP oldbitmap;

      if((oldbitmap=SelectObject(hMemoryDC,hback)) != NULL) {
              BitBlt(hdc,
                      xpos,
                      ypos,
                      ballwide,
                      balldeep,
                      hMemoryDC,
                      0,
                      0,
                      SRCCOPY);
              SelectObject(hMemoryDC,oldbitmap);
      }
}

void DrawCell(HDC hdc,HDC hMemoryDC,HBITMAP hball,HBITMAP hback,WORD xpos,WORD ypos)
```

Figure 5-5   *Continued.*

```
{
        HBITMAP oldbitmap;

        if((oldbitmap=SelectObject(hMemoryDC,hmask)) != NULL) {
                BitBlt(hdc,
                        xpos,
                        ypos,
                        ballwide,
                        balldeep,
                        hMemoryDC,
                        0,
                        0,
                        SRCAND);
                SelectObject(hMemoryDC,oldbitmap);
        }

        if((oldbitmap=SelectObject(hMemoryDC,hball)) != NULL) {
                BitBlt(hdc,
                        xpos,
                        ypos,
                        ballwide,
                        balldeep,
                        hMemoryDC,
                        0,
                        0,
                        SRCINVERT);
                SelectObject(hMemoryDC,oldbitmap);
        }
}

void GetBackground(HDC hdc,HDC hMemoryDC,HBITMAP hback,WORD xpos,WORD ypos)
{
        HBITMAP oldbitmap;

        if((oldbitmap=SelectObject(hMemoryDC,hback)) != NULL) {
                BitBlt(hMemoryDC,
                        0,
                        0,
                        ballwide,
                        balldeep,
                        hdc,
                        xpos,
                        ypos,
                        SRCCOPY);

                SelectObject(hMemoryDC,oldbitmap);
        }
}

DWORD FAR PASCAL AboutDlgProc(HWND hwnd,WORD message,WORD wParam,LONG lParam)
{
```

```
static HANDLE sound;
static LPSTR psound;
HANDLE handle;
POINT point;

switch(message) {
        case WM_INITDIALOG:
                if((handle=FindResource(hInst,"AboutWave",RT_RCDATA)) != NULL) {
                        if((sound=LoadResource(hInst,handle)) != NULL) {
                                if((psound=LockResource(sound)) != NULL)
                                        sndPlaySound(psound,SND_ASYNC |
                                                SND_MEMORY | SND_NOSTOP);
                        }
                }
                CentreWindow(hwnd);
                return(FALSE);
        case WM_CTLCOLOR:
                if(HIWORD(lParam)==CTLCOLOR_STATIC ||
                   HIWORD(lParam)==CTLCOLOR_DLG) {
                        SetBkColor(wParam,RGB(192,192,192));
                        SetTextColor(wParam,RGB(0,0,0));

                        ClientToScreen(hwnd,&point);
                        UnrealizeObject(GetStockObject(LTGRAY_BRUSH));
                        SetBrushOrg(wParam,point.x,point.y);

                        return((DWORD)GetStockObject(LTGRAY_BRUSH));

                }
                if(HIWORD(lParam)==CTLCOLOR_BTN) {
                        SetBkColor(wParam,RGB(192,192,192));
                        SetTextColor(wParam,RGB(0,0,0));

                        ClientToScreen(hwnd,&point);
                        UnrealizeObject(GetStockObject(BLACK_BRUSH));
                        SetBrushOrg(wParam,point.x,point.y);

                        return((DWORD)GetStockObject(BLACK_BRUSH));
                }
                break;
        case WM_COMMAND:
                switch(wParam) {
                        case IDOK:
                                sndPlaySound(NULL,SND_SYNC);
                                if(psound != NULL) UnlockResource(sound);
                                if(sound != NULL) FreeResource(sound);
                                EndDialog(hwnd,wParam);
                                return(FALSE);
                }
                break;
}

return(FALSE);
}
```

Figure 5-5 *Continued.*

```
void lmemset(LPSTR s,int n,unsigned int size)
{
        unsigned int i;

        for(i=0;i<size;++i) *s++=n;
}


void CentreWindow(HWND hwnd)
{
        RECT rect;
        unsigned int x,y;

        GetWindowRect(hwnd,&rect);
        x=(GetSystemMetrics(SM_CXSCREEN)-(rect.right-rect.left))/2;
        y=(GetSystemMetrics(SM_CYSCREEN)-(rect.bottom-rect.top))/2;
        SetWindowPos(hwnd,NULL,x,y,rect.right-rect.left,
            rect.bottom-rect.top,SWP_NOSIZE);
}

WORD AdjustJoyXPOS(WORD n,LPRECT rect)
{

        long wwidth,jwidth;

        wwidth=(long)rect->right-rect->left-ballwide;
        jwidth=joycaps.wXmax-joycaps.wXmin;

        if(wwidth > jwidth) n=((WORD)(double)n*((double)wwidth/(double)jwidth));
        else n=((WORD)(double)n/((double)jwidth/(double)wwidth));

        return(n);
}

WORD AdjustJoyYPOS(WORD n,LPRECT rect)
{
        long wdepth,jdepth;

        wdepth=(long)rect->bottom-rect->top-balldeep;
        jdepth=joycaps.wYmax-joycaps.wYmin;

        if(wdepth > jdepth) n=((WORD)(double)n*((double)wdepth/(double)jdepth));
        else n=((WORD)(double)n/((double)jdepth/(double)wdepth));

        return(n);
}
```

The JOYDEMO.RC resource script.   Figure 5-6

```
MainScreen DIALOG 12, 24, 184, 184
STYLE WS_POPUP | WS_CAPTION | WS_SYSMENU | WS_MINIMIZEBOX | WS_MAXIMIZEBOX
CAPTION "Joystick Demonstration"
BEGIN
END


AboutBox DIALOG 18, 18, 184, 180
STYLE WS_POPUP | WS_CAPTION
CAPTION "About..."
BEGIN
        CONTROL "", 102, "BorShade", BSS_GROUP | WS_CHILD | WS_VISIBLE |
            WS_TABSTOP, 8, 68, 168, 76
        CTEXT "Joystick Demonstration 1.0\n\nCopyright (c) 1994 Alchemy
            Mindworks Inc.\n\nThis program is part of the book Advanced Multimedia
            Programming for Windows by Steven William Rimmer, published by Windcrest/
            McGraw Hill.", -1, 12, 72, 160, WS_CHILD | WS_VISIBLE | WS_GROUP
        CONTROL "Button", IDOK, "BorBtn", BS_DEFPUSHBUTTON | WS_CHILD | WS_VISIBLE |
            WS_TABSTOP, 74, 152, 32, 20
        CONTROL "Button", 801, "BorBtn", BS_PUSHBUTTON | WS_CHILD | WS_VISIBLE |
            WS_TABSTOP, 36, 8, 32, 20
END

1801 BITMAP "smpw.bmp"

AboutWave RCDATA "ABOUT.WAV"

RedBall BITMAP "redball.bmp"

RedMask BITMAP "redmask.bmp"

BlastWave RCDATA "BLAST.WAV"

JoystickDemo ICON
BEGIN
        '00 00 01 00 01 00 20 20 10 00 00 00 00 00 E8 02'
        '00 00 16 00 00 00 28 00 00 00 20 00 00 00 40 00'
        '00 00 01 00 04 00 00 00 00 00 80 02 00 00 00 00'
        '00 00 00 00 00 00 10 00 00 00 00 00 00 00 00 00'
        '00 00 00 00 BF 00 00 BF 00 00 00 BF BF 00 BF 00'
        '00 00 BF 00 BF 00 BF BF 00 00 C0 C0 C0 00 80 80'
        '80 00 00 00 FF 00 00 FF 00 00 00 FF FF 00 FF 00'
        '00 00 FF 00 FF 00 FF FF 00 00 FF FF FF 00 77 77'
        '77 77 77 77 77 77 77 77 77 77 77 77 77 77 7F 88'
        '88 88 88 88 88 88 88 88 88 88 88 88 87 7F F8'
        '88 88 88 88 88 88 88 88 88 88 88 88 87 7F F7'
        '77 77 77 77 70 00 00 00 77 77 77 77 78 87 7F F7'
        '77 77 77 70 09 99 99 99 00 77 77 77 78 87 7F F7'
        '77 77 70 09 99 99 99 99 99 00 77 77 78 87 7F F7'
        '77 77 09 BB BB 99 99 99 99 99 07 77 78 87 7F F7'
        '77 70 99 BB BB B9 99 99 99 99 90 77 78 87 7F F7'
```

Figure 5-6   *Continued.*

```
'77 09 BB BB B9 99 99 99 99 99 99 07 78 87 7F F7'
'77 0B BB BF FB 99 99 99 99 99 99 07 78 87 7F F7'
'70 BB BB 9B FF B9 99 99 99 99 99 90 78 87 7F F7'
'70 BB BB 99 BF B9 99 99 99 99 99 90 78 87 7F F7'
'09 90 00 09 99 B9 99 99 99 00 00 99 08 87 7F F7'
'09 00 00 00 09 9B 99 99 00 00 00 09 08 87 7F F7'
'00 00 00 00 00 9B 99 90 00 00 00 00 08 87 7F F7'
'00 0F 00 00 00 9B B9 90 00 F0 00 00 08 87 7F F7'
'00 FF 00 00 00 0B B9 00 0F F0 00 00 08 87 7F F7'
'00 0F 00 00 00 0B B9 00 0F 00 00 00 08 87 7F F7'
'09 00 00 00 00 00 00 00 00 00 00 00 08 87 7F F7'
'09 00 00 00 00 00 00 00 00 00 00 09 08 87 7F F7'
'70 90 00 00 99 BB BB 99 90 00 00 90 78 87 7F F7'
'70 99 99 99 99 BB BB 99 99 99 99 90 78 87 7F F7'
'77 09 99 99 99 99 9B BB 99 99 99 07 78 87 7F F7'
'77 09 99 99 99 99 9B BB 99 99 99 07 78 87 7F F7'
'77 70 99 99 99 99 99 99 99 99 90 77 78 87 7F F7'
'77 77 00 99 99 99 99 99 99 90 07 77 78 87 7F F7'
'77 77 77 00 99 99 99 99 90 07 77 77 78 87 7F F7'
'77 77 77 77 00 00 00 00 07 77 77 77 78 87 7F F7'
'77 77 77 77 77 77 77 77 77 77 77 77 78 87 7F FF'
'FF FF FF FF FF FF FF FF FF FF FF FF F8 87 7F FF'
'FF FF FF FF FF FF FF FF FF FF FF FF FF 87 77 77'
'77 77 77 77 77 77 77 77 77 77 77 77 77 77 00 00'
'00 00 00 00 00 00 00 00 00 00 00 00 00 00 00 00'
'00 00 00 00 00 00 00 00 00 00 00 00 00 00 00 00'
'00 00 00 00 00 00 00 00 00 00 00 00 00 00 00 00'
'00 00 00 00 00 00 00 00 00 00 00 00 00 00 00 00'
'00 00 00 00 00 00 00 00 00 00 00 00 00 00 00 00'
'00 00 00 00 00 00 00 00 00 00 00 00 00 00 00 00'
'00 00 00 00 00 00 00 00 00 00 00 00 00 00 00 00'
'00 00 00 00 00 00 00 00 00 00 00 00 00 00 00 00'
'00 00 00 00 00 00 00 00 00 00 00 00 00 00 00'
```

END

Having perused the foregoing discussion of animation and the multimedia joystick interface, you probably won't find much about JOYDEMO that's hard to understand. Most of the interesting bits happen in the SelectProc function.

The WM_INITDIALOG message handler in SelectProc does a considerable amount of housekeeping for JOYDEMO. It begins by maximizing the JOYDEMO window by sending itself a WM_SYSCOMMAND message. It then fetches the system menu and adds an item to it to provide access to the JOYDEMO About dialog. There are no conventional menus in this application. Its next function is to load and lock the BlastWave sound bite.

Conventional wisdom dictates that having this object locked in memory for the lifetime of JOYDEMO probably isn't a terribly good idea, and to some extent this is correct. Doing so will place an immovable object in the global memory pool, which will impede Windows' memory management. However, if the object is left unlocked, there's a pretty good chance that Windows will eventually spill it to disk. Because this sound is played whenever the joystick button is belted, finding that it has been spilled to disk would require that everything come to a halt while Windows reloads it.

In reality, having BlastWave locked in memory shouldn't compromise Windows' memory management all that much, as it's a fairly small object. You might have cause to change this arrangement if you create a more complex application with lots of canned sounds.

The next task for the WM_INITDIALOG handler is to load two bitmap resources—the RedBall object is the beach ball graphic and the RedMask object is its mask. The following call to GetObject ascertains the dimensions of the ball bitmap—JOYDEMO assumes that the figure and its mask will be of the same dimensions.

As an aside, while there are many ways to derive a 2-color mask from a 16-color bitmap, one of the easiest is to use the Threshold option of the Dither function of Graphic Workshop for Windows, do a bit of fine tuning if necessary in Windows Paintbrush, and then use the Reverse function of Graphic Workshop to flip the mask black for white.

The call to GetClientRect in the WM_INITDIALOG handler of SelectProc ascertains the dimensions of the window in which the beach ball will ultimately bounce. The xpos and ypos values—the current location of the beach ball when it's moving—are set to the center of the window.

The call to GetDC returns an HDC object compatible with the current screen characteristics. This is used as the device context reference in a call to CreateCompatibleBitmap to generate a bitmap for storing the area behind the ball when it's visible.

Finally, the three joystick calls set up the joystick interface, as discussed earlier.

The WM_PAINT handler for SelectProc is responsible for drawing the background over which the beach ball will bounce. There's nothing particularly sophisticated about what it's drawing. The only mildly tricky element is the bit at the end—aside from being called when the main window of JOYDEMO first opens, the WM_PAINT code can also be invoked if the screen needs to be redrawn after another window has opened on top of it. This might happen if you were to switch applications, for example.

Note that the WM_COMMAND handler in SelectProc is something of a dummy function, as there are no menus or buttons in the main window of the JOYDEMO application to issue WM_COMMAND messages. A WM_COMMAND message with its wParam message set to MAIN_EXIT can occur, however, if you select Close from the system menu—or if you double click on the system menu icon. The WM_SYSCOMMAND handler, earlier on in SelectProc, will see to this. Putting the code to close down the application in the WM_COMMAND handler is good software architecture—there's less juggling of code fragments and less likelihood of bugs being introduced into your software.

Two cases at the top of SelectProc handle messages generated by the joystick interface. The MM_JOY1BUTTONDOWN handler merely invokes sndPlaySound to make noise. The MM_JOY1MOVE handler actually moves the animated graphic around the JOYDEMO window, using the procedure discussed earlier in this chapter.

The AdjustJoyXPOS and AdjustJoyYPOS functions fudge the values returned from the joystick interface into meaningful coordinates for the current application window. In fact, if you happen to find yourself confronted with a joystick and driver combination that don't work quite right together, these functions may return values that are about half what they should be, and the beach ball will be confined to the upper left quarter of its window.

Keep in mind that while it's important that the animation functions work quickly, there are some aspects of the code in the MM_JOY1MOVE handler that are more time-sensitive than others. Specifically, the period between erasing one cell and masking and painting the next should be as short as possible, with heavy emphasis on reducing the time between writing the mask to your screen and then writing the figure. The time

required to calculate the new cell position is not quite so critical. While you wouldn't want to be loading bitmapped resources or allocating memory in this handler, for example, you could permit it to do a reasonable amount of calculation and other housekeeping prior to actually drawing something.

One of the grotty real-world characteristics of joysticks is that even the best of them are relatively unstable. Being essentially mechanical devices interfaced with transducers to return their instantaneous position, they tend to jitter. Specifically, multiple samples returned from an ostensibly stationary joystick will usually differ slightly. Paradoxically, better joysticks tend to exhibit more pronounced jitter.

There are a number of ways to deal with jittered return values from a joystick. The functions of the multimedia joystick interface that deal with the joystick interface threshold can be used to filter out jitter by refusing to issue any joystick movement messages until the joystick has travelled more than a predetermined amount. If the amount is greater than the mechanical uncertainty of the joystick's transducers, the jitter will be eliminated.

I've handled the problem of jitter in JOYDEMO more simply, by maintaining an internal threshold in the software. This requires somewhat more code than would be needed to use the joySetThreshold call, but it results in a slightly more responsive joystick interface.

Obviously, having a responsive interface such that the beach ball in JOYDEMO accurately tracks the movement of your joystick isn't an issue of colossal moment. Responsiveness might prove of greater concern if you were to design a more elaborate application for a joystick controller.

Screen savers
—beware the flying toasters

Windows screen savers have become a peculiar sort of art form in the past few years. The ostensible function of a screen saver is to blank

your screen if you don't do anything for a while, such that your monitor won't be damaged by having a static image painted on it for a prolonged period. While this is a laudable premise, the designers of screen savers realized early on that having blanked the screen, they could then draw something on all that blackness. As long as what's drawn moves around and doesn't appear in consistent locations on your monitor, it won't significantly affect the useful life of your tube.

A number of commercial screen savers have appeared, perhaps the most famous of which is Berkeley Systems' *After Dark*, featuring the now-legendary flying toasters. Berkeley also offers companion flying toaster ties and T-shirts for anyone who really gets into the toaster imagery.

Some while ago a rival software developer created a screen saver which depicted Opus the penguin shooting down flying toasters. Berkeley Systems threatened legal action over the upstart toasters. Famous legal precedents have been set over less.

With the release of Windows 3.1, Microsoft introduced a built-in screen saver interface. It can be accessed through the Control Panel's Desktop applet. You can enable one of a number of canned screen saver effects provided with Windows this way—none of them anywhere near as interesting as the flying toasters, with or without Opus.

The Windows Multimedia Development Kit includes the bones and rags to build additional screen savers compatible with the Windows screen saver interface. While a promising beginning for creating screen savers, this won't prove to be of much help if you're not writing in one of Microsoft's languages. The screen saver library has been hardwired to interface to Microsoft's language runtime. Users of Borland C++ for Windows won't be able to successfully link it into their software.

Perhaps I should qualify this—there does not appear to be any way to link the screen saver libraries into a screen saver written in a non-Microsoft language. Contacting Microsoft about this will eventually get you to a technical support person who will maintain that this is really something to be taken up with Borland. Consulting Borland will

have much the same result—it's something to be resolved by Microsoft. Both companies want money up front to provide technical support for their products, and seem to have a vested interest in making technical support as lengthy an undertaking as possible—the distinction between that which is genuinely impossible and that which is just highly inexplicable grows increasingly meaningless under such circumstances.

While either party might suggest that it sounds a bit like sour grapes under the circumstances, there's a lot to be said for creating screen savers as stand-alone Windows applications, rather than as plug-in savers for the Desktop applet of the Control Panel. Stand-alone screen savers are typically easier to access—installed in your StartUp group, such a screen saver will appear as an icon at the bottom of your Windows desktop. If you want to disable it for the rest of your current session, you can do so simply by closing it. Likewise, you can configure a stand-alone screen saver without having to open the Control Panel and then the Desktop applet.

Finally, of course, writing a stand-alone screen saver doesn't require recourse to the apparently inaccessible Microsoft screen saver library.

A stand-alone Windows screen saver is actually much simpler than it appears. The less than obvious bit is how to actually turn the screen black, and that's only less than obvious because it's so simple that you'd think it couldn't possibly work that way. To blank the screen, all a screen saver need do is figure out how big your screen is, open a window that size, and paint it black.

There's a bit more to a screen saver than this. It has to install a message filter in Windows to tell it when a keypress or some mouse movement has occurred, such that it will know to close the big black window again and return you to your desktop. Installing a message filter in Windows is rather delicate—fortunately, you won't have to figure out how to manage this, as there's a working example of a message filter under glass in the screen saver application discussed later in this chapter.

Finally, you'll have to come up with something trendy, slick, and visually compelling for your screen saver to do while it's busy doing

nothing. The screen saver in this section will roll the beach ball in cheap sunglasses around your screen, optionally making distracting noises whenever it rebounds off one of the edges of your tube. You'll certainly have to improve on this if you want to become renowned in the rarefied world of screen saver design.

As an aside, lest you consider the approach taken by the authors of the alternate flying toaster screen saver discussed earlier in this section, be aware that while the beach ball in cheap sunglasses isn't a copyrighted entity, Opus the penguin most certainly is.

Message filters
—juggling polecats in the dark

A screen saver is an example of a Windows application that must take a global interest in Windows as a whole. Specifically, it must keep a running count of the number of seconds that have elapsed since the last key press or mouse movement and blank the screen after a preset interval. The key presses and mouse movements in question can apply to any currently active application.

In most cases, your message handlers need only concern themselves with messages for your application. In fact, in the normal structure of a Windows application, your message handlers would have no way of knowing about messages for other applications, and as such, no way to keep track of whether any are actually taking place. This makes the prospect of writing a screen saver somewhat questionable.

Perhaps predictably, Windows does provide for a way around this problem. All messages pass through the Windows kernel before making their way to their intended applications. You can install a filter in this structure, so that your filter can have a shot at all the outgoing messages. A message filter can actually trap and modify messages, although in this application we're only interested in one that watches the message queue.

The Windows message filter mechanism isn't terribly well documented, and it's more than a bit fragile if you use it incorrectly.

Because Windows' message queue is fundamental to its continued existence, installing a filter that misbehaves will bring Windows to its knees pretty reliably.

This is a typical Windows message filter—actually, it's the message filter for the screen saver:

```
void FAR PASCAL _export MessageHook(int iCode,
    WORD wParam,LONG lParam)

{
        FILTERMSG FAR *msg;

        msg = (FILTERMSG FAR *)lParam;

        if(!active) {
              if(msg->message==WM_ACTIVATE ||
                msg->message==WM_ACTIVATEAPP ||
                msg->message==WM_LBUTTONDOWN ||
                msg->message==WM_MBUTTONDOWN ||
                msg->message==WM_RBUTTONDOWN ||
                msg->message==WM_KEYDOWN ||
                msg->message==WM_SYSKEYDOWN ||
                msg->message==WM_MOUSEMOVE) count=0;
        }

        if(iCode < 0) DefHookProc(iCode,
                        wParam,lParam,&lpfnOldHook);
}
```

Once installed, the MessageHook function will be called by Windows each time a message appears.

To enhance the general confusion of message filter construction, Windows offers a variety of filter types, each of which requires a filter procedure that works a little differently. The message filter discussed in this section is of the type WH_GETMESSAGE. Specifically, it will be called to process a message whenever GetMessage is called by any application currently running under Windows. As the GetMessage call is the basis of any message-handling loop, it

provides a fairly reliable way for a screen saver to get a shot at all the messages flowing through Windows.

Here's how you'd install MessageHook as a Windows message filter:

```
FARPROC FAR lpfnKeyHook;
FARPROC FAR lpfnOldHook;

lpfnKeyHook = MakeProcInstance((FARPROC)MessageHook,hInstance);
lpfnOldHook = SetWindowsHook(WH_GETMESSAGE,lpfnKeyHook);
```

Having set this hook into Windows, MessageHook will be called to investigate each message processed by any application running under Windows. When the application that MessageHook is part of terminates, it must remove MessageHook from the filter chain like this:

```
UnhookWindowsHook(WH_GETMESSAGE,lpfnKeyHook);
FreeProcInstance(lpfnKeyHook);
```

One of the badly documented things about the Windows message filter facilities is what you can and cannot do within a message filter. There's nothing in MessageHook that's at all contentious—keep the nature of message filters in mind should you have cause to use this facility for other things. A message filter that ties up Windows for a protracted period of time or interferes unduly with the message queue may not be a welcome visitor.

The arguments passed to a message filter like MessageHook aren't quite what they seem. The first argument, iCode, is a flag to tell the filter whether to call the DefHookProc function when it's done with its own intrigues. The DefHookProc function will pass the message on to the default message handler.

The lParam argument to MessageHook is actually a far pointer to a FILTERMSG object. Here's what one looks like:

```
typedef struct {
        WORD hlParam;
        WORD llParam;
        WORD wParam;
        WORD message;
```

```
WORD hWnd;
} FILTERMSG;
```

The FILTERMSG object for a message passed to MessageHook contains the actual information for the message in question. Note that FILTERMSG isn't a defined Windows data type per se. In this version, the conventional lParam element of a message is split into two WORD values. You can redefine this as one DWORD if you like.

The MessageHook for the screen saver is pretty simple—it watches for messages that indicate some activity at your computer and resets a counter if such a message appears. The counter will be incremented by a message handler processing WM_TIMER messages, as we'll get to shortly.

The screen saver

Despite its somewhat exotic nature, a screen saver is a fairly simple Windows application. The difficulty in creating one isn't so much coming up with a lot of code as it is knowing which of a select few very small pieces of code are required to create a workable and stable screen saver. If you go on to write your own screen saver based on the one discussed in this chapter, you'll be able to simply remove the graphical elements from this program and replace them with functions to implement graphics of your own devising.

Figure 5-7 illustrates the SAVER.CPP source code file. Figure 5-8 illustrates SAVER.RC, its resource script. In addition to these files, you'll need PRJ and DEF files for SAVER, and the WAV and BMP files included in SAVER.RC. You will find all these files on the companion CD-ROM for this book.

The structure of the SAVER application is a bit different from that of the other Windows programs that have turned up in this book. Rather than creating a dialog as a principal window, SAVER actually calls CreateWindow directly. In fact, it creates a sort of nonwindow, as its window is displayed minimized and is constrained to stay that way.

Figure 5-7   *The SAVER.CPP source code.*

```
/*
        Copyright (c) 1994 Alchemy Mindworks Inc.
        Bounce a beach ball wearing sunglasses across
        your screen to preserve your monitor...
        sort of thing you see all the time.
*/

#include <windows.h>
#include <stdio.h>
#include <stdlib.h>
#include <dir.h>
#include <ctype.h>
#include <alloc.h>
#include <string.h>
#include <io.h>
#include <bwcc.h>
#include <dos.h>
#include <errno.h>
#include <math.h>
#include <mmsystem.h>

#define say(s)          MessageBox(NULL,s,"Yo...",MB_OK | MB_ICONSTOP);
#define saynumber(f,s)     {char b[128]; sprintf((LPSTR)b,(LPSTR)f,s); \
                        MessageBox(NULL,b,"Debug Message",MB_OK | MB_ICONSTOP); \
                        }

#define CheckOn(item)       SendDlgItemMessage(hwnd,item,BM_SETCHECK,1,0L);
#define CheckOff(item)      SendDlgItemMessage(hwnd,item,BM_SETCHECK,0,0L);
#define IsItemChecked(item)         SendDlgItemMessage(hwnd,item,BM_GETCHECK,0,0L)
#define ItemName(item,string)      { dlgH=GetDlgItem(hwnd,item); \
                            SetWindowText(dlgH,(LPSTR)string); }
#define GetItemName(item,string) { dlgH=GetDlgItem(hwnd,item); \
                            GetWindowText(dlgH,(LPSTR)string,STRINGSIZE); }

#define DoMessage(hwnd,string) BWCCMessageBox(hwnd,string,"Message",\
                        MB_OK | MB_ICONINFORMATION)

#define STRINGSIZE      128             /* how big is a string? */

#define MAINTIMER       1
#define THETIMER        2

#define INTERVAL        10              /* pause between updates */

#define CELLWIDE        48
#define CELLDEEP        48

#define CELLCOUNT       8

#define CELLBASE        1700

#define HOOKTYPE        WH_GETMESSAGE
```

```
#ifndef max
#define max(a,b)            (((a)>(b))?(a):(b))
#endif
#ifndef min
#define min(a,b)            (((a)<(b))?(a):(b))
#endif

#define IDM_ABOUT           101
#define IDM_SETUP           102

#define THRESHOLD           4

#define MINDELAY            30              // thirty seconds
#define MAXDELAY            3600            // one hour

#define SETUP_DELAY         101
#define SETUP_SOUND         102

#define SOUNDKEY            "LoudAnnoyingSound"
#define DELAYKEY            "TimeBeforeUtterBlackness"

typedef struct {
        WORD hlParam;
        WORD llParam;
        WORD wParam;
        WORD message;
        WORD hWnd;
        } FILTERMSG;

/* prototypes */
DWORD FAR PASCAL SetupDlgProc(HWND hwnd,WORD message,WORD wParam,LONG lParam);
DWORD FAR PASCAL AboutDlgProc(HWND hwnd,WORD message,WORD wParam,LONG lParam);
LRESULT FAR PASCAL ScreenSaverProc(HWND hwnd, unsigned int msg,
                  unsigned short wParam, long lParam);
LONG FAR PASCAL DefScreenSaverProc(HWND hwnd,unsigned int msg,
                  unsigned short wParam, long lParam);
void FAR PASCAL _export MessageHook(int iCode,WORD wParam,LONG lParam);
long FAR PASCAL WndProc(HWND hWnd,unsigned int wMessage,
                  unsigned int wParam,LONG lParam);

void DrawImage(HDC hdc,int x,int y,HBITMAP image);
void lmemcpy(LPSTR dest,LPSTR source,unsigned int n);
void EraseCell(HDC hdc,int x,int y);
void MoveCell(int FAR *x,int FAR *y);
void UpdateCurrentCell();
void BlankScreen(HWND hwnd);
void LoadConfig();
void SaveConfig();
void CentreWindow(HWND hwnd);

int FetchAllCells();
int HasMouseMoved(int x,int y);
```

Figure 5-7 *Continued.*

```
void DestroyAllCells();

/* globals */
FARPROC FAR lpfnKeyHook;
FARPROC FAR lpfnOldHook;

GLOBALHANDLE blasthandle;
LPSTR blast;

HANDLE hInst;
HWND hMainWindow;

unsigned int screenwide,screendeep;
char szAppName[] = "ScreenSaver";

char BlankName[]="ScreenSaverBlank";

HBITMAP cell[CELLCOUNT];

int active;
int currentcell=0;
int currentspin=1;
int xdir,ydir;
int xpos,ypos;
int sound=FALSE;
unsigned int delay=20;
unsigned int count=0;

int oldmousex=-1,oldmousey=-1;

#pragma warn -par
int PASCAL WinMain(HANDLE hInstance,HANDLE hPrevInstance,
    LPSTR lpszCmdLine,int nCmdShow)
{
        HWND hWndMain;
        MSG msg;
        WNDCLASS wndclass;

        BWCCGetVersion();
        hInst=hInstance;

        LoadConfig();

        if(!hPrevInstance) {
                wndclass.style = 0;
                wndclass.lpfnWndProc = WndProc;
                wndclass.cbClsExtra = 0;
                wndclass.cbWndExtra = 0;
                wndclass.hInstance = hInst;
                wndclass.hIcon = LoadIcon(hInstance,szAppName);
                wndclass.hCursor = LoadCursor(NULL,IDC_ARROW);
```

```
                wndclass.hbrBackground = COLOR_WINDOW+1;
                wndclass.lpszMenuName = (LPSTR)NULL;
                wndclass.lpszClassName = (LPSTR)szAppName;

                if(!RegisterClass(&wndclass)) return(FALSE);

                hWndMain= CreateWindow(szAppName,
                         "Screen Saver",
                         WS_OVERLAPPEDWINDOW,
                         CW_USEDEFAULT,
                         CW_USEDEFAULT,
                         CW_USEDEFAULT,
                         CW_USEDEFAULT,
                         NULL,
                         NULL,
                         hInstance,
                         NULL);

                ShowWindow(hWndMain,SW_SHOWMINNOACTIVE);
                UpdateWindow(hWndMain);
        }
        else {
                DoMessage(NULL,"The Screen Saver is already running.");
                return(FALSE);
        }

        lpfnKeyHook = MakeProcInstance((FARPROC)MessageHook,hInstance);
        lpfnOldHook = SetWindowsHook(HOOKTYPE,lpfnKeyHook);

        while(GetMessage(&msg,NULL,0,0)) {
                TranslateMessage(&msg);
                DispatchMessage(&msg);
        }

        UnhookWindowsHook(HOOKTYPE,lpfnKeyHook);
        FreeProcInstance(lpfnKeyHook);

        UnregisterClass(szAppName,hInst);

        SaveConfig();

        return(msg.wParam);
}

long FAR PASCAL WndProc(HWND hwnd,unsigned int wMessage,
    unsigned int wParam,LONG lParam)
{
        HANDLE hSysMenu;
        FARPROC lpfnDIALOGSMsgProc;

        switch(wMessage) {
                case WM_CREATE:
                        hSysMenu=GetSystemMenu(hwnd,FALSE);
```

Figure 5-7   *Continued.*

```
                            AppendMenu(hSysMenu,MF_SEPARATOR,0,NULL);
                            AppendMenu(hSysMenu,MF_STRING,IDM_SETUP,
                                (LPSTR)"&Setup");
                            AppendMenu(hSysMenu,MF_STRING,IDM_ABOUT,
                                (LPSTR)"&About Screen Saver...");
                            SetTimer(hwnd,MAINTIMER,1000,NULL);
                            active=FALSE;
                            count=0;

                            return(FALSE);
                    case WM_TIMER:
                            if(!active) {
                                    ++count;
                                    if(count >= delay) {
                                            active=TRUE;
                                            BlankScreen(hwnd);
                                            active=FALSE;
                                            count=0;
                                    }
                            }
                            return(FALSE);
                    case WM_QUERYOPEN:
                            PostMessage(hwnd,WM_SYSCOMMAND,IDM_SETUP,0L);
                            return(FALSE);
                    case WM_SYSCOMMAND:
                            switch(wParam) {
                                    case IDM_ABOUT:
                                            lpfnDIALOGSMsgProc=MakeProcInstance
                                                ((FARPROC)AboutDlgProc,hInst);
                                            DialogBox(hInst,(LPSTR)"AboutBox",
                                                hwnd,lpfnDIALOGSMsgProc);
                                            FreeProcInstance(lpfnDIALOGSMsgProc);
                                            break;
                                    case IDM_SETUP:
                                            lpfnDIALOGSMsgProc = MakeProcInstance
                                                ((FARPROC)SetupDlgProc,hInst);
                                            DialogBox(hInst,(LPSTR)"SetupBox",
                                                hwnd,lpfnDIALOGSMsgProc);
                                            FreeProcInstance(lpfnDIALOGSMsgProc);
                                            break;
                                    default:
                                            return(DefWindowProc(hwnd,wMessage,
                                                wParam,lParam));
                            }
                            return(FALSE);
                    case WM_DESTROY:
                            KillTimer(hwnd,MAINTIMER);
                            PostQuitMessage(0);
                            return(FALSE);
            }
            return(DefWindowProc(hwnd,wMessage,wParam,lParam));
    }
```

```
void BlankScreen(HWND hwnd)
{
        HWND childwindow;
        MSG msg;
        WNDCLASS wndclass;
        int i;

        for(i=0;i<CELLCOUNT;++i) cell[i]=NULL;

        wndclass.style = 0;
        wndclass.lpfnWndProc = (LONG (CALLBACK *)
            (unsigned int,unsigned int,unsigned int,long))ScreenSaverProc;
        wndclass.cbClsExtra = 0;
        wndclass.cbWndExtra = 0;
        wndclass.hInstance = hInst;
        wndclass.hIcon = LoadIcon(hInst,szAppName);
        wndclass.hCursor = LoadCursor(NULL,IDC_ARROW);
        wndclass.hbrBackground = GetStockObject(BLACK_BRUSH);
        wndclass.lpszMenuName = (LPSTR)NULL;
        wndclass.lpszClassName = (LPSTR)BlankName;

        if(!RegisterClass(&wndclass)) return;

        screenwide=GetSystemMetrics(SM_CXSCREEN);
        screendeep=GetSystemMetrics(SM_CYSCREEN);

        childwindow = CreateWindow(BlankName,
                                BlankName,
                                WS_POPUP | WS_MAXIMIZE | WS_BORDER,
                                0,
                                0,
                                screenwide,
                                screendeep,
                                hwnd,
                                NULL,
                                hInst,
                                NULL);

        if(childwindow != NULL) {
                ShowWindow(childwindow,SW_SHOWMAXIMIZED);
                UpdateWindow(childwindow);

                while(GetMessage(&msg,NULL,0,0)) {
                        TranslateMessage(&msg);
                        DispatchMessage(&msg);
                }
        }

        UnregisterClass(BlankName,hInst);
        UpdateWindow(hwnd);
}

void FAR PASCAL _export MessageHook(int iCode,WORD wParam,LONG lParam)
```

265

Figure 5-7   *Continued.*

```
{
        FILTERMSG FAR *msg;

        msg = (FILTERMSG FAR *)lParam;

        if(!active) {
                if(msg->message==WM_ACTIVATE ||
                    msg->message==WM_ACTIVATEAPP ||
                    msg->message==WM_LBUTTONDOWN ||
                    msg->message==WM_MBUTTONDOWN ||
                    msg->message==WM_RBUTTONDOWN ||
                    msg->message==WM_KEYDOWN ||
                    msg->message==WM_SYSKEYDOWN ||
                    msg->message==WM_MOUSEMOVE) count=0;
        }

        if(iCode < 0) DefHookProc(iCode,wParam,lParam,&lpfnOldHook);
}

LRESULT FAR PASCAL ScreenSaverProc(HWND hwnd,unsigned int msg,
    unsigned short wParam,long lParam)
{
        HDC hdc;
        PAINTSTRUCT ps;
        RECT rect;
        static int oldxpos,oldypos;

        switch(msg) {
                case WM_CREATE:
                        randomize();
                        if(FetchAllCells())  {
                                oldmousex=oldmousey=-1;
                                SetTimer(hwnd,THETIMER,INTERVAL,NULL);
                                currentcell=0;
                                oldxpos=xpos=(screenwide-CELLWIDE)/2;
                                oldypos=ypos=(screendeep-CELLDEEP)/2;
                                xdir=CELLWIDE/8;
                                ydir=CELLWIDE/8;
                        }

                        if((blasthandle=LoadResource(hInst,
                            FindResource(hInst,"BlastWave",RT_RCDATA))) != NULL) {
                                blast=LockResource(blasthandle);

                        }
                        return(FALSE);
                case WM_TIMER:
                        InvalidateRect(hwnd,NULL,FALSE);
                        UpdateCurrentCell();
                        oldxpos=xpos;
                        oldypos=ypos;
```

266

```
                              MoveCell(&xpos,&ypos);
                              return(FALSE);
                  case WM_PAINT:
                              hdc=BeginPaint(hwnd,&ps);
                              EraseCell(hdc,oldxpos,oldypos);
                              DrawImage(hdc,xpos,ypos,cell[currentcell]);
                              EndPaint(hwnd,&ps);
                              return(FALSE);
                  case WM_DESTROY:
                              sndPlaySound(NULL,SND_SYNC);
                              KillTimer(hwnd,THETIMER);
                              DestroyAllCells();
                              if(blast != NULL) UnlockResource(blasthandle);
                              if(blasthandle != NULL) FreeResource(blasthandle);
                              PostQuitMessage(0);
                              return(FALSE);
                  case WM_ERASEBKGND:
                              GetClientRect(hwnd,&rect);
                              FillRect(wParam,&rect,GetStockObject(BLACK_BRUSH));
                              return(FALSE);
                  case WM_SETCURSOR:
                              SetCursor(NULL);
                              return(FALSE);
                  case WM_ACTIVATE:
                  case WM_ACTIVATEAPP:
                              if(wParam != FALSE) break;
                  case WM_LBUTTONDOWN:
                  case WM_MBUTTONDOWN:
                  case WM_RBUTTONDOWN:
                  case WM_KEYDOWN:
                  case WM_SYSKEYDOWN:
                              PostMessage(hwnd,WM_CLOSE,0,0L);
                              return(FALSE);
                  case WM_MOUSEMOVE:
                              if(HasMouseMoved((int)LOWORD(lParam),(int)HIWORD(lParam)))
                                  PostMessage(hwnd,WM_CLOSE,0,0L);
                              return(FALSE);
          }
      return(DefWindowProc(hwnd,msg,wParam,lParam));
}

void EraseCell(HDC hdc,int x,int y)
{
      HBRUSH oldbrush;
      HPEN oldpen;

      oldbrush=SelectObject(hdc,GetStockObject(BLACK_BRUSH));
      oldpen=SelectObject(hdc,GetStockObject(NULL_PEN));
      Rectangle(hdc,x,y,x+CELLWIDE+1,y+CELLDEEP+1);
      SelectObject(hdc,oldpen);
      SelectObject(hdc,oldbrush);
}
```

Figure 5-7   *Continued.*

```
void UpdateCurrentCell()
{
        if(currentspin > 0) {
                currentcell+=currentspin;
                if(currentcell >= CELLCOUNT) currentcell=0;
        }
        else {
                currentcell+=currentspin;
                if(currentcell < 0) currentcell=CELLCOUNT-1;
        }
}

void MoveCell(int FAR *x,int FAR *y)
{
        int tx,ty;

        tx=*x+xdir;
        ty=*y+ydir;

        if(tx <= 0 || (tx+CELLWIDE) >= screenwide) {
                xdir=xdir * -1;
                xdir+=random(3)-1;
                currentspin=currentspin*-1;
                if(sound && blast != NULL)
                    sndPlaySound(blast,SND_ASYNC | SND_MEMORY);
        }
        if(ty <= 0 || (ty+CELLDEEP) >= screendeep) {
                ydir=ydir * -1;
                ydir+=random(3)-1;
                currentspin=currentspin*-1;
                if(sound && blast != NULL)
                    sndPlaySound(blast,SND_ASYNC | SND_MEMORY);
        }

        *x+=xdir;
        *y+=ydir;
}

int FetchAllCells()
{
        int i;

        for(i=0;i<CELLCOUNT;++i) {
                if((cell[i]=LoadResource(hInst,FindResource(hInst,
                    MAKEINTRESOURCE(CELLBASE+i),RT_BITMAP))) == NULL)
                        return(FALSE);
        }

        return(TRUE);
}
```

268

```
void DestroyAllCells()
{
        int i;

        for(i=0;i<CELLCOUNT;++i) {
                if(cell[i] != NULL) FreeResource(cell[i]);
                cell[i]=NULL;
        }
}

BOOL RegisterDialogClasses(HANDLE hInst)
{
        return(TRUE);
}

void DrawImage(HDC hdc,int x,int y,HBITMAP image)
{
        LPSTR p,pi;
        HDC hMemoryDC;
        HBITMAP hBitmap,hOldBitmap;
        LPBITMAPINFO bh;
        unsigned int n;

        if(image==NULL) return;

        if((p=LockResource(image))==NULL) return;

        bh=(LPBITMAPINFO)p;
        if(bh->bmiHeader.biBitCount > 8) n=256;
        else n=(1<<bh->bmiHeader.biBitCount);

        pi=p+sizeof(BITMAPINFOHEADER)+n*sizeof(RGBQUAD);

        if((hBitmap=CreateDIBitmap(hdc,(LPBITMAPINFOHEADER)p,CBM_INIT,pi,
           (LPBITMAPINFO)p,DIB_RGB_COLORS)) != NULL) {
                if((hMemoryDC=CreateCompatibleDC(hdc)) != NULL) {
                        hOldBitmap=SelectObject(hMemoryDC,hBitmap);
                        if(hOldBitmap) {
                                BitBlt(hdc,x,y,(int)bh->bmiHeader.biWidth,
                                    (int)bh->bmiHeader.biHeight,hMemoryDC,0,0,SRCCOPY);
                                SelectObject(hMemoryDC,hOldBitmap);
                        }
                        DeleteDC(hMemoryDC);
                }
                DeleteObject(hBitmap);
        }

        UnlockResource(image);
}

void lmemcpy(LPSTR dest,LPSTR source,unsigned int n)
{
        int i;
```

Figure 5-7   *Continued.*

```
                for(i=0;i<n;++i) dest[i]=source[i];
        }

DWORD FAR PASCAL AboutDlgProc(HWND hwnd,WORD message,WORD wParam,LONG lParam)
{
        static HANDLE sound;
        static LPSTR psound;
        HANDLE handle;
        POINT point;

        switch(message) {
                case WM_INITDIALOG:
                        if((handle=FindResource(hInst,
                            "AboutWave",RT_RCDATA)) != NULL) {
                                if((sound=LoadResource(hInst,handle)) != NULL) {
                                        if((psound=LockResource(sound)) != NULL)
                                                sndPlaySound(psound,SND_ASYNC |
                                                    SND_MEMORY | SND_NOSTOP);
                                }
                        }
                        CentreWindow(hwnd);
                        return(FALSE);
                case WM_CTLCOLOR:
                        if(HIWORD(lParam)==CTLCOLOR_STATIC ||
                            HIWORD(lParam)==CTLCOLOR_DLG) {
                                SetBkColor(wParam,RGB(192,192,192));
                                SetTextColor(wParam,RGB(0,0,0));

                                ClientToScreen(hwnd,&point);
                                UnrealizeObject(GetStockObject(LTGRAY_BRUSH));
                                SetBrushOrg(wParam,point.x,point.y);

                                return((DWORD)GetStockObject(LTGRAY_BRUSH));

                        }
                        if(HIWORD(lParam)==CTLCOLOR_BTN) {
                                SetBkColor(wParam,RGB(192,192,192));
                                SetTextColor(wParam,RGB(0,0,0));

                                ClientToScreen(hwnd,&point);
                                UnrealizeObject(GetStockObject(BLACK_BRUSH));
                                SetBrushOrg(wParam,point.x,point.y);

                                return((DWORD)GetStockObject(BLACK_BRUSH));
                        }
                        break;
                case WM_COMMAND:
                        switch(wParam) {
                                case IDOK:
                                        sndPlaySound(NULL,SND_SYNC);
                                        if(psound != NULL) UnlockResource(sound);
```

```
                                        if(sound != NULL) FreeResource(sound);
                                        EndDialog(hwnd,wParam);
                                        return(FALSE);
                                }
                                break;
                        }

        return(FALSE);
}

DWORD FAR PASCAL SetupDlgProc(HWND hwnd,WORD message,WORD wParam,LONG lParam)
{
        POINT point;
        HWND dlgH;
        char b[STRINGSIZE+1];
        int n;

        switch(message) {
                case WM_INITDIALOG:
                        CentreWindow(hwnd);
                        if(sound) CheckOn(SETUP_SOUND);
                        wsprintf(b,"%u",delay);
                        ItemName(SETUP_DELAY,(LPSTR)b);
                        return(FALSE);
                case WM_CTLCOLOR:
                        if(HIWORD(lParam)==CTLCOLOR_STATIC ||
                           HIWORD(lParam)==CTLCOLOR_DLG) {
                                SetBkColor(wParam,RGB(192,192,192));
                                SetTextColor(wParam,RGB(0,0,0));

                                ClientToScreen(hwnd,&point);
                                UnrealizeObject(GetStockObject(LTGRAY_BRUSH));
                                SetBrushOrg(wParam,point.x,point.y);

                                return((DWORD)GetStockObject(LTGRAY_BRUSH));

                        }
                        if(HIWORD(lParam)==CTLCOLOR_BTN) {
                                SetBkColor(wParam,RGB(192,192,192));
                                SetTextColor(wParam,RGB(0,0,0));

                                ClientToScreen(hwnd,&point);
                                UnrealizeObject(GetStockObject(BLACK_BRUSH));
                                SetBrushOrg(wParam,point.x,point.y);

                                return((DWORD)GetStockObject(BLACK_BRUSH));
                        }
                        break;
                case WM_COMMAND:
                        switch(wParam) {
                                case IDOK:
                                        if(IsItemChecked(SETUP_SOUND)) sound=TRUE;
                                        else sound=FALSE;
```

271

Figure 5-7   *Continued.*

```
                                        GetItemName(SETUP_DELAY,b);
                                        n=atoi(b);
                                        if(n >= MINDELAY && n <= MAXDELAY) delay=n;

                                        EndDialog(hwnd,wParam);
                                        return(FALSE);
                        }
                        break;
        }

        return(FALSE);
}


void CentreWindow(HWND hwnd)
{
        RECT rect;
        unsigned int x,y;

        GetWindowRect(hwnd,&rect);
        x=(GetSystemMetrics(SM_CXSCREEN)-(rect.right-rect.left))/2;
        y=(GetSystemMetrics(SM_CYSCREEN)-(rect.bottom-rect.top))/2;
        SetWindowPos(hwnd,NULL,x,y,rect.right-rect.left,
            rect.bottom-rect.top,SWP_NOSIZE);
}

int HasMouseMoved(int x,int y)
{
        int r=FALSE;

        if(oldmousex != -1 && oldmousey != -1) {
                if(abs(x-oldmousex) > THRESHOLD ||
                    abs(y-oldmousey) > THRESHOLD) r=TRUE;
        }

        oldmousex=x;
        oldmousey=y;

        return(r);
}

void LoadConfig()
{
        sound=GetProfileInt(szAppName,SOUNDKEY,sound);
        delay=GetProfileInt(szAppName,DELAYKEY,delay);
}

void SaveConfig()
{
        char b[STRINGSIZE+1];
```

```
            wsprintf(b,"%d",sound);
            WriteProfileString(szAppName,SOUNDKEY,b);

            wsprintf(b,"%d",delay);
            WriteProfileString(szAppName,DELAYKEY,b);
}
```

The SAVER.RC resource script.   Figure 5-8

```
AboutBox DIALOG 18, 18, 184, 180
STYLE WS_POPUP | WS_CAPTION
CAPTION "About..."
BEGIN
        CONTROL "", 102, "BorShade", BSS_GROUP | WS_CHILD | WS_VISIBLE | WS_TABSTOP,
            8, 68, 168, 76
        CTEXT "Screen Saver 1.0\n\nCopyright (c) 1994 Alchemy Mindworks Inc.\n\n
            This program is part of the book Advanced Multimedia Programming for
            Windows by Steven William Rimmer, published by Windcrest/McGraw Hill.",
            -1, 12, 72, 160, 68, WS_CHILD | WS_VISIBLE | WS_GROUP
        CONTROL "Button", IDOK, "BorBtn", BS_DEFPUSHBUTTON | WS_CHILD | WS_VISIBLE |
            WS_TABSTOP, 74, 152, 32, 20
        CONTROL "Button", 801, "BorBtn", BS_PUSHBUTTON | WS_CHILD | WS_VISIBLE |
            WS_TABSTOP, 36, 8, 32, 20
END

1801 BITMAP "smpw.bmp"

BlastWave RCDATA "BLAST.WAV"

1700 BITMAP "ball0.bmp"
1701 BITMAP "ball1.bmp"
1702 BITMAP "ball2.bmp"
1703 BITMAP "ball3.bmp"
1704 BITMAP "ball4.bmp"
1705 BITMAP "ball5.bmp"
1706 BITMAP "ball6.bmp"
1707 BITMAP "ball7.bmp"

AboutWave RCDATA "ABOUT.WAV"

ScreenSaver ICON
BEGIN
        '00 00 01 00 01 00 20 20 10 00 00 00 00 00 E8 02'
        '00 00 16 00 00 00 28 00 00 00 20 00 00 00 40 00'
        '00 00 01 00 04 00 00 00 00 00 80 02 00 00 00 00'
        '00 00 00 00 00 00 10 00 00 00 00 00 00 00 00 00'
        '00 00 00 00 BF 00 00 BF 00 00 00 BF BF 00 BF 00'
        '00 00 BF 00 BF 00 BF BF 00 00 C0 C0 C0 00 80 80'
        '80 00 00 00 FF 00 00 FF 00 00 00 FF FF 00 FF 00'
        '00 00 FF 00 FF 00 FF FF 00 00 FF FF FF 00 77 77'
        '77 77 77 77 77 77 77 77 77 77 77 77 77 77 7F 88'
        '88 88 88 88 88 88 88 88 88 88 88 88 88 87 7F F8'
        '88 88 88 88 88 88 88 88 88 88 88 88 88 87 7F F7'
        '77 77 77 77 77 77 77 77 77 77 77 77 78 87 7F F7'
        '77 77 77 77 77 77 77 77 77 77 77 77 78 87 7F F7'
        '77 77 77 77 77 77 77 77 77 77 77 77 78 87 7F F7'
```

Figure 5-8   *Continued.*

```
'77 00 00 00 00 00 00 00 00 00 00 77 78 87 7F F7'
'77 00 00 00 00 00 00 00 00 00 00 77 78 87 7F F7'
'77 00 00 00 00 00 00 00 00 00 00 77 78 87 7F F7'
'77 00 00 00 00 00 00 00 00 00 00 77 78 87 7F F7'
'77 00 00 00 00 00 00 00 00 00 00 77 78 87 7F F7'
'77 00 00 00 00 00 00 00 00 00 00 77 78 87 7F F7'
'77 00 00 00 00 00 00 00 00 00 00 77 78 87 7F F7'
'77 00 00 00 00 00 00 00 00 00 00 77 78 87 7F F7'
'77 00 00 00 00 00 00 00 00 00 00 77 78 87 7F F7'
'77 00 00 00 00 00 00 00 00 00 00 77 78 87 7F F7'
'77 00 00 00 00 00 00 00 00 00 00 77 78 87 7F F7'
'77 00 00 00 00 00 00 00 00 00 00 77 78 87 7F F7'
'77 00 00 00 00 00 00 00 00 00 00 77 78 87 7F F7'
'77 00 00 00 00 00 00 00 00 00 00 77 78 87 7F F7'
'77 00 00 00 00 00 00 00 00 00 00 77 78 87 7F F7'
'77 00 00 00 00 00 00 00 00 00 00 77 78 87 7F F7'
'77 00 00 00 00 00 00 00 00 00 00 77 78 87 7F F7'
'77 00 00 00 00 00 00 00 00 00 00 77 78 87 7F F7'
'77 00 00 00 00 00 00 00 00 00 00 77 78 87 7F F7'
'77 77 77 77 77 77 77 77 77 77 77 78 87 7F F7'
'77 77 77 77 77 77 77 77 77 77 77 78 87 7F F7'
'77 77 77 77 77 77 77 77 77 77 77 78 87 7F FF'
'FF FF FF FF FF FF FF FF FF FF FF F8 87 7F FF'
'FF FF FF FF FF FF FF FF FF FF FF FF 87 77 77'
'77 77 77 77 77 77 77 77 77 77 77 77 77 00 00'
'00 00 00 00 00 00 00 00 00 00 00 00 00 00 00'
'00 00 00 00 00 00 00 00 00 00 00 00 00 00 00'
'00 00 00 00 00 00 00 00 00 00 00 00 00 00 00'
'00 00 00 00 00 00 00 00 00 00 00 00 00 00 00'
'00 00 00 00 00 00 00 00 00 00 00 00 00 00 00'
'00 00 00 00 00 00 00 00 00 00 00 00 00 00 00'
'00 00 00 00 00 00 00 00 00 00 00 00 00 00 00'
'00 00 00 00 00 00 00 00 00 00 00 00 00 00 00'
END

SetupBox DIALOG 18, 18, 192, 80
STYLE WS_POPUP | WS_CAPTION
CAPTION "Setup..."
BEGIN
        CONTROL "", -1, "BorShade", BSS_GROUP | WS_CHILD | WS_VISIBLE |WS_TABSTOP,
            8, 8, 176, 36
        CONTROL "Button", IDOK, "BorBtn", BS_DEFPUSHBUTTON | WS_CHILD | WS_VISIBLE |
            WS_TABSTOP, 80, 52, 32, 20
        RTEXT "Time until the screen blanks:", -1, 16, 16, 104, 8, SS_RIGHT | WS_CHILD |
            WS_VISIBLE | WS_GROUP
        LTEXT "seconds", -1, 148, 16, 28, 8, WS_CHILD | WS_VISIBLE | WS_GROUP
        EDITTEXT 101, 124, 14, 20, 12, ES_LEFT | WS_CHILD | WS_VISIBLE | WS_BORDER |
            WS_TABSTOP
        CONTROL "Loud, annoying sound when the ball hits a wall", 102, "BorCheck",
            BS_AUTOCHECKBOX | WS_CHILD | WS_VISIBLE | WS_TABSTOP, 16, 28, 164, 10
END
```

The code after the call to CreateWindow in the WinMain function of
SAVER.CPP installs the MessageHook filter function discussed
earlier in this chapter and starts processing messages for the main
window. The while loop that executes GetMessage actually
dispatches the messages for this window.

The WndProc function does all the message handling for the main
window of the screen saver. Its WM_CREATE case adds two new
items to the SAVER system menu to handle About and Setup dialogs.
Admittedly, there isn't all that much to set up in SAVER—more
elaborate savers will presumably have more complicated configuration
dialogs.

Note that while SAVER will never have a visible window, its system
menu can be accessed from its icon.

The WM_CREATE case also sets up a timer for SAVER that sends a
WM_TIMER message to WndProc once each second. This increments
the count value mentioned earlier, as you can see in the WM_TIMER
handler for WndProc. When the value of count reaches the value of
delay—the number of seconds of inactivity required to blank the
screen—the WM_TIMER handler calls BlankScreen to herald the
approach of nightfall.

The BlankScreen function also uses CreateWindow to open a new
window on the screen. Unlike the call in WndMain, this one is
maximized. It has the GDI stock black brush defined as its
hbrBackground brush object. The window has no menu or scroll
bars, and as such fills the entire screen with blackness. As with all
windows, the objects below it will be restored as soon as it closes.

The ScreenSaverProc function handles messages sent to the big
black window. The WM_CREATE handler begins by loading all the
animation cells into memory. There are, in fact, eight of them, as
illustrated in Fig. 5-9. Unlike the JOYDEMO application, the beach
ball in SAVER actually rolls around the screen. This effect is created
by having eight versions of the beach ball graphic, each rotated 45
degrees relative to the last, and animating the ball by stepping
through the cells sequentially.

Figure 5-9

The cells for the screen saver.

Animating the beach ball in SAVER is somewhat less involved than doing so in JOYDEMO. The background of the window in which the beach ball will appear is conveniently black. There's no need to preserve the area under the beach ball before it's drawn, as it can be erased by simply painting a black rectangle over it. There's also no need to mask the beach ball out of its background—it will be drawn inset into a black rectangle, but a small black rectangle painted on a larger black rectangle is pretty well impossible to spot.

The beach ball is animated by progressively moving it until it strikes a wall of the area it's moving in, at which time its direction will reverse. The calculations involved in locating the ball are handled by the MoveCell function declared later in SAVER.CPP. In fact, the SAVER application adds a random element to the ball's travel after it bounces, such that it won't travel the same path over and over again. Each iteration of the beach ball's movement is instigated by WM_TIMER messages appearing at ScreenSaverProc.

The ScreenSaverProc window will always be the top window as long as the screen is blanked, and as such all key press and mouse movement messages will be received by ScreenSaverProc. As you can see at the bottom of the ScreenSaverProc function, the first one that shows up will immediately close the black window.

In fact, WM_MOUSEMOVE messages must be qualified a bit by calling HasMouseMoved, defined later in the SAVER.CPP source listing. This makes sure that the mouse has actually moved a respectable distance, as some inexpensive mice exhibit mechanical jitter not unlike that discussed earlier in this chapter in conjunction with joysticks.

The About item of the system menu of SAVER displays an About dialog pretty much like the ones that have appeared in the applications discussed earlier in this book. The Setup item will call forth the Setup dialog illustrated in Fig. 5-10.

Figure 5-10

Setup...

Time until the screen blanks: 30   seconds
☐ Loud, annoying sound when the ball hits a wall

✓ OK

The screen saver Setup dialog.

The Setup dialog is managed by the SetupDlgProc function in
SAVER.CPP. There are only two configurable items in this screen
saver—a flag to specify whether to make noise when the beach ball
rebounds off one of the window edges, and the number of seconds to
wait before blanking the screen.

The configuration items are stored in WIN.INI. After having run the
screen saver once, you'll find a section like this at the end of your
WIN.INI file:

```
[ScreenSaver]
LoudAnnoyingSound=0
TimeBeforeUtterBlackness=30
```

The LoadConfig function down at the end of SAVER.CPP will fetch
these values when SAVER starts up. The SaveConfig function will
save them when it terminates.

⇨ Animation in the high grass

There's a great deal you can do with animation under Windows
beyond that which has been discussed in this chapter. As with many
areas of multimedia application development, the basic techniques of
making things happen is best augmented by a lot of imagination.

The message-driven nature of Windows can make animating complex graphics, with several moving elements, a lot easier than it might have otherwise been in a DOS application. This may be some compensation for the other restrictions Windows places on bitmapped graphics in general.

While there have been relatively few sophisticated Windows graphic-based games—Windows implementations of Commander Keen or Duke Nukem don't appear to be forthcoming—there's nothing inherent in Windows to make such applications of graphics and sound impractical. A game that you could quickly minimize when the boss came by would certainly be a useful asset.

6

MIDI music

*"If the Buddhist perception of reincarnation is correct, in which we
will all return in the next life with a form dictated by our karma in
this one, the slug population had best brace itself for an influx of
lawyers and politicians."*
—Graffiti

THE MIDI music standard is fairly old as computer structures go.
It dates back to the early eighties, although in its
inception it had little to do with computers. It was based on the
observation that there was a growing application for dedicated
keyboard synthesizers, and that they'd all be a lot more useful if they
could be interconnected.

The acronym MIDI stands for *musical instrument digital interface*.

In a theoretical sense, a keyboard synthesizer consists of two discrete
elements in one box. The keyboard generates information about
which notes to play—along with some secondary things, such as how
hard the keys are struck—and the synthesizer makes sounds based on
the note information being sent to it. This is a very workable model,
as it makes the music being played somewhat device-independent. The
keyboard doesn't have to know what the synthesizer is up to.

The MIDI interface, in its earliest form, was a standardized hardware
and software structure through which note information could pass.
Thus, for example, you could play a Yamaha synthesizer through a
Roland keyboard—assuming that both devices included MIDI
interfaces. You could also control several synthesizers through a single
keyboard.

In this most elemental sort of MIDI application, all MIDI devices can
be seen as generators of note information or sound sources—players
of music based on notes sent to them. All such MIDI devices can be
thought of as black boxes. Thus, while you could drive a MIDI sound
source from a keyboard, you could also drive it from some other sort
of interface, such as a MIDI guitar or a MIDI violin. The sound source

expects note information to be sent to it—it doesn't know or care what sort of hardware generated the notes.

Because a MIDI sound source is independent of whatever is driving it, it can play music in voices that have nothing to do with the hardware used to generate the note data. You could be generating note data with a MIDI guitar, but have the notes played in a voice that sounds like bagpipes, or wind chimes, or cars backfiring.

The information that passes between MIDI instruments is digital data—note numbers and other secondary information, rather than sound. The MIDI interface hardware is actually a sort of specialized high-speed serial port analogous to the modem connector on a PC. The second stage of MIDI development occurred when people began to realize that one of the potential MIDI devices in a complex MIDI system was a computer.

A computer equipped with a MIDI interface can record MIDI information digitally and subsequently pretend to be a MIDI note generator, playing it all back. Because MIDI music is stored as note numbers, rather than as digitized sounds like wave files are, you can actually edit music on screen, much as you might do with words in a word processor.

Figure 6-1 illustrates a MIDI music editor running under Windows.

A computer running suitable software can actually become a sort of digital copyist and recording studio on your desktop. With it you can record and play back tracks, overdub multiple tracks one at a time, save music as disk files, and fine tune your performances note by note if you like. This last facility will help you fix performance mistakes—as well as add grace notes, arpeggios, and other elements that you couldn't actually play in real time.

In an earlier age, this would have been regarded as cheating—with the advent of MIDI it has become almost respectable. One might regard it as "an extension of the human-technological music interface which further augments the creative process." It's still cheating, but it sounds a lot better this way.

Figure 6-1

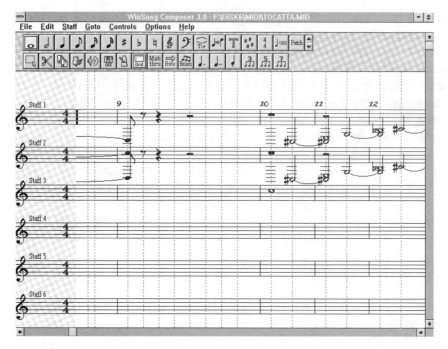

WinSong, a commercial MIDI scoring program. Don't let its appearance here serve as an endorsement.

One of the potentially confusing aspects of MIDI is that the word represents several related but largely distinct elements. A MIDI interface is the mechanical hardware that allows two MIDI devices to communicate. The standard MIDI interface connector is a five-pin DIN plug attached to a special serial port. As we'll see shortly, not all MIDI implementations require physical MIDI connectors.

The information sent over a MIDI interface—properly called MIDI messages—is defined by a fairly simple structure, which we'll discuss in detail in a moment.

Finally, when MIDI messages are stored in a disk file, they represent a third structure. Disk files containing MIDI music have the extension MID. A MIDI file can contain not only note information, but text and voice data as well. Voice data will also turn up later on.

When Windows sprouted its multimedia extensions, it embraced MIDI as its standard for digital music—with a few modifications. This is the context under which MIDI will appear in this chapter. Longtime MIDI purists will complain that Windows' use of MIDI mangled an otherwise pure and noncorporate standard into something only a Microsoft employee could love. You're free to agree with this view if you like—and you're also free to work around it to whatever degree you choose. The MIDI standard as it appears under Windows is pretty flexible. You can use as much or as little of the Windows-specific functions as you require.

⇨ MIDI note messages

The basic structure of MIDI note information is consistent, whether you're playing on a Yamaha DX-7 synthesizer from the early eighties or on a Pentium PC made a decade later. I should note that the keyboard synthesizer used to develop some of the MIDI applications in this chapter really was a Yamaha DX-7 from the early eighties. While no longer even within visual range of the leading edge, it has acquired a patina of funkiness with the passage of time.

To begin with, there are 128 playable notes under MIDI. Each key on a keyboard synthesizer corresponds to one note. Of course, very few keyboards have 128 keys—the range of playable notes extends somewhat beyond both extremes of a conventional keyboard.

As an aside, the voices actually used to play MIDI notes are generated by a number of disparate technologies, which we'll discuss in detail later in this chapter. Few of them sound presentable when confronted with note values at the extremes of this range.

Figure 6-2 illustrates the MIDI note numbers corresponding to the keys on a conventional synthesizer.

As another aside, at this stage MIDI note numbers are fairly abstract. They don't correspond to absolute pitches, nor do they presuppose that they'll be played with specific voices. One of the more abstruse issues of musical instrument technology is that of tuning. Conventional

Figure 6-2

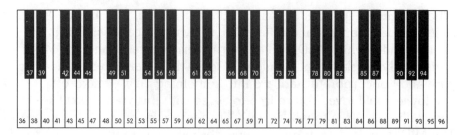

A synthesizer keyboard and the MIDI note numbers that correspond to its keys.

keyboards are tuned using equal temperament. This means that the pitch of each key is separated from that of the previous key by an equal amount. Since the range from C to C' is one octave, and there are 12 notes in an octave, an interval is one-twelfth of an octave.

While equal temperament seems fairly obvious, it's a more or less recent innovation. It turned up at around the time of Johann Sebastian Bach. Prior to its introduction, keyboard instruments were constructed with any of a number of other tunings, such that they sounded best in particular keys—and pretty atonal in others. Detractors of equal temperament at the time of its introduction suggested that it managed to sound atonal in all keys.

Once again, MIDI note numbers don't know what voices they'll be played in, and as such they can play in any tuning you like. Several MIDI synthesizers exist that allow you to select alternate tunings.

It takes two MIDI messages to play a note—one to turn the note on, and a second one to turn the note off:

NOTE ON   90H

NOTE OFF 80H

This probably deserves a bit of explanation. The messages used by MIDI are fairly cunning, and manage to pack a lot of information into relatively few bytes.

To begin with, MIDI supports up to 16 channels of information. This means, for example, that one computer could drive up to 16 discrete MIDI synthesizers. Each channel can be polyphonic—it can play as many notes at once as you like. In practice, specific MIDI sound sources will have finite limits to the number of notes that can play at one time. The MIDI channels are numbered 0 through 15.

A MIDI message can be regarded as consisting of two four-bit nibbles. The upper nibble is the message number, specifying whether the message is NOTE ON, NOTE OFF, CONTROL CHANGE, and so on. The lower nibble is the channel number this particular message applies to. In the hypothetical system of one computer driving 16 MIDI sound sources, a NOTE ON message with its low order nibble set to two—indicating channel two—would be played by the MIDI synthesizer configured to "listen" to channel two and would be ignored by all the others.

A NOTE ON message for channel two would have the value 92H.

Following the message byte of a MIDI message will be its data bytes. Different messages have different numbers of data bytes. Data bytes for messages always have their high-order bits clear—the data in a MIDI data byte must be in the range of 0 through 127. Here's the complete structure of a NOTE ON message:

NOTE ON   90H NOTE VELOCITY

A NOTE ON message has three bytes. The first byte will be 90H with the channel number in its low-order nibble. The second byte will be the note number to turn on, ranging from 0 through 127. The third number will be the key velocity, that is, how hard the key was struck to generate the note. This information might be synthetically generated if the note was actually dispatched from something other than a keyboard.

Some instrument voices use the velocity information and some ignore it. As a few obvious examples, a piano voice will change how a note sounds based on how hard it's played. An organ voice won't—real-world organs aren't velocity-sensitive.

A NOTE ON message with a velocity value of zero should be interpreted as a NOTE OFF message.

A NOTE OFF message has the same data structure as a NOTE ON message. The velocity value is interpreted differently by different synthesizers. My old DX-7 ignores it entirely—it's usually regarded as being a decay value.

Figure 6-3 illustrates the envelope of a note being played and how its data values affect it. This assumes that the voice and hardware in question support velocity sensing.

Figure 6-3

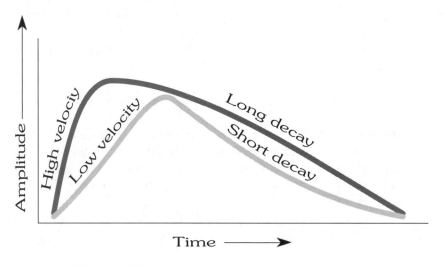

A note and its envelope.

It's important to keep in mind that while real instruments usually have built-in mechanical decays—a piano note will eventually fade out by itself, a note played on a sax will become silent when the sax player runs out of breath, and so on—notes sent over a MIDI interface do not automatically silence themselves after a preset time. If the source of the note information is a MIDI keyboard or other synthesizer controller, NOTE OFF messages will automatically be sent for each NOTE ON message. If you're generating MIDI notes in software— something we'll see in real life shortly—it's important to make sure that NOTE OFF messages are sent for each note you play.

It's convenient to assume that everything sent between MIDI devices happens instantaneously. In fact this isn't true, but the MIDI interface is sufficiently fast so as to make the time lags unnoticeable. As such, if you wanted to play a three-note chord, you could do so by sending three NOTE ON messages and then three corresponding NOTE OFF messages after a suitable interval.

Figure 6-4 illustrates some music and the MIDI messages that would play it.

Figure 6-4

A score and the MIDI messages required to play it.

This discussion of MIDI note messages has largely assumed that they'll be played in real time. In dealing with computer-based MIDI, in which MIDI notes will be played and stored, there's an additional element associated with each MIDI message. A time counter is required to specify when each message is to be sent relative to the beginning of the piece being played. This will turn up in detail when we look at MIDI files.

MIDI voices

A typical MIDI synthesizer—the hardware that plays music when it receives NOTE ON messages—will have a selection of voices to play in. For the sake of this discussion, let's allow that one logical MIDI sound source is one channel and lives in one box. In fact, one sound source could actually be a keyboard synthesizer in which the keyboard

isn't being used—the note information would be coming directly through the MIDI interface—or it could be a keyboard-less synthesizer, a sound source with no input other than a MIDI port. Most sound sources of the latter type can be configured to pretend to be more than one device—that is, to play music on more than one MIDI channel at a time.

Figure 6-5 illustrates the first few bars of Pachelbel's Canon. This is usually scored for three violins and a viola. To play this using a MIDI scoring program and MIDI sound generators, you might assign the first violin to channel zero, the second to channel one, the third to channel two, and the viola to channel three, and arrange to have four sound generators configured to play notes on these channels.

Figure 6-5

The introductory bars of Pachelbel's Canon.

A MIDI score, like the one in Fig. 6-5, can include more than just note information. For example, it can have voice changes interspersed throughout. If you don't like having the first violin line of the Canon played entirely by a violin, you could have it change to a saxophone after a few bars, and perhaps then to a trumpet after a few more. This probably won't result in a particularly listenable performance, but it serves to illustrate how MIDI voices can be controlled.

As an aside, Johannes Pachelbel originally wrote the Canon for organ.
Critics of performers who rearrange it for brass instruments,
synthesizers, or tuned water glasses are wont to forget that the version
for strings that's considered traditional is itself an arrangement.

A MIDI sound source can have up to 128 distinct voices online at a
time. A PROGRAM CHANGE message will tell the sound source in
question to select a new voice. As with NOTE ON and NOTE OFF
messages, a PROGRAM CHANGE message carries its message
number in its high-order nibble and the channel it refers to in its low-
order nibble. The message number for a PROGRAM CHANGE
message is C0H.

A PROGRAM CHANGE message is followed by one byte of data
specifying the new voice to select.

It's actually in dealing with MIDI voices that scoring music for MIDI
gets a bit confusing. In MIDI as it exists outside Windows, there is no
standard assignment for voices. This means that voice number nine
might be a piano on one synthesizer and musical elephants on
another. A PROGRAM CHANGE message specifies which voice
number to use, but not what that voice will sound like.

The Windows MIDI implementation addresses this issue to some
extent, as we'll see.

Additional MIDI messages

There are several other sorts of MIDI messages—less frequently used
than the ones we've covered so far and perhaps not really applicable
to anything you can envision using MIDI for. They're applicable
primarily to instrument parameter control or the exchange of voice
data. Among these are the following:

➤ The AFTERTOUCH message specifies additional note decay
information. Its MIDI message is A0H.

➤ The CONTROL CHANGE message specifies the settings of
specific synthesizer controls, such as foot pedals, a pitch wheel,

and so on, which tend to be system specific. Its MIDI message is B0H.

> The PITCH BEND message specifies how much to adjust the pitch of a note after it has begun playing. Its MIDI message is E0H.

The MIDI specification also defines messages that don't apply to playing music on a particular channel, but rather deal with information for a sound source as a whole. The most commonly encountered such message is a system exclusive, which begins with the message F0H. System exclusive messages are used, among other things, to send voice information between synthesizers.

Voice data is one of those rather large cans of worms that occasionally pops open and begins crawling all over your sheet music under MIDI. Each synthesizer technology uses a different structure to define how its voices will sound. Some of these are extremely exotic. They can range from sampled voices—real sounds that have been digitized—to algorithmic voice synthesizers, such as the FM sound used in Yamaha instruments. Not only is the voice data for one manufacturer's sound source not portable to other instruments, but in many cases you can't even interchange voices among different synthesizers from the same manufacturer. Many of Yamaha's various instruments can't exchange voice banks, for example.

There are certainly applications for sending voice definitions over MIDI. One of the most common is the use of computer-based voice librarians. Assuming you have a voice librarian designed specifically for your synthesizer, you will be able to store banks of voices and download them to your synthesizer as you require them. Most voice librarians also allow you to modify existing voices or create new ones.

Moving voice data about is a subject that could easily fill a book this size. With new and typically incompatible voice formats appearing fairly regularly among MIDI instrument makers, it's probably safe to assume that such a book would be largely out of date by the time it was printed. This is a subject that won't be dealt with in detail in this chapter.

MIDI under Windows

Thus far, we've discussed MIDI in its traditional sense, that of a computer and one or more external MIDI instruments to generate note information and sound sources to play it. Conceptualizing MIDI this way is very useful because it helps you better understand its capabilities. In practice, however, MIDI under Windows usually doesn't work this way. You can do a lot with MIDI under Windows and never get within 20 feet of a MIDI cable.

Old MIDI hands may disparage this "appliance" MIDI implementation, but a good three-quarters of the general frustration level of using complex MIDI implementations can usually be blamed on those cables.

If you have a MIDI-compatible sound card installed in your computer, you have the equivalent of an external MIDI sound source. The "cable" connecting the MIDI interface of your computer to the MIDI input of the sound source is hardwired on your sound card. While this is very much less flexible than using external MIDI instruments and cables, it's orders of magnitude simpler. Furthermore, as we'll see later in this chapter, it doesn't preclude augmenting your MIDI system with external hardware, if you like.

One of the innovations of MIDI as it appears under Windows is the MIDI Mapper. This is a sort of MIDI air traffic controller. It allows software that wants to play MIDI music to do so without having to know what channels various instruments are assigned to, which voices are available, and so on. MIDI note data sent to the MIDI Mapper, rather than to specific MIDI channels, will always be played correctly through your sound card—or at least, it will always be played reasonably well. The MIDI Mapper assigns MIDI channels and maintains a standardized set of voices, shown in Fig. 6-6.

With the Windows MIDI Mapper in place, your sound card or other MIDI sound source will be set up with the standard 128 voices shown in Fig. 6-6. Music scored to use these voices will play in the voices it was intended for, even if it was created on a system with a wholly different sound card than yours. It might not sound precisely the same, as different sound cards generate sound with different

Figure 6-6

Acoustic Grand Piano
Bright Acoustic Piano
Electric Grand Piano
Honky Tonk Piano
Rhodes Piano
Chorused Piano
Harpsichord
Clavinet
Celesta
Glockenspiel
Music Box
Vibraphone
Marimba
Xylophone
Tubular Bells
Dulcimer
Hammond Organ
Percussive Organ
Rock Organ
Church Organ
Reed Organ
Accordion
Harmonica
Tango Accordion
Acoustic Guitar (nylon)
Acoustic Guitar (steel)
Electric Guitar (jazz)
Electric Guitar (clean)
Electric Guitar (muted)
Overdriven Guitar
Distortion Guitar
Guitar Harmonics
Acoustic Bass
Electric Bass (fingered)
Electric Bass (picked)
Fretless Bass
Slap Bass 1
Slap Bass 2
Synth Bass 1
Synth Bass 2
Violin
Viola
Cello
Contrabass
Tremolo Strings
Pizzicato Strings
Orchestral Harp
Timpani
String Ensemble 1
String Ensemble 2
Synth Strings 1
Synth Strings 2

Choir Aahs
Voice Oohs
Synth Voice
Orchestra Hit
Trumpet
Trombone
Tuba
Muted Trumpet
French Horn
Brass Section
Bynth Brass 1
Synth Brass 2
Soprano Sax
Alto Sax
Tenor Sax
Baritone Sax
Oboe
English Horn
Bassoon
Clarinet
Piccolo
Flute
Recorder
Pan Flute
Blown Bottle
Shakuhachi
Whistle
Ocarina
Lead 1 (square)
Lead 2 (sawtooth)
Lead 3 (calliope)
Lead 4 (chiff)
Lead 5 (charang)
Lead 6 (voice)
Lead 7 (fifths)
Lead 8 (bass + lead)
Pad 1 (new age)
Pad 2 (warm)
Pad 3 (polysynth)
Pad 4 (choir)
Pad 5 (bowed)
Pad 6 (metallic)
Pad 7 (halo)
Pad 8 (sweep)
FX 1 (rain)
FX 2 (soundtrack)
FX 3 (crystal)
FX 4 (atmosphere)
FX 5 (brightness)
FX 6 (goblins)
FX 7 (echoes)
FX 8 (sci-fi)

Sitar
Banjo
Shamisen
Koto
Kalimba
Bagpipe
Fiddle
Shanai
Tinkle Bell
Agogo
Steel Drums
Woodblock
Taiko Drum
Melodic Tom
Synth Drum
Reverse Cymbal
Guitar Fret Noise
Breath Noise
Seashore
Bird Tweet
Telephone Ring
Helicopter
Applause
Gunshot

The MIDI voices supported by MIDI Mapper.

technologies. A violin might well sound more like a violin on a high-end Turtle Beach sound card than it does on a low-cost AdLib board, but voice number 40 will sound more or less like a violin in both cases.

The aforementioned old MIDI hands—users of MIDI who don't typically work with the arguable convenience of Windows' MIDI Mapper—will usually respond to this by saying something like "where's the crummhorn voice?" A crummhorn is a medieval instrument that sounds a bit like playing a jar of equally tempered wasps. The important point about crummhorns and crummhorn music is that no crummhorns appear in the Windows MIDI Mapper voice list. Under MIDI as it exists outside Windows, a musician who wants to play MIDI crummhorns could use a voice editor to create a crummhorn voice and select it with a PROGRAM CHANGE message.

Because the voices under the MIDI Mapper are effectively fixed and inalterable, this isn't possible under Windows. Crummhorn music would have to be rescored into one of the existing MIDI Mapper voices.

This is, of course, the price of having a standard and finite voice bank. It would be impractical for the MIDI Mapper to provide a voice editor among its other facilities; as with board synthesizers, sound cards from different manufacturers use wildly different sound generation technologies. In addition, allowing users to define new voices would largely defeat the purpose of the MIDI Mapper—MIDI music would cease to be portable among systems. Windows generally accommodates portability, because it cuts down on technical support calls that Microsoft must answer and subsequently keep on hold.

Playing music with MIDI

In the companion volume to this one, *Multimedia Programming for Windows*, playing MIDI music is handled by letting the MCI interface play MIDI files. This is actually breathlessly simple, as it requires that MCI do all the work. This is all the code you need to play a MIDI file:

```
MCI_OPEN_PARMS mciOpen;
MCI_PLAY_PARMS mciPlay;
char b[STRINGSIZE+1];
unsigned long rtrn;
int id=-1;

mciOpen.wDeviceID=NULL;
mciOpen.lpstrDeviceType="sequencer";
mciOpen.lpstrElementName=path;
if((rtrn=mciSendCommand(NULL,MCI_OPEN,MCI_OPEN_TYPE |
   MCI_OPEN_ELEMENT,(DWORD)(LPVOID)&mciOpen)) != 0L) {
       mciGetErrorString(rtrn,(LPSTR)b,STRINGSIZE);
       DoMessage(hwnd,b);
       return(FALSE);
}

id=mciOpen.wDeviceID;

mciPlay.dwCallback=hwnd;
if((rtrn=mciSendCommand(id,MCI_PLAY,
  MCI_NOTIFY,(DWORD)(LPVOID)&mciPlay)) != 0L) {
       mciSendCommand(id,MCI_CLOSE,0,NULL);
       mciGetErrorString(rtrn,(LPSTR)b,STRINGSIZE);
       DoMessage(hwnd,b);
       return(FALSE);
}
```

You might want to consult *Multimedia Programming for Windows* for a more complete discussion of exactly what this bit of code is up to.

Clearly, there's a great deal more to MIDI music than playing MIDI files. To begin with, you can generate MIDI note data in software, rather than simply having it spring from a canned piece stored on disk. This facility can be used to play fanfares when a menu opens, Bach's Toccata and Fugue when something nasty is about to occur, or uplifting Irish fiddle tunes to brighten your day when your Excel spreadsheet is getting ready to tell you that your overdraft would best be expressed in exponential notation. It's to this latter task that the first sample program in this chapter dedicates itself.

The PLAYSONG application is shown in Fig. 6-7. What it does is less important than how it does it. When you click on the Play button in PLAYSONG, MIDI music will begin playing without a MIDI file in sight. In addition to merely playing music, PLAYSONG will allow you to change the voices it plays in.

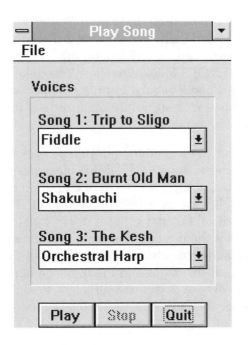

Figure 6-7

The PLAYSONG application.

The PLAYSONG application is deceptively simple. In fact, playing MIDI music directly is exceedingly complicated, as it requires that you deal with something that Windows isn't particularly good at. Inasmuch as PLAYSONG can't use the MCI interface to play MIDI music, the application itself must manage the precise timing involved. This requires recourse to some of the multimedia timer functions discussed earlier in this book. Actually, it requires recourse to the really nasty ones.

For the sake of this example, let's assume that the music to be played is monophonic—that is, that it consists of single notes played one after another. Figure 6-8 illustrates the first few bars of "Trip to Sligo," the first of the tunes played by the PLAYSONG application.

Figure 6-8

Trip to Sligo.

Allowing that the notes in the music illustrated in Fig. 6-8 were to be defined in data in some form, playing them would involve stepping through the list of notes at regular intervals and issuing the appropriate NOTE ON and NOTE OFF MIDI messages. The only awkward aspect of this is the part about regular intervals. Windows isn't really set up to allow for this—at least, not if you approach the problem using conventional Windows facilities.

The most obvious approach to having something happen periodically under Windows is to set up a timer to send WM_TIMER messages to a window, and have the function that's supposed to happen periodically called from the WM_TIMER handler for the window in question. This works reasonably well for less critical functions, but it doesn't play very convincing music. It turns out that the message-handling mechanism of Windows introduces noticeable and somewhat erratic delays into the path between a function that sends messages and the message handler that will ultimately receive them. These delays are sufficient to make WM_TIMER messages useless for the fairly precise timing required to play music.

As mentioned in Chapter 3, more precise timing control can be managed through the use of the timeSetEvent call. This will allow a function of your choice to be called at very precise intervals. There are some catches to this, however. The function in question can in turn call only a very limited number of Windows functions, as explained in Chapter 3. Also, it must reside in a dynamic link library having a fixed code segment.

Later in this chapter we'll take a look at a dedicated dynamic link library for handling MIDI functions.

In its simplest form, sheet music defines each note by its pitch and duration. Creating note information in data, we can do pretty much the same thing. This wouldn't have impressed Bach, but it makes reasonable sense to a computer:

```
typedef struct {
        unsigned int note;
        unsigned int duration;
        } NOTE;
```

In practice, these fields will be used to hold other objects as well in a complex list of notes and other information.

This is a list of note objects defining the first part of the first song that PLAYSONG will generate, "Trip to Sligo":

```
MAKENOTE(D,5,EIGHTH),


MAKENOTE(E,5,QUARTER),
MAKENOTE(E,6,EIGHTH),
MAKENOTE(B,5,EIGHTH),
MAKENOTE(G,5,EIGHTH),
MAKENOTE(E,5,EIGHTH),


MAKENOTE(D,5,QUARTER),
MAKENOTE(D,6,EIGHTH),
MAKENOTE(A,5,EIGHTH),
MAKENOTE(Fs,5,EIGHTH),
MAKENOTE(D,5,EIGHTH),


MAKENOTE(E,5,QUARTER),
MAKENOTE(E,6,EIGHTH),
MAKENOTE(B,5,EIGHTH),
MAKENOTE(G,5,EIGHTH),
MAKENOTE(E,5,EIGHTH),
```

The MAKENOTE macro is a convenient way to store note information in a NOTE object. It looks like this:

```
#define MAKENOTE(note,octave,duration) { note+octave*12,duration}
```

The foregoing list of note objects also presupposes the existence of some additional constants to define the notes to be played and their durations the sharped notes use the letter s to differentiate them from naturals, because the C langauge takes exception to the use of the sharp symbol in defined constants:

297

```
#define C        0
#define Cs       1
#define D        2
#define Ds       3
#define E        4
#define F        5
#define Fs       6
#define G        7
#define Gs       8
#define A        9
#define As       10
#define B        11

#define INTERVAL      136

#define WHOLE         INTERVAL
#define HALF          INTERVAL/2
#define QUARTER       INTERVAL/4
#define EIGHTH        INTERVAL/8
#define SIXTEENTH     INTERVAL/16
```

The value of INTERVAL was chosen to make the music that
PLAYSONG performs sound about right. In a more complicated MIDI
music application you'd want to make this variable.

Finally, most music involves at least a few notes with uncommon
durations—dotted notes and triplets turn up in Celtic music quite
often. Here are two macros to deal with them:

```
#define TRIPLET(n)     ((n*2)/3)
#define DOT(n)         (n+(n/2))
```

To create a dotted note in a list of NOTE objects, you'd do this:

```
MAKENOTE(E,6,DOT(EIGHTH))
```

While a bit too hardwired for a general music package, the approach
to playing music in PLAYSONG is useful if you want to have a few
bars of canned music appear in a larger multimedia application. If you
decide to use this code, you'll probably have to define some additional
macros to handle things like double-dotted notes and other
phenomena that don't appear in PLAYSONG's sample tunes.

Figure 6-9 illustrates the PLAYSONG.CPP source code file. Figure 6-10 illustrates PLAYSONG.RC, its resource script. Figure 6-11 is PLAYSONG.H, which defines the list of NOTE objects for the music to be played. In addition to these files, you'll need PRJ and DEF files for PLAYSONG, and the WAV and BMP files included in PLAYSONG.RC. The PLAYSONG application must link to MIDIMAN.LIB and include MIDIMAN.H. These are discussed in detail later in this chapter. You will find all these files on the companion CD-ROM for this book.

The PLAYSONG.CPP source code.   Figure 6-9

```
/*

        Play Song
        Copyright (c) 1993 Alchemy Mindworks Inc.
*/

#include <windows.h>
#include <stdio.h>
#include <stdlib.h>
#include <dir.h>
#include <ctype.h>
#include <alloc.h>
#include <string.h>
#include <io.h>
#include <bwcc.h>
#include <dos.h>
#include <errno.h>
#include <math.h>
#include <commdlg.h>
#include <mmsystem.h>
#include "midiman.h"
#include "playsong.h"
#include "midimap.h"

#define say(s)      MessageBox(NULL,s,"Yo...",MB_OK | MB_ICONSTOP);
#define saynumber(f,s)    {char b[128]; sprintf((LPSTR)b,(LPSTR)f,s); \
                    MessageBox(NULL,b,"Debug Message",MB_OK | MB_ICONSTOP); \
                    }

#define ItemOn(item)       { dlgH=GetDlgItem(hwnd,item); \
                    EnableWindow(dlgH,TRUE); \
                    EnableMenuItem(hmenu,item,MF_ENABLED);\
                    }

#define ItemOff(item)      { dlgH=GetDlgItem(hwnd,item); \
                    EnableWindow(dlgH,FALSE); \
                    EnableMenuItem(hmenu,item,MF_GRAYED);\
                    }
```

Figure 6-9   *Continued.*

```
#define STRINGSIZE      128                 /* how big is a string? */

#define MAIN_PLAY       101
#define MAIN_STOP       102

#define MAIN_ABOUT      103
#define MAIN_EXIT       199

#define MAIN_MESSAGE    401
#define MAIN_TIME       402

#define MAIN_PATCH1     201
#define MAIN_PATCH2     202
#define MAIN_PATCH3     203

#define VOICE1          110                 //Fiddle
#define VOICE2          77                  //Shakuhachi
#define VOICE3          46                  //Harp

#define DoMessage(hwnd,string)              BWCCMessageBox(hwnd,string,"Message",\
                                            MB_OK | MB_ICONINFORMATION)
#ifndef max
#define max(a,b)              (((a)>(b))?(a):(b))
#endif
#ifndef min
#define min(a,b)              (((a)<(b))?(a):(b))
#endif

/* prototypes */
DWORD FAR PASCAL SelectProc(HWND hwnd,WORD message,WORD wParam,LONG
lParam);
DWORD FAR PASCAL AboutDlgProc(HWND hwnd,WORD message,WORD wParam,LONG
lParam);

int SetPatch(LPNOTE lpnote,unsigned int number,unsigned int voice);

void StopNote(HMIDIOUT hmo,LPNOTE note);
void PlayNote(HMIDIOUT hmo,LPNOTE note,HWND hwnd);
void CentreWindow(HWND hwnd);

/* globals */
char szAppName[] = "PlaySong";
HANDLE hInst;

#pragma warn -par
int PASCAL WinMain(HANDLE hInstance,HANDLE hPrevInstance,
                LPSTR lpszCmdParam,int nCmdShow)
{
        FARPROC dlgProc;
        int r=0;
```

```
                BWCCGetVersion();

                hInst=hInstance;

                dlgProc=MakeProcInstance((FARPROC)SelectProc,hInst);
                r=DialogBox(hInst,"MainScreen",NULL,dlgProc);

                FreeProcInstance(dlgProc);

                return(r);
        }

DWORD FAR PASCAL SelectProc(HWND hwnd,WORD message,WORD wParam,LONG lParam)
{
        static SONG song;
        PAINTSTRUCT ps;
        HICON hIcon;
        FARPROC lpfnDlgProc;
        POINT point;
        HMENU hmenu;
        HWND dlgH;
        long l;
        int i;

        switch(message) {
                case MM_MIDIFINISHED:
                        StopSong(&song);
                        timeBeginPeriod(TIMERESOLUTION);
                        hmenu=GetMenu(hwnd);
                        ItemOn(MAIN_PLAY);
                        ItemOff(MAIN_STOP);
                        ItemOn(MAIN_PATCH1);
                        ItemOn(MAIN_PATCH2);
                        ItemOn(MAIN_PATCH3);
                        break;
                case WM_CTLCOLOR:
                        if(HIWORD(lParam)==CTLCOLOR_STATIC ||
                           HIWORD(lParam)==CTLCOLOR_DLG) {
                                SetBkColor(wParam,RGB(192,192,192));
                                SetTextColor(wParam,RGB(0,0,0));

                                ClientToScreen(hwnd,&point);
                                UnrealizeObject(GetStockObject(LTGRAY_BRUSH));
                                SetBrushOrg(wParam,point.x,point.y);

                                return((DWORD)GetStockObject(LTGRAY_BRUSH));

                        }
                        if(HIWORD(lParam)==CTLCOLOR_BTN) {
                                SetBkColor(wParam,RGB(192,192,192));
                                SetTextColor(wParam,RGB(0,0,0));

                                ClientToScreen(hwnd,&point);
```

Figure 6-9 *Continued.*

```
                                UnrealizeObject(GetStockObject(BLACK_BRUSH));
                                SetBrushOrg(wParam,point.x,point.y);

                                return((DWORD)GetStockObject(BLACK_BRUSH));
                        }
                break;
        case WM_SYSCOMMAND:
                switch(wParam & 0xfff0) {
                        case SC_CLOSE:
                                SendMessage(hwnd,WM_COMMAND,MAIN_EXIT,0L);
                                break;
                }
                break;
        case WM_INITDIALOG:
                hIcon=LoadIcon(hInst,szAppName);
                SetClassWord(hwnd,GCW_HICON,(WORD)hIcon);
                waveOutSetVolume(0,0xffffffffL);

                ItemOn(MAIN_PLAY);
                ItemOff(MAIN_STOP);

                for(i=0;i<PATCHCOUNT;++i) {
                    SendDlgItemMessage(hwnd,MAIN_PATCH1,
                        CB_INSERTSTRING,-1,(LONG)(LPSTR)midiMapPatch[i]);
                    SendDlgItemMessage(hwnd,MAIN_PATCH2,
                        CB_INSERTSTRING,-1,(LONG)(LPSTR)midiMapPatch[i]);
                    SendDlgItemMessage(hwnd,MAIN_PATCH3,
                        CB_INSERTSTRING,-1,(LONG)(LPSTR)midiMapPatch[i]);
                }

                SendDlgItemMessage(hwnd,MAIN_PATCH1,CB_SETCURSEL,VOICE1,0L);
                SendDlgItemMessage(hwnd,MAIN_PATCH2,CB_SETCURSEL,VOICE2,0L);
                SendDlgItemMessage(hwnd,MAIN_PATCH3,CB_SETCURSEL,VOICE3,0L);

                memset((char *)&song,0,sizeof(SONG));

                CentreWindow(hwnd);
                break;
        case WM_PAINT:
                BeginPaint(hwnd,&ps);
                EndPaint(hwnd,&ps);
                break;
        case WM_COMMAND:
                switch(wParam) {
                        case MAIN_STOP:
                                SendMessage(hwnd,MM_MIDIFINISHED,0,0L);
                                break;
                        case MAIN_PLAY:
                                timeBeginPeriod(TIMERESOLUTION);
                                l=SendDlgItemMessage(hwnd,MAIN_PATCH1,
                                        CB_GETCURSEL,0,0L);
                                if(l==CB_ERR) l=0L;
```

```
                              SetPatch(&note[0],0,(unsigned int)l);

                              l=SendDlgItemMessage(hwnd,MAIN_PATCH2,
                                    CB_GETCURSEL,0,0L);
                              if(l==CB_ERR) l=0L;

                              SetPatch(&note[0],1,(unsigned int)l);

                              l=SendDlgItemMessage(hwnd,MAIN_PATCH3,
                                    CB_GETCURSEL,0,0L);
                              if(l==CB_ERR) l=0L;

                              SetPatch(&note[0],2,(unsigned int)l);

                              if(StartSong(&song,hwnd,&note[0])) {
                                    ItemOff(MAIN_PLAY);
                                    ItemOn(MAIN_STOP);
                                    ItemOff(MAIN_PATCH1);
                                    ItemOff(MAIN_PATCH2);
                                    ItemOff(MAIN_PATCH3);
                              } else DoMessage(hwnd,
                                  "Error opening MIDI device");
                              break;
                        case MAIN_ABOUT:
                              if((lpfnDlgProc=MakeProcInstance((FARPROC)
                                  AboutDlgProc,hInst)) != NULL) {
                                    DialogBox(hInst,"AboutBox",
                                        hwnd,lpfnDlgProc);
                                    FreeProcInstance(lpfnDlgProc);
                              }
                              break;
                        case MAIN_EXIT:
                              SendMessage(hwnd,WM_COMMAND,MAIN_STOP,0L);
                              PostQuitMessage(0);
                              break;
                  }
                  break;

            }

      return(FALSE);
}

int SetPatch(LPNOTE lpnote,unsigned int number,unsigned int voice)
{
      int i,count;

      for(i=count=0;lpnote[i].note != ENDSONG;++i) {
            if(lpnote[i].note==VOICE) {
                  if(count==number) {
                        lpnote[i].duration=voice;
                        return(TRUE);
                  }
```

Figure 6-9   *Continued.*

```
                            ++count;
                    }
            }
            return(FALSE);
    }

    DWORD FAR PASCAL AboutDlgProc(HWND hwnd,WORD message,WORD wParam,LONG lParam)
    {
            static HANDLE sound;
            static LPSTR psound;
            HANDLE handle;
            POINT point;

            switch(message) {
                    case WM_INITDIALOG:
                            if((handle=FindResource(hInst,
                                "AboutWave",RT_RCDATA)) != NULL) {
                                    if((sound=LoadResource(hInst,handle)) != NULL) {
                                            if((psound=LockResource(sound)) != NULL)
                                                sndPlaySound(psound,SND_ASYNC |
                                                    SND_MEMORY | SND_NOSTOP);
                                    }
                            }
                            CentreWindow(hwnd);
                            return(FALSE);
                    case WM_CTLCOLOR:
                            if(HIWORD(lParam)==CTLCOLOR_STATIC ||
                                HIWORD(lParam)==CTLCOLOR_DLG) {
                                    SetBkColor(wParam,RGB(192,192,192));
                                    SetTextColor(wParam,RGB(0,0,0));

                                    ClientToScreen(hwnd,&point);
                                    UnrealizeObject(GetStockObject(LTGRAY_BRUSH));
                                    SetBrushOrg(wParam,point.x,point.y);

                                    return((DWORD)GetStockObject(LTGRAY_BRUSH));

                            }
                            if(HIWORD(lParam)==CTLCOLOR_BTN) {
                                    SetBkColor(wParam,RGB(192,192,192));
                                    SetTextColor(wParam,RGB(0,0,0));

                                    ClientToScreen(hwnd,&point);
                                    UnrealizeObject(GetStockObject(BLACK_BRUSH));
                                    SetBrushOrg(wParam,point.x,point.y);

                                    return((DWORD)GetStockObject(BLACK_BRUSH));
                            }
                            break;
                    case WM_COMMAND:
                            switch(wParam) {
```

```
                             case IDOK:
                                     sndPlaySound(NULL,SND_SYNC);
                                     if(psound != NULL) UnlockResource(sound);
                                     if(sound != NULL) FreeResource(sound);
                                     EndDialog(hwnd,wParam);
                                     return(FALSE);
                             }
                             break;
                     }

             return(FALSE);
     }

void CentreWindow(HWND hwnd)
{
        RECT rect;
        unsigned int x,y;

        GetWindowRect(hwnd,&rect);
        x=(GetSystemMetrics(SM_CXSCREEN)-(rect.right-rect.left))/2;
        y=(GetSystemMetrics(SM_CYSCREEN)-(rect.bottom-rect.top))/2;
        SetWindowPos(hwnd,NULL,x,y,rect.right-rect.left,
            rect.bottom-rect.top,SWP_NOSIZE);
}
```

The PLAYSONG.RC resource script.

Figure 6-10

```
MainScreen DIALOG 75, 25, 108, 136
STYLE WS_POPUP | WS_CAPTION | WS_SYSMENU | WS_MINIMIZEBOX
CAPTION "Play Song"
MENU MainMenu
BEGIN
        PUSHBUTTON "Quit", 199, 68, 116, 28, 12, WS_CHILD | WS_VISIBLE | WS_TABSTOP
        PUSHBUTTON "Stop", 102, 40, 116, 28, 12, WS_CHILD | WS_VISIBLE | WS_TABSTOP
        PUSHBUTTON "Play", 101, 12, 116, 28, 12, WS_CHILD | WS_VISIBLE | WS_TABSTOP
        CONTROL "Voices", 104, "BorShade", 32769 | WS_CHILD | WS_VISIBLE, 8, 8, 92, 100
        CONTROL "", 201, "COMBOBOX", CBS_DROPDOWNLIST | WS_CHILD | WS_VISIBLE |
            WS_VSCROLL | WS_TABSTOP, 12, 32, 84, 68
        LTEXT "Song 1: Trip to Sligo", -1, 12, 24, 84, 8, WS_CHILD | WS_VISIBLE | WS_GROUP
        CONTROL "", 202, "COMBOBOX", CBS_DROPDOWNLIST | WS_CHILD | WS_VISIBLE |
            WS_VSCROLL | WS_TABSTOP, 12, 60, 84, 68
        LTEXT "Song 2: Burnt Old Man", -1, 12, 52, 84, 8, WS_CHILD | WS_VISIBLE | WS_GROUP
        CONTROL "", 203, "COMBOBOX", CBS_DROPDOWNLIST | WS_CHILD | WS_VISIBLE |
            WS_VSCROLL | WS_TABSTOP, 12, 88, 84, 68
        LTEXT "Song 3: The Kesh", -1, 12, 80, 84, 8, WS_CHILD | WS_VISIBLE | WS_GROUP
END

MainMenu MENU
BEGIN
        POPUP "&File"
        BEGIN
```

Figure 6-10 *Continued.*

```
                    MENUITEM "&Play", 101
                    MENUITEM "&Stop", 102
                    MENUITEM "&About", 103
                    MENUITEM SEPARATOR
                    MENUITEM "E&xit", 199
            END
    END

    AboutBox DIALOG 18, 18, 184, 180
    STYLE WS_POPUP | WS_CAPTION
    CAPTION "About..."
    BEGIN
            CONTROL "", 102, "BorShade", BSS_GROUP | WS_CHILD | WS_VISIBLE |
                WS_TABSTOP, 8, 68, 168, 76
            CTEXT "Play Song 1.0\n\nCopyright (c) 1994 Alchemy Mindworks Inc.\n\n
                This program is part of the book Advanced Multimedia Programming for
                Windows by Steven William Rimmer, published by Windcrest/McGraw Hill.",
                -1, 12, 72, 160, 68, WS_CHILD | WS_VISIBLE | WS_GROUP
            CONTROL "Button", IDOK, "BorBtn", BS_DEFPUSHBUTTON | WS_CHILD | WS_VISIBLE |
                WS_TABSTOP, 74, 152, 32, 20
            CONTROL "Button", 801, "BorBtn", BS_PUSHBUTTON | WS_CHILD | WS_VISIBLE |
                WS_TABSTOP, 36, 8, 32, 20
    END

    1801 BITMAP "smpw.bmp"

    AboutWave RCDATA "ABOUT.WAV"

    PlaySong ICON
    BEGIN
            '00 00 01 00 01 00 20 20 10 00 00 00 00 00 E8 02'
            '00 00 16 00 00 00 28 00 00 00 20 00 00 00 40 00'
            '00 00 01 00 04 00 00 00 00 00 80 02 00 00 00 00'
            '00 00 00 00 00 00 10 00 00 00 00 00 00 00 00 00'
            '00 00 00 00 BF 00 00 BF 00 00 00 BF BF 00 BF 00'
            '00 00 BF 00 BF 00 BF BF 00 00 C0 C0 C0 00 80 80'
            '80 00 00 00 FF 00 00 FF 00 00 00 FF FF 00 FF 00'
            '00 00 FF 00 FF 00 FF FF 00 00 FF FF FF 00 77 77'
            '77 77 77 77 77 77 77 77 77 77 77 77 77 77 7F 88'
            '88 88 88 88 88 88 88 88 88 88 88 88 88 87 7F F8'
            '88 88 88 88 88 88 88 88 88 88 88 88 88 87 7F F7'
            '77 77 77 77 77 77 77 77 77 77 77 77 78 87 7F F7'
            '77 77 77 77 77 77 77 77 77 77 77 77 78 87 7F F7'
            '77 77 77 77 77 77 77 77 77 77 77 77 78 87 7F F7'
            '77 77 77 77 77 88 88 88 77 77 77 77 78 87 7F F7'
            '77 77 77 77 AA AA AA 77 88 87 77 77 78 87 7F F7'
            '77 77 77 AA 77 88 88 AA A7 88 77 77 78 87 7F F7'
            '77 77 AA 87 AA AA AA 88 AA 78 87 77 78 87 7F F7'
            '77 7A A8 AA 8A AA AA AA 8A A8 88 77 78 87 7F F7'
            '77 AA AA A8 AA AA AA AA AA AA 88 77 78 87 7F F7'
            '77 AA AA 8A AA AA AA AA A8 AA 78 77 78 87 7F F7'
```

```
'77 AA A8 AA AA A8 77 7A AA 7A 88 87 78 87 7F F7'
'7A AA A8 7A AA 87 88 87 7A AA A7 87 78 87 7F F7'
'7A AA 88 78 A7 AA A8 87 8A A7 AA A8 87 78 87 7F F7'
'7A AA 8A 87 A7 AA A7 8A A7 AA A8 87 78 87 7F F7'
'7A AA A8 A7 AA 88 A7 A8 7A 7A A8 87 78 87 7F F7'
'7A AA A8 7A AA 78 AA 8A 8A 8A A8 87 78 87 7F F7'
'7A AA 8A AA 7A AA A7 A7 A7 7A A8 77 78 87 7F F7'
'77 AA A8 87 77 77 77 A7 88 AA 88 77 78 87 7F F7'
'77 AA A8 88 77 77 77 AA A8 AA 78 77 78 87 7F F7'
'77 AA AA 88 88 77 77 AA AA 8A 87 77 78 87 7F F7'
'77 7A AA AA 88 88 8A AA A8 A8 77 77 78 87 7F F7'
'77 77 AA AA AA AA AA AA AA 87 77 77 78 87 7F F7'
'77 77 7A AA AA AA AA AA A7 77 77 77 78 87 7F F7'
'77 77 77 77 AA AA AA 77 77 77 77 77 78 87 7F F7'
'77 77 77 77 77 77 77 77 77 77 77 77 78 87 7F F7'
'77 77 77 77 77 77 77 77 77 77 77 77 78 87 7F FF'
'FF FF FF FF FF FF FF FF FF FF FF FF F8 87 7F FF'
'FF FF FF FF FF FF FF FF FF FF FF FF FF 87 77 77'
'77 77 77 77 77 77 77 77 77 77 77 77 77 00 00'
'00 00 00 00 00 00 00 00 00 00 00 00 00 00 00 00'
'00 00 00 00 00 00 00 00 00 00 00 00 00 00 00 00'
'00 00 00 00 00 00 00 00 00 00 00 00 00 00 00 00'
'00 00 00 00 00 00 00 00 00 00 00 00 00 00 00 00'
'00 00 00 00 00 00 00 00 00 00 00 00 00 00 00 00'
'00 00 00 00 00 00 00 00 00 00 00 00 00 00 00 00'
'00 00 00 00 00 00 00 00 00 00 00 00 00 00 00 00'
'00 00 00 00 00 00 00 00 00 00 00 00 00 00 00'
END
```

The PLAYSONG.H header file.

Figure 6-11

```c
/*
        PLAYSONG.H
*/

NOTE note[]= {
        /* These are three traditional Irish tunes in 6/8 time */

        /* Trip to Sligo */
        MAKEVOICE(0),
        MAKENOTE(D,5,EIGHTH),

        MAKENOTE(E,5,QUARTER),
        MAKENOTE(E,6,EIGHTH),
        MAKENOTE(B,5,EIGHTH),
        MAKENOTE(G,5,EIGHTH),
        MAKENOTE(E,5,EIGHTH),

        MAKENOTE(D,5,QUARTER),
        MAKENOTE(D,6,EIGHTH),
        MAKENOTE(A,5,EIGHTH),
        MAKENOTE(Fs,5,EIGHTH),
        MAKENOTE(D,5,EIGHTH),
```

Figure 6-11   *Continued.*

```
MAKENOTE(E,5,QUARTER),
MAKENOTE(E,6,EIGHTH),
MAKENOTE(B,5,EIGHTH),
MAKENOTE(G,5,EIGHTH),
MAKENOTE(E,5,EIGHTH),

MAKENOTE(G,5,EIGHTH),
MAKENOTE(Fs,5,EIGHTH),
MAKENOTE(E,5,EIGHTH),
MAKENOTE(E,6,QUARTER),
MAKENOTE(Fs,6,EIGHTH),

MAKENOTE(G,6,EIGHTH),
MAKENOTE(Fs,6,EIGHTH),
MAKENOTE(E,6,EIGHTH),
MAKENOTE(D,6,QUARTER),
MAKENOTE(B,5,EIGHTH),

MAKENOTE(A,5,EIGHTH),
MAKENOTE(B,5,EIGHTH),
MAKENOTE(G,5,EIGHTH),
MAKENOTE(Fs,5,EIGHTH),
MAKENOTE(E,5,EIGHTH),
MAKENOTE(D,5,EIGHTH),

MAKENOTE(E,5,EIGHTH),
MAKENOTE(Fs,5,EIGHTH),
MAKENOTE(G,5,EIGHTH),
MAKENOTE(A,5,EIGHTH),
MAKENOTE(B,5,EIGHTH),
MAKENOTE(C,6,EIGHTH),

MAKENOTE(B,5,EIGHTH),
MAKENOTE(A,5,EIGHTH),
MAKENOTE(Fs,5,EIGHTH),
MAKENOTE(E,5,QUARTER),
MAKENOTE(REST,0,EIGHTH),

MAKENOTE(E,6,EIGHTH),
MAKENOTE(B,5,EIGHTH),
MAKENOTE(E,6,EIGHTH),
MAKENOTE(G,6,EIGHTH),
MAKENOTE(Fs,6,EIGHTH),
MAKENOTE(E,6,EIGHTH),

MAKENOTE(D,6,EIGHTH),
MAKENOTE(A,5,EIGHTH),
MAKENOTE(D,6,EIGHTH),
MAKENOTE(Fs,6,EIGHTH),
MAKENOTE(E,6,EIGHTH),
MAKENOTE(D,6,EIGHTH),
```

```
        MAKENOTE(E,6,EIGHTH),
        MAKENOTE(B,5,EIGHTH),
        MAKENOTE(E,6,EIGHTH),
        MAKENOTE(G,6,EIGHTH),
        MAKENOTE(Fs,6,EIGHTH),
        MAKENOTE(E,6,EIGHTH),

        MAKENOTE(Fs,6,TRIPLET(EIGHTH)),
        MAKENOTE(G,6,TRIPLET(EIGHTH)),
        MAKENOTE(B,6,TRIPLET(EIGHTH)),
        MAKENOTE(Fs,6,EIGHTH),
        MAKENOTE(G,6,EIGHTH),
        MAKENOTE(Fs,6,EIGHTH),
        MAKENOTE(E,6,EIGHTH),

        MAKENOTE(Fs,6,TRIPLET(EIGHTH)),
        MAKENOTE(G,6,TRIPLET(EIGHTH)),
        MAKENOTE(B,6,TRIPLET(EIGHTH)),
        MAKENOTE(Fs,6,EIGHTH),
        MAKENOTE(G,6,EIGHTH),
        MAKENOTE(Fs,6,EIGHTH),
        MAKENOTE(E,6,EIGHTH),

        MAKENOTE(D,6,QUARTER),
        MAKENOTE(B,5,EIGHTH),
        MAKENOTE(A,5,EIGHTH),
        MAKENOTE(B,5,EIGHTH),
        MAKENOTE(G,5,EIGHTH),

        MAKENOTE(Fs,5,EIGHTH),
        MAKENOTE(E,5,EIGHTH),
        MAKENOTE(D,5,EIGHTH),
        MAKENOTE(E,5,EIGHTH),
        MAKENOTE(Fs,5,EIGHTH),
        MAKENOTE(G,5,EIGHTH),

        MAKENOTE(A,5,EIGHTH),
        MAKENOTE(B,5,EIGHTH),
        MAKENOTE(C,6,EIGHTH),
        MAKENOTE(B,5,EIGHTH),
        MAKENOTE(G,5,EIGHTH),
        MAKENOTE(Fs,5,EIGHTH),

        MAKENOTE(E,5,DOT(QUARTER)),

        MAKENOTE(REST,0,QUARTER),                /* pause between tunes */

        /* Burnt Old Man */
        MAKEVOICE(0),
        MAKENOTE(D,5,EIGHTH),

        MAKENOTE(D,5,EIGHTH),
```

Figure 6-11 *Continued.*

```
MAKENOTE(Fs,5,EIGHTH),
MAKENOTE(B,5,EIGHTH),
MAKENOTE(A,5,EIGHTH),
MAKENOTE(Fs,5,EIGHTH),
MAKENOTE(D,5,EIGHTH),

MAKENOTE(Fs,5,EIGHTH),
MAKENOTE(G,5,EIGHTH),
MAKENOTE(Fs,5,EIGHTH),
MAKENOTE(Fs,5,QUARTER),
MAKENOTE(E,5,EIGHTH),

MAKENOTE(D,5,EIGHTH),
MAKENOTE(Fs,5,EIGHTH),
MAKENOTE(B,5,EIGHTH),
MAKENOTE(A,5,EIGHTH),
MAKENOTE(Fs,5,EIGHTH),
MAKENOTE(D,5,EIGHTH),

MAKENOTE(E,5,DOT(QUARTER)),
MAKENOTE(E,5,EIGHTH),
MAKENOTE(Fs,5,EIGHTH),
MAKENOTE(E,5,EIGHTH),

MAKENOTE(D,5,EIGHTH),
MAKENOTE(Fs,5,EIGHTH),
MAKENOTE(B,5,EIGHTH),
MAKENOTE(A,5,EIGHTH),
MAKENOTE(Fs,5,EIGHTH),
MAKENOTE(D,5,EIGHTH),

MAKENOTE(D,5,EIGHTH),
MAKENOTE(Fs,5,EIGHTH),
MAKENOTE(A,5,EIGHTH),
MAKENOTE(D,6,QUARTER),
MAKENOTE(E,6,EIGHTH),

MAKENOTE(Fs,6,EIGHTH),
MAKENOTE(E,6,EIGHTH),
MAKENOTE(D,6,EIGHTH),
MAKENOTE(B,5,EIGHTH),
MAKENOTE(Cs,6,EIGHTH),
MAKENOTE(D,6,EIGHTH),

MAKENOTE(A,5,EIGHTH),
MAKENOTE(Fs,5,EIGHTH),
MAKENOTE(Fs,5,EIGHTH),
MAKENOTE(E,5,QUARTER),
MAKENOTE(D,5,EIGHTH),
```

```
        MAKENOTE(D,6,DOT(QUARTER)),
        MAKENOTE(D,6,EIGHTH),
        MAKENOTE(E,6,EIGHTH),
        MAKENOTE(Fs,6,EIGHTH),

        MAKENOTE(A,5,EIGHTH),
        MAKENOTE(Fs,5,EIGHTH),
        MAKENOTE(A,5,EIGHTH),
        MAKENOTE(A,5,EIGHTH),
        MAKENOTE(Fs,5,EIGHTH),
        MAKENOTE(A,5,EIGHTH),

        MAKENOTE(E,6,DOT(QUARTER)),
        MAKENOTE(E,6,EIGHTH),
        MAKENOTE(D,6,EIGHTH),
        MAKENOTE(E,6,EIGHTH),

        MAKENOTE(Fs,6,EIGHTH),
        MAKENOTE(E,6,EIGHTH),
        MAKENOTE(D,6,EIGHTH),
        MAKENOTE(B,5,QUARTER),
        MAKENOTE(A,5,EIGHTH),

        MAKENOTE(D,6,DOT(QUARTER)),
        MAKENOTE(D,6,EIGHTH),
        MAKENOTE(E,6,EIGHTH),
        MAKENOTE(Fs,6,EIGHTH),

        MAKENOTE(A,5,EIGHTH),
        MAKENOTE(Fs,5,EIGHTH),
        MAKENOTE(A,5,EIGHTH),
        MAKENOTE(D,6,QUARTER),
        MAKENOTE(E,6,EIGHTH),

        MAKENOTE(Fs,6,EIGHTH),
        MAKENOTE(E,6,EIGHTH),
        MAKENOTE(D,6,EIGHTH),
        MAKENOTE(B,5,EIGHTH),
        MAKENOTE(Cs,6,EIGHTH),
        MAKENOTE(D,6,EIGHTH),

        MAKENOTE(A,5,EIGHTH),
        MAKENOTE(Fs,5,EIGHTH),
        MAKENOTE(Fs,5,EIGHTH),
        MAKENOTE(E,5,QUARTER),
        MAKENOTE(D,5,EIGHTH),

        MAKENOTE(D,5,DOT(WHOLE)),

        MAKENOTE(REST,0,QUARTER),          /* pause between tunes */

        /* The Kesh */
        MAKEVOICE(0),
        MAKENOTE(D,5,EIGHTH),
```

Figure 6-11   *Continued.*

```
                    MAKENOTE(G,5,EIGHTH),
                    MAKENOTE(Fs,5,EIGHTH),
                    MAKENOTE(G,5,EIGHTH),
                    MAKENOTE(G,5,EIGHTH),
                    MAKENOTE(A,5,EIGHTH),
                    MAKENOTE(B,5,EIGHTH),

                    MAKENOTE(A,5,EIGHTH),
                    MAKENOTE(G,5,EIGHTH),
                    MAKENOTE(A,5,EIGHTH),
                    MAKENOTE(A,5,EIGHTH),
                    MAKENOTE(B,5,EIGHTH),
                    MAKENOTE(D,6,EIGHTH),

                    MAKENOTE(E,6,EIGHTH),
                    MAKENOTE(D,6,EIGHTH),
                    MAKENOTE(D,6,EIGHTH),
                    MAKENOTE(G,6,EIGHTH),
                    MAKENOTE(D,6,EIGHTH),
                    MAKENOTE(D,6,EIGHTH),

                    MAKENOTE(E,6,EIGHTH),
                    MAKENOTE(D,6,EIGHTH),
                    MAKENOTE(B,5,EIGHTH),
                    MAKENOTE(D,6,EIGHTH),
                    MAKENOTE(B,5,EIGHTH),
                    MAKENOTE(A,5,EIGHTH),

                    MAKENOTE(G,5,EIGHTH),
                    MAKENOTE(A,5,EIGHTH),
                    MAKENOTE(G,5,EIGHTH),
                    MAKENOTE(G,5,EIGHTH),
                    MAKENOTE(A,5,EIGHTH),
                    MAKENOTE(B,5,EIGHTH),

                    MAKENOTE(A,5,EIGHTH),
                    MAKENOTE(B,5,EIGHTH),
                    MAKENOTE(A,5,EIGHTH),
                    MAKENOTE(A,5,EIGHTH),
                    MAKENOTE(B,5,EIGHTH),
                    MAKENOTE(D,6,EIGHTH),

                    MAKENOTE(E,6,EIGHTH),
                    MAKENOTE(D,6,EIGHTH),
                    MAKENOTE(D,6,EIGHTH),
                    MAKENOTE(G,6,EIGHTH),
                    MAKENOTE(D,6,EIGHTH),
                    MAKENOTE(B,5,EIGHTH),

                    MAKENOTE(A,5,EIGHTH),
                    MAKENOTE(G,5,EIGHTH),
```

```
MAKENOTE(Fs,5,EIGHTH),
MAKENOTE(G,5,QUARTER),
MAKENOTE(A,5,EIGHTH),

MAKENOTE(B,5,QUARTER),
MAKENOTE(B,5,EIGHTH),
MAKENOTE(D,6,EIGHTH),
MAKENOTE(B,5,EIGHTH),
MAKENOTE(D,6,EIGHTH),

MAKENOTE(E,6,EIGHTH),
MAKENOTE(G,6,EIGHTH),
MAKENOTE(E,6,EIGHTH),
MAKENOTE(D,6,EIGHTH),
MAKENOTE(B,5,EIGHTH),
MAKENOTE(A,5,EIGHTH),

MAKENOTE(B,5,EIGHTH),
MAKENOTE(A,5,EIGHTH),
MAKENOTE(B,5,EIGHTH),
MAKENOTE(D,6,EIGHTH),
MAKENOTE(B,5,EIGHTH),
MAKENOTE(G,5,EIGHTH),

MAKENOTE(A,5,EIGHTH),
MAKENOTE(B,5,EIGHTH),
MAKENOTE(A,5,EIGHTH),
MAKENOTE(A,5,EIGHTH),
MAKENOTE(G,5,EIGHTH),
MAKENOTE(A,5,EIGHTH),

MAKENOTE(B,5,EIGHTH),
MAKENOTE(A,5,EIGHTH),
MAKENOTE(B,5,EIGHTH),
MAKENOTE(D,6,EIGHTH),
MAKENOTE(B,5,EIGHTH),
MAKENOTE(D,6,EIGHTH),

MAKENOTE(E,6,EIGHTH),
MAKENOTE(G,6,EIGHTH),
MAKENOTE(E,6,EIGHTH),
MAKENOTE(D,6,EIGHTH),
MAKENOTE(B,5,EIGHTH),
MAKENOTE(D,6,EIGHTH),

MAKENOTE(G,6,EIGHTH),
MAKENOTE(Fs,6,EIGHTH),
MAKENOTE(G,6,EIGHTH),
MAKENOTE(A,6,EIGHTH),
MAKENOTE(G,6,EIGHTH),
MAKENOTE(A,6,EIGHTH),
```

Figure **6-11**   *Continued.*

```
MAKENOTE(B,6,EIGHTH),
MAKENOTE(G,6,EIGHTH),
MAKENOTE(Fs,6,EIGHTH),

MAKENOTE(G,6,DOT(QUARTER)),

MAKENOTE(ENDSONG,0,0),
};
```

The PLAYSONG application is exceedingly simple, mostly because it expects its companion dynamic link library, MIDIMAN.DLL, to do all the work. You can see pretty well the entire application in the SelectProc function of PLAYSONG.CPP. When you click on the Play button, SelectProc thinks for a moment and then calls StartSong, one of the functions in the MIDIMAN.DLL library. It gets passed a pointer to a SONG object, the HWND window handle for the main window of PLAYSONG, and a list of NOTE objects.

A SONG object is a collection of data that pertains to a list of notes being played. It will turn up in detail when we take a look at MIDIMAN later in this chapter.

The StartSong function will begin playing music. When it's done, it will send the message MM_MIDIFINISHED to SelectProc. The handler for MM_MIDIFINISHED must call StopSong, which does some internal housekeeping in MIDIMAN and frees some buffers referenced by the SONG object for the music being played.

The only other aspect of PLAYSONG that's specific to the task of playing music is the SetPatch function. It's defined further down in PLAYSONG.CPP. The list of NOTE objects in PLAYSONG.H also includes several voice-change items, which MIDIMAN will interpret as PROGRAM CHANGE messages when it generates MIDI data based on this list. By default, these objects are patched by SetPatch just before the music starts to play in the following voices:

"Trip to Sligo"   Fiddle
"Burnt Old Man"   Shakuhachi
"The Kesh"   Orchestral Harp

A shakuhachi is a large Japanese flute. It's by no means part of traditional Celtic music, but it sounds interesting.

The SetPatch function counts through the list of NOTE objects passed to it looking for voice changes. When SetPatch has skipped over the requisite number, as defined by its second argument, it sets the next one it locates to the voice number passed as its third argument.

You can change the voices for the songs handled by PLAYSONG through the three combo boxes in its main window. You'll find this mildly diverting for a few minutes—you can experiment, playing the tunes with unusual voices. They sound very New Age played on wind chimes or African log drums.

The names in the PLAYSONG voice combo boxes are stored in MIDIMAP.H, which you'll find on the companion CD-ROM for this book. It's illustrated in Fig. 6-12.

The MIDIMAP.H header file.

Figure 6-12

```
/*
        MIDI Mapper patch map
*/
LPSTR midiMapPatch[]= {
        "Accoustic Grand Piano",
        "Bright Accoustic Piano",
        "Electric Grand Piano",
        "Honky Tonk Piano",
        "Rhodes Piano",
        "Chorused Piano",
        "Harpsichord",
        "Clavinet",
        "Celesta",
        "Glockenspiel",
        "Music Box",
        "Vibraphone",
        "Marimba",
        "Xylophone",
        "Tubular Bells",
        "Dulcimer",
        "Hammond Organ",
        "Percussive Organ",
        "Rock Organ",
        "Church Organ",
        "Reed Organ",
        "Accordion",
        "Harmonica",
        "Tango Accordion",
        "Acoustic Guitar (nylon)",
        "Acoustic Guitar (steel)",
```

Figure 6-12 *Continued.*

```
"Electric Guitar (jazz)",
"Electric Guitar (clean)",
"Electric Guitar (muted)",
"Overdriven Guitar",
"Distortion Guitar",
"Guitar Harmonics",
"Acoustic Bass",
"Electric Bass (fingered)",
"Electric Bass (picked)",
"Fretless Bass",
"Slap Bass 1",
"Slap Bass 2",
"Synth Bass 1",
"Synth Bass 2",
"Violin",
"Viola",
"Cello",
"Contrabass",
"Tremolo Strings",
"Pizzicato Strings",
"Orchestral Harp",
"Timpani",
"String Ensemble 1",
"String Ensemble 2",
"Synth Strings 1",
"Synth Strings 2",
"Choir Aahs",
"Voice Oohs",
"Synth Voice",
"Orchestra Hit",
"Trumpet",
"Trombone",
"Tuba",
"Muted Trumpet",
"French Horn",
"Brass Section",
"Synth Brass 1",
"Synth Brass 2",
"Soprano Sax",
"Alto Sax",
"Tenor Sax",
"Baritone Sax",
"Oboe",
"English Horn",
"Bassoon",
"Clarinet",
"Piccolo",
"Flute",
"Recorder",
"Pan Flute",
"Blown Bottle",
```

```
                  "Shakuhachi",
                  "Whistle",
                  "Ocarina",
                  "Lead 1 (square)",
                  "Lead 2 (sawtooth)",
                  "Lead 3 (calliope)",
                  "Lead 4 (chiff)",
                  "Lead 5 (charang)",
                  "Lead 6 (voice)",
                  "Lead 7 (fifths)",
                  "Lead 8 (bass + lead)",
                  "Pad 1 (new age)",
                  "Pad 2 (warm)",
                  "Pad 3 (polysynth)",
                  "Pad 4 (choir)",
                  "Pad 5 (bowed)",
                  "Pad 6 (metallic)",
                  "Pad 7 (halo)",
                  "Pad 8 (sweep)",
                  "FX 1 (rain)",
                  "FX 2 (soundtrack)",
                  "FX 3 (crystal)",
                  "FX 4 (atmosphere)",
                  "FX 5 (brightness)",
                  "FX 6 (goblins)",
                  "FX 7 (echoes)",
                  "FX 8 (sci-fi)",
                  "Sitar",
                  "Banjo",
                  "Shamisen",
                  "Koto",
                  "Kalimba",
                  "Bagpipe",
                  "Fiddle",
                  "Shanai",
                  "Tinkle Bell",
                  "Agogo",
                  "Steel Drums",
                  "Woodblock",
                  "Taiko Drum",
                  "Melodic Tom",
                  "Synth Drum",
                  "Reverse Cymbal",
                  "Guitar Fret Noise",
                  "Breath Noise",
                  "Seashore",
                  "Bird Tweet",
                  "Telephone Ring",
                  "Helicopter",
                  "Applause",
                  "Gunshot",
                  };

        #define      PATCHCOUNT      (sizeof(midiMapPatch)/sizeof(LPSTR))
```

Running PLAYSONG on systems with different sound hardware will produce fairly noticeable variations in the sound quality of the instruments. I use several computers with MIDI sound hardware. The system I developed PLAYSONG on has one of the cheapest and generally low-tech 8-bit sound cards available, driving two speakers that could have been compact headphones in another life. Predictably, the sound thus generated was a bit weedy. Moving PLAYSONG over to the computer with a good 16-bit card driving a stereo made a big difference—the music really came to life and sounded interesting.

MIDI input

If you have a MIDI keyboard or other external source of note information—and assuming that your system has a MIDI port of some type—you can write applications that will accept MIDI input from external instruments. We'll look at two such applications. The first, MIDIVIEW, will display a running list of all the interesting MIDI messages. This is handy for both understanding what MIDI messages really look like as well as for debugging more complex MIDI software. The second, MIDIREC, will record notes and other MIDI messages generated by a MIDI keyboard and store them in a standard MIDI file.

The MIDIVIEW application is functionally similar to the MIDI monitor included with the Microsoft Multimedia Development Kit. If you've experimented with the Microsoft MIDI monitor, you have probably found that it doesn't compile correctly, and that if you fix its compile time problems, it crashes. You might find MIDIVIEW a less confusing place to start working with the intricacies of MIDI input.

Figure 6-13 illustrates the main window of MIDIVIEW. You can select the channel number of the MIDI messages you're interested in viewing and which specific message types are to be displayed using its controls.

Dealing with MIDI messages sent from an external keyboard is another example of something that computers in general—and Windows in particular—don't really like to get involved with. MIDI messages are asynchronous events—they can occur at any time and in daunting numbers. Even simple message processing—in this case decoding each message and adding it to the list box in the main window of MIDIVIEW—can be fairly time-consuming.

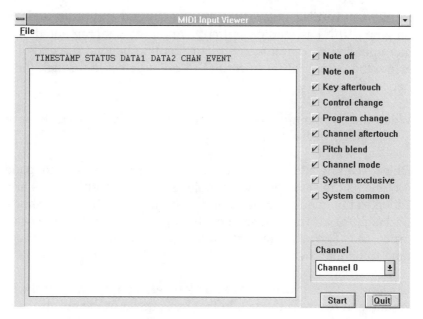

Figure 6-13

The MIDIVIEW application.

The obvious way to deal with MIDI messages is to poll the MIDI port—that is, to wait in a loop until a message appears, deal with it, and then return to the loop. As with other applications of polling, Windows abhors this one, because it wastes a great deal of processor time. In fact, it's less than desirable for other reasons as well. In the time it takes to handle one message, several additional messages might have appeared and been ignored.

On the assumption that most performers can't play a constant stream of thirty-second notes indefinitely without a few rests every so often, a more practical approach to handling incoming messages would be to store them somewhere as they appear and then process them when there's a moment with nothing much happening. The mechanism for doing this is a circular queue.

Allowing that one MIDI message is stored in an object called EVENT, a circular queue is an array of EVENT objects with two index pointers, called the head and the tail. The head points to the next entry in the list where an incoming EVENT object can be written. The tail points

to the next EVENT object in the list to be read and processed. Each time an EVENT is read or written, its pointer is incremented. If incrementing a pointer would see it pointing beyond the end of the array, the pointer is set to zero. The pointers circle through the array, hence its name.

When the two pointers point to the same EVENT object, there are no events in the queue to be read.

Objects can be added to and read from a circular queue independently. As long as the same number of objects are ultimately read as are added to the queue over time, it doesn't matter if there's a short onslaught of incoming messages that appear faster than they can be processed. They'll accumulate in the queue for a while until there's time to handle them.

Obviously, if this process carries on long enough, the head will wrap around and overtake the tail. In that case, some of the events stored in the queue will be lost. When you design a circular queue, you should make sure its array of objects is large enough to preclude this possibility.

The Windows multimedia extensions allow applications like MIDIVIEW to set up interrupt-driven MIDI message handlers—that is, to define a function that will be called whenever a MIDI message appears. The function can write the MIDI message to the head of a circular queue. It can also post a message to a window handle specifying that there are events in the queue to be processed as soon as it's convenient.

The MIDI input interface under Windows is supremely complicated, requiring among other things another recourse to code stashed in a dynamic link library. However, it does provide a solid MIDI input path. The MIDI information supplied by the multimedia extensions is in a particularly useful form, too, as each message is accompanied by the precise time it appeared. While of no significant importance to MIDIVIEW, this is extremely important to applications that want to actually do something musical with MIDI messages. The MIDIREC application discussed in the next section of this chapter will work out things like note duration based on the time codes of incoming MIDI messages.

As with the PLAYSONG application discussed earlier in this chapter, many of the tricky bits associated with MIDI input are handled by the MIDIMAN dynamic link library. The MIDIMAN DLL deals with adding EVENT objects to the MIDIVIEW circular queue, and it will post messages back to MIDIVIEW to tell it that something is waiting to be picked up. The MIDIVIEW application is responsible for allocating the queue itself.

The circular queue logic and related functions in MIDIVIEW are derived from the Microsoft MIDIMON application.

Figure 6-14 illustrates the MIDIVIEW.CPP source code file. Figure 6-15 illustrates MIDIVIEW.RC, its resource script. In addition to these files, you'll need PRJ and DEF files for MIDIVIEW, and the WAV and BMP files included in MIDIVIEW.RC. You will find all these files on the companion CD-ROM for this book.

The MIDIVIEW.CPP source code.   Figure 6-14

```
/*

        MIDI Input Viewer
        Copyright (c) 1993 Alchemy Mindworks Inc.

        With reference to Microsoft's MIDIMON

*/

#include <windows.h>
#include <stdio.h>
#include <stdlib.h>
#include <dir.h>
#include <ctype.h>
#include <alloc.h>
#include <string.h>
#include <io.h>
#include <bwcc.h>
#include <dos.h>
#include <errno.h>
#include <math.h>
#include <commdlg.h>
#include <mmsystem.h>
#include "midiman.h"

#define say(s)      MessageBox(NULL,s,"Yo...",MB_OK | MB_ICONSTOP);
#define saynumber(f,s)     {char b[128]; sprintf((LPSTR)b,(LPSTR)f,s); \
        MessageBox(NULL,b,"Debug Message",MB_OK | MB_ICONSTOP); \
        }
```

Figure 6-14 *Continued.*

```
#define ItemName(item,string)       { dlgH=GetDlgItem(hwnd,item); \
                                     SetWindowText(dlgH,(LPSTR)string); \
                                     }

#define ItemOn(item)          { dlgH=GetDlgItem(hwnd,item); \
                                EnableWindow(dlgH,TRUE); \
                                EnableMenuItem(hmenu,item,MF_ENABLED); \
                                }

#define ItemOff(item)         { dlgH=GetDlgItem(hwnd,item); \
                                EnableWindow(dlgH,FALSE); \
                                EnableMenuItem(hmenu,item,MF_GRAYED); \
                                }

#define IsItemChecked(item) SendDlgItemMessage(hwnd,item,BM_GETCHECK,0,0L)

#define CheckOn(item)       SendDlgItemMessage(hwnd,item,BM_SETCHECK,1,0L);
#define CheckOff(item)      SendDlgItemMessage(hwnd,item,BM_SETCHECK,0,0L);

#define SetCurrentChannel(n) { \
        SendDlgItemMessage(hwnd,MAIN_CHANNELS,CB_SETCURSEL,n,0L); \
        currentchannel=n; \
        }

#define TurnItemOn(item) { CheckOn(item); \
        SetEventFlag(item-MAIN_EVENTBASE,TRUE); }

#define GetEventFlag(n)     (eventflags & (1 << (n)))

#define MESSAGETYPE(n)      (n-MAIN_EVENTBASE)

#define IsActiveChannel(n) (n==currentchannel ? TRUE : FALSE)

#define STRINGSIZE          128

#define MAIN_START          101
#define MAIN_ABOUT          102
#define MAIN_EXIT           199

#define MAIN_LIST           301
#define MAIN_LISTTITLE      302

#define MAIN_CHANNELS       401

#define MAIN_NOTEOFF        201
#define MAIN_NOTEON         202
#define MAIN_KEYAFTER       203
#define MAIN_CONTROLCH      204
#define MAIN_PROGCH         205
#define MAIN_CHAFTER        206
#define MAIN_PITCHBEND      207
```

```
#define MAIN_CHMODE        208
#define MAIN_SYSEX         209
#define MAIN_SYSCOM        210

#define MAIN_EVENTBASE     201
#define MAIN_EVENTCOUNT    10

#define MAX_DEVICES        8
#define INPUT_BUFFER_SIZE  200

#define NOTEON             0x90
#define NOTEOFF            0x80
#define KEYAFTERTOUCH      0xa0
#define CONTROLCHANGE      0xb0
#define PROGRAMCHANGE      0xc0
#define CHANAFTERTOUCH     0xd0
#define PITCHBEND          0xe0
#define SYSTEMMESSAGE      0xf0
#define BEGINSYSEX         0xf0
#define MTCQUARTERFRAME    0xf1
#define SONGPOSPTR         0xf2
#define SONGSELECT         0xf3

#define VELOCITY           64

#define MAX_LINES          27

#define FORMAT3  " %08lX   %02X      %02X      %02X      %2d   %s "
#define FORMAT2  " %08lX   %02X      %02X      --       %2d   %-21s "
#define FORMAT3X " %08lX   %02X      %02X      %02X      --   %-21s "
#define FORMAT2X " %08lX   %02X      %02X      --       --   %-21s "
#define FORMAT1X " %08lX   %02X      --       --       --   %-21s "

#define DoMessage(hwnd,string) BWCCMessageBox(hwnd,string,"Message",\
                        MB_OK | MB_ICONINFORMATION)

#define CreateControlFont()         if(ControlFontName[0]) \
                   controlfont=CreateFont(10,0,0,0,0,0,0,0,0,\
                   ANSI_CHARSET,OUT_DEFAULT_PRECIS,CLIP_DEFAULT_PRECIS,\
                   DEFAULT_QUALITY,DEFAULT_PITCH | FF_DONTCARE,\
                   ControlFontName)

#define SetControlFont(hwnd,id) {HWND dlgH;\
             if(controlfont != NULL) {\
                   dlgH=GetDlgItem(hwnd,id);\
                   SendMessage(dlgH,WM_SETFONT,(WORD)controlfont,FALSE);\
             }\
             }

#define DestroyControlFont() \
      if(controlfont != NULL) DeleteObject(controlfont)

#define MIDI_CHANNELS         16
```

Figure 6-14 *Continued.*

```
#ifndef max
#define max(a,b)              (((a)>(b))?(a):(b))
#endif
#ifndef min
#define min(a,b)              (((a)<(b))?(a):(b))
#endif


/* prototypes */
LPCIRCULARBUFFER AllocCircularBuffer(DWORD dwSize);
LPCALLBACKINSTANCEDATA FAR PASCAL AllocCallbackInstanceData(void);

DWORD FAR PASCAL SelectProc(HWND hwnd,WORD message,WORD wParam,LONG
lParam);
DWORD FAR PASCAL AboutDlgProc(HWND hwnd,WORD message,WORD wParam,LONG
lParam);
DWORD FAR PASCAL MessageDlgProc(HWND hwnd,WORD message,WORD wParam,LONG
lParam);

int StartMidiInput(HWND hwnd);
int IsInterestingMessage(LPEVENT lpEvent);

WORD FAR PASCAL GetEvent(LPCIRCULARBUFFER lpBuf,LPEVENT lpEvent);
LPSTR NoteToName(int number);

void StopMidiInput();
void lmemset(LPSTR s,int n,unsigned int size);
void CentreWindow(HWND hwnd);
void FreeCircularBuffer(LPCIRCULARBUFFER lpBuf);
void FAR PASCAL FreeCallbackInstanceData(LPCALLBACKINSTANCEDATA lpBuf);
void AddToList(HWND hwnd,unsigned int list,LPEVENT event);
void SetEventFlag(int n,int state);

/* globals */
char ControlFontName[STRINGSIZE+1]="Courier";
HFONT controlfont=NULL;
LPCIRCULARBUFFER lpInputBuffer;

MIDIINCAPS midiInCaps[MAX_DEVICES];
HMIDIIN hMidiIn[MAX_DEVICES];

LPCALLBACKINSTANCEDATA lpCallbackInstanceData[MAX_DEVICES];
HMIDIOUT hMapper=0;
char szAppName[] = "MidiView";
HANDLE hInst;

unsigned int currentchannel=0;
unsigned int eventflags=0;
unsigned int active=FALSE;

#pragma warn -par
int PASCAL WinMain(HANDLE hInstance,HANDLE hPrevInstance,
                LPSTR lpszCmdParam,int nCmdShow)
```

```
{
        FARPROC dlgProc;
        int r=0;

        BWCCGetVersion();

        hInst=hInstance;

        dlgProc=MakeProcInstance((FARPROC)SelectProc,hInst);
        r=DialogBox(hInst,"MainScreen",NULL,dlgProc);

        FreeProcInstance(dlgProc);

        return(r);
}

DWORD FAR PASCAL SelectProc(HWND hwnd,WORD message,WORD wParam,LONG lParam)
{
        EVENT event;
        PAINTSTRUCT ps;
        HICON hIcon;
        FARPROC lpfnDlgProc;
        POINT point;
        long l;
        char b[STRINGSIZE+1];
        int i;

        switch(message) {
                case MM_MIDIINPUT:
                        while(GetEvent(lpInputBuffer,(LPEVENT)&event)) {
                                if(!active) continue;

                                 if(IsInterestingMessage(&event))
                                     AddToList(hwnd,MAIN_LIST,&event);
                        }
                        break;
                case WM_CTLCOLOR:
                        if(HIWORD(lParam)==CTLCOLOR_STATIC ||
                           HIWORD(lParam)==CTLCOLOR_DLG) {
                                SetBkColor(wParam,RGB(192,192,192));
                                SetTextColor(wParam,RGB(0,0,0));

                                ClientToScreen(hwnd,&point);
                                UnrealizeObject(GetStockObject(LTGRAY_BRUSH));
                                SetBrushOrg(wParam,point.x,point.y);

                                return((DWORD)GetStockObject(LTGRAY_BRUSH));

                        }
                        if(HIWORD(lParam)==CTLCOLOR_BTN) {
                                SetBkColor(wParam,RGB(192,192,192));
                                SetTextColor(wParam,RGB(0,0,0));
```

Figure 6-14 *Continued.*

```
                        ClientToScreen(hwnd,&point);
                        UnrealizeObject(GetStockObject(BLACK_BRUSH));
                        SetBrushOrg(wParam,point.x,point.y);

                        return((DWORD)GetStockObject(BLACK_BRUSH));
                }
            break;
        case WM_SYSCOMMAND:
            switch(wParam & 0xfff0) {
                    case SC_CLOSE:
                            SendMessage(hwnd,WM_COMMAND,MAIN_EXIT,0L);
                            break;
            }
            break;
        case WM_INITDIALOG:
            hIcon=LoadIcon(hInst,szAppName);
            SetClassWord(hwnd,GCW_HICON,(WORD)hIcon);

            for(i=0;i<MIDI_CHANNELS;++i) {
                    wsprintf(b,"Channel %u",i);
                    SendDlgItemMessage(hwnd,MAIN_CHANNELS,
                        CB_INSERTSTRING,-1,(LONG)(LPSTR)b);
            }

            SetCurrentChannel(0);

            CreateControlFont();

            SetControlFont(hwnd,MAIN_LIST);

            SetControlFont(hwnd,MAIN_LISTTITLE);

            TurnItemOn(MAIN_NOTEOFF);
            TurnItemOn(MAIN_NOTEON);
            TurnItemOn(MAIN_KEYAFTER);
            TurnItemOn(MAIN_CONTROLCH);
            TurnItemOn(MAIN_PROGCH);
            TurnItemOn(MAIN_CHAFTER);
            TurnItemOn(MAIN_PITCHBEND);
            TurnItemOn(MAIN_CHMODE);
            TurnItemOn(MAIN_SYSEX);
            TurnItemOn(MAIN_SYSCOM);

            CentreWindow(hwnd);
            break;
        case WM_PAINT:
            BeginPaint(hwnd,&ps);
            EndPaint(hwnd,&ps);
            break;
        case WM_COMMAND:
            switch(wParam) {
```

```
case MAIN_START:
        if(active) {
                SetWindowText(GetDlgItem(hwnd,
                    wParam),"Start");
                active=FALSE;
                StopMidiInput();
        }
        else {
                SetWindowText(GetDlgItem(hwnd,
                    wParam),"Stop");
                active=TRUE;
                if(!StartMidiInput(hwnd))
                    PostMessage(hwnd,WM_COMMAND,
                        MAIN_START,0L);
        }
        break;
case MAIN_ABOUT:
        if((lpfnDlgProc=MakeProcInstance((FARPROC)
            AboutDlgProc,hInst)) != NULL) {
                DialogBox(hInst,"AboutBox",
                    hwnd,lpfnDlgProc);
                FreeProcInstance(lpfnDlgProc);
        }
        break;
case MAIN_EXIT:
        if(active) StopMidiInput();
        DestroyControlFont();
        PostQuitMessage(0);
        break;
case MAIN_CHANNELS:
        if((l=SendDlgItemMessage(hwnd,
            MAIN_CHANNELS,CB_GETCURSEL,0,0L))
                != CB_ERR)
            currentchannel=(unsigned int)l;
        break;
case MAIN_NOTEOFF:
case MAIN_NOTEON:
case MAIN_KEYAFTER:
case MAIN_CONTROLCH:
case MAIN_PROGCH:
case MAIN_CHAFTER:
case MAIN_PITCHBEND:
case MAIN_CHMODE:
case MAIN_SYSEX:
case MAIN_SYSCOM:
        SetEventFlag(wParam-MAIN_EVENTBASE,
            (int)IsItemChecked(wParam));
        break;
}
break;

}
```

Figure 6-14 *Continued.*

```
                  return(FALSE);
         }

DWORD FAR PASCAL AboutDlgProc(HWND hwnd,WORD message,WORD wParam,LONG lParam)
{
         static HANDLE sound;
         static LPSTR psound;
         HANDLE handle;
         POINT point;

         switch(message) {
               case WM_INITDIALOG:
                        if((handle=FindResource(hInst,"AboutWave",
                           RT_RCDATA)) != NULL) {
                                if((sound=LoadResource(hInst,handle)) != NULL) {
                                        if((psound=LockResource(sound)) != NULL)
                                             sndPlaySound(psound,SND_ASYNC |
                                                  SND_MEMORY | SND_NOSTOP);
                                }
                        }
                        CentreWindow(hwnd);
                        return(FALSE);
               case WM_CTLCOLOR:
                        if(HIWORD(lParam)==CTLCOLOR_STATIC ||
                           HIWORD(lParam)==CTLCOLOR_DLG) {
                                SetBkColor(wParam,RGB(192,192,192));
                                SetTextColor(wParam,RGB(0,0,0));

                                ClientToScreen(hwnd,&point);
                                UnrealizeObject(GetStockObject(LTGRAY_BRUSH));
                                SetBrushOrg(wParam,point.x,point.y);

                                return((DWORD)GetStockObject(LTGRAY_BRUSH));

                        }
                        if(HIWORD(lParam)==CTLCOLOR_BTN) {
                                SetBkColor(wParam,RGB(192,192,192));
                                SetTextColor(wParam,RGB(0,0,0));

                                ClientToScreen(hwnd,&point);
                                UnrealizeObject(GetStockObject(BLACK_BRUSH));
                                SetBrushOrg(wParam,point.x,point.y);

                                return((DWORD)GetStockObject(BLACK_BRUSH));
                        }
                        break;
               case WM_COMMAND:
                        switch(wParam) {
                               case IDOK:
                                        sndPlaySound(NULL,SND_SYNC);
                                        if(psound != NULL) UnlockResource(sound);
```

```
                                        if(sound != NULL) FreeResource(sound);
                                        EndDialog(hwnd,wParam);
                                        return(FALSE);
                            }
                            break;
            }

            return(FALSE);
}

void lmemset(LPSTR s,int n,unsigned int size)
{
            unsigned int i;

            for(i=0;i<size;++i) *s++=n;
}

void CentreWindow(HWND hwnd)
{
            RECT rect;
            unsigned int x,y;

            GetWindowRect(hwnd,&rect);
            x=(GetSystemMetrics(SM_CXSCREEN)-(rect.right-rect.left))/2;
            y=(GetSystemMetrics(SM_CYSCREEN)-(rect.bottom-rect.top))/2;
            SetWindowPos(hwnd,NULL,x,y,rect.right-rect.left,
                rect.bottom-rect.top,SWP_NOSIZE);
}

int StartMidiInput(HWND hwnd)
{
            char b[STRINGSIZE+1];
            int i,r,devcount;

            if((devcount=midiInGetNumDevs())==0) {
                    DoMessage(hwnd,"There are no MIDI devices installed");
                    return(FALSE);
            }

            if((lpInputBuffer = AllocCircularBuffer((long)INPUT_BUFFER_SIZE
                * (long)sizeof(EVENT)))==NULL) {
                    DoMessage(hwnd,"Error allocating memory");
                    return(FALSE);
            }

            for(i=0;i<devcount && i<MAX_DEVICES;++i) {
                    if((lpCallbackInstanceData[i] =
                        AllocCallbackInstanceData()) == NULL) {
                            DoMessage(hwnd,"Error allocating memory");
                            return(FALSE);
                    }
                    lpCallbackInstanceData[i]->hWnd = hwnd;
                    lpCallbackInstanceData[i]->dwDevice = i;
```

329

Figure 6-14 *Continued.*

```
                      lpCallbackInstanceData[i]->lpBuf = lpInputBuffer;
                      lpCallbackInstanceData[i]->hMapper = hMapper;

                      if((r=midiInOpen((LPHMIDIIN)&hMidiIn[i],i,
                         (DWORD)midiInputHandler,
                         (DWORD)lpCallbackInstanceData[i],CALLBACK_FUNCTION)) != 0) {

                             FreeCallbackInstanceData(lpCallbackInstanceData[i]);
                             midiInGetErrorText(r,b,STRINGSIZE);
                             DoMessage(hwnd,b);
                      }
              }

              for(i=0;i<devcount && i<MAX_DEVICES;++i) {
                      if(hMidiIn[i]) midiInStart(hMidiIn[i]);
              }
              return(TRUE);
      }

      void StopMidiInput()
      {
              int i,devcount;

              devcount=midiInGetNumDevs();

              for(i=0;i<devcount && i<MAX_DEVICES;++i) {
                      if(hMidiIn[i]) {
                              midiInStop(hMidiIn[i]);
                                 midiInReset(hMidiIn[i]);
                                 midiInClose(hMidiIn[i]);
                                 FreeCallbackInstanceData(lpCallbackInstanceData[i]);
                      }
              }

              if(hMapper) midiOutClose(hMapper);

              FreeCircularBuffer(lpInputBuffer);
      }

      LPCIRCULARBUFFER AllocCircularBuffer(DWORD dwSize)
      {
              HANDLE hMem;
              LPCIRCULARBUFFER lpBuf;
              LPEVENT lpMem;

              if((hMem=GlobalAlloc(GMEM_SHARE | GMEM_MOVEABLE,
              (DWORD)sizeof(CIRCULARBUFFER)))==NULL)
                  return(NULL);

              if((lpBuf = (LPCIRCULARBUFFER)GlobalLock(hMem))==NULL) {
                  GlobalFree(hMem);
```

```
                        return(NULL);
                }

        GlobalPageLock(HIWORD(lpBuf));

        lpBuf->hSelf=hMem;

        if((hMem = GlobalAlloc(GMEM_SHARE | GMEM_MOVEABLE,
            dwSize*sizeof(EVENT)))==NULL) {
                GlobalPageUnlock(HIWORD(lpBuf));
                GlobalUnlock(lpBuf->hSelf);
                GlobalFree(lpBuf->hSelf);
                return(NULL);
        }

        if((lpMem=(LPEVENT)GlobalLock(hMem))==NULL) {
                GlobalFree(hMem);
                GlobalPageUnlock(HIWORD(lpBuf));
                GlobalUnlock(lpBuf->hSelf);
                GlobalFree(lpBuf->hSelf);
                return(NULL);
        }

        GlobalPageLock(HIWORD(lpMem));

        lpBuf->hBuffer = hMem;
        lpBuf->wError = 0;
        lpBuf->dwSize = dwSize;
        lpBuf->dwCount = 0L;
        lpBuf->lpStart = lpMem;
        lpBuf->lpEnd = lpMem+(WORD)dwSize;
        lpBuf->lpTail = lpMem;
        lpBuf->lpHead = lpMem;

        return(lpBuf);
}

void FreeCircularBuffer(LPCIRCULARBUFFER lpBuf)
{
        HANDLE hMem;

        GlobalPageUnlock(HIWORD(lpBuf->lpStart));
        GlobalUnlock(lpBuf->hBuffer);
        GlobalFree(lpBuf->hBuffer);

        hMem = lpBuf->hSelf;
        GlobalPageUnlock(HIWORD(lpBuf));
        GlobalUnlock(hMem);
        GlobalFree(hMem);
}

WORD FAR PASCAL GetEvent(LPCIRCULARBUFFER lpBuf,LPEVENT lpEvent)
{
        if(lpBuf->dwCount <= 0) return(FALSE);
```

Figure 6-14 *Continued.*

```
            *lpEvent=*lpBuf->lpTail;

            -lpBuf->dwCount;
            ++lpBuf->lpTail;

            if(lpBuf->lpTail >= lpBuf->lpEnd)
                lpBuf->lpTail = lpBuf->lpStart;
            return(TRUE);
}

LPCALLBACKINSTANCEDATA FAR PASCAL AllocCallbackInstanceData(void)
{
            HANDLE hMem;
            LPCALLBACKINSTANCEDATA lpBuf;

            if((hMem=GlobalAlloc(GMEM_SHARE | GMEM_MOVEABLE,
                (DWORD)sizeof(CALLBACKINSTANCEDATA)))==NULL)
                    return(NULL);

            if((lpBuf=(LPCALLBACKINSTANCEDATA)GlobalLock(hMem))==NULL) {
                    GlobalFree(hMem);
                    return(NULL);
            }

            GlobalPageLock(HIWORD(lpBuf));

            lpBuf->hSelf=hMem;

            return(lpBuf);
}

void FAR PASCAL FreeCallbackInstanceData(LPCALLBACKINSTANCEDATA lpBuf)
{
            HANDLE hMem;

            hMem=lpBuf->hSelf;

            GlobalPageUnlock(HIWORD(lpBuf));
            GlobalUnlock(hMem);
            GlobalFree(hMem);
}

int IsInterestingMessage(LPEVENT lpEvent)
{
            BYTE bStatus,bStatusRaw,bChannel;

            bStatusRaw = LOBYTE(LOWORD(lpEvent->data));
            bStatus = bStatusRaw & (BYTE) 0xf0;
            bChannel = LOBYTE(LOWORD(lpEvent->data)) & (BYTE) 0x0f;

            switch(bStatus){
```

```
                        case NOTEOFF:
                                if(GetEventFlag(MESSAGETYPE(MAIN_NOTEOFF)))
                                    return(IsActiveChannel(bChannel));
                                break;
                        case NOTEON:
                                if(GetEventFlag(MESSAGETYPE(MAIN_NOTEON)))
                                    return(IsActiveChannel(bChannel));
                                break;
                        case KEYAFTERTOUCH:
                                if(GetEventFlag(MESSAGETYPE(MAIN_KEYAFTER)))
                                    return(IsActiveChannel(bChannel));
                                break;
                        case CONTROLCHANGE:
                                if(GetEventFlag(MESSAGETYPE(MAIN_CONTROLCH)))
                                    return(IsActiveChannel(bChannel));
                                break;
                        case PROGRAMCHANGE:
                                if(GetEventFlag(MESSAGETYPE(MAIN_PROGCH)))
                                    return(IsActiveChannel(bChannel));
                                break;
                        case CHANAFTERTOUCH:
                                if(GetEventFlag(MESSAGETYPE(MAIN_CHAFTER)))
                                    return(IsActiveChannel(bChannel));
                                break;
                        case PITCHBEND:
                                if(GetEventFlag(MESSAGETYPE(MAIN_PITCHBEND)))
                                    return(IsActiveChannel(bChannel));
                                break;
                        case SYSTEMMESSAGE:
                                if(bStatusRaw < 0xf8 &&
                                    GetEventFlag(MESSAGETYPE(MAIN_SYSCOM)))
                                            return(TRUE);
                                break;

                }
                return(FALSE);
        }


void AddToList(HWND hwnd,unsigned int list,LPEVENT lpEvent)
{
        static char szEventNames[8][24]={
                "Note Off",
                "Note On",
                "Key Aftertouch",
                "Control Change",
                "Program Change",
                "Channel Aftertouch",
                "Pitch Bend",
                "System Message"
                };

        static char szSysMsgNames[16][24]={
                "System Exclusive",
```

Figure 6-14 *Continued.*

```
                        "MTC Quarter Frame",
                        "Song Position Pointer",
                        "Song Select",
                        "Undefined",
                        "Undefined",
                        "Tune Request",
                        "System Exclusive End",
                        "Timing Clock",
                        "Undefined",
                        "Start",
                        "Continue",
                        "Stop",
                        "Undefined",
                        "Active Sensing",
                        "System Reset"
                        };

        char npText[STRINGSIZE+1];
        BYTE bStatus, bStatusRaw, bChannel, bData1, bData2;
        DWORD dwTimestamp,count;

        bStatusRaw=LOBYTE(LOWORD(lpEvent->data));
        bStatus=bStatusRaw & (BYTE) 0xf0;
        bChannel=bStatusRaw & (BYTE) 0x0f;
        bData1=HIBYTE(LOWORD(lpEvent->data));
        bData2=LOBYTE(HIWORD(lpEvent->data));
        dwTimestamp=lpEvent->timestamp;

        switch(bStatus) {
                case NOTEOFF:
                case NOTEON:
                case KEYAFTERTOUCH:
                case CONTROLCHANGE:
                case PITCHBEND:
                        if(bStatus == NOTEON && bData2==0) bStatus=NOTEOFF;

                        sprintf(npText,FORMAT3,dwTimestamp,
                            bStatusRaw,bData1,bData2,bChannel,
                                &szEventNames[(bStatus-0x80) > 4][0]);

                        if(bStatus==NOTEON) lstrcat(npText,NoteToName(bData1));

                        break;
                case PROGRAMCHANGE:
                case CHANAFTERTOUCH:
                        sprintf(npText, FORMAT2, dwTimestamp, bStatusRaw, bData1,
                            bChannel, &szEventNames[(bStatus-0x80) > 4][0]);
                        break;
                case SYSTEMMESSAGE:
                        switch(bStatusRaw) {
```

```
                                          case MTCQUARTERFRAME:
                                          case SONGSELECT:
                                                    sprintf(npText,FORMAT2X,dwTimestamp,
                                                        bStatusRaw,bData1,
                                                        &szSysMsgNames[(bStatusRaw & 0x0f)][0]);
                                                    break;

                                          case SONGPOSPTR:
                                                    sprintf(npText,FORMAT3X,dwTimestamp,
                                                        bStatusRaw,bData1,bData2,
                                                        &szSysMsgNames[(bStatusRaw & 0x0f)][0]);
                                                    break;
                                          default:
                                                    sprintf(npText,FORMAT1X,dwTimestamp,
                                                        bStatusRaw,
                                                        &szSysMsgNames[(bStatusRaw & 0x0f)][0]);
                                                    break;
                                  }
                                  break;
                       default:
                                  sprintf(npText,FORMAT3X,dwTimestamp,bStatusRaw,bData1,
                                      bData2, "Unknown Event");
                                  break;
            }

            if((count=SendDlgItemMessage(hwnd,list,LB_GETCOUNT,0,0L)) != LB_ERR) {
                     if(count >= MAX_LINES)
                            SendDlgItemMessage(hwnd,list,LB_DELETESTRING,0,0L);

                     SendDlgItemMessage(hwnd,list,LB_INSERTSTRING,-1,(LONG)(LPSTR)npText);
            }
}

LPSTR NoteToName(int number)
{
            static char note[12][3]={"C","C#","D","D#","E","F",
                                    "F#","G","G#","A","A#","B"};
            static char b[STRINGSIZE+1];

            wsprintf(b," %s(%u)",(LPSTR)note[number % 12],(number/12)+1);

            return(b);
}

void SetEventFlag(int n,int state)
{
            if(state) eventflags |= (1 << (n));
            else eventflags &= ~(1 << (n));
}
```

Figure 6-15 *The MIDIVIEW.RC resource script.*

```
MainScreen DIALOG 48, 24, 316, 216
STYLE WS_POPUP | WS_CAPTION | WS_SYSMENU | WS_MINIMIZEBOX
CAPTION "MIDI Input Viewer"
MENU MainMenu
BEGIN
        PUSHBUTTON "Quit", 199, 280, 196, 28, 12, WS_CHILD | WS_VISIBLE | WS_TABSTOP
        CONTROL "", -1, "BorShade", 32769 | WS_CHILD | WS_VISIBLE, 8, 8, 220, 200
        CONTROL "", 301, "LISTBOX", LBS_NOTIFY | LBS_USETABSTOPS | WS_CHILD |
            WS_VISIBLE | WS_BORDER | WS_TABSTOP, 12, 24, 212, 180
        PUSHBUTTON "Start", 101, 244, 196, 28, 12, WS_CHILD | WS_VISIBLE | WS_TABSTOP
        CONTROL "Note off", 201, "BorCheck", BS_AUTOCHECKBOX | WS_CHILD | WS_VISIBLE |
            WS_TABSTOP, 236, 8, 72, 10
        CONTROL "Note on", 202, "BorCheck", BS_AUTOCHECKBOX | WS_CHILD | WS_VISIBLE |
            WS_TABSTOP, 236, 20, 72, 10
        CONTROL "Key aftertouch", 203, "BorCheck", BS_AUTOCHECKBOX | WS_CHILD |
            WS_VISIBLE | WS_TABSTOP, 236, 32, 72, 10
        CONTROL "Control change", 204, "BorCheck", BS_AUTOCHECKBOX | WS_CHILD |
            WS_VISIBLE | WS_TABSTOP, 236, 44, 72, 10
        CONTROL "Program change", 205, "BorCheck", BS_AUTOCHECKBOX | WS_CHILD |
            WS_VISIBLE | WS_TABSTOP, 236, 56, 72, 10
        CONTROL "Channel aftertouch", 206, "BorCheck", BS_AUTOCHECKBOX | WS_CHILD |
            WS_VISIBLE | WS_TABSTOP, 236, 68, 72, 10
        CONTROL "Pitch bend", 207, "BorCheck", BS_AUTOCHECKBOX | WS_CHILD |
            WS_VISIBLE | WS_TABSTOP, 236, 80, 72, 10
        CONTROL "Channel mode", 208, "BorCheck", BS_AUTOCHECKBOX | WS_CHILD |
            WS_VISIBLE | WS_TABSTOP, 236, 92, 72, 10
        CONTROL "System exclusive", 209, "BorCheck", BS_AUTOCHECKBOX | WS_CHILD |
            WS_VISIBLE | WS_TABSTOP, 236, 104, 72, 10
        CONTROL "System common", 210, "BorCheck", BS_AUTOCHECKBOX | WS_CHILD |
            WS_VISIBLE | WS_TABSTOP, 236, 116, 72, 10
        CONTROL "", -1, "BorShade", 32769 | WS_CHILD | WS_VISIBLE, 236, 156, 72, 32
        CONTROL "", 401, "COMBOBOX", CBS_DROPDOWNLIST | WS_CHILD | WS_VISIBLE |
            WS_VSCROLL | WS_TABSTOP, 240, 171, 64, 64
        LTEXT "Channel", -1, 240, 159, 64, 8, WS_CHILD | WS_VISIBLE | WS_GROUP
        LTEXT " TIMESTAMP STATUS DATA1 DATA2 CHAN EVENT                ", 302,
            12, 12, 212, 8, WS_CHILD | WS_VISIBLE | WS_GROUP
END

MainMenu MENU
BEGIN
        POPUP "&File"
        BEGIN
                MENUITEM "&Start", 101
                MENUITEM "&About", 102
                MENUITEM SEPARATOR
                MENUITEM "E&xit", 199
        END

END
```

```
AboutBox DIALOG 18, 18, 184, 180
STYLE WS_POPUP | WS_CAPTION
CAPTION "About..."
BEGIN
        CONTROL "", 102, "BorShade", BSS_GROUP | WS_CHILD | WS_VISIBLE |
            WS_TABSTOP, 8, 68, 168, 76
        CTEXT "MIDI Input Viewer 1.0\n\nCopyright (c) 1994 Alchemy Mindworks Inc.\n\n
            This program is part of the book Advanced Multimedia Programming for
            Windows by Steven William Rimmer, published by Windcrest/McGraw Hill.",
            -1, 12, 72, 160, 68, WS_CHILD | WS_VISIBLE | WS_GROUP
        CONTROL "Button", IDOK, "BorBtn", BS_DEFPUSHBUTTON | WS_CHILD | WS_VISIBLE |
            WS_TABSTOP, 74, 152, 32, 20
        CONTROL "Button", 801, "BorBtn", BS_PUSHBUTTON | WS_CHILD | WS_VISIBLE |
            WS_TABSTOP, 36, 8, 32, 20
END

1801 BITMAP "smpw.bmp"

AboutWave RCDATA "ABOUT.WAV"

MidiView ICON
BEGIN
        '00 00 01 00 01 00 20 20 10 00 00 00 00 00 E8 02'
        '00 00 16 00 00 00 28 00 00 00 20 00 00 00 40 00'
        '00 00 01 00 04 00 00 00 00 00 80 02 00 00 00 00'
        '00 00 00 00 00 00 10 00 00 00 00 00 00 00 00 00'
        '00 00 00 00 BF 00 00 BF 00 00 00 BF BF 00 BF 00'
        '00 00 BF 00 BF 00 BF BF 00 00 C0 C0 C0 00 80 80'
        '80 00 00 00 FF 00 00 FF 00 00 00 FF FF 00 FF 00'
        '00 00 FF 00 FF 00 FF FF 00 00 FF FF FF 00 77 77'
        '77 77 77 77 77 77 77 77 77 77 77 77 77 77 7F 88'
        '88 88 88 88 88 88 88 88 88 88 88 88 88 87 7F F8'
        '88 88 88 88 88 88 88 88 88 88 88 88 88 87 7F F7'
        '77 77 77 77 77 77 77 77 77 77 77 77 78 87 7F F7'
        '77 77 77 77 77 77 77 77 77 77 77 77 78 87 7F F7'
        '77 77 77 77 7A AA A0 77 77 77 77 77 78 87 7F F7'
        '77 77 77 77 7A A0 7A 07 77 77 77 77 78 87 7F F7'
        '77 77 77 77 77 77 7A 07 77 77 77 77 78 87 7F F7'
        '77 77 77 77 77 77 7A 07 77 77 77 77 78 87 7F F7'
        '77 77 77 77 77 77 7A 07 77 77 77 77 78 87 7F F7'
        '77 77 77 77 7A AA A0 77 77 77 77 77 78 87 7F F7'
        '77 77 77 77 A0 77 7A 07 77 77 77 77 78 87 7F F7'
        '77 77 77 7A 07 A0 A0 A0 77 77 77 77 78 87 7F F7'
        '77 77 77 7A 0A 07 A0 A0 77 77 77 77 78 87 7F F7'
        '77 77 77 7A 0A AA 0A A0 77 77 77 77 78 87 7F F7'
        '77 77 77 7A 07 AA AA 07 77 77 77 77 78 87 7F F7'
        '77 77 77 77 7A A0 7A 07 77 77 77 77 78 87 7F F7'
        '77 77 77 77 AA A0 77 77 77 77 77 77 78 87 7F F7'
        '77 77 77 77 7A A0 77 77 77 77 77 77 78 87 7F F7'
        '77 77 77 77 7A AA 07 77 77 77 77 77 78 87 7F F7'
        '77 77 77 77 77 AA A0 77 77 77 77 77 78 87 7F F7'
        '77 77 77 77 7A 07 AA 07 77 77 77 77 78 87 7F F7'
        '77 77 77 77 7A 07 AA 07 77 77 77 77 78 87 7F F7'
```

337

Figure 6-15 *Continued.*

```
'77 77 77 77 77 A0 7A 07 77 77 77 77 78 87 7F F7'
'77 77 77 77 77 A0 7A 07 77 77 77 77 78 87 7F F7'
'77 77 77 77 77 AA AA 07 77 77 77 77 78 87 7F F7'
'77 77 77 77 77 7A A0 77 77 77 77 77 78 87 7F F7'
'77 77 77 77 77 77 77 77 77 77 77 77 78 87 7F F7'
'77 77 77 77 77 77 77 77 77 77 77 77 78 87 7F FF'
'FF FF FF FF FF FF FF FF FF FF FF FF F8 87 7F FF'
'FF FF FF FF FF FF FF FF FF FF FF FF FF 87 77 77'
'77 77 77 77 77 77 77 77 77 77 77 77 77 77 00 00'
'00 00 00 00 00 00 00 00 00 00 00 00 00 00 00 00'
'00 00 00 00 00 00 00 00 00 00 00 00 00 00 00 00'
'00 00 00 00 00 00 00 00 00 00 00 00 00 00 00 00'
'00 00 00 00 00 00 00 00 00 00 00 00 00 00 00 00'
'00 00 00 00 00 00 00 00 00 00 00 00 00 00 00 00'
'00 00 00 00 00 00 00 00 00 00 00 00 00 00 00 00'
'00 00 00 00 00 00 00 00 00 00 00 00 00 00 00 00'
'00 00 00 00 00 00 00 00 00 00 00 00 00 00 00'
END
```

The MIDIVIEW application will begin displaying incoming MIDI messages when you click on its Start button. The real work is done down in the MAIN_START case of the WM_COMMAND handler of SelectProc. It calls StartMidiInput, which is defined later in MIDIVIEW.CPP. The MAIN_START case also handles shutting down the MIDI input—the Start button will change to a Stop button when MIDIVIEW is displaying messages.

The MM_MIDIINPUT handler of SelectProc hands messages from MIDIMAN.DLL indicating that there are MIDI messages in the circular queue waiting to be retrieved. Because MM_MIDIINPUT messages are posted rather than sent, there may be more than one message in the queue by the time an MM_MIDIINPUT message reaches SelectProc. For this reason, the while loop in the MM_MIDIINPUT handler retrieves all the waiting events, rather than assuming there's just one.

The GetEvent function called from the MM_MIDIINPUT handler fetches the event indicated by the tail pointer for the circular event queue and increments the pointer. The IsInterestingMessage function decides whether the message just retrieved should be displayed—it consults the list of check boxes in the main window of MIDIVIEW to see whether the one that corresponds to the message in question has been checked. Finally, AddToList formats the message and adds it to the list box in the main window of MIDIVIEW.

The StartMidiInput function in MIDIVIEW.CPP does all the housekeeping required to initiate the reception of MIDI messages through MIDIMAN.DLL. It begins by calling midiInGetDevs to make sure there's at least one MIDI device available. It then allocates an EVENT buffer by calling AllocateCircularBuffer. The large for loop in StartMidiInput sets up a callback instance for each available MIDI device and then opens it by calling midiInOpen. Finally, the function starts MIDI input on each channel by calling midiInStart.

When the whole dog and pony show is over, MIDIVIEW will stop MIDI input by calling—perhaps predictably—StopMidiInput. It reverses what StartMidiInput began, closing down each of the opened MIDI channels, freeing the callbacks, and finally freeing the circular buffer.

The message formatting functions of MIDIVIEW, IsInterestingMessage and AddToList, can be found toward the bottom of MIDIVIEW.CPP. Both functions split a MIDI message stored in an EVENT object into its component parts. The IsInterestingMessage function ascertains whether the check box corresponding to a message type is checked, and whether the message channel corresponds to the channel number set in the main window of MIDIVIEW. The AddToList function formats the message into something more easily read by humans than by a MIDI interface and adds it to the MIDIVIEW list box. This is a somewhat unusual application of a list box, as it's never actually allowed to become full enough to scroll. After enough lines have been added to fill it, adding subsequent lines will involve removing the oldest line first.

The NoteToName function will return the real name of a note, based on its MIDI note number.

Once again, the really complex, technical bits of MIDIVIEW aren't in MIDIVIEW.CPP. They're in the MIDIMAN dynamic link library. Being the nastiest part of the MIDI software interface under discussion in this chapter, it will turn up last.

Writing MIDI files

In what must qualify as a singularly unusual degree of flexibility, Microsoft didn't define its own standard for MIDI files when it

created the multimedia extensions. Rather, it adopted the standard MIDI file structure being used in other environments. Admittedly, the voice assignments used by other MIDI applications are rarely correct for Windows applications playing through the MIDI Mapper, but the note data and other MIDI messages will be interpreted as they should be.

The MIDI file standard is a bit peculiar and has been created rather cunningly to store as much information in as little space as possible. This is very much in keeping with the nature of MIDI itself, which does all sorts of bitwise tricks to make MIDI messages small and easily interpretable in hardware.

You'll probably find MIDI files to be a bit unfathomable. The MIDI file player in *Multimedia Programming for Windows* includes a function to unpack them and format their contents in somewhat understandable English, should you be of a mind to know how they're read. This section deals with creating them.

The MIDI file functions discussed in this section have been adapted from MIDILIB, by Michael Czeiszperger as were the ones in *Multimedia Programming for Windows*. This is a wonderful bit of code, as it provides a complete MIDI file interface that has been thoroughly debugged and well thought out. The original MIDILIB source files, found on the Internet, are included on the companion CD-ROM for this book. They're named PART01 and PART02. While these are simple ASCII text files, they'll typically require some massaging if you want to use anything in them.

A complete discussion of the structure of MIDI files can be found in *Multimedia Programming for Windows*. While you can certainly immerse yourself in their lore if you wish, there's no need to do so just to use the functions provided by MIDILIB. One of the agreeable aspects of the MIDILIB interface is that it's pretty modular. It does all the hard work for you.

You'll also find the MIDI file specification extremely useful if you want to create applications that write MIDI files. It's available as *Standard MIDI Files 1.0* for $10 as of this writing from:

The International MIDI Association
5316 West 57th Street
Los Angeles, CA 90056

Figure 6-16 illustrates the main window for the WRITESNG
application. While it looks superficially like PLAYSONG, it doesn't
actually make any noise. Rather, if you click on its Save button, it will
prompt you for a file name and then write a MIDI file containing the
three Irish fiddle tunes from PLAYSONG. The source code for
WRITESNG is far more useful than its function.

Figure 6-16

The WRITESNG application.

The MIDI file created by WRITESNG will subsequently play correctly,
but it won't look particularly attractive if you open it in a MIDI scoring
package. The eighth notes, which were tied in Fig. 6-4, will appear as
discrete notes in the file created by WRITESNG. You can certainly
elaborate on this program, should you plan on creating software that
stores more sophisticated scores in MIDI files.

Also, as with PLAYSONG, the music handled by WRITESNG is
monophonic.

Figure 6-17 illustrates the WRITESNG.CPP source code file. Figure
6-18 illustrates WRITESNG.RC, its resource script. In addition to
these files, you'll need PRJ and DEF files for WRITESNG, and the
WAV and BMP files included in WRITESNG.RC. You'll find all these
files on the companion CD-ROM for this book.

Figure 6-17 *The WRITESNG.CPP source code.*

```
/*
        Write Song
        Copyright (c) 1993 Alchemy Mindworks Inc.
*/

#include <windows.h>
#include <stdio.h>
#include <stdlib.h>
#include <dir.h>
#include <ctype.h>
#include <alloc.h>
#include <string.h>
#include <io.h>
#include <bwcc.h>
#include <dos.h>
#include <errno.h>
#include <math.h>
#include <commdlg.h>
#include <mmsystem.h>
#include "midiman.h"
#include "playsong.h"
#include "midimap.h"

#define say(s)      MessageBox(NULL,s,"Yo...",MB_OK | MB_ICONSTOP);
#define saynumber(f,s)    {char b[128]; sprintf((LPSTR)b,(LPSTR)f,s); \
                      MessageBox(NULL,b,"Debug Message",MB_OK | MB_ICONSTOP); \
                      }

#define ItemOn(item)       { dlgH=GetDlgItem(hwnd,item); \
                      EnableWindow(dlgH,TRUE); \
                      EnableMenuItem(hmenu,item,MF_ENABLED);\
                      }

#define ItemOff(item)      { dlgH=GetDlgItem(hwnd,item); \
                      EnableWindow(dlgH,FALSE); \
                      EnableMenuItem(hmenu,item,MF_GRAYED);\
                      }

#define STRINGSIZE      128             /* how big is a string? */

#define MAIN_SAVE       101

#define MAIN_ABOUT      103
#define MAIN_EXIT       199

#define MAIN_PATCH1     201
#define MAIN_PATCH2     202
#define MAIN_PATCH3     203

#define VOICE1          110             //Fiddle
#define VOICE2          77              //Shakuhachi
#define VOICE3          46              //Harp
```

```
#define CHANNEL            1
#define DoMessage(hwnd,string)                 BWCCMessageBox(hwnd,string,"Message",\
                                               MB_OK | MB_ICONINFORMATION)
#ifndef max
#define max(a,b)           (((a)>(b))?(a):(b))
#endif
#ifndef min
#define min(a,b)           (((a)<(b))?(a):(b))
#endif

#define MThd 0x4d546864L
#define MTrk 0x4d54726bL
#define lowerbyte(x) ((unsigned char)(x & 0xff))
#define upperbyte(x) ((unsigned char)((x & 0xff00)>>8))

#define note_off           0x80
#define note_on            0x90
#define poly_aftertouch    0xa0
#define control_change     0xb0
#define program_chng       0xc0
#define channel_aftertouch 0xd0
#define pitch_wheel        0xe0
#define system_exclusive   0xf0
#define delay_packet       (1111)

#define damper_pedal       0x40
#define portamento         0x41
#define sostenuto          0x42
#define soft_pedal         0x43
#define general_4          0x44
#define hold_2             0x45
#define general_5          0x50
#define general_6          0x51
#define general_7          0x52
#define general_8          0x53
#define tremolo_depth      0x5c
#define chorus_depth       0x5d
#define detune             0x5e
#define phaser_depth       0x5f

#define data_inc           0x60
#define data_dec           0x61

#define non_reg_lsb        0x62
#define non_reg_msb        0x63
#define reg_lsb            0x64
#define reg_msb            0x65

#define meta_event         0xFF
#define sequence_number    0x00
#define text_event         0x01
#define copyright_notice   0x02
```

Figure 6-17 *Continued.*

```
#define sequence_name           0x03
#define instrument_name         0x04
#define lyric                   0x05
#define marker                  0x06
#define cue_point               0x07
#define channel_prefix          0x20
#define end_of_track            0x2f
#define set_tempo               0x51
#define smpte_offset            0x54
#define time_signature          0x58
#define key_signature           0x59
#define sequencer_specific      0x74

/* prototypes */
DWORD FAR PASCAL SelectProc(HWND hwnd,WORD message,WORD wParam,LONG lParam);
DWORD FAR PASCAL AboutDlgProc(HWND hwnd,WORD message,WORD wParam,LONG lParam);
void CentreWindow(HWND hwnd);

void mf_write_header_chunk(int format,int ntracks,int division);
void mf_write_tempo(unsigned long tempo);
void write32bit(unsigned long data);
void write16bit(int data);
void WriteVarLen(unsigned long value);
void mf_write_timesig(unsigned int numerator,unsigned int denominator,
                      unsigned int clocks,unsigned int quotes);
void mf_write_keysig(int flats,int minor);

int mf_write_track_chunk(int which_track,FILE *fp);
int mfwrite(int format,int ntracks,int division,FILE *fp);
int mf_write_midi_event(unsigned long delta_time, unsigned int type,
    unsigned int chan, unsigned char *data, unsigned long size);
int mf_write_meta_event(unsigned long delta_time, unsigned char type,
    unsigned char *data, unsigned long size);
int eputc(unsigned char c);
int mywritetrack(int track);
int GetSaveFileName(HWND hwnd,LPSTR path);
int WriteSong(char *path);
int SetPatch(LPNOTE lpnote,unsigned int number,unsigned int voice);

int myputc(int c);

unsigned long mf_sec2ticks(float secs,int division,unsigned int tempo);

float mf_ticks2sec(unsigned long ticks,int division,unsigned int tempo);

/* globals */
char szAppName[] = "WriteSong";
HANDLE hInst;
FILE *fp;

int (*Mf_putc)(int c) = NULL;
int (*Mf_writetrack)(int which_track) = NULL;
```

```
int (*Mf_writetempotrack)() = NULL;
static long Mf_numbyteswritten = 0L;

#pragma warn -par
int PASCAL WinMain(HANDLE hInstance,HANDLE hPrevInstance,
            LPSTR lpszCmdParam,int nCmdShow)
{
      FARPROC dlgProc;
      int r=0;

      BWCCGetVersion();

      hInst=hInstance;

      dlgProc=MakeProcInstance((FARPROC)SelectProc,hInst);
      r=DialogBox(hInst,"MainScreen",NULL,dlgProc);

      FreeProcInstance(dlgProc);

      return(r);
}

DWORD FAR PASCAL SelectProc(HWND hwnd,WORD message,WORD wParam,LONG lParam)
{
      PAINTSTRUCT ps;
      HICON hIcon;
      FARPROC lpfnDlgProc;
      POINT point;
      char b[STRINGSIZE+1];
      long l;
      int i;

      switch(message) {
            case WM_CTLCOLOR:
                  if(HIWORD(lParam)==CTLCOLOR_STATIC ||
                    HIWORD(lParam)==CTLCOLOR_DLG) {
                        SetBkColor(wParam,RGB(192,192,192));
                        SetTextColor(wParam,RGB(0,0,0));

                        ClientToScreen(hwnd,&point);
                        UnrealizeObject(GetStockObject(LTGRAY_BRUSH));
                        SetBrushOrg(wParam,point.x,point.y);

                        return((DWORD)GetStockObject(LTGRAY_BRUSH));

                  }
                  if(HIWORD(lParam)==CTLCOLOR_BTN) {
                        SetBkColor(wParam,RGB(192,192,192));
                        SetTextColor(wParam,RGB(0,0,0));

                        ClientToScreen(hwnd,&point);
                        UnrealizeObject(GetStockObject(BLACK_BRUSH));
                        SetBrushOrg(wParam,point.x,point.y);
```

Figure 6-17 *Continued.*

```
                            return((DWORD)GetStockObject(BLACK_BRUSH));
                }
            break;
        case WM_SYSCOMMAND:
                switch(wParam & 0xfff0) {
                        case SC_CLOSE:
                                SendMessage(hwnd,WM_COMMAND,MAIN_EXIT,0L);
                                break;
                }
            break;
        case WM_INITDIALOG:
                hIcon=LoadIcon(hInst,szAppName);
                SetClassWord(hwnd,GCW_HICON,(WORD)hIcon);

                for(i=0;i<PATCHCOUNT;++i) {
                    SendDlgItemMessage(hwnd,MAIN_PATCH1,
                        CB_INSERTSTRING,-1,(LONG)(LPSTR)midiMapPatch[i]);
                    SendDlgItemMessage(hwnd,MAIN_PATCH2,
                        CB_INSERTSTRING,-1,(LONG)(LPSTR)midiMapPatch[i]);
                    SendDlgItemMessage(hwnd,MAIN_PATCH3,
                        CB_INSERTSTRING,-1,(LONG)(LPSTR)midiMapPatch[i]);
                }

                SendDlgItemMessage(hwnd,MAIN_PATCH1,CB_SETCURSEL,VOICE1,0L);
                SendDlgItemMessage(hwnd,MAIN_PATCH2,CB_SETCURSEL,VOICE2,0L);
                SendDlgItemMessage(hwnd,MAIN_PATCH3,CB_SETCURSEL,VOICE3,0L);

                CentreWindow(hwnd);
                break;
        case WM_PAINT:
                BeginPaint(hwnd,&ps);
                EndPaint(hwnd,&ps);
                break;
        case WM_COMMAND:
                switch(wParam) {
                        case MAIN_SAVE:
                                l=SendDlgItemMessage(hwnd,MAIN_PATCH1,
                                        CB_GETCURSEL,0,0L);
                                if(l==CB_ERR) l=0L;

                                SetPatch(&note[0],0,(unsigned int)l);

                                l=SendDlgItemMessage(hwnd,MAIN_PATCH2,
                                        CB_GETCURSEL,0,0L);
                                if(l==CB_ERR) l=0L;

                                SetPatch(&note[0],1,(unsigned int)l);

                                l=SendDlgItemMessage(hwnd,MAIN_PATCH3,
                                        CB_GETCURSEL,0,0L);
                                if(l==CB_ERR) l=0L;
```

```
                                    SetPatch(&note[0],2,(unsigned int)1);

                                    if(GetSaveFileName(hwnd,b)){
                                            if(WriteSong(b))
                                                    DoMessage(hwnd,"Done");
                                            else
                                                    DoMessage(hwnd,
                                                            "Error writing file");
                                    }
                                    break;
                            case MAIN_ABOUT:
                                    if((lpfnDlgProc=MakeProcInstance((FARPROC)
                                        AboutDlgProc,hInst)) != NULL) {
                                            DialogBox(hInst,"AboutBox",
                                                    hwnd,lpfnDlgProc);
                                            FreeProcInstance(lpfnDlgProc);
                                    }
                                    break;
                            case MAIN_EXIT:
                                    PostQuitMessage(0);
                                    break;
                    }
                    break;

        }

        return(FALSE);
}

DWORD FAR PASCAL AboutDlgProc(HWND hwnd,WORD message,WORD wParam,LONG lParam)
{
        static HANDLE sound;
        static LPSTR psound;
        HANDLE handle;
        POINT point;

        switch(message) {
                case WM_INITDIALOG:
                        if((handle=FindResource(hInst,
                            "AboutWave",RT_RCDATA)) != NULL) {
                                if((sound=LoadResource(hInst,handle)) != NULL) {
                                        if((psound=LockResource(sound)) != NULL)
                                            sndPlaySound(psound,SND_ASYNC |
                                                SND_MEMORY | SND_NOSTOP);
                                }
                        }
                        CentreWindow(hwnd);
                        return(FALSE);
                case WM_CTLCOLOR:
                        if(HIWORD(lParam)==CTLCOLOR_STATIC ||
                            HIWORD(lParam)==CTLCOLOR_DLG) {
                                SetBkColor(wParam,RGB(192,192,192));
                                SetTextColor(wParam,RGB(0,0,0));
```

Figure 6-17 *Continued.*

```
                                    ClientToScreen(hwnd,&point);
                                    UnrealizeObject(GetStockObject(LTGRAY_BRUSH));
                                    SetBrushOrg(wParam,point.x,point.y);

                                    return((DWORD)GetStockObject(LTGRAY_BRUSH));

                            }
                            if(HIWORD(lParam)==CTLCOLOR_BTN) {
                                    SetBkColor(wParam,RGB(192,192,192));
                                    SetTextColor(wParam,RGB(0,0,0));

                                    ClientToScreen(hwnd,&point);
                                    UnrealizeObject(GetStockObject(BLACK_BRUSH));
                                    SetBrushOrg(wParam,point.x,point.y);

                                    return((DWORD)GetStockObject(BLACK_BRUSH));
                            }
                            break;
                    case WM_COMMAND:
                            switch(wParam) {
                                    case IDOK:
                                            sndPlaySound(NULL,SND_SYNC);
                                            if(psound != NULL) UnlockResource(sound);
                                            if(sound != NULL) FreeResource(sound);
                                            EndDialog(hwnd,wParam);
                                            return(FALSE);

                            }
                            break;
            }

            return(FALSE);
    }

    void CentreWindow(HWND hwnd)
    {
            RECT rect;
            unsigned int x,y;

            GetWindowRect(hwnd,&rect);
            x=(GetSystemMetrics(SM_CXSCREEN)-(rect.right-rect.left))/2;
            y=(GetSystemMetrics(SM_CYSCREEN)-(rect.bottom-rect.top))/2;
            SetWindowPos(hwnd,NULL,x,y,rect.right-rect.left,
                rect.bottom-rect.top,SWP_NOSIZE);
    }

    int GetSaveFileName(HWND hwnd,LPSTR path)
    {
            OPENFILENAME ofn;
            char szDirName[256],szFileTitle[256],szFilter[256];

            getcwd(szDirName,sizeof(szDirName)-1);
```

```
        lstrcpy(szFilter,"*.MID");

        memset((char *)&ofn,0,sizeof(OPENFILENAME));

        lstrcpy(path,"*.MID");
        szFileTitle[0]=0;

        ofn.lStructSize=sizeof(OPENFILENAME);
        ofn.hwndOwner=hwnd;
        ofn.lpstrFilter="MIDI files (*.MID)\000*.MID\000";
        ofn.lpstrFile=path;
        ofn.nFilterIndex=2;
        ofn.nMaxFile=STRINGSIZE;
        ofn.lpstrFileTitle=szFileTitle;
        ofn.nMaxFileTitle=sizeof(szFileTitle);
        ofn.lpstrInitialDir=szDirName;
        ofn.Flags=OFN_OVERWRITEPROMPT | OFN_HIDEREADONLY;
        ofn.lpstrTitle="Save File";

        if(!GetSaveFileName(&ofn)) {
                path[0]=0;
                return(0);
        } else return(1);
}

int WriteSong(char *path)
{
        int r;

        Mf_putc=myputc;
        Mf_writetrack=mywritetrack;

        if((fp=fopen(path,"wb"))==NULL) return(FALSE);

        r=mfwrite(0,1,INTERVAL,fp);

        fclose(fp);
        return(r);
}

int SetPatch(LPNOTE lpnote,unsigned int number,unsigned int voice)
{
        int i,count;

        for(i=count=0;lpnote[i].note != ENDSONG;++i) {
                if(lpnote[i].note==VOICE) {
                        if(count==number) {
                                lpnote[i].duration=voice;
                                return(TRUE);
                        }
                        ++count;
                }
        }
```

Figure 6-17 *Continued.*

```
            return(FALSE);
    }

    /* This is from MIDILIB, by M. Czeiszperger */

    /* Functions to implement in order to write a MIDI file */


    /*
     * mfwrite() - The only function you'll need to call to write out
     *             a midi file.
     *
     * format      0 - Single multi-channel track
     *             1 - Multiple simultaneous tracks
     *             2 - One or more sequentially independent
     *                 single track patterns
     * ntracks     The number of tracks in the file.
     * division    This is kind of tricky, it can represent two
     *             things, depending on whether it is positive or negative
     *             (bit 15 set or not).  If  bit  15  of division  is zero,
     *             bits 14 through 0 represent the number of delta-time
     *             "ticks" which make up a quarter note.  If bit  15 of
     *             division  is  a one, delta-times in a file correspond to
     *             subdivisions of a second similiar to  SMPTE  and  MIDI
     *             time code.  In  this format bits 14 through 8 contain
     *             one of four values - 24, -25, -29, or -30,
     *             corresponding  to  the  four standard  SMPTE and MIDI
     *             time code frame per second formats, where  -29
     *             represents  30  drop  frame.  The  second  byte
     *             consisting  of  bits 7 through 0 corresponds to the
     *             resolution within a frame.  Refer to the Standard MIDI
     *             Files 1.0 spec for more details.
     * fp          This should be the open file pointer to the file you
     *             want to write.  It will have be a global in order
     *             to work with Mf_putc.
     */
    int mfwrite(int format,int ntracks,int division,FILE *fp)
    {
            int i;

            if(Mf_putc==NULL || Mf_writetrack == NULL) return(FALSE);

            mf_write_header_chunk(format,ntracks,division);

            if(format == 1 && (Mf_writetempotrack))
                (*Mf_writetempotrack)();

            for(i=0;i<ntracks;i++) {
                    if(!mf_write_track_chunk(i,fp)) return(FALSE);
            }
```

```
        return(TRUE);
}

int mf_write_track_chunk(int which_track,FILE *fp)
{
        unsigned long trkhdr,trklength;
        long offset, place_marker;

        trkhdr = MTrk;
        trklength = 0;

        offset = ftell(fp);

        write32bit(trkhdr);
        write32bit(trklength);

        Mf_numbyteswritten = 0L;

        if( Mf_writetrack )
            (*Mf_writetrack)(which_track);

        eputc(0);
        eputc(meta_event);
        eputc(end_of_track);

        eputc(0);

        place_marker = ftell(fp);

        if(fseek(fp,offset,0) < 0) return(FALSE);

        trklength = Mf_numbyteswritten;

        write32bit(trkhdr);
        write32bit(trklength);

        fseek(fp,place_marker,0);
        return(TRUE);
}


void mf_write_header_chunk(int format,int ntracks,int division)
{
        unsigned long ident,length;

            ident = MThd;
            length = 6;

            write32bit(ident);
            write32bit(length);
            write16bit(format);
            write16bit(ntracks);
            write16bit(division);
}
```

Figure 6-17 *Continued.*

```
int mf_write_midi_event(unsigned long delta_time, unsigned int type,
    unsigned int chan, unsigned char *data, unsigned long size)
{
        int i;
        unsigned char c;

        WriteVarLen(delta_time);

        c = type | chan;

        eputc(c);

        for(i = 0; i < size; i++) eputc(data[i]);

        return((int)size);
}

int mf_write_meta_event(unsigned long delta_time, unsigned char type,
    unsigned char *data, unsigned long size)
{
        int i;

        WriteVarLen(delta_time);

        eputc(meta_event);

        eputc(type);

        WriteVarLen(size);

        for(i=0;i<size;i++) {
                if(eputc(data[i]) != data[i])
                        return(-1);
        }
        return((int)size);
}

void mf_write_tempo(unsigned long tempo)
{
        eputc(0);
        eputc(meta_event);
        eputc(set_tempo);

        eputc(3);
        eputc((unsigned)(0xff & (tempo >> 16)));
        eputc((unsigned)(0xff & (tempo >> 8)));
        eputc((unsigned)(0xff & tempo));
}

void mf_write_timesig(unsigned int numerator,unsigned int denominator,
                      unsigned int clocks,unsigned int quotes)
```

```
{
        eputc(0);
        eputc(meta_event);
        eputc(time_signature);

        eputc(4);
        eputc(numerator);
        eputc(denominator);
        eputc(clocks);
        eputc(quotes);
}

void mf_write_keysig(int flats,int minor)
{
        eputc(0);
        eputc(meta_event);
        eputc(key_signature);

        eputc(2);
        eputc(flats);
        eputc(minor);
}


unsigned long mf_sec2ticks(float secs,int division,unsigned int tempo)
{
        return (long)(((secs * 1000.0) / 4.0 * division) / tempo);
}

void WriteVarLen(unsigned long value)
{
        unsigned long buffer;

          buffer = value & 0x7f;
          while((value >>= 7) > 0) {
                buffer <<= 8;
                buffer |= 0x80;
                buffer += (value & 0x7f);
          }
          while(1){
                eputc((unsigned)(buffer & 0xff));

                if(buffer & 0x80) buffer >>= 8;
                else return;
          }
}

float mf_ticks2sec(unsigned long ticks,int division,unsigned int tempo)
{
        float smpte_format, smpte_resolution;

            if(division > 0)
                return((float) (((float)(ticks)*(float)(tempo))/
```

Figure **6-17** *Continued.*

```
                                ((float)(division) * 1000000.0)));
                else {
                    smpte_format = upperbyte(division);
                    smpte_resolution = lowerbyte(division);
                    return(float)((float) ticks/
                        (smpte_format * smpte_resolution * 1000000.0));
        }
}

void write32bit(unsigned long data)
{
        eputc((unsigned)((data >> 24) & 0xff));
        eputc((unsigned)((data >> 16) & 0xff));
        eputc((unsigned)((data >> 8 ) & 0xff));
        eputc((unsigned)(data & 0xff));
}

void write16bit(int data)
{
        eputc((unsigned)((data & 0xff00) >> 8));
        eputc((unsigned)(data & 0xff));
}

int eputc(unsigned char c)
{
        int return_val;

        if((Mf_putc) == NULL) return(-1);

        return_val=(Mf_putc)(c);

        if(return_val == EOF ) return(-1);

        Mf_numbyteswritten++;
        return(return_val);
}

int mywritetrack(int track)
{
        static char textmessage[]="Some traditional Irish music";
        char data[2];
        int i,duration=0;

        mf_write_tempo(544000L);

        mf_write_timesig(6,3,36,8);

        mf_write_keysig(KEY_G,KEY_MAJOR);

        if(mf_write_meta_event(0,text_event,textmessage,sizeof(textmessage)) < 0)
            return(-1);
```

```
        for(i=0;note[i].note != ENDSONG;++i) {
                if(note[i].note==VOICE) {
                        data[0] = note[i].duration; /* note number */
                        if(!mf_write_midi_event(0,program_chng,CHANNEL,data,1))
                                return(-1);
                }
                else if(note[i].note==REST) {
                        data[0] = 0; /* note number */
                        data[1] = 0; /* velocity */

                        if(!mf_write_midi_event(duration,note_off,CHANNEL,data,2))
                                return(-1);
                        duration=note[i].duration;
                }
                else {
                        data[0] = note[i].note; /* note number */
                        data[1] = VELOCITY; /* velocity */
                        if(!mf_write_midi_event(duration,note_on,CHANNEL,data,2))
                                return(-1);
                        data[1] = 0; /* velocity */
                        if(!mf_write_midi_event(duration,note_off,CHANNEL,data,2))
                                return(-1);
                        duration=note[i].duration;
                }


        }
        return(1);
}

int myputc(int c)
{
        return(fputc(c,fp));
}
```

The WRITESNG.RC resource script.

Figure 6-18

```
MainScreen DIALOG 75, 25, 108, 136
STYLE WS_POPUP | WS_CAPTION | WS_SYSMENU | WS_MINIMIZEBOX
CAPTION "Write Song"
MENU MainMenu
BEGIN
        PUSHBUTTON "Quit", 199, 56, 116, 28, 12, WS_CHILD | WS_VISIBLE | WS_TABSTOP
        PUSHBUTTON "Save", 101, 24, 116, 28, 12, WS_CHILD | WS_VISIBLE | WS_TABSTOP
        CONTROL "Voices", 104, "BorShade", 32769 | WS_CHILD | WS_VISIBLE, 8, 8, 92, 100
        CONTROL "", 201, "COMBOBOX", CBS_DROPDOWNLIST | WS_CHILD | WS_VISIBLE |
            WS_VSCROLL | WS_TABSTOP, 12, 32, 84, 68
        LTEXT "Song 1: Trip to Sligo", -1, 12, 24, 84, 8, WS_CHILD | WS_VISIBLE | WS_GROUP
        CONTROL "", 202, "COMBOBOX", CBS_DROPDOWNLIST | WS_CHILD | WS_VISIBLE |
            WS_VSCROLL | WS_TABSTOP, 12, 60, 84, 68
        LTEXT "Song 2: Burnt Old Man", -1, 12, 52, 84, 8, WS_CHILD | WS_VISIBLE | WS_GROUP
        CONTROL "", 203, "COMBOBOX", CBS_DROPDOWNLIST | WS_CHILD | WS_VISIBLE |
```

Figure 6-18 *Continued.*

```
                        WS_VSCROLL | WS_TABSTOP, 12, 88, 84, 68
                LTEXT "Song 3: The Kesh", -1, 12, 80, 84, 8, WS_CHILD | WS_VISIBLE | WS_GROUP
        END

        MainMenu MENU
        BEGIN
                POPUP "&File"
                BEGIN
                        MENUITEM "&Save", 101
                        MENUITEM "&About", 103
                        MENUITEM SEPARATOR
                        MENUITEM "E&xit", 199
                END
        END

        AboutBox DIALOG 18, 18, 184, 180
        STYLE WS_POPUP | WS_CAPTION
        CAPTION "About..."
        BEGIN
                CONTROL "", 102, "BorShade", BSS_GROUP | WS_CHILD | WS_VISIBLE |
                        WS_TABSTOP, 8, 68, 168, 76
                CTEXT "Write Song 1.0\n\nCopyright (c) 1994 Alchemy Mindworks Inc.\n\n
                        This program is part of the book Advanced Multimedia Programming
                        for Windows by Steven William Rimmer, published by Windcrest/McGraw
                        Hill.", -1, 12, 72, 160, 68, WS_CHILD | WS_VISIBLE | WS_GROUP
                CONTROL "Button", IDOK, "BorBtn", BS_DEFPUSHBUTTON | WS_CHILD | WS_VISIBLE |
                        WS_TABSTOP, 74, 152, 32, 20
                CONTROL "Button", 801, "BorBtn", BS_PUSHBUTTON | WS_CHILD | WS_VISIBLE |
                        WS_TABSTOP, 36, 8, 32, 20
        END

        1801 BITMAP "smpw.bmp"

        AboutWave RCDATA "ABOUT.WAV"

        WriteSong ICON
        BEGIN
                '00 00 01 00 01 00 20 20 10 00 00 00 00 00 E8 02'
                '00 00 16 00 00 00 28 00 00 00 20 00 00 00 40 00'
                '00 00 01 00 04 00 00 00 00 00 80 02 00 00 00 00'
                '00 00 00 00 00 00 10 00 00 00 00 00 00 00 00 00'
                '00 00 00 00 BF 00 00 BF 00 00 00 BF BF 00 BF 00'
                '00 00 BF 00 BF 00 BF BF 00 00 C0 C0 C0 00 80 80'
                '80 00 00 00 FF 00 00 FF 00 00 00 FF FF 00 FF 00'
                '00 00 FF 00 FF 00 FF FF 00 00 FF FF FF 00 77 77'
                '77 77 77 77 77 77 77 77 77 77 77 77 77 77 7F 88'
                '88 88 88 88 88 88 88 88 88 88 88 88 88 87 7F F8'
                '88 88 88 88 88 88 88 88 88 88 88 88 88 87 7F F7'
                '77 99 99 77 77 77 77 77 77 77 77 77 78 87 7F F7'
                '79 97 79 97 77 77 77 77 77 77 77 77 78 87 7F F7'
                '79 99 79 97 77 77 77 77 77 77 77 77 78 87 7F F7'
```

```
'77 99 77 97 77 77 77 77 77 77 77 77 78 87 7F F7'
'77 77 79 77 77 77 77 77 77 77 77 77 78 87 7F F7'
'77 77 79 77 77 74 48 88 88 88 44 44 78 87 7F F7'
'77 99 97 77 77 4C C8 77 88 88 CC C4 78 87 7F F7'
'79 77 79 97 74 CC C8 77 88 88 CC C4 78 87 7F F7'
'97 79 97 97 74 CC C8 77 88 88 CC C4 78 87 7F F9'
'77 97 97 79 74 CC C8 77 88 88 CC C4 78 87 7F F9'
'77 99 77 79 74 CC C8 88 88 88 CC C4 78 87 7F F9'
'77 99 77 99 74 CC CC CC CC CC CC C4 78 87 7F F9'
'97 79 99 97 74 CC 44 44 44 44 44 C4 78 87 7F F7'
'97 77 99 77 74 CC 4B BB BB BB B4 C4 78 87 7F F7'
'99 79 77 77 74 CC 4B BB BB BB B4 C4 78 87 7F F7'
'79 99 77 77 74 CC 4B BB BB BB B4 C4 78 87 7F F7'
'77 99 77 77 74 CC 4B BB BB BB B4 C4 78 87 7F F7'
'77 79 97 77 74 CC 4B BB BB BB B4 C4 78 87 7F F7'
'77 97 97 77 74 CC 4B BB BB BB B4 C4 78 87 7F F7'
'77 97 99 77 74 44 44 44 44 44 44 44 78 87 7F F7'
'77 97 79 77 77 77 77 77 77 77 77 77 78 87 7F F7'
'77 79 79 77 77 77 77 77 77 77 77 77 78 87 7F F7'
'77 79 79 77 77 77 77 77 77 77 77 77 78 87 7F F7'
'77 79 97 77 77 77 77 77 77 77 77 77 78 87 7F F7'
'77 77 97 77 77 77 77 77 77 77 77 77 78 87 7F FF'
'FF FF FF FF FF FF FF FF FF FF FF FF F8 87 7F FF'
'FF FF FF FF FF FF FF FF FF FF FF FF FF 87 77 77'
'77 77 77 77 77 77 77 77 77 77 77 77 77 77 00 00'
'00 00 00 00 00 00 00 00 00 00 00 00 00 00 00 00'
'00 00 00 00 00 00 00 00 00 00 00 00 00 00 00 00'
'00 00 00 00 00 00 00 00 00 00 00 00 00 00 00 00'
'00 00 00 00 00 00 00 00 00 00 00 00 00 00 00 00'
'00 00 00 00 00 00 00 00 00 00 00 00 00 00 00 00'
'00 00 00 00 00 00 00 00 00 00 00 00 00 00 00 00'
'00 00 00 00 00 00 00 00 00 00 00 00 00 00 00 00'
'00 00 00 00 00 00 00 00 00 00 00 00 00 00 00'
END
```

Being a one-trick pony of truly galactic proportions, absolutely
everything of interest in WRITESNG.CPP is initiated from the
MAIN_SAVE case of the WM_COMMAND handler of SelectProc. As
with the earlier PLAYSONG application, SelectProc patches a list of
NOTE objects containing the music to be written to disk based on the
settings of its three combo boxes. It then calls GetSaveFileName to
prompt for a file name to write to. The GetSaveFileName function
makes a call to the Windows common dialog library for a Save To
dialog. If GetSaveFileName returns a true value, indicating that it has
a valid file name, SelectProc calls the WriteSong function, which in
turn sets up a call to the MIDILIB code at the bottom of the
WRITESNG.CPP file.

The interface to the MIDI file-writing functions of MIDILIB is mfwrite. It expects four arguments, as follows:

```
mfwrite(format,ntracks,division,fp)
```

The format argument to mfwrite is a constant to specify which of several possible types of MIDI files should be created. This value should be zero for a MIDI file containing one multiple-channel score, one for a MIDI file containing multiple simultaneous tracks, or two for multiple independent single tracks. Most applications, including this one, call for this value to be zero.

The ntracks argument represents the number of tracks in the MIDI file to be created—one, in this case.

The division argument is, as the author of MIDILIB notes, kind of tricky. You'll find an explanation of it in the WRITESNG source code and in the MIDI file specification. For the sake of this application, the division value represents the number of time intervals, or *ticks*, required to play one quarter note.

Finally, the fp argument to mfwrite is a standard C language streamed file pointer, as returned by fopen.

MIDILIB also expects you to supply a function to actually write tracks. It doesn't know how the information defining the MIDI note data to be written is stored. It also has only a vague idea about how you plan to manage delta times. You can see an example of this function as mywritetrack at the end of WRITESNG.CPP.

Most of the work done by a custom track writer is handled by calls back into the MIDILIB code, and as such it needn't be quite as fearsome as you might think. The mywritetrack function actually has an easier time than most, as all it needs to do is parse the information, out of the list of NOTE objects, that defines the fiddle tunes to be written and then call mf_write_midi_event.

The mf_write_midi_event call from MIDILIB expects the following arguments:

```
mf_write_midi_event(delta_time,type,channel,data,size)
```

The delta_time argument to mf_write_midi_event represents the duration of the note to be played if the event to be written is in fact a NOTE ON message. The type argument is the MIDI message to be written. The channel argument is the MIDI channel the message applies to, ranging from 0 through 15. The data argument is a pointer to the data pertaining to this message. Finally, the size argument specifies the number of bytes of valid data that exist at data.

The only really tricky bit of mywritetrack is keeping track of the note durations, or delta time values. In fact, this is usually the nettlesome aspect of creating MIDI files from note information—it's quite a bit more so in the MIDI recorder application we'll look at in the next section of this chapter. In this case, the note duration values can be derived from the NOTE objects involved. In dealing with real-time MIDI information, the delta time values must be derived by comparing the time stamps of NOTE ON with their corresponding NOTE OFF messages.

Prior to writing its note data, mywritetrack makes several calls back into MIDILIB to write some preliminary track information. The first is mf_write_tempo, which sets the playback tempo. Its argument is the number of microseconds to hold a quarter note. In this case, a quarter note would hold for about .54 seconds.

The mf_write_timesig function writes the current time signature. Its first argument is the numerator of the time signature. Its second argument is the number that two must be raised to the power of to form the numerator. The third argument is the number of MIDI clocks in one metronome tick. The last argument is the number of notated thirty-second notes in 24 MIDI clock ticks, or one quarter note. This is usually eight.

The mf_write_keysig function writes the key signature. The keys are defined in MIDIMAN.H. The first argument to mf_write_keysig is actually the number of sharps or flats in the key signature in question—positive numbers represent sharps and negative numbers represent flats. The key constants in MIDIMAN.H will take care of this for you. The second argument should be zero for a major key and one for a minor key. Again, there are constants in MIDIMAN.H to use for this value.

The mf_write_timesig and mf_write_keysig functions are not part of MIDILIB, but were derived from the MIDILIB source code.

Finally, the mf_write_meta_event call in mywritetrack is used to write a text event to the file under construction. In this case it will store a bit of text to describe the music about to be played. Meta events are discussed in detail in the MIDI file specification—this is a trivial example of their use. In creating MIDI files that will simply store music, you won't have to get into meta event records in any greater depth.

One possible comfort in this discussion of MIDI files is that unless you specifically intend to write a MIDI scoring program or other fairly specialized MIDI application, you'll probably not have to deal with them. While MIDI can be very useful for playing short canned tunes using a structure along the lines of the one in PLAYSONG, storing MIDI music in files is the province of fairly specialized music software.

MIDI scoring programs exist in uncounted legions, but good ones are somewhat thinner on the ground. Most MIDI music packages seem to start and end with scoring jingles for beer commercials. If you have read this far and have not come up with any really catchy ideas for software that works with MIDI, consider that civilization as we know it probably wouldn't object to some serious music software.

⇨ Recording MIDI files

Having looked at how to deal with incoming MIDI data in MIDIVIEW and how to write MIDI files in WRITESNG, we should find that creating an application to record MIDI data and write it to MIDI files is fairly elementary. In fact, the task isn't quite as simple as it probably should be. The inherent complexity has to do with handling note delta times, as touched on in the previous section.

Figure 6-19 illustrates the principal window of the MIDIREC application. It's similar in structure to the WAVEREC program back in Chapter 2. In the interest of keeping the sample source code in this section down to a manageable level, this is a very basic MIDI recorder. It will only correctly record monophonic MIDI music—that is, no more than one note at a time. You might want to expand on its capabilities if you require more elaborate MIDI recording. Nevertheless, it does illustrate the basic structure of software to record real-time MIDI.

Figure 6-19

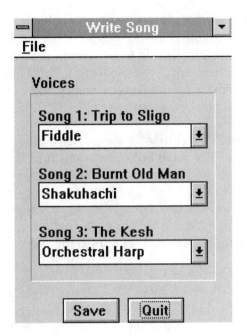

The MIDIREC application.

As mentioned earlier in this chapter, the awkward aspect of incoming MIDI messages is that there's no way to predict when they'll appear, or how many might appear in a short time. This problem is further compounded in an application to record real-time MIDI messages, because there's no easy way to know how many of them might comprise the entirety of the piece to be recorded.

In its simplest sense, a MIDI recorder would be the circular queue logic from MIDIVIEW, with the EVENT handler modified to fetch the incoming messages and store them in a fixed buffer, rather than writing them to a list box. It's impossible to know how large the buffer might have to be. In the WAVEREC recorder, this was dealt with by assigning a maximum value for the input buffer and stopping the recorder if the buffer limit was reached. This is arguably less practical in a MIDI recorder—imagine getting to within 10 seconds of the conclusion of a flawless performance of an entire Mozart opera, arranged for five synthesizers and a MIDI saxophone, only to discover that your MIDI recording software has run out of virtual tape.

One solution to this apparent impasse would be to have the buffer periodically write its contents to a disk file. The drawback to this is that disk access can be very slow, especially if the file being written is on a floppy drive or must be handled by a relatively busy network. Unless the circular event buffer is enormous, there will be a pretty respectable chance of losing a few MIDI messages during a disk access.

There is a way around this problem, of course. It's a bit hairy in theory, but works well in practice. The fixed buffer into which EVENT objects are written after they're fetched from the circular queue by GetEvent can be reallocated when it gets full. The Windows GlobalRealloc function allows a previously allocated buffer to be expanded. In fact, what typically happens is that GlobalRealloc allocates a new buffer larger than the old one and copies the old contents to it.

The hairy aspect of this is that if GlobalRealloc is unable to expand a previously allocated buffer, it will trash the old contents and free the buffer they were stored in. This means you could still get to within 10 seconds of the conclusion of that flawless performance of an entire Mozart opera, arranged for five synthesizers and a MIDI saxophone, only to discover that your MIDI recording software had run out of virtual tape—if Windows runs out of available memory (although it's considerably less likely that you'll do so).

Another potential problem in this approach is that Windows might choose to spill something to disk during a buffer reallocation in order to satisfy a memory request from GlobalRealloc—this is another example of a slow disk access possibly allowing the circular event queue to become full and overflow, losing some MIDI messages.

In practice, neither eventuality is particularly likely. The EVENT messages in question aren't very big, and even a lot of them won't occupy all that much memory. If Windows does have to spill some memory contents to disk during a recording, it will be writing to a hard disk file, which should be fairly quick.

This is one of those situations in which the phrase "requires eight megabytes or more of memory" might well be prominently displayed on the packaging for your application.

Having successfully stored the EVENT objects representing a recorded performance, a MIDI recorder must write the messages contained there to a MIDI file. This, too, is somewhat more difficult than it might seem at first. Unlike the NOTE objects in WRITESNG, recorded note events don't have specific durations. A single note will be represented by a NOTE ON message with a time stamp, followed by a NOTE OFF message some time thereafter, with another time stamp. The two messages need not be sequential—the only thing relating the two is that they'll both have the same note number as data. To further confuse the issue, the NOTE OFF message could actually be a NOTE ON message with its velocity value set to zero—many MIDI keyboards send NOTE OFF messages in this form.

In the single-note MIDI recorder discussed in this section, a duration value for the note to be written can be ascertained by locating the NOTE OFF message for each NOTE ON and calculating the differences in their time stamps. If you wish to expand this MIDI recorder to allow for polyphony—that is, to handle multiple-note chords—you'll have to install a lookup table for pending notes, because a multiple-note chord will consist of multiple NOTE ON messages followed by multiple NOTE OFF messages, and the latter may not appear in the same sequence as the former.

Figure 6-20 illustrates the MIDIREC.CPP source code file. Figure 6-21 illustrates MIDIREC.RC, its resource script. In addition to these files, you'll need PRJ and DEF files for MIDIREC, and the WAV and BMP files included in MIDIREC.RC. You will find all these files on the companion CD-ROM for this book.

The MIDIREC.CPP source code.   Figure 6-20

```
/*

        MIDI Recorder
        Copyright (c) 1993 Alchemy Mindworks Inc.
*/

#include <windows.h>
#include <stdio.h>
#include <stdlib.h>
#include <dir.h>
#include <ctype.h>
#include <alloc.h>
#include <string.h>
```

Figure 6-20 *Continued.*

```
#include <io.h>
#include <bwcc.h>
#include <dos.h>
#include <errno.h>
#include <math.h>
#include <commdlg.h>
#include <mmsystem.h>
#include "midiman.h"

#define say(s)       MessageBox(NULL,s,"Yo...",MB_OK | MB_ICONSTOP);
#define saynumber(f,s)    {char b[128]; sprintf((LPSTR)b,(LPSTR)f,s); \
                       MessageBox(NULL,b,"Debug Message",MB_OK | MB_ICONSTOP); \
                       }

#define ItemName(item,string)   { dlgH=GetDlgItem(hwnd,item); \
                                SetWindowText(dlgH,(LPSTR)string); \
                                }

#define ItemOn(item)          { dlgH=GetDlgItem(hwnd,item); \
                              EnableWindow(dlgH,TRUE); \
                              EnableMenuItem(hmenu,item,MF_ENABLED);\
                              }

#define ItemOff(item)         { dlgH=GetDlgItem(hwnd,item); \
                              EnableWindow(dlgH,FALSE); \
                              EnableMenuItem(hmenu,item,MF_GRAYED);\
                              }

#define STRINGSIZE       128              /* how big is a string? */

#define THETIMER         1

#define MAIN_OPEN        101
#define MAIN_ABOUT       102

#define MAIN_RECORD      202
#define MAIN_STOP        204
#define MAIN_SAVE        205
#define MAIN_EXIT        199

#define MAIN_MESSAGE     401
#define MAIN_TIME        402

#define BLOCKSIZE        1024

#define MAX_DEVICES          8
#define INPUT_BUFFER_SIZE    200


#define UpdateRecordTime(hwnd,n)      { char bxx[STRINGSIZE+1];\
                                      wsprintf(bxx,"%u.%u sec.",n/10,n%10);\
```

```
                                        ItemName(MAIN_TIME,bxx);\
                                        }

#define SetUntitledFile(hwnd)            { getcwd(soundpath,STRINGSIZE-16);\
                                        lstrcat(soundpath,"\\UNTITLED.MIDI");\
                                        strlwr(soundpath);\
                                        ItemName(MAIN_MESSAGE,soundpath);\
                                        }

#define DoMessage(hwnd,string)           BWCCMessageBox(hwnd,string,"Message",\
                                        MB_OK | MB_ICONINFORMATION)

#define SetSoundPath(hwnd,bxx)           { lstrcpy(soundpath,bxx);\
                                        strlwr(soundpath);\
                                        ItemName(MAIN_MESSAGE,soundpath);\
                                        }

#ifndef max
#define max(a,b)          (((a)>(b))?(a):(b))
#endif
#ifndef min
#define min(a,b)          (((a)<(b))?(a):(b))
#endif

#define MThd 0x4d546864L
#define MTrk 0x4d54726bL
#define lowerbyte(x) ((unsigned char)(x & 0xff))
#define upperbyte(x) ((unsigned char)((x & 0xff00)>8))

#define note_off              0x80
#define note_on               0x90
#define poly_aftertouch       0xa0
#define control_change        0xb0
#define program_chng          0xc0
#define channel_aftertouch    0xd0
#define pitch_wheel           0xe0
#define system_exclusive      0xf0
#define delay_packet          (1111)

#define damper_pedal          0x40
#define portamento            0x41
#define sostenuto             0x42
#define soft_pedal            0x43
#define general_4             0x44
#define hold_2                0x45
#define general_5             0x50
#define general_6             0x51
#define general_7             0x52
#define general_8             0x53
#define tremolo_depth         0x5c
#define chorus_depth          0x5d
#define detune                0x5e
#define phaser_depth          0x5f
```

Figure 6-20 *Continued.*

```
#define data_inc                0x60
#define data_dec                0x61

#define non_reg_lsb             0x62
#define non_reg_msb             0x63
#define reg_lsb                 0x64
#define reg_msb                 0x65

#define meta_event              0xFF
#define sequence_number         0x00
#define text_event              0x01
#define copyright_notice        0x02
#define sequence_name           0x03
#define instrument_name         0x04
#define lyric                   0x05
#define marker                  0x06
#define cue_point               0x07
#define channel_prefix          0x20
#define end_of_track            0x2f
#define set_tempo               0x51
#define smpte_offset            0x54
#define time_signature          0x58
#define key_signature           0x59
#define sequencer_specific      0x74

/* prototypes */
LPCIRCULARBUFFER AllocCircularBuffer(DWORD dwSize);
LPCALLBACKINSTANCEDATA FAR PASCAL AllocCallbackInstanceData(void);

DWORD FAR PASCAL SelectProc(HWND hwnd,WORD message,WORD wParam,LONG lParam);
DWORD FAR PASCAL AboutDlgProc(HWND hwnd,WORD message,WORD wParam,LONG lParam);
DWORD FAR PASCAL MessageDlgProc(HWND hwnd,WORD message,WORD wParam,LONG lParam);

WORD FAR PASCAL GetEvent(LPCIRCULARBUFFER lpBuf,LPEVENT lpEvent);

int GetOpenFileName(HWND hwnd,LPSTR path);
int GetSaveFileName(HWND hwnd,LPSTR path);
int StartMidiInput(HWND hwnd);
int IsInterestingMessage(LPEVENT lpEvent);

int AllocateBuffer();
int FreeBuffer();
int RecordMIDI(HWND hwnd);
int FetchMidiEvent(LPEVENT lpevent,unsigned long number);
int AddMidiEvent(LPEVENT lpevent);

void FreeCircularBuffer(LPCIRCULARBUFFER lpBuf);
void FAR PASCAL FreeCallbackInstanceData(LPCALLBACKINSTANCEDATA lpBuf);
void SayLoadedSound(HWND hwnd,int flag);
void lmemset(LPSTR s,int n,unsigned int size);
void CentreWindow(HWND hwnd);
void StopMidiInput();
```

```c
void mf_write_header_chunk(int format,int ntracks,int division);
void mf_write_tempo(unsigned long tempo);
void write32bit(unsigned long data);
void write16bit(int data);
void WriteVarLen(unsigned long value);
void mf_write_timesig(unsigned int numerator,unsigned int denominator,
                      unsigned int clocks,unsigned int quotes);
void mf_write_keysig(int flats,int minor);

int mf_write_track_chunk(int which_track,FILE *fp);
int mfwrite(int format,int ntracks,int division,FILE *fp);
int mf_write_midi_event(unsigned long delta_time, unsigned int type,
    unsigned int chan, unsigned char *data, unsigned long size);
int mf_write_meta_event(unsigned long delta_time, unsigned char type,
    unsigned char *data, unsigned long size);
int eputc(unsigned char c);
int mywritetrack(int track);
int GetSaveFileName(HWND hwnd,LPSTR path);
int WriteSong(char *path);
int SetPatch(LPNOTE lpnote,unsigned int number,unsigned int voice);

int myputc(int c);

long GetDuration(long pos);

unsigned long mf_sec2ticks(float secs,int division,unsigned int tempo);

float mf_ticks2sec(unsigned long ticks,int division,unsigned int tempo);

/* globals */
char szAppName[] = "MIDIRecorder";
HANDLE hInst;

LPCIRCULARBUFFER lpInputBuffer;

MIDIINCAPS midiInCaps[MAX_DEVICES];
HMIDIIN hMidiIn[MAX_DEVICES];

LPCALLBACKINSTANCEDATA lpCallbackInstanceData[MAX_DEVICES];
HMIDIOUT hMapper=0;

char soundpath[256];

GLOBALHANDLE midibuffer=NULL;
unsigned long buffersize=0L;
unsigned long nextbufferitem=0L;

FILE *fp;
int active=FALSE;
int channel=0;

int (*Mf_putc)(int c) = NULL;
int (*Mf_writetrack)(int which_track) = NULL;
int (*Mf_writetempotrack)() = NULL;
```

Figure 6-20 *Continued.*

```
static long Mf_numbyteswritten = 0L;

#pragma warn -par
int PASCAL WinMain(HANDLE hInstance,HANDLE hPrevInstance,
                LPSTR lpszCmdParam,int nCmdShow)
{
        FARPROC dlgProc;
        int r=0;

        BWCCGetVersion();

        hInst=hInstance;

        dlgProc=MakeProcInstance((FARPROC)SelectProc,hInst);
        r=DialogBox(hInst,"MainScreen",NULL,dlgProc);

        FreeProcInstance(dlgProc);

        return(r);
}

DWORD FAR PASCAL SelectProc(HWND hwnd,WORD message,WORD wParam,LONG lParam)
{
        static unsigned int recordtime;
        EVENT event;
        PAINTSTRUCT ps;
        HICON hIcon;
        FARPROC lpfnDlgProc;
        POINT point;
        HMENU hmenu;
        HWND dlgH;
        char b[STRINGSIZE+1];

        switch(message) {
                case MM_MIDIINPUT:
                        while(GetEvent(lpInputBuffer,(LPEVENT)&event)) {

                                if(IsInterestingMessage(&event)) {
                                        if(!AddMidiEvent(&event)) {
                                                SendMessage(hwnd,MAIN_STOP,0,0L);
                                                DoMessage(hwnd,"Out of memory");
                                        }
                                }
                        }
                        break;

                case WM_CTLCOLOR:
                        if(HIWORD(lParam)==CTLCOLOR_STATIC ||
                            HIWORD(lParam)==CTLCOLOR_DLG) {
                                SetBkColor(wParam,RGB(192,192,192));
                                SetTextColor(wParam,RGB(0,0,0));
```

```
                            ClientToScreen(hwnd,&point);
                            UnrealizeObject(GetStockObject(LTGRAY_BRUSH));
                            SetBrushOrg(wParam,point.x,point.y);

                            return((DWORD)GetStockObject(LTGRAY_BRUSH));

                    }
                    if(HIWORD(lParam)==CTLCOLOR_BTN) {
                            SetBkColor(wParam,RGB(192,192,192));
                            SetTextColor(wParam,RGB(0,0,0));

                            ClientToScreen(hwnd,&point);
                            UnrealizeObject(GetStockObject(BLACK_BRUSH));
                            SetBrushOrg(wParam,point.x,point.y);

                            return((DWORD)GetStockObject(BLACK_BRUSH));
                    }
                    break;
            case WM_SYSCOMMAND:
                    switch(wParam & 0xfff0) {
                            case SC_CLOSE:
                                    SendMessage(hwnd,WM_COMMAND,MAIN_EXIT,0L);
                                    break;
                    }
                    break;
            case WM_TIMER:
                    ++recordtime;
                    UpdateRecordTime(hwnd,recordtime);
                    break;
            case WM_INITDIALOG:
                    hIcon=LoadIcon(hInst,szAppName);
                    SetClassWord(hwnd,GCW_HICON,(WORD)hIcon);
                    midiOutSetVolume(0,0xffffffffL);

                    recordtime=0;

                    hmenu=GetMenu(hwnd);

                    ItemOn(MAIN_OPEN);
                    ItemOn(MAIN_RECORD);
                    ItemOff(MAIN_STOP);
                    ItemOff(MAIN_SAVE);

                    SetUntitledFile(hwnd);
                    UpdateRecordTime(hwnd,recordtime);
                    CentreWindow(hwnd);
                    break;
            case WM_PAINT:
                    BeginPaint(hwnd,&ps);
                    EndPaint(hwnd,&ps);
                    break;
            case WM_COMMAND:
                    switch(wParam) {
```

Figure 6-20 *Continued.*

```
                                case MAIN_SAVE:
                                        if(GetSaveFileName(hwnd,b)) {
                                                if(WriteSong(b))
                                                        DoMessage(hwnd,"Done");
                                                else
                                                        DoMessage(hwnd,
                                                            "Error writing the file");
                                                SetSoundPath(hwnd,b);
                                        }
                                        break;
                                case MAIN_RECORD:
                                        FreeBuffer();

                                        ItemOff(MAIN_RECORD);
                                        if(RecordMIDI(hwnd)) {

                                                recordtime=0;
                                                SetTimer(hwnd,THETIMER,100,NULL);

                                                hmenu=GetMenu(hwnd);
                                                ItemOn(MAIN_STOP);
                                                ItemOff(MAIN_RECORD);
                                                ItemOff(MAIN_SAVE);
                                                ItemOff(MAIN_OPEN);

                                                SetUntitledFile(hwnd);
                                                UpdateRecordTime(hwnd,recordtime);
                                        }
                                        else {
                                                SayLoadedSound(hwnd,FALSE);
                                                soundpath[0]=0;
                                                DoMessage(hwnd,
                                                    "Can't initiate recording");
                                        }
                                        ItemName(MAIN_MESSAGE,soundpath);
                                        break;
                                case MAIN_STOP:
                                        KillTimer(hwnd,THETIMER);

                                        StopMidiInput();
                                        ItemName(MAIN_MESSAGE,soundpath);
                                        UpdateRecordTime(hwnd,recordtime);

                                        hmenu=GetMenu(hwnd);
                                        ItemOn(MAIN_RECORD);
                                        ItemOff(MAIN_STOP);
                                        ItemOn(MAIN_SAVE);
                                        ItemOn(MAIN_OPEN);

                                        SayLoadedSound(hwnd,TRUE);
                                        break;
```

```
                                case MAIN_ABOUT:
                                        if((lpfnDlgProc=MakeProcInstance((FARPROC)
                                            AboutDlgProc,hInst)) != NULL) {
                                                DialogBox(hInst,"AboutBox",
                                                    hwnd,lpfnDlgProc);
                                                FreeProcInstance(lpfnDlgProc);
                                        }
                                        break;
                                case MAIN_EXIT:
                                        SendMessage(hwnd,WM_COMMAND,MAIN_STOP,0L);
                                        FreeBuffer();
                                        PostQuitMessage(0);
                                        break;
                        }
                        break;

        }

        return(FALSE);
}

DWORD FAR PASCAL AboutDlgProc(HWND hwnd,WORD message,WORD wParam,LONG lParam)
{
        static HANDLE sound;
        static LPSTR psound;
        HANDLE handle;
        POINT point;

        switch(message) {
                case WM_INITDIALOG:
                        if((handle=FindResource(hInst,
                            "AboutWave",RT_RCDATA)) != NULL) {
                                if((sound=LoadResource(hInst,handle)) != NULL) {
                                        if((psound=LockResource(sound)) != NULL)
                                                sndPlaySound(psound,SND_ASYNC |
                                                    SND_MEMORY | SND_NOSTOP);
                                }
                        }
                        CentreWindow(hwnd);
                        return(FALSE);
                case WM_CTLCOLOR:
                        if(HIWORD(lParam)==CTLCOLOR_STATIC ||
                            HIWORD(lParam)==CTLCOLOR_DLG) {
                                SetBkColor(wParam,RGB(192,192,192));
                                SetTextColor(wParam,RGB(0,0,0));

                                ClientToScreen(hwnd,&point);
                                UnrealizeObject(GetStockObject(LTGRAY_BRUSH));
                                SetBrushOrg(wParam,point.x,point.y);

                                return((DWORD)GetStockObject(LTGRAY_BRUSH));
                        }
```

Figure 6-20 *Continued.*

```
                            if(HIWORD(lParam)==CTLCOLOR_BTN) {
                                    SetBkColor(wParam,RGB(192,192,192));
                                    SetTextColor(wParam,RGB(0,0,0));

                                    ClientToScreen(hwnd,&point);
                                    UnrealizeObject(GetStockObject(BLACK_BRUSH));
                                    SetBrushOrg(wParam,point.x,point.y);

                                    return((DWORD)GetStockObject(BLACK_BRUSH));
                            }
                            break;
                    case WM_COMMAND:
                            switch(wParam) {
                                    case IDOK:
                                            sndPlaySound(NULL,SND_SYNC);
                                            if(psound != NULL) UnlockResource(sound);
                                            if(sound != NULL) FreeResource(sound);
                                            EndDialog(hwnd,wParam);
                                            return(FALSE);
                            }
                            break;
            }

            return(FALSE);
    }

    void lmemset(LPSTR s,int n,unsigned int size)
    {
            unsigned int i;

            for(i=0;i<size;++i) *s++=n;
    }

    void SayLoadedSound(HWND hwnd,int flag)
    {
            HMENU hmenu;
            HWND dlgH;

            hmenu=GetMenu(hwnd);

            if(flag) {
                    ItemOn(MAIN_SAVE);
            }
            else {
                    ItemOff(MAIN_SAVE);
            }
    }

    int GetOpenFileName(HWND hwnd,LPSTR path)
    {
            OPENFILENAME ofn;
            char szDirName[256],szFileTitle[256],szFilter[256];
```

```
        getcwd(szDirName,sizeof(szDirName)-1);

        lstrcpy(szFilter,"*.MID");

        lmemset((LPSTR)&ofn,0,sizeof(OPENFILENAME));

        lstrcpy(path,"*.MID");
        szFileTitle[0]=0;

        ofn.lStructSize=sizeof(OPENFILENAME);
        ofn.hwndOwner=hwnd;
        ofn.lpstrFilter="All files (*.*)\000*.*\000MIDI files (*.MID)\000*.MID\000";
        ofn.lpstrFile=path;
        ofn.nFilterIndex=2;
        ofn.nMaxFile=STRINGSIZE;
        ofn.lpstrFileTitle=szFileTitle;
        ofn.nMaxFileTitle=sizeof(szFileTitle);
        ofn.lpstrInitialDir=szDirName;
        ofn.Flags=OFN_PATHMUSTEXIST | OFN_HIDEREADONLY;
        ofn.lpstrTitle="Open File";
        ofn.lpstrDefExt="MID";

        if(!GetOpenFileName(&ofn)) {
                path[0]=0;
                return(0);
        } else return(1);
}

int GetSaveFileName(HWND hwnd,LPSTR path)
{
        OPENFILENAME ofn;
        char szDirName[256],szFileTitle[256],szFilter[256];

        getcwd(szDirName,sizeof(szDirName)-1);

        lstrcpy(szFilter,"*.MID");

        lmemset((LPSTR)&ofn,0,sizeof(OPENFILENAME));

        lstrcpy(path,"*.MID");
        szFileTitle[0]=0;

        ofn.lStructSize=sizeof(OPENFILENAME);
        ofn.hwndOwner=hwnd;
        ofn.lpstrFilter="MIDI files (*.MID)\000*.MID\000";
        ofn.lpstrFile=path;
        ofn.nFilterIndex=2;
        ofn.nMaxFile=STRINGSIZE;
        ofn.lpstrFileTitle=szFileTitle;
        ofn.nMaxFileTitle=sizeof(szFileTitle);
        ofn.lpstrInitialDir=szDirName;
        ofn.Flags=OFN_OVERWRITEPROMPT | OFN_HIDEREADONLY;
        ofn.lpstrTitle="Save File";
```

Figure 6-20 *Continued.*

```
        if(!GetSaveFileName(&ofn)) {
                path[0]=0;
                return(0);
        } else return(1);
}

int OpenWave(HWND hwnd,LPSTR path)
{
        MCI_OPEN_PARMS mciopen;
        DWORD rtrn;
        char b[STRINGSIZE+1];

        mciopen.lpstrDeviceType="waveaudio";
        mciopen.lpstrElementName=path;
        if((rtrn=mciSendCommand(0,MCI_OPEN,MCI_OPEN_TYPE |
            MCI_OPEN_ELEMENT,(DWORD)(LPVOID)&mciopen)) != 0L) {
                mciGetErrorString(rtrn,(LPSTR)b,STRINGSIZE);
                DoMessage(hwnd,b);
                return(-1);
        }

        return(mciopen.wDeviceID);
}

void CentreWindow(HWND hwnd)
{
        RECT rect;
        unsigned int x,y;

        GetWindowRect(hwnd,&rect);
        x=(GetSystemMetrics(SM_CXSCREEN)-(rect.right-rect.left))/2;
        y=(GetSystemMetrics(SM_CYSCREEN)-(rect.bottom-rect.top))/2;
        SetWindowPos(hwnd,NULL,x,y,rect.right-rect.left,
            rect.bottom-rect.top,SWP_NOSIZE);
}

int FetchMidiEvent(LPEVENT lpevent,unsigned long number)
{
        char huge *event;

        if((event=(char huge *)GlobalLock(midibuffer))==NULL)
            return(FALSE);

        hmemcpy((char huge *)lpevent,event+number*(long)sizeof(EVENT),
                (long)sizeof(EVENT));

        GlobalUnlock(midibuffer);
        return(TRUE);
}


int AddMidiEvent(LPEVENT lpevent)
```

```
{
        char huge *event;

        if(nextbufferitem >= buffersize) {
                buffersize+=(long)BLOCKSIZE;
                if((midibuffer=GlobalReAlloc(midibuffer,
                    buffersize*(long)sizeof(EVENT),
                        GMEM_MOVEABLE | GMEM_ZEROINIT))==NULL)
                            return(FALSE);

        }

        if((event=(char huge *)GlobalLock(midibuffer))==NULL)
            return(FALSE);

        hmemcpy(event+nextbufferitem*(long)sizeof(EVENT),
                (char huge *)lpevent,(long)sizeof(EVENT));

        ++nextbufferitem;

        GlobalUnlock(midibuffer);
        return(TRUE);

}

int AllocateBuffer()
{
        if((midibuffer=GlobalAlloc(GMEM_MOVEABLE | GMEM_SHARE | GMEM_ZEROINIT,
            (long)BLOCKSIZE*(long)sizeof(EVENT)))==NULL) return(FALSE);
        buffersize=(long)BLOCKSIZE;
        nextbufferitem=0L;

        return(TRUE);
}

int FreeBuffer()
{
        if(midibuffer == NULL) return(FALSE);
        GlobalFree(midibuffer);
        midibuffer=NULL;
        return(TRUE);
}

int RecordMIDI(HWND hwnd)
{
        FreeBuffer();

        if(!AllocateBuffer()) return(FALSE);

        if(!StartMidiInput(hwnd)) {
                FreeBuffer();
                return(FALSE);
        }
```

Figure 6-20 *Continued.*

```
        return(TRUE);
}

void hmemcpy(char huge *dest,char huge *source,unsigned long length)
{
        unsigned long n;

        for(n=0;n<length;++n) *dest++=*source++;
}

int StartMidiInput(HWND hwnd)
{
        char b[STRINGSIZE+1];
        int i,r,devcount;

        if(active) StopMidiInput();

        if((devcount=midiInGetNumDevs())==0) return(FALSE);

        if((lpInputBuffer = AllocCircularBuffer((long)INPUT_BUFFER_SIZE
            * (long)sizeof(EVENT)))==NULL) return(FALSE);

        for(i=0;i<devcount && i<MAX_DEVICES;++i) {
                if((lpCallbackInstanceData[i] =
                    AllocCallbackInstanceData()) == NULL)
                        return(FALSE);

                lpCallbackInstanceData[i]->hWnd = hwnd;
                lpCallbackInstanceData[i]->dwDevice = i;
                lpCallbackInstanceData[i]->lpBuf = lpInputBuffer;
                lpCallbackInstanceData[i]->hMapper = hMapper;

                if((r=midiInOpen((LPHMIDIIN)&hMidiIn[i],i,
                    (DWORD)midiInputHandler,
                    (DWORD)lpCallbackInstanceData[i],CALLBACK_FUNCTION)) != 0) {

                        FreeCallbackInstanceData(lpCallbackInstanceData[i]);
                        midiInGetErrorText(r,b,STRINGSIZE);
                        DoMessage(hwnd,b);
                }
        }

        for(i=0;i<devcount && i<MAX_DEVICES;++i) {
                if(hMidiIn[i]) midiInStart(hMidiIn[i]);
        }

        active=TRUE;

        return(TRUE);
}
```

```
void StopMidiInput()
{
        int i,devcount;

        if(!active) return;

        devcount=midiInGetNumDevs();

        for(i=0;i<devcount && i<MAX_DEVICES;++i) {
                if(hMidiIn[i]) {
                        midiInStop(hMidiIn[i]);
                        midiInReset(hMidiIn[i]);
                        midiInClose(hMidiIn[i]);
                        FreeCallbackInstanceData(lpCallbackInstanceData[i]);
                }
        }

        if(hMapper) midiOutClose(hMapper);

        FreeCircularBuffer(lpInputBuffer);
        active=FALSE;
}

LPCIRCULARBUFFER AllocCircularBuffer(DWORD dwSize)
{
        HANDLE hMem;
        LPCIRCULARBUFFER lpBuf;
        LPEVENT lpMem;

        if((hMem=GlobalAlloc(GMEM_SHARE \ GMEM_MOVEABLE,
            (DWORD)sizeof(CIRCULARBUFFER)))==NULL)
                return(NULL);

        if((lpBuf = (LPCIRCULARBUFFER)GlobalLock(hMem))==NULL) {
                GlobalFree(hMem);
                return(NULL);
        }

        GlobalPageLock(HIWORD(lpBuf));

        lpBuf->hSelf=hMem;

        if((hMem = GlobalAlloc(GMEM_SHARE | GMEM_MOVEABLE,
            dwSize*sizeof(EVENT)))==NULL) {
                GlobalPageUnlock(HIWORD(lpBuf));
                GlobalUnlock(lpBuf->hSelf);
                GlobalFree(lpBuf->hSelf);
                return(NULL);
        }

            if((lpMem=(LPEVENT)GlobalLock(hMem))==NULL) {
                GlobalFree(hMem);
                GlobalPageUnlock(HIWORD(lpBuf));
```

377

Figure 6-20   *Continued.*

```
                        GlobalUnlock(lpBuf->hSelf);
                        GlobalFree(lpBuf->hSelf);
                        return(NULL);
                }

                GlobalPageLock(HIWORD(lpMem));

                lpBuf->hBuffer = hMem;
                lpBuf->wError = 0;
                lpBuf->dwSize = dwSize;
                lpBuf->dwCount = 0L;
                lpBuf->lpStart = lpMem;
                lpBuf->lpEnd = lpMem+(WORD)dwSize;
                lpBuf->lpTail = lpMem;
                lpBuf->lpHead = lpMem;

                return(lpBuf);
        }

        void FreeCircularBuffer(LPCIRCULARBUFFER lpBuf)
        {
                HANDLE hMem;

                GlobalPageUnlock(HIWORD(lpBuf->lpStart));
                GlobalUnlock(lpBuf->hBuffer);
                GlobalFree(lpBuf->hBuffer);

                hMem = lpBuf->hSelf;
                GlobalPageUnlock(HIWORD(lpBuf));
                GlobalUnlock(hMem);
                GlobalFree(hMem);
        }

        WORD FAR PASCAL GetEvent(LPCIRCULARBUFFER lpBuf,LPEVENT lpEvent)
        {
                if(lpBuf->dwCount <= 0) return(FALSE);

                *lpEvent=*lpBuf->lpTail;

                --lpBuf->dwCount;
                ++lpBuf->lpTail;

                if(lpBuf->lpTail >= lpBuf->lpEnd)
                    lpBuf->lpTail = lpBuf->lpStart;
                return(TRUE);
        }

        LPCALLBACKINSTANCEDATA FAR PASCAL AllocCallbackInstanceData(void)
        {
                HANDLE hMem;
                LPCALLBACKINSTANCEDATA lpBuf;
```

```
            if((hMem=GlobalAlloc(GMEM_SHARE | GMEM_MOVEABLE,
                (DWORD)sizeof(CALLBACKINSTANCEDATA)))==NULL)
                    return(NULL);

            if((lpBuf=(LPCALLBACKINSTANCEDATA)GlobalLock(hMem))==NULL) {
                    GlobalFree(hMem);
                    return(NULL);
            }

            GlobalPageLock(HIWORD(lpBuf));

            lpBuf->hSelf=hMem;

            return(lpBuf);
    }

    void FAR PASCAL FreeCallbackInstanceData(LPCALLBACKINSTANCEDATA lpBuf)
    {
            HANDLE hMem;

            hMem=lpBuf->hSelf;

            GlobalPageUnlock(HIWORD(lpBuf));
            GlobalUnlock(hMem);
            GlobalFree(hMem);
    }

    int IsInterestingMessage(LPEVENT lpEvent)
    {
            BYTE bStatus,bStatusRaw;

            bStatusRaw = LOBYTE(LOWORD(lpEvent->data));
            bStatus = bStatusRaw & (BYTE) 0xf0;

             switch(bStatus){
                    case NOTEOFF:
                    case NOTEON:
                    case KEYAFTERTOUCH:
                    case CONTROLCHANGE:
                    case PROGRAMCHANGE:
                    case CHANAFTERTOUCH:
                    case PITCHBEND:
                            return(TRUE);

            }
            return(FALSE);
    }

    int WriteSong(char *path)
    {
            int r;
```

Figure 6-20 *Continued.*

```
            Mf_putc=myputc;
            Mf_writetrack=mywritetrack;

            if((fp=fopen(path,"wb"))==NULL) return(FALSE);

            r=mfwrite(0,1,INTERVAL,fp);

            fclose(fp);
            return(r);
}

int SetPatch(LPNOTE lpnote,unsigned int number,unsigned int voice)
{
            int i,count;

            for(i=count=0;lpnote[i].note != ENDSONG;++i) {
                    if(lpnote[i].note==VOICE) {
                            if(count==number) {
                                    lpnote[i].duration=voice;
                                    return(TRUE);
                            }
                            ++count;
                    }
            }
            return(FALSE);
}

/* This is from MIDILIB, by M. Czeiszperger */

/* Functions to implement in order to write a MIDI file */


/*
 * mfwrite() - The only function you'll need to call to write out
 *             a midi file.
 *
 * format      0 - Single multi-channel track
 *             1 - Multiple simultaneous tracks
 *             2 - One or more sequentially independent
 *                 single track patterns
 * ntracks     The number of tracks in the file.
 * division    This is kind of tricky, it can represent two
 *             things, depending on whether it is positive or negative
 *             (bit 15 set or not). If bit 15 of division is zero,
 *             bits 14 through 0 represent the number of delta-time
 *             "ticks" which make up a quarter note. If bit 15 of
 *             division is a one, delta-times in a file correspond to
 *             subdivisions of a second similiar to SMPTE and MIDI
 *             time code. In this format bits 14 through 8 contain
 *             one of four values - 24, -25, -29, or -30,
 *             corresponding to the four standard SMPTE and MIDI
```

```
 *              time code frame per second formats, where  -29
 *              represents  30  drop  frame.   The  second  byte
 *              consisting  of  bits 7 through 0 corresponds the the
 *              resolution within a frame.  Refer the Standard MIDI
 *              Files 1.0 spec for more details.
 * fp           This should be the open file pointer to the file you
 *              want to write.  It will have be a global in order
 *              to work with Mf_putc.
 */
int mfwrite(int format,int ntracks,int division,FILE *fp)
{
        int i;

        if(Mf_putc==NULL ¦¦ Mf_writetrack == NULL) return(FALSE);

        mf_write_header_chunk(format,ntracks,division);

        if(format == 1 && (Mf_writetempotrack))
            (*Mf_writetempotrack)();

        for(i=0;i<ntracks;i++) {
                if(!mf_write_track_chunk(i,fp)) return(FALSE);
        }

        return(TRUE);
}


int mf_write_track_chunk(int which_track,FILE *fp)
{
        unsigned long trkhdr,trklength;
        long offset, place_marker;

        trkhdr = MTrk;
        trklength = 0;

        offset = ftell(fp);

        write32bit(trkhdr);
        write32bit(trklength);

        Mf_numbyteswritten = 0L;

        if( Mf_writetrack )
            (*Mf_writetrack)(which_track);

        eputc(0);
        eputc(meta_event);
        eputc(end_of_track);

        eputc(0);

        place_marker = ftell(fp);

        if(fseek(fp,offset,0) < 0) return(FALSE);
```

Figure 6-20 *Continued.*

```
        trklength = Mf_numbyteswritten;

        write32bit(trkhdr);
        write32bit(trklength);

        fseek(fp,place_marker,0);
        return(TRUE);
}


void mf_write_header_chunk(int format,int ntracks,int division)
{
        unsigned long ident,length;

        ident = MThd;
        length = 6;

        write32bit(ident);
        write32bit(length);
        write16bit(format);
        write16bit(ntracks);
        write16bit(division);
}

int mf_write_midi_event(unsigned long delta_time, unsigned int type,
    unsigned int chan, unsigned char *data, unsigned long size)
{
        int i;
        unsigned char c;

        WriteVarLen(delta_time);

        c = type | chan;

        eputc(c);

        for(i = 0; i < size; i++) eputc(data[i]);

        return((int)size);
}

int mf_write_meta_event(unsigned long delta_time, unsigned char type,
    unsigned char *data, unsigned long size)
{
        int i;

        WriteVarLen(delta_time);

        eputc(meta_event);

        eputc(type);
```

```
        WriteVarLen(size);

        for(i=0;i<size;i++) {
                if(eputc(data[i]) != data[i])
                        return(-1);
        }
        return((int)size);
}

void mf_write_tempo(unsigned long tempo)
{
        eputc(0);
        eputc(meta_event);
        eputc(set_tempo);

        eputc(3);
        eputc((unsigned)(0xff & (tempo >> 16)));
        eputc((unsigned)(0xff & (tempo >> 8)));
        eputc((unsigned)(0xff & tempo));
}

void mf_write_timesig(unsigned int numerator,unsigned int denominator,
                      unsigned int clocks,unsigned int quotes)
{
        eputc(0);
        eputc(meta_event);
        eputc(time_signature);

        eputc(4);
        eputc(numerator);
        eputc(denominator);
        eputc(clocks);
        eputc(quotes);
}

void mf_write_keysig(int flats,int minor)
{
        eputc(0);
        eputc(meta_event);
        eputc(key_signature);

        eputc(2);
        eputc(flats);
        eputc(minor);
}


unsigned long mf_sec2ticks(float secs,int division,unsigned int tempo)
{
        return (long)(((secs * 1000.0) / 4.0 * division) / tempo);
}

void WriteVarLen(unsigned long value)
```

Figure 6-20 *Continued.*

```
{
        unsigned long buffer;

          buffer = value & 0x7f;
          while((value >>= 7) > 0) {
                buffer <<= 8;
                buffer |= 0x80;
                buffer += (value & 0x7f);
          }
          while(1){
                eputc((unsigned)(buffer & 0xff));

                if(buffer & 0x80) buffer >>= 8;
                else return;
          }
}

float mf_ticks2sec(unsigned long ticks,int division,unsigned int tempo)
{
        float smpte_format, smpte_resolution;

        if(division > 0)
                return((float) (((float)(ticks)*(float)(tempo))/
                        ((float)(division) * 1000000.0)));
        else {
                smpte_format = upperbyte(division);
                smpte_resolution = lowerbyte(division);
                return(float)((float) ticks/
                        (smpte_format * smpte_resolution * 1000000.0));
        }
}

void write32bit(unsigned long data)
{
        eputc((unsigned)((data >> 24) & 0xff));
        eputc((unsigned)((data >> 16) & 0xff));
        eputc((unsigned)((data >> 8 ) & 0xff));
        eputc((unsigned)(data & 0xff));
}

void write16bit(int data)
{
        eputc((unsigned)((data & 0xff00) >> 8));
        eputc((unsigned)(data & 0xff));
}

int eputc(unsigned char c)
{
        int return_val;

        if((Mf_putc) == NULL) return(-1);
```

```
        return_val=(Mf_putc)(c);

        if(return_val == EOF ) return(-1);

        Mf_numbyteswritten++;
        return(return_val);
}

int mywritetrack(int track)
{
        EVENT event;
        static char textmessage[]="Music recorded by MIDIREC";
        BYTE bStatus, bStatusRaw, bChannel, bData1, bData2;
        char data[2];
        long l,duration=0L;

        mf_write_tempo(125000L);

        /*
        you might want to write additional information here, such
        as the time signature and the key, for example

        mf_write_timesig(6,3,36,8);

        mf_write_keysig(KEY_G,KEY_MAJOR);
        */

        if(mf_write_meta_event(0,text_event,textmessage,sizeof(textmessage)) < 0)
            return(-1);

        if(!FetchMidiEvent(&event,0)) return(-1);


        for(l=0L;l<nextbufferitem;++l) {
                if(!FetchMidiEvent(&event,l)) return(-1);

                bStatusRaw=LOBYTE(LOWORD(event.data));
                bStatus=bStatusRaw & (BYTE) 0xf0;
                bChannel=bStatusRaw & (BYTE) 0x0f;
                bData1=HIBYTE(LOWORD(event.data));
                bData2=LOBYTE(HIWORD(event.data));

                if(bStatus==NOTEON && bData2 != 0) duration=GetDuration(l);

                switch(bStatus) {
                        case NOTEOFF:
                                data[0] = bData1; /* note number */
                                data[1] = bData2; /* velocity */
                                if(!mf_write_midi_event(duration,bStatus,
                                   bChannel,data,2))
                                    return(-1);
                                break;
                        case NOTEON:
```

Figure 6-20 *Continued.*

```
                                    data[0] = bData1; /* note number */
                                    data[1] = bData2; /* velocity */
                                    if(!mf_write_midi_event(duration,bStatus,
                                      bChannel,data,2))
                                        return(-1);
                                    break;
                            case KEYAFTERTOUCH:
                                    data[0] = bData1;
                                    if(!mf_write_midi_event(0,bStatus,
                                      bChannel,data,1))
                                        return(-1);
                                    break;
                            case CONTROLCHANGE:
                                    data[0] = bData1;
                                    if(!mf_write_midi_event(0,bStatus,
                                      bChannel,data,1))
                                        return(-1);
                                    break;
                            case PITCHBEND:
                                    data[0] = bData1;
                                    if(!mf_write_midi_event(0,bStatus,
                                      bChannel,data,1))
                                        return(-1);
                                    break;
                            case PROGRAMCHANGE:
                                    data[0] = bData1;
                                    if(!mf_write_midi_event(0,bStatus,
                                      bChannel,data,1))
                                        return(-1);
                                    break;
                            case CHANAFTERTOUCH:
                                    data[0] = bData1;
                                    if(!mf_write_midi_event(0,bStatus,
                                      bChannel,data,1))
                                        return(-1);
                                    break;
                    }
            }
            return(1);
    }

    long GetDuration(long pos)
    {
            EVENT event;
            long l,time;
            BYTE bStatus,bStatusRaw,bData1,bData2;
            int note;
            if(!FetchMidiEvent(&event,pos)) return(0L);
            note=HIBYTE(LOWORD(event.data));
            time=event.timestamp;
```

```
        for(l=pos+1;l<nextbufferitem;++l) {
                if(!FetchMidiEvent(&event,l)) return(0L);

                bStatusRaw=LOBYTE(LOWORD(event.data));
                bStatus=bStatusRaw & (BYTE) 0xf0;
                bData1=HIBYTE(LOWORD(event.data));
                bData2=LOBYTE(HIWORD(event.data));

                if(bData1 != note) continue;

                if((bStatus==NOTEON && bData2==0) || bStatus==NOTEOFF)
                    return(event.timestamp-time);
        }

        return(0L);
}

int myputc(int c)
{
        return(fputc(c,fp));

}
```

The MIDIREC.RC resource script.

Figure 6-21

```
MainScreen DIALOG 9, 24, 184, 48
STYLE WS_POPUP | WS_CAPTION | WS_SYSMENU | WS_MINIMIZEBOX
CAPTION "MIDI Recorder"
MENU MainMenu
BEGIN
        CONTROL "", -1, "BorShade", BSS_GROUP | WS_CHILD | WS_VISIBLE, 8, 4, 124, 16
        LTEXT "", 401, 12, 8, 116, 8, WS_CHILD | WS_VISIBLE | WS_GROUP
        PUSHBUTTON "Quit", 199, 148, 28, 28, 12, WS_CHILD | WS_VISIBLE | WS_TABSTOP
        PUSHBUTTON "Save", 205, 120, 28, 28, 12, WS_CHILD | WS_VISIBLE | WS_TABSTOP
        PUSHBUTTON "Stop", 204, 92, 28, 28, 12, WS_CHILD | WS_VISIBLE | WS_TABSTOP
        PUSHBUTTON "Record", 202, 64, 28, 28, 12, WS_CHILD | WS_VISIBLE | WS_TABSTOP
        CONTROL "", 102, "BorShade", 32769 | WS_CHILD | WS_VISIBLE, 136, 4, 40, 16
        CTEXT "", 402, 140, 8, 32, 8, WS_CHILD | WS_VISIBLE | WS_GROUP
END

MainMenu MENU
BEGIN
        POPUP "&File"
        BEGIN
                MENUITEM "&Save", 205
                MENUITEM "&About", 102
                MENUITEM SEPARATOR
                MENUITEM "E&xit", 199
        END

        POPUP "&Edit"
        BEGIN
                MENUITEM "&Record", 202
```

Figure 6-21 *Continued.*

```
                        MENUITEM "&Stop", 204
                END

        END

        AboutBox DIALOG 18, 18, 184, 180
        STYLE WS_POPUP | WS_CAPTION
        CAPTION "About..."
        BEGIN
                CONTROL "", 102, "BorShade", BSS_GROUP | WS_CHILD | WS_VISIBLE |
                    WS_TABSTOP, 8, 68, 168, 76
                CTEXT "MIDI Recorder 1.0\n\nCopyright (c) 1994 Alchemy Mindworks Inc.\n\n
                    This program is part of the book Advanced Multimedia
                    Programming for Windows by Steven William Rimmer, published by
                    Windcrest/McGraw Hill.", -1, 12, 72, 160, 68, WS_CHILD |
                    WS_VISIBLE | WS_GROUP
                CONTROL "Button", IDOK, "BorBtn", BS_DEFPUSHBUTTON | WS_CHILD |
                    WS_VISIBLE | WS_TABSTOP, 74, 152, 32, 20
                CONTROL "Button", 801, "BorBtn", BS_PUSHBUTTON | WS_CHILD |
                    WS_VISIBLE | WS_TABSTOP, 36, 8, 32, 20
        END

        1801 BITMAP "smpw.bmp"

        AboutWave RCDATA "ABOUT.WAV"

        MIDIRecorder ICON
        BEGIN
                '00 00 01 00 01 00 20 20 10 00 00 00 00 00 E8 02'
                '00 00 16 00 00 00 28 00 00 00 20 00 00 00 40 00'
                '00 00 01 00 04 00 00 00 00 00 80 02 00 00 00 00'
                '00 00 00 00 00 00 10 00 00 00 00 00 00 00 00 00'
                '00 00 00 00 BF 00 00 BF 00 00 00 BF BF 00 BF 00'
                '00 00 BF 00 BF 00 BF BF 00 00 C0 C0 C0 00 80 80'
                '80 00 00 00 FF 00 00 FF 00 00 00 FF FF 00 FF 00'
                '00 00 FF 00 FF 00 FF FF 00 00 FF FF FF 00 77 77'
                '77 77 77 77 77 77 77 77 77 77 77 77 77 77 7F 88'
                '88 88 88 88 88 88 88 88 88 88 88 88 87 7F F8'
                '88 88 88 88 88 88 88 88 88 88 88 88 87 7F F7'
                '77 77 77 77 77 77 77 77 77 77 77 77 78 87 7F F7'
                '77 77 77 77 77 77 77 77 77 77 77 77 78 87 7F F7'
                '77 77 77 77 77 77 77 77 77 77 77 77 78 87 7F F7'
                '77 77 77 77 77 77 00 00 00 00 00 00 08 87 7F F7'
                '77 77 77 77 77 0C CC CC CC CC CC CC 78 87 7F F7'
                '77 77 77 77 7C CC 77 CC C0 07 77 77 78 87 7F F7'
                '77 77 77 77 CC 77 07 07 CC 07 77 77 78 87 7F F7'
                '77 77 77 77 C0 0C 0C 00 0C 00 77 77 78 87 7F F7'
                '77 77 77 7C CC CC CC CC CC C0 77 77 78 87 7F F7'
                '77 77 77 7C 07 CC CC CC 77 C0 77 77 78 87 7F F7'
                '77 77 77 7C 07 0C 0C C0 77 C0 77 77 78 87 7F F7'
                '77 77 77 CC 0C 7C 7C C7 77 C0 77 77 78 87 7F F7'
```

```
'77 77 77 CC C0 77 77 77 7C C7 77 77 78 87 7F F7'
'77 77 77 CC C7 07 77 77 0C 77 77 77 78 87 7F F7'
'77 77 7C CC 0C 70 00 0C C7 77 77 77 78 87 7F F7'
'77 77 7C CC C0 CC CC CC 77 77 77 77 78 87 7F F7'
'77 77 CC CC CC 00 77 77 77 77 77 77 78 87 7F F7'
'77 77 CC CC CC C0 07 77 77 77 77 77 78 87 7F F7'
'77 7C CC CC CC CC 00 77 77 77 77 77 78 87 7F F7'
'77 CC CC CC CC CC C0 00 77 77 77 77 78 87 7F F7'
'7C CC CC CC CC CC CC C0 07 77 77 77 78 87 7F F7'
'CC CC CC CC CC CC CC CC 77 77 77 77 78 87 7F F7'
'77 77 77 77 77 77 77 77 77 77 77 77 78 87 7F F7'
'77 77 77 77 77 77 77 77 77 77 77 77 78 87 7F F7'
'77 77 77 77 77 77 77 77 77 77 77 77 78 87 7F F7'
'77 77 77 77 77 77 77 77 77 77 77 77 78 87 7F FF'
'FF FF FF FF FF FF FF FF FF FF FF FF F8 87 7F FF'
'FF FF FF FF FF FF FF FF FF FF FF FF FF 87 77 77'
'77 77 77 77 77 77 77 77 77 77 77 77 77 77 00 00'
'00 00 00 00 00 00 00 00 00 00 00 00 00 00 00 00'
'00 00 00 00 00 00 00 00 00 00 00 00 00 00 00 00'
'00 00 00 00 00 00 00 00 00 00 00 00 00 00 00 00'
'00 00 00 00 00 00 00 00 00 00 00 00 00 00 00 00'
'00 00 00 00 00 00 00 00 00 00 00 00 00 00 00 00'
'00 00 00 00 00 00 00 00 00 00 00 00 00 00 00 00'
'00 00 00 00 00 00 00 00 00 00 00 00 00 00 00 00'
'00 00 00 00 00 00 00 00 00 00 00 00 00 00 00'
```

END

Virtually everything in MIDIREC.CPP has turned up in other forms
earlier in this book. The MM_MIDIINPUT message handler in
SelectProc works pretty much as it did in MIDIVIEW, except that
interesting messages are handled by AddMidiEvent. The
AddMidiEvent function, defined in MIDIREC.CPP, will reallocate the
MIDI event buffer if it gets full and stash the event passed to it in the
next free entry. It uses huge pointers to access the buffer, as a long
performance might well see it grow to beyond 64 kilobytes.

The circular queue logic and interface to the MIDIMAN dynamic link
library are unchanged from MIDIVIEW. All the real work starts when
you click on the Record button, and SelectProc calls RecordMIDI.
The RecordMIDI function calls StartMidiInput, and the
MM_MIDIINPUT message should begin appearing at SelectProc.

As with WAVEREC, the main window of MIDIREC keeps a running
time counter by sending itself WM_TIMER messages once every tenth
of a second.

If you click on the Save button of MIDIREC after recording some music, the MIDI file code from MIDILIB will be invoked to write your recorded music to a file. Once again, this is almost identical to what happened in WRITESNG, except for the logic in the mywritetrack function at the bottom of the MIDIREC.CPP source listing. This function walks through the list of recorded EVENT objects by calling FetchMidiEvent, parses each event into its component parts, and works out the direction of NOTE ON messages by calling GetDuration. The GetDuration function looks at the event list to find the NOTE OFF message that corresponds to a NOTE ON message and calculates the difference in their time stamps.

As an aside, this is the logic you'll have to expand on if you'd like to make MIDIREC polyphonic.

The MIDI manager DLL
—all the really nasty bits

While perhaps not as difficult to write as they might appear at first, Windows dynamic link libraries probably qualify as a bit of a black art. There are few good reasons for undertaking a DLL if your programming doesn't stray into applications that are either very large, seethingly complex, or highly exotic.

Regrettably, applications that work with MIDI qualify as exotic as far as Windows is concerned. The extremely high speed of the MIDI interface requires drastic measures for Windows. Specifically, Windows would like to be able to call a function to handle incoming MIDI messages without having to figure out where it's gotten to in memory. In conventional Windows applications, code segments are not constrained to stay in the same place. When a Windows application calls a function indirectly, Windows must make sure it hasn't gone for a wander, and modify the call if it has.

Windows does not allow for fixed code segments in applications—that is, code which can't be relocated. It only allows for them in a dynamic link library.

As touched on earlier in this book, the same problem besets applications that want to have the precision timers afforded by the Windows multimedia extensions call a function at regular intervals. If the function to be called is permitted to move around, Windows will have to expend a variable amount of time tracking it down, and the precision timers will cease to be particularly precise.

Both these situations require the use of a dynamic link library with a fixed code segment to store critical bits of code. In the applications discussed in this chapter, the timers appeared in PLAYSONG and the MIDI input handler was used by MIDIVIEW and WRITESNG. To keep the DLL count down, they all use the same MIDIMAN.DLL library.

Figure 6-22 illustrates the MIDIMAN.CPP source code. Figure 6-23 illustrates the MIDIMAN.H header file that should be included in any application that calls MIDIMAN. In addition, of course, you'll need the by now traditional PRJ and DEF files to compile MIDIMAN.CPP into MIDIMAN.DLL.

The MIDIMAN.CPP source code.   Figure 6-22

```
/*
        MIDI Manager
*/

#include <windows.h>
#include <stdio.h>
#include <stdlib.h>
#include <dir.h>
#include <ctype.h>
#include <alloc.h>
#include <string.h>
#include <io.h>
#include <bwcc.h>
#include <dos.h>
#include <errno.h>
#include <math.h>
#include <mmsystem.h>
#include "midiman.h"

#define say(s)      MessageBox(NULL,s,"Yo...",MB_OK | MB_ICONSTOP);
#define saynumber(f,s)    {char b[128]; sprintf((LPSTR)b,(LPSTR)f,s); \
                        MessageBox(NULL,b,"Debug Message",MB_OK | MB_ICONSTOP); \
                        }

void StopNote(LPSONG lpsong);
```

Figure 6-22 *Continued.*

```
void PlayNote(LPSONG lpsong);
void FAR PASCAL TimeFunc(unsigned int id,unsigned int msg,
    DWORD dwUser,DWORD dw1,DWORD dw2);

HANDLE hInst;
static EVENT event;

#pragma argsused
extern "C" int FAR PASCAL LibMain(HANDLE hInstance,WORD wDataSeg,
    WORD wHeapSize, LPSTR lpCmdLine)
{
        hInst=hInstance;
        if(wHeapSize > 0) UnlockData(0);
        return(1);
}

#pragma argsused
extern "C" int FAR PASCAL _export WEP(int nParameter)
{
        return(1);
}

#pragma argsused
extern "C" void FAR PASCAL _export midiInputHandler(HMIDIIN hMidiIn,WORD wMsg,
    DWORD dwInstance,DWORD dwParam1,DWORD dwParam2)
{
            switch(wMsg) {
                case MIM_OPEN:
                        break;
                case MIM_ERROR:
                case MIM_DATA:
                        event.dwDevice =
                            ((LPCALLBACKINSTANCEDATA)dwInstance)->dwDevice;
                        event.data = dwParam1;
                        event.timestamp = dwParam2;
                        if(((LPCALLBACKINSTANCEDATA)dwInstance)->hMapper)
                                midiOutShortMsg(((LPCALLBACKINSTANCEDATA)
                                    dwInstance)->hMapper,dwParam1);

                        PutEvent(((LPCALLBACKINSTANCEDATA)dwInstance)->lpBuf,
                            (LPEVENT)&event);
                        PostMessage(((LPCALLBACKINSTANCEDATA)dwInstance)->hWnd,
                            MM_MIDIINPUT,0,0L);

                        break;
                default:
                        break;
        }
}

extern "C" void FAR PASCAL _export PutEvent(LPCIRCULARBUFFER lpBuf,LPEVENT lpEvent)
```

```
{
        if(lpBuf->dwCount >= lpBuf->dwSize){
                lpBuf->wError = 1;
                return;
        }

        *lpBuf->lpHead = *lpEvent;

        ++lpBuf->lpHead;
        ++lpBuf->dwCount;

        if(lpBuf->lpHead >= lpBuf->lpEnd) lpBuf->lpHead = lpBuf->lpStart;
}

extern "C" int FAR PASCAL _export StartSong(LPSONG lpsong,HWND hwnd,LPNOTE lpnote)
{
        lpsong->timeleft=0;
        lpsong->hwnd=hwnd;
        lpsong->note=lpnote;
        lpsong->noteindex=0;

        if(midiOutOpen(&lpsong->hmo,MIDIMAPPER,NULL,NULL,0L)) return(FALSE);
        else {
                midiOutGetVolume(lpsong->hmo,&lpsong->oldvolume);
                midiOutSetVolume(lpsong->hmo,0xffffffffL);
        }

        PlayNote(lpsong);

        if((lpsong->timeid=timeSetEvent(SIXTEENTH,TIMERESOLUTION,TimeFunc,
            (DWORD)(LPSTR)lpsong,TIME_PERIODIC))==NULL) {
                midiOutSetVolume(lpsong->hmo,lpsong->oldvolume);
                midiOutClose(lpsong->hmo);
                return(FALSE);
        }

        return(TRUE);
}

extern "C" void FAR PASCAL _export StopSong(LPSONG lpsong)
{
        if(lpsong->hmo==NULL) return;

        StopNote(lpsong);

        midiOutSetVolume(lpsong->hmo,lpsong->oldvolume);
        midiOutClose(lpsong->hmo);
        timeKillEvent(lpsong->timeid);
}

#pragma argsused
void FAR PASCAL TimeFunc(unsigned int id,unsigned int msg,
    DWORD dwUser,DWORD dw1,DWORD dw2)
```

Figure 6-22 *Continued.*

```
{
        LPSONG lpsong;

        lpsong=(LPSONG)dwUser;

        if(lpsong->timeleft==0) {
                if(lpsong->noteindex &&
                    lpsong->note[lpsong->noteindex].note != VOICE)
                        StopNote(lpsong);

                ++lpsong->noteindex;

                if(lpsong->note[lpsong->noteindex].note==ENDSONG)
                    PostMessage(lpsong->hwnd,MM_MIDIFINISHED,0,0L);
                else
                        PlayNote(lpsong);
        } else —lpsong->timeleft;
}

void StopNote(LPSONG lpsong)
{
        if(lpsong->note[lpsong->noteindex].note != REST &&
            lpsong->note[lpsong->noteindex].note != VOICE)
            midiSendEvent(lpsong->hmo,NOTEOFF,lpsong->note[lpsong->noteindex].note,0);
}

void PlayNote(LPSONG lpsong)
{

        if(lpsong->note[lpsong->noteindex].note==VOICE) {
                lpsong->timeleft=0;
                midiSendEvent(lpsong->hmo,PROGRAMCHANGE,
                    lpsong->note[lpsong->noteindex].duration,0);
                return;
        }

        lpsong->timeleft=lpsong->note[lpsong->noteindex].duration;

        if(lpsong->note[lpsong->noteindex].note != REST)
            midiSendEvent(lpsong->hmo,NOTEON,
                lpsong->note[lpsong->noteindex].note,VELOCITY);
}

extern "C" WORD FAR PASCAL _export midiSendEvent(HMIDIOUT hmo,
    WORD status,WORD data1,WORD data2)
{
        union {
                DWORD dwData;
                BYTE bData[4];
        } u;
```

```
        u.bData[0]=status;
        u.bData[1]=data1;
        u.bData[2]=data2;
        u.bData[3]=0;

        return(midiOutShortMsg(hmo,u.dwData));
}
```

The MIDIMAN.H header file.

Figure 6-23

```
/*
        MIDI Manager header
*/

#define MM_MIDIINPUT            WM_USER + 0
#define MM_MIDIFINISHED         WM_USER + 1

#define C       0
#define Cs      1
#define D       2
#define Ds      3
#define E       4
#define F       5
#define Fs      6
#define G       7
#define Gs      8
#define A       9
#define As      10
#define B       11

#define KEY_Aff -11
#define KEY_Eff -10
#define KEY_Bff -9
#define KEY_Ff  -8
#define KEY_Cf  -7
#define KEY_Gf  -6
#define KEY_Df  -5
#define KEY_Af  -4
#define KEY_Ef  -3
#define KEY_Bf  -2
#define KEY_F   -1
#define KEY_C   0
#define KEY_G   1
#define KEY_D   2
#define KEY_A   3
#define KEY_E   4
#define KEY_B   5
#define KEY_Fs  6
#define KEY_Cs  7
#define KEY_Gs  8
#define KEY_Ds  9
#define KEY_As  10
```

Figure 6-23   *Continued.*

```
#define KEY_Es   11

#define KEY_MAJOR        0
#define KEY_MINOR        1

#define TIMER_INTERVAL  1

#define VOICE     0xfffd
#define REST      0xfffe
#define ENDSONG   0xffff

#define INTERVAL         136           // Number of milliconds for a whole
note

#define WHOLE             INTERVAL
#define HALF              INTERVAL/2
#define QUARTER           INTERVAL/4
#define EIGHTH            INTERVAL/8
#define SIXTEENTH         INTERVAL/16

#define TIMERESOLUTION   SIXTEENTH

#define NOTEON            0x90
#define NOTEOFF           0x80
#define KEYAFTERTOUCH     0xa0
#define CONTROLCHANGE     0xb0
#define PROGRAMCHANGE     0xc0
#define CHANAFTERTOUCH    0xd0
#define PITCHBEND         0xe0
#define SYSTEMMESSAGE     0xf0
#define BEGINSYSEX        0xf0
#define MTCQUARTERFRAME   0xf1
#define SONGPOSPTR        0xf2
#define SONGSELECT        0xf3

#define VELOCITY          64

#define TRIPLET(n)        ((n*2)/3)
#define DOT(n)            (n+(n/2))

#define MAKENOTE(note,octave,duration) { note+octave*12,duration}
#define MAKEVOICE(number)        { VOICE,number}

typedef struct event_tag {
        DWORD dwDevice;
        DWORD timestamp;
        DWORD data;
        } EVENT;

typedef EVENT FAR *LPEVENT;
```

```
typedef struct circularBuffer_tag {
        HANDLE hSelf;
        HANDLE hBuffer;
        WORD wError;
        DWORD dwSize;
        DWORD dwCount;
        LPEVENT lpStart;
        LPEVENT lpEnd;
        LPEVENT lpHead;
        LPEVENT lpTail;
        } CIRCULARBUFFER;

typedef CIRCULARBUFFER FAR *LPCIRCULARBUFFER;

typedef struct callbackInstance_tag {
        HWND hWnd;
        HANDLE hSelf;
        DWORD dwDevice;
        LPCIRCULARBUFFER lpBuf;
        HMIDIOUT hMapper;
        } CALLBACKINSTANCEDATA;

typedef CALLBACKINSTANCEDATA FAR *LPCALLBACKINSTANCEDATA;

typedef struct {
        unsigned int note;
        unsigned int duration;
        } NOTE;

typedef struct {
        HMIDIOUT hmo;
        HWND hwnd;
        WORD timeid;
        LPNOTE note;
        unsigned int timeleft;
        unsigned int noteindex;
        DWORD oldvolume;
        } SONG;

typedef SONG FAR *LPSONG;

extern "C" void FAR PASCAL _export midiInputHandler(HMIDIIN hMidiIn,WORD wMsg,
    DWORD dwInstance,DWORD dwParam1,DWORD dwParam2);
extern "C" void FAR PASCAL _export PutEvent(LPCIRCULARBUFFER lpBuf, LPEVENT lpEvent);
extern "C" int FAR PASCAL _export StartSong(LPSONG lpsong,HWND hwnd,LPNOTE lpnote);
extern "C" void FAR PASCAL _export StopSong(LPSONG lpsong);
extern "C" WORD FAR PASCAL _export midiSendEvent(HMIDIOUT hmo,
                                    WORD status,WORD data1,WORD data2);
```

Note that the PRJ file for a dynamic link library is set up differently from that of a conventional Borland PRJ file for compiling a Windows application. Note also that the MIDIMAN.DEF file is a bit peculiar, as it specifies a fixed code segment. As an aside, one of the problems with the Microsoft MIDI Monitor application that accompanies the Multimedia Development Kit is that its equivalent DLL doesn't do this.

The MIDIMAN.DLL file is included on the companion CD-ROM for this book. You won't have to recompile it unless you want to modify it. If you do so, you should also rebuild its import library, MIDIMAN.LIB. This is handled by opening MIDIMAN.DLL with the Import Librarian application that accompanies Borland C++ for Windows. For a DLL of this size, the Import Librarian may work so quickly as to make you think that nothing has happened. It will create a new LIB file from any DLL.

If you'd like to read a more complete discussion of the dark terrors of dynamic link libraries, take a look at my book *Constructing Windows Dialogs*.

The first bit of MIDIMAN.DLL deals with handling MIDI input. The hard work is handled by the midiInput handler function. It's called whenever a MIDI message shows up asking to be processed and is really only concerned with MIM_DATA messages. It stores each message in an EVENT object and calls PutEvent to store it in the circular event queue. It then posts an MM_MIDIINPUT message to the parent window that set the whole works up.

The latter portion of MIDIMAN.CPP handles playing music from an array of NOTE objects. The externally callable functions are StartSong and StopSong, which will be familiar from their appearance in the PLAYSONG application. The StartSong function opens a MIDI device for output—in this case, it's hardwired to play through the MIDI mapper. It preserves the old volume level in its SONG object and cranks up the volume to full orchestral strength. It seems fair to note that on a cheap sound card with little cat-scratch speakers, this amounts to a fairly low-rent orchestra.

The really high-tech aspect of StartSong is timeSetEvent, which causes the precision timer functions of the Windows multimedia

extensions to call TimeFunc once every so often with demonic precision. In this case, every so often is once for every sixteenth note, as defined by the constants in MIDIMAN.H. More elaborate music software would want to increase the timer frequency, at least to deal with thirty-second notes.

The StopSong function restores the MIDI output volume, closes the MIDI channel, and powers down the timer.

All the music is actually played by TimeFunc. Each time it's called, TimeFunc locates the next note in the array of NOTE objects it's working with and processes it. It will send a MIDI NOTE ON message by calling PlayNote when it encounters a NOTE containing note information, and set the timeleft element of the SONG object it's dealing with to indicate how many timer intervals should elapse until the note can be considered well and truly played.

NOTE objects might also contain voice changes and the ENDSONG constant, which TimeFunc will interpret as the day the music died. It will send an MM_MIDIFINISHED message to the window it was initially called from and speak no more.

Once it has initiated the playing of a note, TimeFunc will do nothing on subsequent invocations of itself save for decrementing the timeleft field of the SONG object for the tune being played. When this value hits zero, TimeFunc will call StopNote to send a MIDI NOTE OFF message and step along to the next note in the list.

The structure of the NOTE object array used by the StartSong function in MIDIMAN.DLL is somewhat arbitrary—it has been contrived to deal with the Irish fiddle tunes that PLAYSONG performs. If you want to implement MIDI music in software, you'll no doubt have cause to expand on it somewhat.

Any application that wants to do more with MIDI than play canned music from a file will require something along these lines. Unlike the situation with wave files, there are no provisions in the Windows multimedia extensions to play directly MIDI information stored in memory. The StartSong function and its associated elements can be used as the basis of a complete in-memory MIDI playing facility.

Video for Windows

CHAPTER 7

"Send more tourists. . .. The last ones were delicious."
—Graffiti

THE initial premise of Video for Windows was likely something along the lines of showing video clips in small windows, with little more in the cards. This probably wasn't an unreasonable notion—a technology that doesn't do anything particularly useful can be forgiven for offering a dearth of options while it's busy not doing it. To be sure, productive uses for Video for Windows remain thin on the ground.

Despite requiring a high-end display card, lots of hard drive space, and a state-of-the-art computer to make it go, the image quality of Video for Windows can typically be surpassed by a hundred-dollar portable television from Sears with the rabbit ears connected. On anything less than a Pentium system with local-bus video, AVI movies tend to play erratically, skipping frames to maintain their playback speeds and gradually slipping out of sync with their sound tracks as a result.

For practical purposes, AVI files of a length and size to make them interesting are too large to distribute on anything other than CD-ROMs. Most CD-ROM readers are too slow to play such files in real time. There are numerous subtle penalties inherent in riding the leading edge.

Despite the limitations, there are certainly potential uses for Video for Windows—if you become involved in creating complex multimedia applications for Windows, the facility to produce canned animation might well be a genuinely interesting feature. Rather than describing it as largely unproductive, it might be fairer to say of Video for Windows that it's a nascent technology, something beyond the state of the art that the rest of us just lack the insight to appreciate.

Having survived into technological adolescence, Video for Windows has expanded somewhat from its early specifications. If you have explored the Video for Windows facilities discussed in *Multimedia*

Programming for Windows, you'll know that the basic AVI interface allowed for AVI movie files to be played—and that's about it.

Not long ago as I write this, Microsoft released version 1.1 of its Video for Windows Software Development Kit. Fairly seething with new facilities, it offers considerable extensions over the basic AVI interface facilities hitherto available. While this chapter doesn't discuss them all in detail, it will provide you with a comfortable introduction to the blackest of the black arts surrounding Video for Windows. It will also get you over one somewhat troubling detail of the Version 1.1 Video for Windows SDK.

If you're not writing in a Microsoft language, the whole thing's wholly unusable. At least, it certainly appears to be. We'll look at how to work around this little inconvenience as well.

AVI behind the screen

A Video for Windows movie—an AVI file—is a species of RIFF file. The RIFF file format is discussed at length in *Windows Multimedia Programming*. In theory, the RIFF format is *extremely elegant*, made more so by the RIFF file software interface that's part of the Windows multimedia extensions.

Without getting too deeply into the RIFF file structure, RIFF allows applications to store blocks of data in a flexible, extensible way. It also allows complex data—such as the images and sound track of a Video for Windows movie—to be structured such that they can be accessed quickly and without severe memory penalties. At least, they can be accessed with memory penalties no more severe than need be inherent in something as cumbersome as real-time video handled in software.

The RIFF format is also used to store wave files, among other things.

While a wonderful concept in theory, the RIFF file structure was beset by mutant cybernetic lawyers when it came time to define AVI files. There's no single RIFF structure applicable to Video for Windows. While

each image in a video sequence is stored individually, AVI files can be created compressed, uncompressed, interleaved, in sequence, almost in sequence, in streams, with no sound track, with one sound track, with many sound tracks, with and without JUNK chunks, and so on. The permutations are daunting, and most software authors who have tried to use the RIFF file functions to work with AVI files have found the experience to be a lot like trying to teach skunks to tap dance.

One of the many improvements offered by the new Video for Windows Software Development Kit is that your applications will never again have to deal with another RIFF file chunk. The new SDK will seamlessly read and write individual AVI image frames, handling them as conventional Windows device-independent bitmaps. This makes the creation of software to read, write, or modify AVI files breathtakingly easy to manage.

You can simply command the AVI libraries to fetch a frame for you and let them do all the RIFF chunk management behind the scenes. They'll handle all the AVI variations, too.

The only catch is that the libraries performing all this magic behind your back won't work with versions of Video for Windows older than 1.1. Specifically, the original 1.0 release of the software will not get along well with the libraries, or with your applications that use them.

If you create commercial software that uses Video for Windows, you're permitted to distribute with it a run-time version of Video for Windows. It can all live on a single high-density floppy disk. The contents of such a disk, including a convenient installation function, are provided in a subdirectory of the Video for Windows Software Development Kit CD-ROM. This makes the process of ensuring that users of your software have a suitable version of Video for Windows installed in their systems fairly painless.

Another highly attractive aspect of the new Video for Windows Software Development Kit is that it offers an alternative to the rather pedestrian display window that pops up to contain an AVI file played through the default MCI interface discussed in *Multimedia Programming for Windows*. Figure 7-1 illustrates what Video for Windows can look like with its new window dressing.

Figure 7-1

An AVI file playing with an MCIWnd *window.*

While AVI files are still played through the MCI interface—and as such embody all the convenient playback controls it offers—the new AVI libraries offer you a much greater degree of control over the creation of AVI windows, and over how an AVI file can communicate with the application that spawned it.

The window in Fig. 7-1 includes a number of handy controls. You can play an AVI file normally by clicking on the Play button in the lower left corner of the window. If you hold down the Shift key when you do so, the movie in question will play backwards. The button to the right of the Play button will sprout a menu if you click on it, allowing you to configure how the movie will appear. It will also give you access to some fairly exotic facilities, such as a command-line interface for entering MCI command strings. You can adjust the playback volume for a movie with a sound track—often something of a mercy for AVI files recorded with everything cranked up to 10.

Figure 7-2 illustrates the options menu of an AVI movie.

Figure 7-2

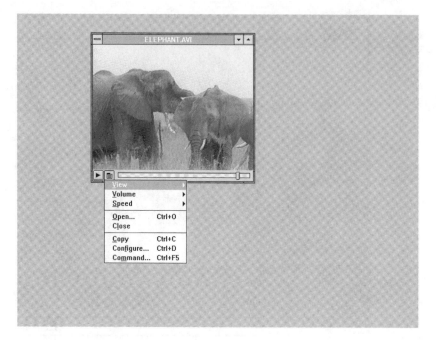

The options menu of an AVI movie.

The scroll bar at the bottom of the window in Fig. 7-1 allows you to manually select the current frame in an animation sequence. If you drag the scroll bar's thumb around, the video will change accordingly. This can be used either when a movie is running or after it has been stopped. As discussed later in this chapter, an AVI movie can be instructed to notify your application when this control is operated.

In addition to being very slick and state of the art, the alternate Video for Windows playback window actually requires less work to implement than conventional MCI interface playback. The whole works requires fewer than a dozen lines of code.

The Video for Windows Software Development Kit comes on two CD-ROMs—you'll need a CD-ROM drive to work with it. This probably won't be much of a limitation, since you'll need one to access most elements of multimedia. The package includes Video for Windows 1.1 as well, and a CD-ROM of sample AVI files.

The first potential catch in using the Video for Windows SDK is that it insists on installing itself in its entirety. In addition to the libraries and header files and such that are needed for accessing the new facilities of Video for Windows, the SDK will also grace your hard drive with all manner of executable files, examples, and so on which you probably won't need.

The whole works occupies about 11 megabytes. Something like 10 megabytes of this can be deleted. You will, however, need at least this much free space to survive the installation procedure.

One of the things notable by its absence from the Video for Windows SDK is any sort of printed manual. The documentation for the package is provided in an extensive Windows Help file, which can be accessed either through the conventional Help function or through a somewhat more elaborate stand-alone search engine installed with the rest of the package. As you might imagine, it's singularly inconvenient to use if you're trying to get familiar with the new libraries. There's no obvious way to just print the beast.

You can access the Video for Windows Help file as a stand-alone application by clicking on the Programmer's Guide icon in the Video for Windows 1.1 SDK Program Manager group that's created when the package is installed.

A printed manual is available for the Video for Windows SDK—it just costs a bit more. At the bottom of the first screen of the Help file, you'll find a toll-free number to call to order it. The manual purports to have a price associated with it to cover the cost of printing and shipping. As of this writing, the price is $30, plus $6 more for shipping.

It would be unfair to say that the Video for Windows SDK is wholly unworkable without its printed documentation—you can bash your way through it by frequent recourse to the Help file and the sample application source code files installed with the package. Most of the code discussed in this chapter, and the entire AVI section of the Graphic Workshop for Windows application on the companion CD-ROM for this book, were written prior to the arrival of the

manual. I think it would have taken about a third of the time had the book arrived with the CD-ROMs, however.

When I called to order the manual, I was told that Microsoft wouldn't ship it outside the United States. Being, in fact, outside the United States, I was forced to cheat and have them send it to the offices of Windcrest Books, which then forwarded it to me. If you'll be ordering the manual from distant parts of the world as well, either plan to have a convenient front man in the States, or see if your local Microsoft office can get it for you.

There is one more catch to working with the Video for Windows SDK. It's quite a nasty catch, too. The approved method of getting access to all the exciting new functions in the AVI libraries is to include the VFW.H header file in your application source code and then add the VFW.LIB library to the module list for the application being compiled. In the case of Borland C++ for Windows, you'd add it to your project file list.

Actually, when you compile your application—assuming your compiler wasn't written by Microsoft—you'll encounter a fatal linker error when your linker attempts to ingest a 32-bit object module record in VFW.LIB, and that will be the end of the whole works. The VFW.LIB library, the interface to the Video for Windows 1.1 facilities, appears to have been hardwired to use Microsoft's languages. It wants nothing to do with anything from Borland.

As an aside, you'll also encounter at least four spurious warnings from VFW.H when a Borland compiler attempts to work with it. These can be ignored.

Needless to say, there is a way to get around this apparent impasse, although it's not mentioned in the Video for Windows SDK documentation and it will probably be less than obvious. It turns out that VFW.LIB is a peculiar sort of DLL import library—peculiar because it actually supports several DLL files and because it has a 32-bit record in it.

You can work around the problem with VFW.LIB by simply ignoring it. Use the Import Librarian application that accompanies Borland

C++ for Windows to create new import libraries for the relevant DLLs from the Video for Windows SDK, add these to your application's project file rather than VFW.LIB, and all will be well.

The aforementioned four spurious warnings will still appear, but with the great triple-headed 32-bit swamp dragon slain, it's fairly easy to just pretend they aren't there.

Suitable import libraries are included with the source code on the companion CD-ROM for this book, along with the DLL files they support. If you use these, you needn't even warm up the Import Librarian. Note, however, that you must have the Video for Windows Software Development Kit Version 1.1 or better to compile the applications discussed in this section. You must also have Version 1.1 or better of Video for Windows itself installed on your system.

The AVI player

The window in Fig. 7-1 was created by the VIEWAVI.CPP application. A bear of very little brain, it will open and immediately play the AVI movie of your choice. This will include both the video—in a sophisticated window with a scroll bar and such—and a sound track, if one is present. While arguably not much to look at as movie players go, it serves to illustrate how to use the MCIWndCreate function and its dependent library calls.

Figure 7-3 illustrates the VIEWAVI.CPP source code file. Figure 7-4 illustrates VIEWAVI.RC, its resource script. In addition to these files, you'll need PRJ and DEF files for VIEWAVI, and the WAV and BMP files included in VIEWAVI.RC. You will find all these files on the companion CD-ROM for this book.

The VIEWAVI.CPP source code.   Figure 7-3

```
/*
        View AVI
        Copyright (c) 1993 Alchemy Mindworks Inc.

        NOTE: This program... any anything else that includes
        VFW.H... will compile with four warnings:
```

Figure 7-3   *Continued.*

```
                    Redefinition of 'mmioFOURCC' is not identical
                    Redefinition of 'ACMFORMATCHOOSE_STYLEF_ENABLETEM' is not identical
                    Redefinition of 'ACMFILTERCHOOSE_STYLEF_ENABLETEM' is not identical
                    'dwICValue' is declared but never used

                    These are a peculiarity of the Video for Windows SDK... ignore them.

*/
#include <windows.h>
#include <stdio.h>
#include <dir.h>
#include <string.h>
#include <bwcc.h>
#include <commdlg.h>
#include <vfw.h>

#define say(s)        MessageBox(NULL,s,"Yo...",MB_OK ¦ MB_ICONSTOP);
#define saynumber(f,s)     {char b[128]; sprintf((LPSTR)b,(LPSTR)f,s); \
                    MessageBox(NULL,b,"Debug Message",MB_OK ¦ MB_ICONSTOP); \
                    }

#define ItemName(item,string)      { dlgH=GetDlgItem(hwnd,item); \
                           SetWindowText(dlgH,(LPSTR)string); \
                           }

#define ItemOn(item)       { dlgH=GetDlgItem(hwnd,item); \
                    EnableWindow(dlgH,TRUE); \
                    EnableMenuItem(hmenu,item,MF_ENABLED);\
                    }

#define ItemOff(item)      { dlgH=GetDlgItem(hwnd,item); \
                    EnableWindow(dlgH,FALSE); \
                    EnableMenuItem(hmenu,item,MF_GRAYED);\
                    }

#define STRINGSIZE     128            /* how big is a string? */

#define MAIN_OPEN      101
#define MAIN_ABOUT     104
#define MAIN_EXIT      199

#define MCIWNDF_SHOWNAME        0x0010  // show name in caption
#define MCIWNDF_SHOWPOS         0x0020  // show position in caption
#define MCIWNDF_SHOWMODE        0x0040  // show mode in caption
#define MCIWNDF_SHOWALL         0x0070  // show all

#define DoMessage(hwnd,string) BWCCMessageBox(hwnd,string,"Message",\
                    MB_OK ¦ MB_ICONINFORMATION)

#ifndef max
#define max(a,b)               (((a)>(b))?(a):(b))
```

```
#endif
#ifndef min
#define min(a,b)               (((a)<(b))?(a):(b))
#endif

/* prototypes */
DWORD FAR PASCAL SelectProc(HWND hwnd,WORD message,WORD wParam,LONG lParam);
DWORD FAR PASCAL AboutDlgProc(HWND hwnd,WORD message,WORD wParam,LONG lParam);

DWORD HandleCtlColour(HWND hwnd,WORD wParam,DWORD lParam);

HWND PlayFile(HWND hwnd,LPSTR path);

int GetOpenFileName(HWND hwnd,LPSTR path);

void lmemset(LPSTR s,int n,unsigned int size);
void CentreWindow(HWND hwnd);

/* globals */
char szAppName[] = "ViewAVI";
HANDLE hInst;
LPSTR messagehook;

#pragma warn -par
int PASCAL WinMain(HANDLE hInstance,HANDLE hPrevInstance,
               LPSTR lpszCmdParam,int nCmdShow)
{
        FARPROC dlgProc;
        int r=0;

        BWCCGetVersion();

        if(lstrlen(lpszCmdParam)) messagehook=lpszCmdParam;
        else messagehook=NULL;

        hInst=hInstance;

        dlgProc=MakeProcInstance((FARPROC)SelectProc,hInst);
        r=DialogBox(hInst,"MainScreen",NULL,dlgProc);

        FreeProcInstance(dlgProc);

        return(r);
}

DWORD FAR PASCAL SelectProc(HWND hwnd,WORD message,WORD wParam,LONG lParam)
{
        static HWND hwndMovie;
        HWND dlgH;
        PAINTSTRUCT ps;
        HICON hIcon;
        FARPROC lpfnDlgProc;
        char b[STRINGSIZE+1];
```

Figure 7-3   *Continued.*

```
switch(message) {
        case WM_CTLCOLOR:
                return(HandleCtlColour(hwnd,wParam,lParam));
        case WM_SYSCOMMAND:
                switch(wParam & 0xfff0) {
                        case SC_CLOSE:
                                SendMessage(hwnd,WM_COMMAND,MAIN_EXIT,0L);
                                break;
                }
                break;
        case WM_INITDIALOG:
                hwndMovie=NULL;

                if(HIWORD(VideoForWindowsVersion()) < 0x010a) {
                        DoMessage(hwnd,
                            "Your version of Video for Windows is too old.");
                        PostMessage(hwnd,WM_COMMAND,MAIN_EXIT,0L);
                }

                if(MCIWndRegisterClass(hInst)==NULL) {
                        DoMessage(hwnd,
                            "Unable to register the MCI window.");
                        PostMessage(hwnd,WM_COMMAND,MAIN_EXIT,0L);
                }

                hIcon=LoadIcon(hInst,szAppName);
                SetClassWord(hwnd,GCW_HICON,(WORD)hIcon);

                CentreWindow(hwnd);

                if(messagehook != NULL) {
                        if((hwndMovie=PlayFile(hwnd,messagehook))==NULL)
                            DoMessage(hwnd,"Error playing file");
                }
                break;
        case WM_PAINT:
                BeginPaint(hwnd,&ps);
                EndPaint(hwnd,&ps);
                break;
        case WM_COMMAND:
                switch(wParam) {
                        case MAIN_OPEN:
                                if(hwndMovie != NULL) MCIWndDestroy(hwndMovie);
                                if(GetOpenFileName(hwnd,b)) {
                                        if((hwndMovie=PlayFile(hwnd,b))==NULL)
                                                DoMessage(hwnd,
                                                        "Error playing file");
                                }
                                break;
                        case MAIN_ABOUT:
                                if((lpfnDlgProc=MakeProcInstance((FARPROC)
```

```
                                          AboutDlgProc,hInst)) != NULL) {
                                          DialogBox(hInst,"AboutBox",
                                              hwnd,lpfnDlgProc);
                                          FreeProcInstance(lpfnDlgProc);
                                      }
                                      break;
                              case MAIN_EXIT:
                                      if(hwndMovie != NULL) MCIWndDestroy(hwndMovie);
                                      PostQuitMessage(0);
                                      break;
                      }
                      break;
          }

          return(FALSE);
}

DWORD FAR PASCAL AboutDlgProc(HWND hwnd,WORD message,WORD wParam,LONG lParam)
{
          static HANDLE sound;
          static LPSTR psound;
          HANDLE handle;

          switch(message) {
                  case WM_INITDIALOG:
                          if((handle=FindResource(hInst,"AboutWave",
                              RT_RCDATA)) != NULL) {
                                  if((sound=LoadResource(hInst,handle)) != NULL) {
                                          if((psound=LockResource(sound)) != NULL)
                                              sndPlaySound(psound,SND_ASYNC |
                                                  SND_MEMORY | SND_NOSTOP);
                                  }
                          }
                          CentreWindow(hwnd);
                          return(FALSE);
                  case WM_CTLCOLOR:
                          return(HandleCtlColour(hwnd,wParam,lParam));
                  case WM_COMMAND:
                          switch(wParam) {
                                  case IDOK:
                                          sndPlaySound(NULL,SND_SYNC);
                                          if(psound != NULL) UnlockResource(sound);
                                          if(sound != NULL) FreeResource(sound);
                                          EndDialog(hwnd,wParam);
                                          return(FALSE);
                          }
                          break;
          }

          return(FALSE);
}

void lmemset(LPSTR s,int n,unsigned int size)
```

Figure 7-3 *Continued.*

```
{
        unsigned int i;

        for(i=0;i<size;++i) *s++=n;
}

int GetOpenFileName(HWND hwnd,LPSTR path)
{
        OPENFILENAME ofn;
        char szDirName[256],szFileTitle[256],szFilter[256];

        getcwd(szDirName,sizeof(szDirName)-1);

        lstrcpy(szFilter,"*.AVI");

        lmemset((LPSTR)&ofn,0,sizeof(OPENFILENAME));

        lstrcpy(path,"*.AVI");
        szFileTitle[0]=0;

        ofn.lStructSize=sizeof(OPENFILENAME);
        ofn.hwndOwner=hwnd;
        ofn.lpstrFilter="All files (*.*)\000*.*\000AVI files (*.AVI)\000*.AVI\000";
        ofn.lpstrFile=path;
        ofn.nFilterIndex=2;
        ofn.nMaxFile=STRINGSIZE;
        ofn.lpstrFileTitle=szFileTitle;
        ofn.nMaxFileTitle=sizeof(szFileTitle);
        ofn.lpstrInitialDir=szDirName;
        ofn.Flags=OFN_PATHMUSTEXIST | OFN_HIDEREADONLY;
        ofn.lpstrTitle="Open File";
        ofn.lpstrDefExt="AVI";

        if(!GetOpenFileName(&ofn)) {
                path[0]=0;
                return(FALSE);
        } else return(TRUE);
}
void CentreWindow(HWND hwnd)
{
        RECT rect;
        unsigned int x,y;

        GetWindowRect(hwnd,&rect);
        x=(GetSystemMetrics(SM_CXSCREEN)-(rect.right-rect.left))/2;
        y=(GetSystemMetrics(SM_CYSCREEN)-(rect.bottom-rect.top))/2;
        SetWindowPos(hwnd,NULL,x,y,rect.right-rect.left,
            rect.bottom-rect.top,SWP_NOSIZE);
}

DWORD HandleCtlColour(HWND hwnd,WORD wParam,DWORD lParam)
```

```
{
        POINT point;
        HBRUSH hBrush;

        if(HIWORD(lParam)==CTLCOLOR_STATIC ||
           HIWORD(lParam)==CTLCOLOR_DLG) {
                hBrush=GetStockObject(LTGRAY_BRUSH);
                SetBkColor(wParam,RGB(192,192,192));
                SetTextColor(wParam,RGB(0,0,0));

                ClientToScreen(hwnd,&point);
                UnrealizeObject(hBrush);
                SetBrushOrg(wParam,point.x,point.y);

                return((DWORD)hBrush);

        }
        if(HIWORD(lParam)==CTLCOLOR_BTN) {
                hBrush=GetStockObject(LTGRAY_BRUSH);
                SetBkColor(wParam,RGB(192,192,192));
                SetTextColor(wParam,RGB(0,0,0));

                ClientToScreen(hwnd,&point);
                UnrealizeObject(hBrush);
                SetBrushOrg(wParam,point.x,point.y);

                return((DWORD)hBrush);
        }
        return(FALSE);
}

HWND PlayFile(HWND hwnd,LPSTR path)
{
        HWND hwndMci;

        if((hwndMci=MCIWndCreate(hwnd,hInst,WS_DISABLED | WS_SYSMENU |
            WS_THICKFRAME | WS_MINIMIZEBOX | WS_MAXIMIZEBOX |
            MCIWNDF_SHOWNAME,NULL)) == NULL)
                return(NULL);

        MCIWndOpen(hwndMci,path,0);
        MCIWndPlay(hwndMci);

        CentreWindow(hwndMci);
        EnableWindow(hwndMci,TRUE);
        ShowWindow(hwndMci,SW_SHOWNORMAL);

        return(hwndMci);
}
```

Figure 7-4   *The VIEWAVI.RC resource script.*

```
MainScreen DIALOG 73, 50, 128, 48
STYLE WS_POPUP | WS_CAPTION | WS_SYSMENU | WS_MINIMIZEBOX
CAPTION "View AVI"
MENU MainMenu
BEGIN
        PUSHBUTTON "Open", 101, 32, 24, 28, 12, WS_CHILD | WS_VISIBLE | WS_TABSTOP
        PUSHBUTTON "Quit", 199, 68, 24, 28, 12, WS_CHILD | WS_VISIBLE | WS_TABSTOP
END

MainMenu MENU
BEGIN
        POPUP "&File"
        BEGIN
                MENUITEM "&Open", 101
                MENUITEM "&About", 104
                MENUITEM SEPARATOR
                MENUITEM "E&xit", 199
        END

END

AboutBox DIALOG 18, 18, 184, 180
STYLE WS_POPUP | WS_CAPTION
CAPTION "About..."
BEGIN
        CONTROL "", 102, "BorShade", BSS_GROUP | WS_CHILD |
            WS_VISIBLE | WS_TABSTOP, 8, 68, 168, 76
        CTEXT "View AVI 1.0\n\nCopyright (c) 1994 Alchemy Mindworks Inc.\n\n
            This program is part of the book Advanced Multimedia Programming
            for Windows by Steven William Rimmer, published by Windcrest/McGraw
            Hill.", -1, 12, 72, 160, 68, WS_CHILD | WS_VISIBLE | WS_GROUP
        CONTROL "Button", IDOK, "BorBtn", BS_DEFPUSHBUTTON | WS_CHILD | WS_VISIBLE |
            WS_TABSTOP, 74, 152, 32, 20
        CONTROL "Button", 801, "BorBtn", BS_PUSHBUTTON | WS_CHILD | WS_VISIBLE |
            WS_TABSTOP, 36, 8, 32, 20
END

ViewAVI ICON
BEGIN
            '00 00 01 00 01 00 20 20 10 00 00 00 00 00 E8 02'
            '00 00 16 00 00 00 28 00 00 00 20 00 00 00 40 00'
            '00 00 01 00 04 00 00 00 00 00 80 02 00 00 00 00'
            '00 00 00 00 00 00 10 00 00 00 00 00 00 00 00 00'
            '00 00 00 00 BF 00 00 00 BF 00 00 00 BF BF 00 00'
            '00 00 BF 00 BF 00 BF BF 00 00 C0 C0 C0 00 80 80'
            '80 00 00 00 FF 00 00 00 FF 00 00 00 FF FF 00 FF 00'
            '00 00 FF 00 FF 00 FF FF 00 00 FF FF FF 00 77 77'
            '77 77 77 77 77 77 77 77 77 77 77 77 77 77 7F 88'
            '88 88 88 88 88 88 88 88 88 88 88 88 88 87 7F F8'
            '88 88 88 88 88 88 88 88 88 88 88 88 88 87 7F F0'
            '00 07 77 F7 77 00 77 77 F7 77 70 00 08 87 7F F0'
```

```
'00 07 77 7F 77 70 77 7F 77 77 70 00 08 87 7F F0'
'00 07 77 77 F7 7F 77 F7 77 77 70 00 08 87 7F F0'
'00 07 77 77 7F FF FF 77 77 77 70 00 08 87 7F F0'
'FF 07 77 77 77 7F 77 77 77 77 70 FF 08 87 7F F0'
'FF 00 00 00 00 00 00 00 00 00 00 FF 08 87 7F F0'
'00 07 77 77 77 7F 77 77 77 77 70 00 08 87 7F F0'
'00 07 77 77 7F FF FF 77 77 77 70 00 08 87 7F F0'
'00 07 77 77 F7 7F 77 F7 77 77 70 00 08 87 7F F0'
'00 07 77 7F 70 00 00 7F 77 77 70 00 08 87 7F F0'
'00 07 77 F7 77 0F 77 77 F7 77 70 00 08 87 7F F0'
'FF 07 77 F7 77 70 77 77 F7 77 70 FF 08 87 7F F0'
'FF 07 FF FF FF FF 0F FF FF F7 70 FF 08 87 7F F0'
'00 07 77 F7 77 7F 70 77 F7 77 70 00 08 87 7F F0'
'00 07 77 F7 70 7F 70 77 F7 77 70 00 08 87 7F F0'
'00 07 77 7F 77 00 07 7F 77 77 70 00 08 87 7F F0'
'00 07 77 77 F7 7F 77 F7 77 77 70 00 08 87 7F F0'
'00 07 77 77 7F FF FF 77 77 77 70 00 08 87 7F F0'
'FF 07 77 77 77 7F 77 77 77 77 70 FF 08 87 7F F0'
'FF 00 00 00 00 00 00 00 00 00 00 FF 08 87 7F F0'
'00 07 77 77 77 7F 77 77 77 77 70 00 08 87 7F F0'
'00 07 77 77 7F FF FF 77 77 77 70 00 08 87 7F F0'
'00 07 77 77 F7 7F 77 F7 77 77 70 00 08 87 7F F0'
'00 07 77 7F 77 00 07 7F 77 77 70 00 08 87 7F F0'
'00 07 77 F7 70 7F 70 77 F7 77 70 00 08 87 7F F0'
'FF 07 77 F7 77 77 70 77 F7 77 70 FF 08 87 7F FF'
'FF FF FF FF FF FF FF FF FF FF FF FF F8 87 7F FF'
'FF FF FF FF FF FF FF FF FF FF FF FF 87 77 77'
'77 77 77 77 77 77 77 77 77 77 77 77 77 77 00 00'
'00 00 00 00 00 00 00 00 00 00 00 00 00 00 00 00'
'00 00 00 00 00 00 00 00 00 00 00 00 00 00 00 00'
'00 00 00 00 00 00 00 00 00 00 00 00 00 00 00 00'
'00 00 00 00 00 00 00 00 00 00 00 00 00 00 00 00'
'00 00 00 00 00 00 00 00 00 00 00 00 00 00 00 00'
'00 00 00 00 00 00 00 00 00 00 00 00 00 00 00 00'
'00 00 00 00 00 00 00 00 00 00 00 00 00 00 00 00'
'00 00 00 00 00 00 00 00 00 00 00 00 00 00 00'
END

1801 BITMAP "smpw.bmp"

AboutWave RCDATA "ABOUT.WAV"
```

You must also have the Video for Windows SDK installed on your hard drive—the VIEWAVI project file included on the companion CD-ROM for this book assumes that the VFW.H header and all its dependent headers are installed in the directory C:\VFWDK\INC. Make sure you change this prior to compiling VIEWAVI if you've installed the Video for Windows SDK elsewhere.

The VIEWAVI program will probably look largely familiar, as almost everything it does has turned up in earlier applications in this book. The only new element is the PlayFile function, the very last thing in VIEWAVI.CPP. Deceptively simple, this is the code that generates complex AVI windows and plays movies in them.

Note that many of the new MCI functions offered by the Video for Windows SDK are actually implemented as macros.

The MCIWndCreate function is extremely flexible. Analogous to the common CreateWindow function, it allows you to define a window to play AVI files in such a way that you can specify which elements of the window and the video-specific control objects will be visible. The arguments for MCIWndCreate are as follows:

```
MCIWndCreate(hwnd,hInst,flags,device)
```

The hwnd argument for MCIWndCreate is the window handle of the parent window from which the new AVI window will be spawned. This can also be left as NULL, although there are good reasons for not doing so, as we'll discuss in a moment. The hInst argument is the instance handle for your application, as passed to its WinMain function. The device argument is a string defining the name of the device that will generate whatever is to appear in the window about to be created. This should be NULL for AVI files.

The flags argument is a complicated little beast. It can embody both the WS_ flags appropriate for use with the traditional CreateWindows API call, as well as a few additional flags that pertain specifically to MCIWndCreate. If no WS_ flags are used to explicitly define the appearance of the window to be created, MCIWndCreate will use WS_CHILD | WS_BORDER | WS_VISIBLE if its hwnd argument is not NULL, or WS_OVERLAPPEDWINDOW | WS_VISIBLE otherwise. By using explicit WS_ flags, you can create AVI windows with any appearance you like. For example, you can have MCIWndCreate open a window without the usual system menu, caption, and such that AVI files usually find themselves surrounded by.

The additional flags which can be ORed with the flags argument include:

MCIWNDF_NOAUTOSIZEWINDOW	Prevents the window size from changing to suit the dimensions of the AVI file being displayed.
MCIWNDF_NOAUTOSIZEMOVIE	Prevents the AVI file being played from stretching to suit a resized window.
MCIWNDF_NOPLAYBAR	Prevents the appearance of the display controls bar below the AVI file being played. This bar includes the Play and Menu buttons and the position slider.
MCIWNDF_NOMENU	Prevents the appearance of a Menu button in the display controls bar.
MCIWNDF_RECORD	Adds a Record button to the display controls bar, and a Record item to its menu.
MCIWNDF_NOERRORDLG	Prevents the appearance of error dialogs, should an error be encountered during the playing of an AVI file. As discussed in a moment, you can have an AVI file notify your application if an error occurs.
MCIWNDF_NOTIFYMODE	Causes the parent window indicated by the hwnd argument to MCIWndCreate to be notified when the AVI file being displayed changes state. We'll discuss this in greater detail in a moment.
MCIWNDF_NOTIFYPOS	Causes the parent window indicated by the hwnd argument to MCIWndCreate to be notified when the AVI file being displayed changes position.

MCIWNDF_NOTIFYMEDIA	Causes the parent window indicated by the hwnd argument to MCIWndCreate to be notified when the AVI file being displayed changes media, as when a new file is opened.
MCIWNDF_NOTIFYSIZE	Causes the parent window indicated by the hwnd argument to MCIWndCreate to be notified when the AVI file being displayed changes size.
MCIWNDF_NOTIFYERROR	Causes the parent window indicated by the hwnd argument to MCIWndCreate to be notified when the AVI file being displayed encounters an error.
MCIWNDF_NOTIFYALL	Causes the parent window indicated by the hwnd argument to MCIWndCreate to be notified when the AVI file being displayed does almost anything at all. It's a combination of all the MCIWNDF_NOTIFY flags.
MCIWNDF_SHOWNAME	Allows the device name to be displayed in the title bar of the display window.
MCIWNDF_SHOWPOS	Allows the current file position— the frame number—to be displayed in the title bar of the display window.
MCIWNDF_SHOWMODE	Allows the device mode to be displayed in the title bar of the display window.
MCIWNDF_SHOWALL	Allows all the foregoing options to be displayed in the title bar of the display window. Note that the default window size for most AVI files will not create a title bar large enough to support all these items.

Perhaps the most useful of all these flags are the MCIWNDF_NOTIFY options. They can be used to have your AVI file tell the parent window that spawned it—or any other window you like—what it's up to. For example, if you include the MCIWNDF_NOTIFYMODE flag in the flags list, an MCIWNDM_NOTIFYMODE message will appear at the message handler of the window specified by the hwnd argument to MCIWndCreate whenever the mode of the AVI file being played changes. When this message appears, the low-order word of its lParam argument will contain a constant that defines the new mode of the AVI file being played. The constant will be one of the following:

MCI_MODE_NOT_READY	The avivideo device is not ready.
MCI_MODE_STOP	The movie has been stopped.
MCI_MODE_PLAY	The movie has started playing.
MCI_MODE_RECORD	A movie has begun recording.
MCI_MODE_SEEK	The movie is seeking a new location.
MCI_MODE_PAUSE	The movie has been paused.
MCI_MODE_OPEN	The avivideo device is being opened.

You can use the MCIWNDM_NOTIFYMODE message to present a status display of the AVI movie being played, or to control it in the event that specific conditions appear. For example, by default, a window created by MCIWndCreate will play the movie it's associated with and then hang around until it's explicitly closed. Assuming that the window had been created with the MCIWNDF_NOTIFYMODE flag, you could have it terminate immediately upon the completion of its performance by adding the following case to the message handler for its parent window:

```
case MCIWNDM_NOTIFYMODE:
        if(LOWORD(lParam)==MCI_MODE_STOP)
            MCIWndDestroy(hwndMovie);
```

The hwndMovie window handle will be the value returned by PlayFile. The MCIWndDestroy function will both close an MCI window if it's open and release any objects associated with it.

Note that the MCIWNDM_NOTIFY messages are actually WM_USER messages. They're defined like this:

```
#define MCIWNDM_NOTIFYMODE      (WM_USER + 200)
#define MCIWNDM_NOTIFYPOS       (WM_USER + 201)
#define MCIWNDM_NOTIFYSIZE      (WM_USER + 202)
#define MCIWNDM_NOTIFYMEDIA     (WM_USER + 203)
#define MCIWNDM_NOTIFYERROR     (WM_USER + 205)
```

If your application makes use of WM_USER messages for other purposes, be certain they don't have the same offsets as the MCIWNDM_NOTIFY messages.

The arguments to MCIWndCreate in PlayFile include WS_ flags to set up a conventional AVI window with most of its interesting elements enabled. This does not include a Record button—you can add one if you like—nor does it include the aforementioned MCIWNDF_NOTIFYMODE flag, because an AVI player as simple as VIEWAVI arguably has no good reason to be sending status messages to its parent window. You'll note, however, that the window is created initially disabled. In theory this shouldn't be necessary, but theories under Windows are often cheaper than year-old Hondas.

In reality, it takes a noticeable amount of time for an AVI file to begin playing after MCIWndCreate opens its window. In the interim, a peculiar window consisting of nothing but a title bar and a system menu will appear. By creating the playback window disabled, this unwanted object will not be visible.

Once a suitable playback window has been created by MCIWndCreate, the AVI file to be played can be opened with a call to MCIWndOpen. The MCIWndPlay function starts it playing. The EnableWindow and ShowWindow calls make the previously hidden window visible.

The PlayFile function returns an HWND window handle to the playing AVI file. This object should be preserved by the calling function—in this case by SelectProc—and passed to MCIWndDestroy when the window is to be closed.

The MCIWndCreate function and the other enhanced MCI resources included with the Video for Windows Software Development Kit offer

a wealth of playback features. They're well worth exploring if you can think up some exotic applications for Video for Windows.

One of the sample applications included with the Video for Windows Software Development Kit—and present on your hard drive, if you haven't deleted all the unnecessary files yet—is MCIPLAY, a much more complex AVI player. It uses many of the same function calls as VIEWAVI, but it's a complete multiple-document interface application, allowing several AVI files to be open at once. It also manages to work in some additional MCIWnd calls, illustrating their use. The MCIPLAY.C source file is exceedingly daunting, especially if it's the first thing you come across in trying to implement the MCIWnd facilities. However, once you have VIEWAVI on the mats you might want to look at MCIPLAY.C, should you be interested in extending these facilities further.

Working with AVI files

As discussed earlier in this chapter, the RIFF file structure that forms the basis of Video for Windows movies is elegant and easy to work with in theory, but something of an incensed Burmese tiger in a roomful of poodles when it comes to actually implementing real-world AVI files with it. In earlier times this would have required the creation of very complex functions to deal with all the permutations. The release 1.1 of Video for Windows lets you ignore the whole works—it will do all the file handling for you.

The AVI file-handling functions of Video for Windows are accessed through the AVIFILE.DLL library included with the Video for Windows Software Development Kit. This is one of the DLLs intended to be supported by VFW.LIB. For reasons discussed earlier in this chapter, its appearance in the application presented in this section will involve its having an import library of its own, AVIFILE.LIB, as created by the Import Librarian. You can either create one yourself or use the AVIFILE.LIB included with the source code on the companion CD-ROM for this book.

You will still need the Video for Windows SDK to compile the program we'll be looking at here, however, as it provides VFW.H and the other dependent header files.

The AVI file functions will allow you to extract individual frames from AVI movies and have them available in a useful form. While we won't discuss the details here, these functions will also allow you to create AVI movies from an initial array of device-independent bitmaps. The Graphic Workshop for Windows application on the companion CD-ROM for this book uses these resources to handle AVI files.

The application discussed in this section is called STORYBRD, or StoryBoard. It will read the frames from an AVI file and display a matrix of them in a window. Figure 7-5 illustrates StoryBoard at work. This is the starship Enterprise going into warp drive, a special effect for which Industrial Light and Magic is said to have spent a great deal of time while working out the mechanics. You can see it in detail in StoryBoard.

Figure 7-5

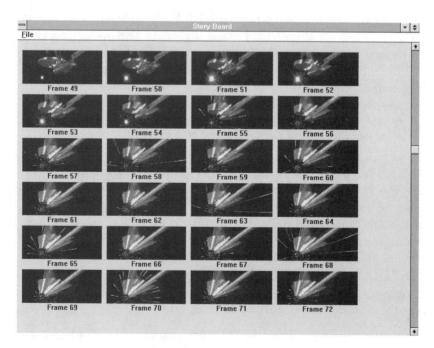

The AVI StoryBoard application.

The operation of StoryBoard is pretty elementary. It begins reading frames at an arbitrary location in the AVI file to be displayed. The location is the first frame by default, but if more frames exist than can be displayed at once, the scroll bar in the StoryBoard window can be used to start viewing part way down the list. Each frame is fetched from the AVI file as a device-independent bitmap and displayed. The techniques involved work more or less like those discussed in detail in Chapter 3 of this book.

In fact, because multiple individual bitmaps are involved in this application, you should be able to do only one of the images in the matrix correctly at a time, as each one could have a different palette. The StoryBoard window gets away with ignoring this problem because AVI files typically don't change palettes part way through an animation sequence. This is actually not a particularly good assumption to make in real-world software that works with AVI files, as there's nothing stopping an AVI file from changing palettes.

AVI files having 24-bit frames do exist. If you attempt to display one with StoryBoard on a system with a 256-color Windows display driver installed, you'll see fairly coarse color-remapped frames.

Figure 7-6 illustrates the STORYBRD.CPP source code file. Figure 7-7 illustrates STORYBRD.RC, its resource script. In addition to these files, you'll need PRJ and DEF files for StoryBoard, and the WAV and BMP files included in STORYBRD.RC. You will find all these files on the companion CD-ROM for this book.

The STORYBRD.CPP source code.　　　　　　　　　　　　　　Figure 7-6

```
/*

        Story Board
        Copyright (c) 1993 Alchemy Mindworks Inc.

        NOTE: This program... any anything else that includes
        VFW.H... will compile with four warnings:

        Redefinition of 'mmioFOURCC' is not identical
        Redefinition of 'ACMFORMATCHOOSE_STYLEF_ENABLETEM' is not identical
        Redefinition of 'ACMFILTERCHOOSE_STYLEF_ENABLETEM' is not identical
        'dwICValue' is declared but never used

        These are a peculiarity of the Video for Windows SDK... ignore them.
```

Figure 7-6 *Continued.*

```c
*/
#include <windows.h>
#include <stdio.h>
#include <dir.h>
#include <alloc.h>
#include <string.h>
#include <bwcc.h>
#include <commdlg.h>
#include <vfw.h>

#define say(s)          MessageBox(NULL,s,"Yo...",MB_OK | MB_ICONSTOP);
#define saynumber(f,s)      {char b[128]; sprintf((LPSTR)b,(LPSTR)f,s); \
                        MessageBox(NULL,b,"Debug Message",MB_OK | MB_ICONSTOP); \
                        }

#define ItemName(item,string)    { dlgH=GetDlgItem(hwnd,item); \
                            SetWindowText(dlgH,(LPSTR)string); \
                            }

#define ItemOn(item)        { dlgH=GetDlgItem(hwnd,item); \
                        EnableWindow(dlgH,TRUE); \
                        EnableMenuItem(hmenu,item,MF_ENABLED);\
                        }

#define ItemOff(item)       { dlgH=GetDlgItem(hwnd,item); \
                        EnableWindow(dlgH,FALSE); \
                        EnableMenuItem(hmenu,item,MF_GRAYED);\
                        }

#define STRINGSIZE      128             /* how big is a string? */

#define MAIN_OPEN       101
#define MAIN_ABOUT      104
#define MAIN_EXIT       199

#define HMARGIN         10
#define VMARGIN         20

#define  DoMessage(hwnd,string) BWCCMessageBox(hwnd,string,"Message",\
                            MB_OK | MB_ICONINFORMATION)

#ifndef max
#define max(a,b)            (((a)>(b))?(a):(b))
#endif
#ifndef min
#define min(a,b)            (((a)<(b))?(a):(b))
#endif

/* prototypes */
DWORD FAR PASCAL SelectProc(HWND hwnd,WORD message,WORD wParam,LONG lParam);
DWORD FAR PASCAL AboutDlgProc(HWND hwnd,WORD message,WORD wParam,LONG lParam);
```

```
DWORD HandleCtlColour(HWND hwnd,WORD wParam,DWORD lParam);

int GetOpenFileName(HWND hwnd,LPSTR path);

void lmemset(LPSTR s,int n,unsigned int size);
void CentreWindow(HWND hwnd);

int OpenAVIFile(LPSTR path);
int DrawDib(HDC hdc,int x,int y,LPBITMAPINFOHEADER lpbi);

LPBITMAPINFOHEADER GetAVIFrame(unsigned int number);
void CloseAVIFile();

/* globals */
char szAppName[] = "StoryBoard";
HANDLE hInst;
LPSTR messagehook;
PAVIFILE pfile;
PAVISTREAM pstream;
PGETFRAME pget;

#pragma warn -par
int PASCAL WinMain(HANDLE hInstance,HANDLE hPrevInstance,
                LPSTR lpszCmdParam,int nCmdShow)
{
        FARPROC dlgProc;
        int r=0;

        BWCCGetVersion();

        if(lstrlen(lpszCmdParam)) messagehook=lpszCmdParam;
        else messagehook=NULL;

        hInst=hInstance;

        dlgProc=MakeProcInstance((FARPROC)SelectProc,hInst);
        r=DialogBox(hInst,"MainScreen",NULL,dlgProc);

        FreeProcInstance(dlgProc);

        return(r);
}

DWORD FAR PASCAL SelectProc(HWND hwnd,WORD message,WORD wParam,LONG lParam)
{
        static int frames,framesacross;
        LPBITMAPINFOHEADER lpbi;
        PAINTSTRUCT ps;
        HICON hIcon;
        HDC hdc;
        FARPROC lpfnDlgProc;
        RECT rect;
        int i,j,n,x,y;
```

427

Figure 7-6 *Continued.*

```
            char b[STRINGSIZE+1];

            switch(message) {
                    case WM_CTLCOLOR:
                            return(HandleCtlColour(hwnd,wParam,lParam));
                    case WM_SYSCOMMAND:
                            switch(wParam & 0xfff0) {
                                    case SC_CLOSE:
                                            SendMessage(hwnd,WM_COMMAND,MAIN_EXIT,0L);
                                            break;
                            }
                            break;
                    case WM_INITDIALOG:
                            frames=-1;

                            if(HIWORD(VideoForWindowsVersion()) < 0x010a) {
                                    DoMessage(hwnd,
                                            "Your version of Video for Windows is too old.");
                                    PostMessage(hwnd,WM_COMMAND,MAIN_EXIT,0L);
                            }

                            hIcon=LoadIcon(hInst,szAppName);
                            SetClassWord(hwnd,GCW_HICON,(WORD)hIcon);

                            CentreWindow(hwnd);

                            if(messagehook != NULL) {
                                    if(!OpenAVIFile(messagehook))
                                            DoMessage(hwnd,"Error opening file");
                                    else
                                            frames=(int)AVIStreamLength(pstream);
                            }
                    case WM_SIZE:
                            if(frames != -1) {
                                    GetClientRect(hwnd,&rect);
                                    if((lpbi=GetAVIFrame(0)) != NULL) {
                                            framesacross=max((rect.right-rect.left)/
                                                    ((int)lpbi->biWidth+HMARGIN),1);
                                            y=(rect.bottom-rect.top)/
                                                    ((int)lpbi->biHeight+VMARGIN);
                                            n=(frames/framesacross)-y+1;
                                            SetScrollRange(hwnd,SB_VERT,0,n,FALSE);
                                    }
                            }

                            i=GetScrollPos(hwnd,SB_VERT);
                            if(i > n) i=n;

                            SetScrollPos(hwnd,SB_VERT,i,TRUE);

                            InvalidateRect(hwnd,NULL,TRUE);
```

```
                break;
case WM_VSCROLL:
        n=GetScrollPos(hwnd,SB_VERT);
        GetScrollRange(hwnd,SB_VERT,&x,&y);
        i=max(y/8,1);
        switch(wParam) {
                case SB_LINEUP:
                        n-=1;
                        break;
                case SB_LINEDOWN:
                        n+=1;
                        break;
                case SB_PAGEUP:
                        n-=i;
                        break;
                case SB_PAGEDOWN:
                        n+=i;
                        break;
                case SB_THUMBPOSITION:
                        n=LOWORD(lParam);
                        break;
        }

        if(n < 0) n=0;
        else if(n > y) n=y;

        if(n != GetScrollPos(hwnd,SB_VERT)) {
                SetScrollPos(hwnd,SB_VERT,n,TRUE);
                InvalidateRect(hwnd,NULL,TRUE);
        }
        return(FALSE);
case WM_PAINT:
        hdc=BeginPaint(hwnd,&ps);
        SetTextAlign(hdc,TA_CENTER);
        SetBkColor(hdc,RGB(192,192,192));

        if(frames != -1) {
                GetClientRect(hwnd,&rect);
                x=HMARGIN;
                y=VMARGIN;
                for(i=GetScrollPos(hwnd,SB_VERT)*framesacross,j=0;
                    i<frames;++i,++j) {
                        if((lpbi=GetAVIFrame(i)) == NULL)
                            continue;

                        if(j && (x+(int)lpbi->biWidth+HMARGIN) >=
                            (rect.right-rect.left)) {
                                x=HMARGIN;
                                y+=(int)lpbi->biHeight+VMARGIN;
                                if((y+(int)lpbi->biHeight+VMARGIN) >=
                                    (rect.bottom-rect.top)) break;
                        }
```

Figure 7-6   *Continued.*

```
                                DrawDib(hdc,x,y,lpbi);
                                n=wsprintf(b,"Frame %u",i+1);
                                TextOut(hdc,
                                    x+((int)lpbi->biWidth/2),
                                    y+(int)lpbi->biHeight,b,n);

                                x+=(int)lpbi->biWidth+HMARGIN;
                            }
                        }
                        EndPaint(hwnd,&ps);
                        break;
                case WM_COMMAND:
                        switch(wParam) {
                            case MAIN_OPEN:
                                if(frames != -1) CloseAVIFile();
                                if(GetOpenFileName(hwnd,b)) {
                                    if(!OpenAVIFile(b))
                                        DoMessage(hwnd,
                                            "Error opening file");
                                    else {
                                        frames=(int)
                                            AVIStreamLength(pstream);
                                        InvalidateRect(hwnd,NULL,TRUE);
                                    }
                                }
                                break;
                            case MAIN_ABOUT:
                                if((lpfnDlgProc=MakeProcInstance((FARPROC)
                                    AboutDlgProc,hInst)) != NULL) {
                                    DialogBox(hInst,"AboutBox",
                                        hwnd,lpfnDlgProc);
                                    FreeProcInstance(lpfnDlgProc);
                                }
                                break;
                            case MAIN_EXIT:
                                if(frames != -1) CloseAVIFile();
                                PostQuitMessage(0);
                                break;
                        }
                        break;
            }

        return(FALSE);
}

DWORD FAR PASCAL AboutDlgProc(HWND hwnd,WORD message,WORD wParam,LONG lParam)
{
        static HANDLE sound;
        static LPSTR psound;
        HANDLE handle;
```

```
        switch(message) {
                case WM_INITDIALOG:
                        if((handle=FindResource(hInst,"AboutWave",
                            RT_RCDATA)) != NULL) {
                                if((sound=LoadResource(hInst,handle)) != NULL) {
                                        if((psound=LockResource(sound)) != NULL)
                                                sndPlaySound(psound,SND_ASYNC |
                                                    SND_MEMORY | SND_NOSTOP);
                                }
                        }
                        CentreWindow(hwnd);
                        return(FALSE);
                case WM_CTLCOLOR:
                        return(HandleCtlColour(hwnd,wParam,lParam));
                case WM_COMMAND:
                        switch(wParam) {
                                case IDOK:
                                        sndPlaySound(NULL,SND_SYNC);
                                        if(psound != NULL) UnlockResource(sound);
                                        if(sound != NULL) FreeResource(sound);
                                        EndDialog(hwnd,wParam);
                                        return(FALSE);
                        }
                        break;
        }

        return(FALSE);
}

void lmemset(LPSTR s,int n,unsigned int size)
{
        unsigned int i;

        for(i=0;i<size;++i) *s++=n;
}

int GetOpenFileName(HWND hwnd,LPSTR path)
{
        OPENFILENAME ofn;
        char szDirName[256],szFileTitle[256],szFilter[256];

        getcwd(szDirName,sizeof(szDirName)-1);

        lstrcpy(szFilter,"*.AVI");

        lmemset((LPSTR)&ofn,0,sizeof(OPENFILENAME));

        lstrcpy(path,"*.AVI");
        szFileTitle[0]=0;

        ofn.lStructSize=sizeof(OPENFILENAME);
        ofn.hwndOwner=hwnd;
        ofn.lpstrFilter="All files (*.*)\000*.*\000AVI files (*.AVI)\000*.AVI\000";
```

Figure 7-6   *Continued.*

```
            ofn.lpstrFile=path;
            ofn.nFilterIndex=2;
            ofn.nMaxFile=STRINGSIZE;
            ofn.lpstrFileTitle=szFileTitle;
            ofn.nMaxFileTitle=sizeof(szFileTitle);
            ofn.lpstrInitialDir=szDirName;
            ofn.Flags=OFN_PATHMUSTEXIST | OFN_HIDEREADONLY;
            ofn.lpstrTitle="Open File";
            ofn.lpstrDefExt="AVI";

            if(!GetOpenFileName(&ofn)) {
                    path[0]=0;
                    return(FALSE);
            } else return(TRUE);
    }
    void CentreWindow(HWND hwnd)
    {
            RECT rect;
            unsigned int x,y;

            GetWindowRect(hwnd,&rect);
            x=(GetSystemMetrics(SM_CXSCREEN)-(rect.right-rect.left))/2;
            y=(GetSystemMetrics(SM_CYSCREEN)-(rect.bottom-rect.top))/2;
            SetWindowPos(hwnd,NULL,x,y,rect.right-rect.left,
                rect.bottom-rect.top,SWP_NOSIZE);
    }

    DWORD HandleCtlColour(HWND hwnd,WORD wParam,DWORD lParam)
    {
            POINT point;
            HBRUSH hBrush;

            if(HIWORD(lParam)==CTLCOLOR_STATIC ||
               HIWORD(lParam)==CTLCOLOR_DLG) {
                    hBrush=GetStockObject(LTGRAY_BRUSH);
                    SetBkColor(wParam,RGB(192,192,192));
                    SetTextColor(wParam,RGB(0,0,0));

                    ClientToScreen(hwnd,&point);
                    UnrealizeObject(hBrush);
                    SetBrushOrg(wParam,point.x,point.y);

                    return((DWORD)hBrush);

            }
            if(HIWORD(lParam)==CTLCOLOR_BTN) {
                    hBrush=GetStockObject(LTGRAY_BRUSH);
                    SetBkColor(wParam,RGB(192,192,192));
                    SetTextColor(wParam,RGB(0,0,0));

                    ClientToScreen(hwnd,&point);
```

```
                    UnrealizeObject(hBrush);
                    SetBrushOrg(wParam,point.x,point.y);

                    return((DWORD)hBrush);
            }
            return(FALSE);
}

int OpenAVIFile(LPSTR path)
{
            AVIFileInit();

            if(AVIFileOpen(&pfile,(LPCSTR)path,OF_READ,NULL)) {
                    AVIFileExit();
                    return(FALSE);
            }

            if(AVIFileGetStream(pfile,&pstream,streamtypeVIDEO,0)) {
                    AVIFileRelease(pfile);
                    AVIFileExit();
                    return(FALSE);
            }

            if((pget=AVIStreamGetFrameOpen(pstream,NULL)) == NULL) {
                    AVIStreamRelease(pstream);
                    AVIFileRelease(pfile);
                    AVIFileExit();
                    return(FALSE);
            }

            return(TRUE);
}

LPBITMAPINFOHEADER GetAVIFrame(unsigned int number)
{
            return((LPBITMAPINFOHEADER)AVIStreamGetFrame(pget,number));
}

void CloseAVIFile()
{
            AVIStreamGetFrameClose(pget);
            AVIStreamRelease(pstream);
            AVIFileRelease(pfile);
            AVIFileExit();
}

int DrawDib(HDC hdc,int x,int y,LPBITMAPINFOHEADER lpbi)
{
            LPBITMAPINFO lpbp;
            LOGPALETTE *pLogPal=NULL;
            HANDLE hPal=NULL;
            char huge *p;
            unsigned int i;
```

Figure 7

434

Figure 7-6   *Continued.*

```
        lpbp=(LPBITMAPINFO)lpbi;
        if(lpbi->biBitCount <= 8) {

                if((pLogPal=(LOGPALETTE *)malloc(sizeof(LOGPALETTE)+
                    ((unsigned int)lpbi->biClrUsed*sizeof(PALETTEENTRY)))) == NULL)
                        return(FALSE);

                pLogPal->palVersion=0x0300;
                pLogPal->palNumEntries=lpbi->biClrUsed;

                for(i=0;i<pLogPal->palNumEntries;i++) {
                        pLogPal->palPalEntry[i].peRed=lpbp->bmiColors[i].rgbRed;
                        pLogPal->palPalEntry[i].peGreen=lpbp->bmiColors[i].rgbGreen;
                        pLogPal->palPalEntry[i].peBlue=lpbp->bmiColors[i].rgbBlue;
                        pLogPal->palPalEntry[i].peFlags=0;
                }

                hPal=CreatePalette(pLogPal);

                SelectPalette(hdc,hPal,0);
                RealizePalette(hdc);

                free(pLogPal);
        }
        p=(char huge *)(lpbi)+(long)lpbi->biSize+(long)
            (lpbi->biClrUsed*sizeof(RGBQUAD));

        SetDIBitsToDevice(hdc,
                          x,
                          y,
                          (unsigned int)lpbi->biWidth,
                          (unsigned int)lpbi->biHeight,
                          0,
                          0,
                          0,
                          (unsigned int)lpbi->biHeight,
                          p,
                          (LPBITMAPINFO)lpbi,
                          DIB_RGB_COLORS);

        if(hPal != NULL) DeleteObject(hPal);
        return(TRUE);

}
```

7-7   *The STORYBRD.RC resource script.*

```
MainScreen DIALOG 19, 21, 272, 184
STYLE WS_POPUP | WS_CAPTION | WS_VSCROLL | WS_SYSMENU |
    WS_THICKFRAME | WS_MINIMIZEBOX | WS_MAXIMIZEBOX
CAPTION "Story Board"
```

```
MENU MainMenu
BEGIN
END

MainMenu MENU
BEGIN
        POPUP "&File"
        BEGIN
                MENUITEM "&Open", 101
                MENUITEM "&About", 104
                MENUITEM SEPARATOR
                MENUITEM "E&xit", 199
        END
END

AboutBox DIALOG 18, 18, 184, 180
STYLE WS_POPUP | WS_CAPTION
CAPTION "About..."
BEGIN
        CONTROL "", 102, "BorShade", BSS_GROUP | WS_CHILD | WS_VISIBLE |
            WS_TABSTOP, 8, 68, 168, 76
        CTEXT "Story Board 1.0\n\nCopyright (c) 1994 Alchemy Mindworks Inc.\n\n
            This program is part of the book Advanced Multimedia Programming for
            Windows by Steven William Rimmer, published by Windcrest/McGraw
            Hill.", -1, 12, 72, 160, 68, WS_CHILD | WS_VISIBLE | WS_GROUP
        CONTROL "Button", IDOK, "BorBtn", BS_DEFPUSHBUTTON | WS_CHILD | WS_VISIBLE |
            WS_TABSTOP, 74, 152, 32, 20
        CONTROL "Button", 801, "BorBtn", BS_PUSHBUTTON | WS_CHILD | WS_VISIBLE |
            WS_TABSTOP, 36, 8, 32, 20
END

ViewAVI ICON
BEGIN
        '00 00 01 00 01 00 20 20 10 00 00 00 00 00 E8 02'
        '00 00 16 00 00 00 28 00 00 00 20 00 00 00 40 00'
        '00 00 01 00 04 00 00 00 00 00 80 02 00 00 00 00'
        '00 00 00 00 00 00 10 00 00 00 00 00 00 00 00 00'
        '00 00 00 00 BF 00 00 BF 00 00 00 BF BF 00 BF 00'
        '00 00 BF 00 BF 00 BF BF 00 00 C0 C0 C0 00 80 80'
        '80 00 00 00 FF 00 00 FF 00 00 00 FF FF 00 FF 00'
        '00 00 FF 00 FF 00 FF FF 00 00 FF FF FF 00 77 77'
        '77 77 77 77 77 77 77 77 77 77 77 77 77 77 7F 88'
        '88 88 88 88 88 88 88 88 88 88 88 88 88 87 7F F8'
        '88 88 88 88 88 88 88 88 88 88 88 88 88 87 7F F0'
        '00 07 77 F7 77 00 77 77 F7 77 70 00 08 87 7F F0'
        '00 07 77 7F 77 70 77 7F 77 77 70 00 08 87 7F F0'
        '00 07 77 77 F7 7F 77 F7 77 77 70 00 08 87 7F F0'
        '00 07 77 77 7F FF FF 77 77 77 70 00 08 87 7F F0'
        'FF 07 77 77 77 7F 77 77 77 77 70 FF 08 87 7F F0'
        'FF 00 00 00 00 00 00 00 00 00 00 FF 08 87 7F F0'
        '00 07 77 77 77 7F 77 77 77 77 70 00 08 87 7F F0'
        '00 07 77 77 7F FF FF 77 77 77 70 00 08 87 7F F0'
        '00 07 77 77 F7 7F 77 F7 77 77 70 00 08 87 7F F0'
```

435

Figure 7-7   *Continued.*

```
            '00 07 77 7F 70 00 00 7F 77 77 70 00 08 87 7F F0'
            '00 07 77 F7 77 0F 77 77 F7 77 70 00 08 87 7F F0'
            'FF 07 77 F7 77 70 77 77 F7 77 70 FF 08 87 7F F0'
            'FF 07 FF FF FF FF 0F FF FF F7 70 FF 08 87 7F F0'
            '00 07 77 F7 77 7F 70 77 F7 77 70 00 08 87 7F F0'
            '00 07 77 F7 70 7F 70 77 F7 77 70 00 08 87 7F F0'
            '00 07 77 7F 77 00 07 7F 77 77 70 00 08 87 7F F0'
            '00 07 77 77 F7 7F 77 F7 77 77 70 00 08 87 7F F0'
            '00 07 77 77 7F FF FF 77 77 77 70 00 08 87 7F F0'
            'FF 07 77 77 77 7F 77 77 77 77 70 FF 08 87 7F F0'
            'FF 00 00 00 00 00 00 00 00 00 00 FF 08 87 7F F0'
            '00 07 77 77 77 7F 77 77 77 77 70 00 08 87 7F F0'
            '00 07 77 77 7F FF FF 77 77 77 70 00 08 87 7F F0'
            '00 07 77 77 F7 7F 77 F7 77 77 70 00 08 87 7F F0'
            '00 07 77 7F 77 00 07 7F 77 77 70 00 08 87 7F F0'
            '00 07 77 F7 70 7F 70 77 F7 77 70 00 08 87 7F F0'
            'FF 07 77 F7 77 77 70 77 F7 77 70 FF 08 87 7F FF'
            'FF FF FF FF FF FF FF FF FF FF FF FF F8 87 7F FF'
            'FF FF FF FF FF FF FF FF FF FF FF FF FF 87 77 77'
            '77 77 77 77 77 77 77 77 77 77 77 77 77 77 00 00'
            '00 00 00 00 00 00 00 00 00 00 00 00 00 00 00 00'
            '00 00 00 00 00 00 00 00 00 00 00 00 00 00 00 00'
            '00 00 00 00 00 00 00 00 00 00 00 00 00 00 00 00'
            '00 00 00 00 00 00 00 00 00 00 00 00 00 00 00 00'
            '00 00 00 00 00 00 00 00 00 00 00 00 00 00 00 00'
            '00 00 00 00 00 00 00 00 00 00 00 00 00 00 00 00'
            '00 00 00 00 00 00 00 00 00 00 00 00 00 00 00 00'
            '00 00 00 00 00 00 00 00 00 00 00 00 00 00 00'
END

1801 BITMAP "smpw.bmp"

AboutWave RCDATA "ABOUT.WAV"
```

You must also have the Video for Windows SDK installed on your
hard drive—the STORYBRD project file included on the companion
CD-ROM for this book assumes that the VFW.H header and all its
dependent headers will be installed in the directory C:\VFWDK\INC.
Make sure you change this prior to compiling StoryBoard if you've
installed the Video for Windows SDK elsewhere.

The structure of StoryBoard should be familiar if you've worked with
some of the other sample applications in this book. Its main window
consists of a very simple dialog, a window with a scroll bar down its
right side. This window could also have been created using the more

traditional approach of registering a window class and calling CreateWindow.

Once again, all the work is done in the SelectProc function, the message handler for the main window of StoryBoard. Note that the WM_INITDIALOG function gets under way by calling VideoForWindowsVersion. Make sure that the version of Video for Windows installed on the system running this application is capable of responding correctly to all the system calls it uses.

As an aside, it's worth noting that if you remove the check for the Video for Windows version and run StoryBoard on a system with Version 1.0 of Video for Windows installed, StoryBoard will correctly display some AVI files. Others will show up as meaningless rectangles of colored dots.

The MAIN_OPEN case of the WM_COMMAND handler for SelectProc calls up a standard Windows File Open dialog to select an AVI file to unpack, and then passes the name it returns to OpenAVIFile. This is the first of the functions that make calls to the AVIFILE.DLL library.

The OpenAVIFile function in STORYBRD.CPP begins by calling AVIFileInit to initialize the AVI file system. AVIFileInit should always be called before you do anything with the AVI file functions.

The AVIFileOpen call will open the AVI file passed to it, in this case for reading. It will initialize the PAVIFILE object to which it's passed a pointer in its first argument. Note that this is a pointer to a pointer to an AVIFILE object—the AVIFileOpen will actually allocate space in the common data segment of your application to store the AVIFILE object in and then store a pointer to it in the PAVIFILE object it's passed a pointer to.

Video for Windows presentations are handled as data streams. A data stream is either the audio or video portion of an AVI movie. The AVIFileGetStream function will rummage around in an open AVI file and locate the stream you're after. An AVI file can contain one video stream and any number of audio streams—none for silent movies, one for normal AVI files, and multiple audio streams for multilingual

presentations. An example of an AVI with multiple audio streams is included with the Video for Windows Software Development Kit.

In this case, we're interested in the video stream. The third argument to AVIFileGetStream would be the constant streamtypeVIDEO to access it.

The AVIStreamGetFrameOpen function prepares to unpack frames from a video stream. It accepts the stream pointer object filled in by AVIFileGetStream and returns a PGETFRAME pointer.

The structure of the code that accesses AVI files through the AVIFILE.DLL library is somewhat more complex than it needs to be for applications like StoryBoard. Actually, you'll probably find that it's much more complicated than it needs to be for most AVI file software. In somewhat exotic—and perhaps highly improbable—situations, you can use this flexibility to deal with very complex AVI files. For example, it would allow you to deal with AVI files having multiple video streams, even though no such files exist at the moment.

Software authors who decried the early inflexibility and general lack of forethought in the AVI interface will no doubt applaud the high level of foresight built into this second attempt at it—even if it does make the simple act of opening an AVI to read a few frames from it singularly complicated.

In looking at the OpenAVIFile function, note the calls used in the error conditions for the various calls to the AVIFILE functions—or take a look at the CloseAVIFile function further down the STORYBRD.CPP listing. Always shut things down correctly when you use the AVIFILE.DLL interface, lest a number of memory objects be orphaned. Specifically, call AVIStreamGetFrameClose to free up the resources allocated by AVIStreamGetFrameOpen. Call AVIStreamRelease to tidy up after a successful call to AVIFileGetStream. Call AVIFileRelease to close an AVI file opened by AVIFileOpen. Finally, call AVIFileExit to shut down the AVI file system when it's no longer required.

If you've had a look at OpenAVIFile and CloseAVIFile, you probably had a hard time missing GetAVIFrame, strategically located between them in STORYBRD.CPP. This represents all the code required to fetch any frame you like from an AVI file after a successful call to OpenAVIFrame. The number argument is the frame number, starting with zero for the first frame in the file.

The value returned by the AVIStreamGetFrame call used by GetAVIFrame is a far pointer to the BITMAPINFOHEADER structure of a device-independent bitmap. This will prove to be a singularly accommodating object—not only is it in precisely the right format to be displayed in a window, but it's already locked in memory. It actually points to a buffer allocated by AVIFILE.DLL, which is filled in with the appropriate image information when you call AVIStreamGetFrame. You don't even have to free it when it's no longer required.

The only catch to this object is that it can only contain one frame at a time. Should you have cause to buffer more than one frame, you'll have to allocate some storage and copy to your allocated memory block the contents of the buffer pointed to by the return value of AVIStreamGetFrame. Beware the temptation to buffer large numbers of AVI file frames—or, worse still, a whole AVI movie. Individually they don't seem to require much storage, but put a few hundred of them in memory and things may start getting a bit crowded.

As an aside, attempting to buffer all the frames in a movie can leave your software staring at one of the inflexible perversities of Windows' memory management. For example, a single frame of a movie with the dimensions 160 by 100 pixels at 256 colors would occupy a bit under 16 kilobytes—plus something over one kilobyte more for the device-independent bitmap header and RGBQUAD palette array. A movie with 200 such frames would occupy something over 3 megabytes. This isn't a lot of memory on a 16-megabyte system, but it will prove impossible to allocate entirely out of real memory on a 4-megabyte machine. Keep in mind that DOS, Windows, and your software will each want memory as well.

Assuming that each frame is stored in its own buffer—and allowing that each buffer is to be stored unlocked, referenced by a handle

rather than a pointer—Windows would be free to spill to disk the contents of the buffers in question in order to free up real memory.

The usual reason for buffering lots of AVI movie frames in memory, rather than reading them from an AVI file one at a time as they're required, is to make them faster to access. However, if you allocate buffers for them, store them in these buffers, and Windows subsequently spills them to disk, they'll be read from disk files in any case. Admittedly, it's slightly faster to fetch objects from a Windows spill file than it is to uncompress frames from an AVI file, but the difference can be all but unnoticeable.

Most of the interesting bits of StoryBoard appear in the WM_PAINT handler for SelectProc. Its for loop runs from the number of the first frame to be displayed to the total number of frames in the AVI file in question, as set down in the MAIN_OPEN case of the WM_COMMAND handler. The AVIStreamLength function returns different values for different sorts of streams—it returns the frame count for a video stream. The loop will terminate prematurely if enough frames have been painted to fill the main window of StoryBoard.

Each iteration of the WM_PAINT for loop fetches an LPBITMAPINFOHEADER pointer to a frame with a call to GetAVIFrame. It then calculates the appropriate place to paint it in the current display window based on the window dimensions. The dimensions of the frames in question, as located in the LPBITMAPINFOHEADER object returned by GetAVIFrame, are padded out a bit with the values of the HMARGIN and VMARGIN constants to make the frame matrix look attractive.

Each frame is also given a title.

The DrawDib function illustrated at the bottom of the STORYBRD.CPP source listing actually handles displaying the frames fetched by GetAVIFrame. Its operation was discussed in detail in Chapter 3. You can improve on its performance somewhat by realizing the display palette once and then using the DIB_PAL_COLORS constant as the final argument to SetDIBitsToDevice, rather than DIB_RGB_COLORS, as is done in

this version of DrawDib. In practice, this has somewhat less effect than you might think, as the time required to locate and unpack a frame from an AVI file is far greater than the time required to display one.

Video for Windows II: the wrath of Microsoft

There's a great deal more to the AVI interface available through Version 1.1 of the Video for Windows Software Development Kit. This chapter has touched on some of the most useful facilities it offers. If your intended application for Video for Windows is reasonably undemanding, this will probably be all you'll require. There's acres of room for experimentation, however, and all sorts of things that haven't even been hinted at here. As with so many areas of multimedia software development, this is a subject that could easily encompass a whole book and still not be thoroughly covered.

The AVI interface is flexible enough to accommodate just about anything you can imagine using Video for Windows for. Unfortunately, imagination by its nature is a bit tricky to document.

Having said all this, I should warn you that Microsoft's documentation for the Video for Windows Software Development Kit is a bit anorexic. Even with the printed manual for the package in hand, plan to undertake rather more fruitless speculation and general head bashing to get things done with the AVI libraries than you'd normally expect to get into for other areas of Windows software development. There are lots of sample applications to extract code from—some of them quite useful—but scavenging about in them can also be pretty time-consuming. Some of them elevate spaghetti code to a higher art form.

The bit of graffiti that appears at the beginning of the first chapter of this book is singularly applicable to Video for Windows: "You can always spot the pioneers—they're the ones with the arrows in their backs." Video for Windows is a promising but still fairly undeveloped technology. It's very much a blank canvas, ready for the colors of

your inspiration. However, as with so many things in a technology that seems to have invented the phrase "rushed to market" specifically for its own use, it has a few quickly plastered-over holes, inexpertly bridged crevasses, and arrows flying about in all directions.

When you get frustrated, you might consider the Zen of software architecture, and try to see these things not as drawbacks but as opportunities.

If it were easy, everyone would be doing it.

Appendix

What's on
the CD-ROM

The companion CD-ROM for this book includes the following files:

➤ The \SOURCE directory includes all the C-language source
code, resource scripts, DEF and PRJ files, and resource files for
the applications in this book. It also includes the DLL and
import library LIB files required to compile the applications
created for this book. You'll still need the Microsoft Multimedia
Development Kit and Video for Windows Software
Development Kit to compile the applications, of course.

➤ The \APPS directory includes all the compiled applications
from this book, should you want to see what they're up to. You
can run them individually from the CD-ROM by selecting the

Run item from the File menu of the Windows Program Manager, or you can install them on your hard drive by running \APPS\SETUP from the CD-ROM.

➤ The \GWSWIN directory contains a shareware version of the Graphic Workshop for Windows application. You can't run this from the CD-ROM. It must be installed on your hard drive. To do this, run \GWSWIN\SETUP.

➤ The \QSHOW directory contains a shareware version of the QuickShow Light for Windows multimedia slide-show package. You can't run this from the CD-ROM. It must be installed on your hard drive. To do this, run \QSHOW\SETUP.

➤ The \PAGANDAY directory contains a shareware version of The Pagan Daybook, a Windows calendar application. This has nothing at all to do with this book, but there was lots of room on the CD-ROM and it's an interesting application. You can install it on your hard drive by running \PAGANDAY\SETUP.

➤ The \PICTURES directory contains a library of public domain GIF files. You can view these with Graphic Workshop for Windows. You might find them more useful if you use Graphic Workshop to convert the images you're interested in to the BMP format. Once converted to BMP, they can be edited with Windows Paintbrush and used as sample files in the BMP-FX application in this book.

➤ The \MIDI directory includes a library of MIDI music files.

➤ The \WAVE directory includes a library of WAV files.

➤ The \AVI directory includes several Video for Windows AVI movies.

➤ The \VFW directory includes the Video for Windows 1.1 runtime. To install it on your hard drive, run \VFW\SETUP. You won't need this version of Video for Windows if you have installed Video for Windows from the Video for Windows Software Development Kit Version 1.1 or better.

Read the README.TXT file in the root directory of the CD-ROM for more information.

Index

Illustration page numbers are in **boldface**.

About the Author

Steve Rimmer lives in rural central Ontario with his wife Megan, two dogs, and a variety of unusual cars. All his neighbors are cows. He is the president of Alchemy Mindworks Inc., which is a small software company that creates graphics applications. He has written over a dozen books about computer-related topics and several novels about witchcraft and pagan magic. His computer books include *Bitmapped Graphics* and *Windows Multimedia Programming*, published by Windcrest/McGraw-Hill. His most recent works of fiction include *The Order* and *Wyccad*, published by Jam Ink Books.

His hobbies include archery and playing Celtic music with a local band.

DISK WARRANTY

This software is protected by both United States copyright law and international copyright treaty provision. You must treat this software just like a book, except that you may copy it into a computer in order to be used and you may make archival copies of the software for the sole purpose of backing up our software and protecting your investment from loss.

By saying "just like a book," McGraw-Hill means, for example, that this software may be used by any number of people and may be freely moved from one computer location to another, so long as there is no possibility of its being used at one location or on one computer while it also is being used at another. Just as a book cannot be read by two different people in two different places at the same time, neither can the software be used by two different people in two different places at the same time (unless, of course, McGraw-Hill's copyright is being violated).

LIMITED WARRANTY

Windcrest/McGraw-Hill takes great care to provide you with top-quality software, thoroughly checked to prevent virus infections. McGraw-Hill warrants the physical diskette(s) contained herein to be free of defects in materials and workmanship for a period of sixty days from the purchase date. If McGraw-Hill receives written notification within the warranty period of defects in materials or workmanship, and such notification is determined by McGraw-Hill to be correct, McGraw-Hill will replace the defective diskette(s). Send requests to:

> Customer Service
> Windcrest/McGraw-Hill
> 13311 Monterey Lane
> Blue Ridge Summit, PA 17294-0850

The entire and exclusive liability and remedy for breach of this Limited Warranty shall be limited to replacement of defective diskette(s) and shall not include or extend to any claim for or right to cover any other damages, including but not limited to, loss of profit, data, or use of the software, or special, incidental, or consequential damages or other similar claims, even if McGraw-Hill has been specifically advised of the possibility of such damages. In no event will McGraw-Hill's liability for any damages to you or any other person ever exceed the lower of suggested list price or actual price paid for the license to use the software, regardless of any form of the claim.

McGRAW-HILL, INC. SPECIFICALLY DISCLAIMS ALL OTHER WARRANTIES, EXPRESS OR IMPLIED, INCLUDING, BUT NOT LIMITED TO, ANY IMPLIED WARRANTY OF MERCHANTABILITY OR FITNESS FOR A PARTICULAR PURPOSE.

Specifically, McGraw-Hill makes no representation or warranty that the software is fit for any particular purpose and any implied warranty of merchantability is limited to the sixty-day duration of the Limited Warranty covering the physical diskette(s) only (and not the software) and is otherwise expressly and specifically disclaimed.

This limited warranty gives you specific legal rights; you may have others which may vary from state to state. Some states do not allow the exclusion of incidental or consequential damages, or the limitation on how long an implied warranty lasts, so some of the above may not apply to you.